Praise for

Communication

"The book begins with a bold claim that communication competence is the single most important factor in determining quality of life. As it turns out, I agree, and I think that after reading this book, students will too. Starting with an emphasis on basic competencies in language, nonverbal communication, and listening, the book then clearly and effectively explicates knowledge and skills in the traditional areas of communication studies—interpersonal communication, small group communication, and public speaking."

—Phil Backlund, Director, National Communication Association's
Educational Policies Board, Central Washington University

"Clear, concise, and comprehensive, the third edition of *Communication: Motivation, Knowledge, Skills* highlights a contextual applied approach to communication competence without sacrificing the big picture, the philosophical aspects of communication foundational to any introductory class. Its mix of micro- and macro-level concepts, including media literacy, will likely meet the demands of any course curriculum. Students and teachers alike will benefit from the book's easy-to-understand and conversational tone."

—Kurt Lindemann, Associate Professor and Basic Course Director,
San Diego State University

"The diverse expertise of the three authors makes for a comprehensive and substantive learning experience for students in the basic communication course. Students are introduced to the discipline in a way that grounds them for future studies in communication. The inclusion of the impact of media and technology in this third edition provides insight into a phenomenon that will continue to influence the ways in which we communicate."

—Laura Austin-Eurich, Director of Undergraduate Studies,
University of Colorado, Colorado Springs

"The model of communication competence on which the third edition of this textbook is based is one I also have used in my own writings. Morreale, Spitzberg, and Barge effectively discuss the three main contexts in the basic communication course—interpersonal, group, and public speaking—using communication competence as the foundation and unifying framework for this useful textbook."

—Pamela Shockley-Zalabak, Chancellor, University of Colorado, Colorado Springs

Communication

This book is part of the Peter Lang Media and Communication list.
Every volume is peer reviewed and meets
the highest quality standards for content and production.

PETER LANG
New York • Washington, D.C./Baltimore • Bern
Frankfurt • Berlin • Brussels • Vienna • Oxford

Sherwyn P. Morreale,
Brian H. Spitzberg,
J. Kevin Barge

Communication

Motivation,
Knowledge,
Skills

THIRD EDITION

PETER LANG
New York • Washington, D.C./Baltimore • Bern
Frankfurt • Berlin • Brussels • Vienna • Oxford

Library of Congress Cataloging-in-Publication Data

Morreale, Sherwyn P., author.
[Human communication]
Communication: Motivation, Knowledge, Skills / Sherwyn P. Morreale,
Brian H. Spitzberg, Kevin Barge. — Third Edition.
pages cm
Previously published as: Human communication, 2nd ed., 2007.
Includes bibliographical references and index.
1. Communication. I. Spitzberg, Brian H., author.
II. Barge, J. Kevin. author. III. Title.
P90.M637 302.2—dc23 2012041673
ISBN 978-1-4331-1714-5 (paperback)
ISBN 978-1-4539-0257-8 (e-book)

Bibliographic information published by **Die Deutsche Nationalbibliothek**.
Die Deutsche Nationalbibliothek lists this publication in the "Deutsche
Nationalbibliografie"; detailed bibliographic data is available
on the Internet at http://dnb.d-nb.de/.

Cover art and photography: *Desert Mantra* by Heather Sweeney
Interior photos by Shaan Couture

The paper in this book meets the guidelines for permanence and durability
of the Committee on Production Guidelines for Book Longevity
of the Council of Library Resources.

© 2013 Peter Lang Publishing, Inc., New York
29 Broadway, 18th floor, New York, NY 10006
www.peterlang.com

Printed in the United States of America

CONTENTS IN BRIEF

PART FIVE: 21ST-CENTURY COMMUNICATION

DETAILED TABLE OF CONTENTS

PREFACE

Almost everything that is important to the human condition, both good and bad, is a product of communication. Conflict and cooperation, society and family, love and friendship, and the engines of commerce and organizations are all made possible through communication. It follows that the more competent this communication, the better these vital institutions and relationships are likely to be. This third edition of *Communication: Motivation, Knowledge, and Skills* promises to be a key player in the development of competent communication by all students in any basic communication course. Our book is intended for use in basic courses focusing on interpersonal and group communication and public speaking—this course is sometimes referred to as the "hybrid course." Several good textbooks are already available for the hybrid communication course, but the third edition of this book is a bit different in several key ways.

UNIQUE FEATURES OF
COMMUNICATION: MOTIVATION, KNOWLEDGE, AND SKILLS

- The entire book is the result of the collaborative work of three recognized experts in the communication discipline, each of whom specializes in one of the three areas covered in the hybrid, basic course—interpersonal communication (Brian Spitzberg), small-group communication (Kevin Barge), and public speaking (Sherwyn [Sherry] Morreale).
- The book's content offers a unified approach for understanding human communication, based on a communication competence model pioneered by author, Brian Spitzberg. This model describes competent communication as both appropriate (communicating in ways acceptable to the norms and expectations of the communication context) and effective (achieving the most desirable objectives or outcomes in the context or situation).
- To be effective and appropriate, communication competence is made up of three components—motivation, knowledge, and skills. This conceptual model of appropriateness and effectiveness, combined with motivation, knowledge, and skills provides a solid theoretical foundation for studying communication.
- And finally, this textbook includes a brand-new chapter on mass communication, media convergence, and computer-mediated communication—topics critical to communicating effectively and appropriately in the technologically mediated 21st century.

SPECIAL FEATURES IN THIS THIRD EDITION

Beginning with the premise that all forms of communication have the potential to be viewed as competent, this text helps students develop a framework for choosing among communication messages and behaviors that will allow them to communicate most competently in any situation. The third edition is written in five parts with 15 chapters.

- Part One, Chapters One to Six, introduces students to the essential foundations of communication, and a chapter on our model of communication competence also is included.
- Part Two, Chapters Seven and Eight, focuses on the knowledge and skills related to interpersonal communication.
- Part Three, Chapters Nine and Ten, is about knowledge and skills for small-group communication, decision making, and leadership in groups.
- Part Four, Chapters Eleven to Fourteen, covers public speaking, including speech preparation and presentation, and speaking to inform and to persuade.
- Part Five, Chapter Fifteen, acquaints students with the latest research and recommendations for communicating competently in two crucial contexts in the 21st century—mass communication and technologically and computer-mediated communication.

SPECIAL FEATURES IN EVERY CHAPTER

In addition to theoretically based but accessible content, all 15 chapters of *Communication: Motivation, Knowledge, and Skills* include features designed to enhance teaching and learning. Each chapter contains the following features:

- A *story of a student experience* opens each chapter and is discussed and used as an example to illustrate the chapter's content.
- *Tables and boxes* related to important topics in each chapter are presented to intrigue student readers and "lock in learning."
- A *self-assessment tool* students can use to evaluate their own motivation, knowledge, and skills related to real world situations and the chapter's content concludes each chapter.
- *Building knowledge discussion questions* and *building competence activities* for home assignments or in-class groups also conclude each chapter.

A past president of the National Communication Association, Dan O'Hair, once said something profound in its simplicity: "The promise of communication is understanding." We agree with Dan, and believe improved communication—developing your own communication competence—will help you deliver on that promise by enhancing your relationships, bridging differences, and encouraging productive dialogues in organizations and in society.

The three authors of this third edition wish you well, and sincerely hope that this third edition of *Communication: Motivation, Knowledge, and Skills* contributes to all students' development as competent communicators.

Cordially,
Sherry Morreale, Brian Spitzberg,
and Kevin Barge

ACKNOWLEDGMENTS

We first express our gratitude to the communication colleagues, researchers, instructors, and leaders in the communication discipline who, over the years, have expressed their belief in our approach to communication competence and related pedagogy.

With regard to this textbook, special thanks go to Mary Savigar and Bernadette Shade at Peter Lang, who guided the third edition skillfully through conceptualization and production to completion. Committed graduate research assistants contributed immeasurably over several years to the book's development. At University of Colorado–Colorado Springs, we are appreciative of the work of Rose Fortune, Mireya Garcia, Rayven Irons, Kelly Lynch, and Lindsey McCormick. Their research efforts and continuous reading and rereading of all 15 chapters helped ensure an error-free manuscript—we hope! At San Diego State University, Shaan Couture spent countless hours serving as our staff photographer (see Shaan's other works at http://www.wediawix.com). We are appreciative of her high level of professionalism and competence, which is obvious when you look at the photographs of students that open each chapter of this book. We also thank Heather Sweeney for her amazing artwork, *Desert Mantra*, that graces the cover of this third edition (see her other works at http://heathersweeney.net/).

On the home front, our families continued to understand, as we spent countless hours writing and revising each and every chapter over the last several years.

Finally, as coauthors, we acknowledge and appreciate each other's commitment to a third edition of this textbook.

PART ONE

FOUNDATIONS OF COMMUNICATION

CHAPTER ONE

INTRODUCING COMMUNICATION

- **What Is Communication?**
  Messages
  Media
  Meaning
  Managing

- **Models of Communication**
  Communication as Informing
  Communication as Persuading
  Communication as Relating

- **Assumptions About Communication**
  Communication Is a Process
  Communication Creates Our Social Worlds
  Communication Is Functional and Adaptive

- **The Importance of Communication**

- **Chapter Summary**
  Building Motivation: Self-Assessment Tool
  Building Knowledge: Discussion Questions
  Building Skills: Student Activities

Communication—the human connection—is the key to personal and career success. —Paul J. Meyer, Businessman and Motivational Author, 1928–2009

• • •

Monday, 8:00 p.m.—Kathryn returned to her apartment after attending a team-building workshop hosted by her university's Student Life Department. Even though she had extensive experience as a committee chair, Kathryn had been looking forward to this workshop, because her new position as chair for her service club's fund-raising committee held many challenges.

As she walked into her apartment, she checked her phone and noticed that she had received six text messages, eight e-mail messages, two tweets, and some comments on a picture she had put up on Facebook. One of the e-mails was from a friend confirming a lunch date, some of the messages were from classmates, and one text message was from a coworker asking if Kathryn would take a shift at their retail store that week. She responded to a couple messages, but quickly got to work on a presentation for her 9:00 a.m. marketing class. She had done all her research; it was now time to outline her presentation of the marketing plan. She knew speaking to large groups was not her strength, and she always felt nervous in front of an audience. She began typing an outline for her presentation.

Tuesday, 10:30 a.m.—The speech had gone poorly. Despite the fact that she had prepared thoroughly and knew the information, she still had not overcome her nervousness. She lost her place on more than one occasion, and made awkward pauses during the presentation. Her classmates looked embarrassed for her, and the professor's feedback was a bit negative.

Tuesday, 1:00 p.m.—Kathryn's lunch with her friend Kwan went much more smoothly than her presentation. Kwan was conflicted about whether to transfer to another college. Kathryn did not have a hard time listening to him, but felt awkward giving advice. She wanted to tell Kwan how she really felt but could not find a way of putting her feelings into words.

Tuesday, 5:00 p.m.—The fund-raising committee meeting had gone very well. Kathryn received several compliments from committee members about how well she had organized the meeting and how effective she was at keeping the discussion on track.

Tuesday, 8:00 p.m.—Kathryn returned to her apartment, exhausted after a long day. She looked at her phone and saw all kinds of new messages. She had a voicemail from her mother and another from her boyfriend that she had not answered due to her meetings. She glanced at her calendar and made note of her two other meetings in addition to her two classes on Wednesday. What would tomorrow be like?

Most of our waking hours are spent communicating with other people. Whether we are talking, texting, tweeting, or responding to e-mail; listening to a lecture or at a meeting; or just chatting with a friend, we are communicating with and relating to people. A reality of contemporary life is that we must continually engage with others to do work, to maintain relationships, and to enjoy happy and healthy lives. This chapter begins our discussion of human communication, and lays the foundation for all the concepts and information that will follow in subsequent chapters. We start with an explanation of what communication is and how it works.

WHAT IS COMMUNICATION?

Consider first this ambitious claim—your communication competence is the single most important factor in determining your quality of life. You may think it overly bold—surely health, or love, or family, or economic security matter more. However, try to imagine how you would go about achieving any of these vital objectives without the motivation to do so, the knowledge of how to do so, and the skills to do so. In short, all the things that matter to us are, to a significant degree, dependent on the ability to communicate well. This book seeks to illuminate how people like you, and like Kathryn in the scenario just described, use communication to achieve their goals. We will demonstrate how an understanding of the most essential aspects of communication can make you happier, and significantly improve your ability to succeed throughout life.

COMPETENT COMMUNICATION is appropriate and effective for a particular situation.

Indeed, if most of our life is spent communicating, then the quality of our communication matters greatly. The quality of our communication is defined by how well, or how competently, we communicate. **Competent communication** is both appropriate and effective. **Appropriate communication** means behaving in ways acceptable to the valued norms and expectations of a given context. **Effective communication** means achieving the most desirable objectives or outcomes possible in a given context. Your communication competence can vary from context to context. For example, Kathryn was perceived as very competent by her fellow committee members, but as less competent by her professor and classmates during her marketing presentation.

APPROPRIATE COMMUNICATION occurs when you act in ways suitable to the norms and expectations of contexts and situations you encounter.

EFFECTIVE COMMUNICATION occurs when you are able to achieve the most desirable objectives or outcomes in contexts.

COMMUNICATION is the process of managing messages and media for the purpose of creating meaning.

It takes only a moment to think back to instances in which your communication may have been perceived as less than competent. You said something awkward, felt embarrassed by what you said, or were unable to persuade someone to see things your way. In any of these situations, more awareness and a better understanding of communication would have made a difference, and that understanding begins with looking at what we actually mean by *communication*. Even though you communicate every day, there is a difference between an intuitive approach to it and this scholarly definition: **Communication** is the process of managing messages and media for the purpose of creating meaning.[1] Although there are numerous concepts embedded in this definition,[2] the following four key terms are now discussed in more detail: messages, media, meaning, and managing.

MESSAGES.

Messages are the words, sounds, actions, and gestures that people express to one another when they interact. Messages may be expressed verbally in words or nonverbally in sounds, actions, and gestures. Messages may be symbolic. A **symbol** is a word, sound, action, or gesture that refers to something else. The relationship between symbols and the things or concepts to which they refer is arbitrary.

The arbitrary relation between symbols and their **referent**, or the thing to which they refer, deserves further consideration. Think of the word *nuts*. To begin with, it has several potential conventional meanings, as in "That guy is nuts!" or "Let's get down to nuts and bolts," or "The mixed nuts they served at that party were great." But to what reality do these words really refer? In fact, what we call something is merely a product of history, culture, and our ability to communicate using these arbitrary labels we place on things.

> MESSAGES are the words, sounds, actions, and gestures that people express to one another when they interact.
>
> A SYMBOL is a word, sound, action, or gesture that refers to something else.
>
> A REFERENT is the thing to which symbols refer.

The basic relationship between symbol and referent is illustrated in Figure 1.1, depicting a speaker trying to persuade an audience on a position regarding capital punishment. There is the actual act of executing a person, and then there are the various symbols we use to refer to the act (e.g., capital

Figure 1.1: The Components of Messages

Every communication process involves at least one person translating ideas or meanings into behaviors and symbols intended to express those ideas and meanings. Those ideas and meanings, in turn, have an arbitrary but conventional association with the things to which they refer, or the referent.

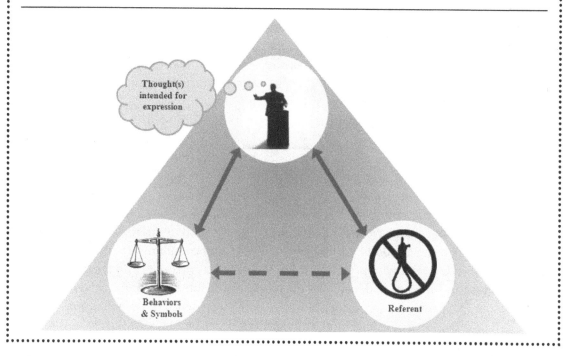

punishment, execution, death penalty, etc.), and there are the ideas we conjure up in our minds when we interpret such symbols, and then there is the actual act of executing somebody. Each person will process the relationship among these symbols, acts, and meanings somewhat differently. Therefore, messages themselves may be varyingly interpreted, which often results in misunderstandings.

The arbitrary nature of the relationship between symbols and referents is often central to understanding communication problems in many different situations. For example, when a politician says that we need to spread democracy around the world, what exactly does that mean in terms of actual political changes: does it mean changes in the constitution, voting processes, marketplace, authority of the military, family and gender relations, or all of the above? And if you interpret democracy as a verbal symbol differently than someone else does, how could you determine who has the more "true" conception of its meaning?

The most common set of verbal symbols we use is language. **Language** is a verbal symbol system that allows us to take messages and utterances, in the form of words, and translate them into meaning. For example, in the English language, we use words such as *house* and *car* to refer to physical objects in our world, and words such as *love* and *anger* to refer to our inner feelings. Most verbal symbols take either spoken or written form. Verbal communication and language is discussed in detail in Chapter Four.

Symbolic behavior is not limited to verbal messages; it can be nonverbal as well. **Nonverbal communication** consists of those sounds, actions, or gestures to which people attribute meaning. When such behavior has commonly shared meanings, it can be understood as a form of **nonverbal symbol**. An example of a nonverbal symbol in North America is the joining of the forefinger and thumb to signal to others that we are OK. However, in some cultures, this same symbol sends an obscene message![3] Nonverbal communication is explored more in Chapter Five.

> LANGUAGE is a verbal symbol system that allows us to take messages and utterances, in the form of words, and translate them into meaning.

> NONVERBAL COMMUNICATION consists of those sounds, actions, or gestures—other than words—to which people attribute meaning.

> NONVERBAL SYMBOLS are sounds, actions, or gestures that people agree have a common meaning.

> MEDIA are any means through which symbols are transmitted and meanings are represented.

MEDIA.

Media are any means through which symbols are transmitted and meanings are represented. Humankind's earliest efforts at communication probably used their natural abilities as a medium—such as through grunts, growls, howls, and other vocalizations. Later, they probably employed various instruments of nature as a medium, by making sounds on tree trunks, signals with smoke, and painted representations on cave walls. Over time, elaborate symbol systems, complete with grammar and alphabets developed. When we use our own voice, gestures, and body to communicate directly to someone within sensory proximity to us, it represents a form of **natural media**.

Another addition to natural media today is **technological media**. Pens and papers were early media for writing, which became the printing press and, subsequently, all the various electronic and digital forms of communicating. Telephones now routinely transfer voice, text, and images. The Internet, e-mail, and instant messaging permit the transfer of written, visual, and audio information. The options for communicating through technological media have vastly expanded in recent decades.

Ultimately, the fundamentals of human endeavors, such as seeking belonging, seeking autonomy, seeking confirmation, mating, and so forth, remain fundamentally unchanged. However, the speed, efficiency, and scale with which we use media to accomplish these tasks are changing at an unprecedented rate, and this forecasts many changes for how we adapt to and communicate in the world around us.

MEANING.

Meaning refers to the interpretation people assign to a message—how it is recognized or understood. Meaning for words and events may be personal and unique or it may be shared with others. As people are socialized into a group or culture, they develop meanings for certain words and events they share with others. Take, for example, the words *spam*, *virus*, and *firewall*. If you are a cook, *spam* refers to spiced ham in a can. If you are a doctor, the term *virus* refers to an infectious agent that invades and takes over human cells. If you are a forest firefighter, the word *firewall* refers to a line of defense where you will attempt to stop a fire. But if you are a computer programmer, these words take on different meanings: The word, *spam*, refers to junk mail you receive via e-mail; *virus* refers to a rogue computer program that corrupts your files or does other damage; and a *firewall* restricts access to data on a computer network.

> MEANING is the interpretation people assign to a message—how it is recognized or understood.
>
> MANAGING is the handling or supervising of people or some process or material.

People may agree at some level on the meaning of particular words or events, but meaning can also be personal and unique, and can depend on your own personal history, your culture, your political and religious beliefs, the volunteer organizations to which you belong, and so on. It is not enough to ask, "What does that mean?" Instead, the question needs to be rephrased as "What does that mean **to you**?"

MANAGING.

In our earlier definition, **managing** means making choices about how to behave in any given context of communication. Our job as communicators is to manage the process of creating, receiving, and responding to verbal and nonverbal messages and media. One way to sort out messages, media, meanings, and their management is to examine the models communication researchers have created to describe the communication process.[3] Engineers, architects, artists, military strategists, economists, and others use models to help them understand complex processes and plan their strategies for more competent action. The models play an important role in changing awareness of a process and, therefore, in changing the process itself. In the same way, models of communication can play an important role in understanding communication as a process and guiding our actions and behaviors.

MODELS OF COMMUNICATION

Three different models that depict the communication process have evolved over the last century:

1. Communication as informing.
2. Communication as persuading.
3. Communication as relating.

COMMUNICATION AS INFORMING.

An informational model of communication has a long history, ranging from philosophers speculating on the nature of symbolic behavior and language, to engineers working on communication technologies such as telephone systems. An early model of communication still used today views **communicating as informing.**[4]

In this information transfer model, a **source**, or sender, is the original producer of the message, and in human communication it is a person. The **channel** is the medium through which a message is sent. Channels may be written, as in letters, memos, or text messages; oral, as in face-to-face verbal communication and telephone conversations; nonverbal, as in shared looks or raised eyebrows; or mediated, as in e-mail or videoconferencing. The **receiver** of the message is the person or group of people who are the ultimate audience for the message.

The most direct version of this model, and the one for which it was originally developed, is a telephone call or television program in which a source creates the content of a message, and sends this content through cable or television signals and transmitters to telephones or television sets where people receive the content. At every stage of the transmission process, there is potential loss of information due to forms of **noise**, which distort or interfere with the original content. For example, in receiving a cell phone call, there may be poor signal strength where the sender is, or a lot of activity in the environment of the receiver, both of which may act as noise and affect the message. Or the sender or receiver may simply be distracted by internal noise, such as mental or psychological distractions.

This model of communication suggests we can understand a communication situation by answering five simple questions: Who? Says what? To whom? Through what channel?[5] And with what effect? These questions lead to two more general key questions: "Did the source successfully convey the intended meaning to the receiver of the message? Did the receiver understand precisely what the speaker intended?"[6]

Since its earliest articulation in the 1950s, this basic model has continued to see communication simply as a conduit or channel for sending and receiving information.[7] But despite its intuitive appeal, the informing model is limited in significant ways. First, it is overly linear, assuming that when a message is being sent and received, the sender and receiver are not simultaneously sending and receiving messages. The suggestion is that the sender sends a message, and the receiver does not communicate until she or he replies and sends a message back to the sender in the form of feedback. This **feedback loop** represents the information that allows communicators in the system to interpret the effects of their messages. For example, in talking to someone on the phone, the person might send feedback by saying, "What—I didn't hear what you said." In speaking to a small group, a presenter might see from someone's facial expression that this group member is distracted by something on that person's com-

COMMUNICATION AS INFORMING is an informational transfer model that identifies a source, channel, receiver, noise, and feedback loop.

A **SOURCE** is the original producer of the message and in human communication it is a person.

THE **CHANNEL** is the medium through which a message is sent.

A **RECEIVER** is the person or group of people who are the ultimate audience for the message.

NOISE is any type of interference coming from the environment that distorts the message or distracts us from the communication.

THE **FEEDBACK LOOP** represents the information that allows communicators in the system to interpret the effects of their messages.

puter screen. These forms of feedback allow a communicator to realize the extent to which a message is getting through to an audience. In both instances, the feedback is itself a form of sending a message, so the receiver is both sending and receiving information simultaneously.

Efforts to adapt this model and make it less linear led to a more complex version of communication as informing that sees the process more as a transaction. These more transactional models recognize that there is no clear distinction between a sender and receiver. They suggest that all communicators in any interaction are continuously acting as senders and receivers. With technologies converging and becoming more interactive, everyone is increasingly both an information producer of messages and a consumer. An example of such a transactional model of communication as informing is presented in Figure 1.2.

The revised communication as informing model, a transactional model of communication, focuses on identifying areas where shared meaning exists, areas where people disagree about meaning, and the communication processes people can use to create shared meaning. This model recognizes that individuals come to situations with different personal meanings that may or may not overlap. This transactional model highlights a second limitation of communication-as-informing models. That is, these models assume the primary purpose of all communication is to achieve shared meaning. Yet, there are many functions communication serves. Not only is shared meaning only one of these functions, there are situations where communicators intentionally hope to be ambiguous, deceptive, or seek outcomes that have little to do with sharing information or creating shared meaning. One of these other functions communication serves is influence, or persuasion.

Figure 1.2: The Communication-as-Informing Model

The transactional model of communication as informing views the source and receiver as engaging in encoding and decoding simultaneously. Furthermore, it accounts for personal fields of meaning. The personal fields of meaning of the two communicators can overlap, creating a shared field of meaning.

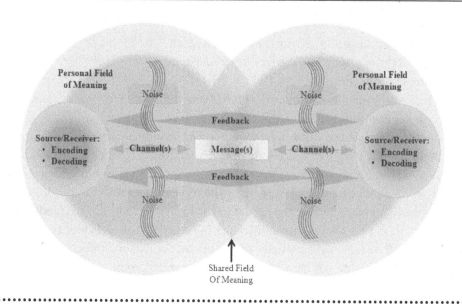

COMMUNICATION AS PERSUADING.

Since Aristotle offered his first course in rhetoric in the fourth century B.C.E., communication scholars have studied the way speakers use the tools of persuasion to influence audiences. **Persuasion** is the use of communication to reinforce, change, or modify an audience's attitudes, values, beliefs, or actions. This definition is explored more in Chapter Fourteen, as it relates to public speaking. However, as a form of influence, persuasion occurs in many different contexts; for example, when we talk a friend into seeing a movie she does not want to see, when a salesperson persuades us to purchase a product or service, or when we convince members of a group or team to follow our recommendations.

The **communication as persuading** model sees communication as a process of influencing others to achieve your own goals. When trying to persuade others, you might typically ask yourself questions such as these:

- Who am I attempting to persuade? Who is the target of my persuasive attempt? What are the target person's key attitudes, values, and beliefs?
- What kinds of arguments can I use to persuade the target person? How do these arguments fit the target person's key attitudes, values, and beliefs?
- What kinds of appeals or arguments would most successfully persuade this person?
- How will the target of my persuasion need to act for me to know I have succeeded?

From this viewpoint, communication is successful to the degree that you are able to get other people to believe, value, or do what you want. Successful communication is measured by your ability to persuade others, and move them in the direction you choose. As Figure 1.3 shows, across messages and times, the more your communication moves others to see or do things the way you want, the more you have persuaded them.

Using communication to accomplish the function of persuading others may be enhanced by our ability to relate to those others.

PERSUASION is the use of communication to reinforce, change, or modify an audience's attitudes, values, beliefs, or actions.

COMMUNICATION AS PERSUADING sees communication as a process of influencing others to achieve your own goals.

COMMUNICATION AS RELATING focuses on the power of communication to create, maintain, and dissolve relationships with others.

A RELATIONSHIP is any actual or perceived interdependence between or among communicators.

COMMUNICATION AS RELATING.

Every time you communicate with someone, you are creating a relationship with that person. Some relationships last moments—others a lifetime. As we participate and communicate in relationships, we are creating our social worlds together. In this sense, communication is so powerful that it creates our social worlds.[8] This is easy to see in messages such as "I want a divorce," or "I hate you," or "I love you." When such messages are said, they create the nature of the relationship among the communicators. This power of communication to create, maintain, and dissolve relationships with others is illustrated in models of **communication as relating**.

A **relationship** is any actual or perceived interdependence between or among communicators. *Interdependence* means that each person's goals or actions are affected by the other's actions.

Figure 1.3: The Communication-as-Persuading Model

Communication is used to influence others. In this model, as Person A communicates with Person B, the communication process achieves changes in Person B's attitudes, values, beliefs, or behaviors to increasingly reflect Person A's views or intended effects.

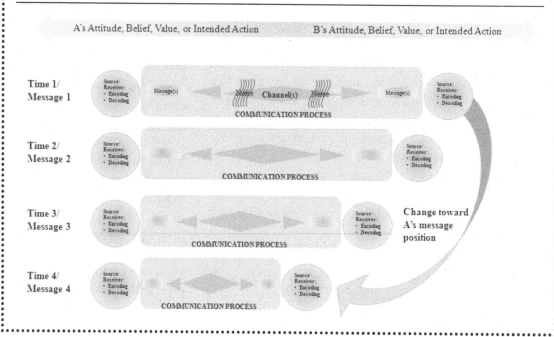

Dependence is one-way influence, whereas *inter*dependence is a situation in which both or everyone's goals and actions are achieved or blocked based on the actions of the others in the relationship. Some relationships are very temporary, such as returning an item of clothing to a salesperson. But most of the time when we think of a relationship, we tend to think of *close* or *personal* relationships, which exist over time and significantly influence who we are and what we do. When such relationships exist among a larger collective of people, it often generates a community, and communication plays a significant role in forming a sense of community.

A **community** is a group of people who come together in the same physical, mental, or virtual space to interact or pursue a common goal. Public institutions such as governments and schools, organizations such as Microsoft and Apple, groups such as families, work teams, and even those people on institutional *Facebook* and *Twitter* accounts—all of these represent the vast variety of communities to which we belong. How do these various kinds of communities get created? As Figure 1.4 illustrates, communication permeates and creates the various communities we belong to. Moreover, different forms of communication create different forms of community. For example, when people in a group communicate little interest in completing an assigned task, the kind of community these members create is significantly different from the community created by a group whose members feel passionate about the task and communicate a willingness to devote the time and energy necessary to complete it. Speech

A COMMUNITY is a group of people who come together in the same physical, mental, or virtual space to interact or pursue a common goal.

Figure 1.4: The Communication-as-Relating Model

The communication-as-relating model portrays how every act of communication is a process of establishing or defining a relationship with others. We all exist in an interconnected set of relationships with others, which are created, maintained, and dissolved through communication.

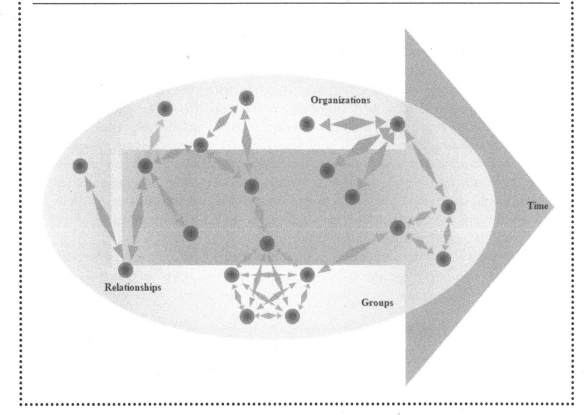

works to regulate such groups, and also becomes a marker or signal of a person's group relationships and affiliations.

One notable communication theorist, Basil Bernstein, explains how language and communication, what he terms **communication codes**, reflect the group a communicator is from, and the group in which that person is communicating.[9] Communication codes are the set of principles and meanings underlying and guiding the language used by members of any social group. For example, when communicating within a community or group of people highly familiar with one another, you can use a code of language in which symbols and expressions have evolved over time within the group. Taken-for-granted understandings allow insiders to understand one another and recognize those who are not group members. When those group members communicate with people outside the group or community, they are more inclined to use a language code in which ideas are clearly spelled out in order for the same meaning to be conveyed. If you have ever been the outsider trying to communicate with a close-knit community or group, Bernstein's description of communication codes needs no further explanation.

COMMUNICATION CODES are the set of principles and meanings underlying and guiding the language used by members of any social group.

That said, this notion that a communication code can alter how people respond to and understand one another led other theorists to believe language is a filter for how we understand the entire world around us. Few scholars believe now that language actually determines thought or reality, but there is also little doubt that how people think is significantly influenced by their language and the language codes of their communities and culture. In Chapter Four, we examine in more detail how language affects, to some extent, our perceptions of reality. For now, the challenge for you as a competent communicator is figuring out how to align your own communication codes with those of people in groups and communities you encounter regularly.

All three models of communication—communication as informing, as persuading, and as relating—are useful when deciding how to communicate in different situations. For example, the informing model is useful in mass communication, or when giving instructions to a large group of people. Viewing communication as persuading may help a salesperson fulfill a quota to keep his or her job. Communication as relating helps us understand the importance of relationships and communities. However, each model provides only partial insight into the communication process, because it allows us to focus on only what it highlights as important. If we believe in communication as informing, we neglect the way shared meaning is created and the persuasive elements of communication. If we believe in communication as persuasion, we do not focus on how people create shared meaning and mutual relationships. If we focus only on relationships, we may ignore the importance of achieving personal goals through persuasive communication.

These limiting beliefs about communication may affect our ability to communicate as competently as we would prefer. But by considering any faulty assumptions you may think are true about the nature of communication, you will move a step closer to enhancing your own communication competence.

ASSUMPTIONS ABOUT COMMUNICATION

If we view communication as community and as the process of managing messages to create meaning, what assumptions do we make about communication? Test your own beliefs about communication in Box 1.1: Test Your Assumptions. Then read the following descriptions of these common assumptions and compare them to your answers on the test.

COMMUNICATION IS A PROCESS.

Communication as a process means every facet or aspect of a communication context affects every other aspect of that context. To say it is **holistic** is to say the entire communication process forms a system in which all the parts of the system attempt to collaborate in helping the system work. Collectively, the parts of the system produce an outcome different than the parts alone would allow. Just as every component of a car engine needs to function in relationship to every other component for it to work optimally, so in a communication process all the relationships and personal histories of those involved, their messages, actions, thoughts, feelings, and their surroundings all interact to affect the outcomes of any encounter.

One of the turning points in any romantic relationship occurs when two people look each other in the eye and say, "I love you." Does uttering the phrase mean the same thing the

HOLISTIC means the entire communication process forms a system in which all the parts of the system attempt to collaborate in helping the system work.

Box 1.1: Test Your Assumptions About Communication

Instructions: Please read the following statements and decide whether you think each is true or false.

TRUE	FALSE	
☐	☐	1. Saying something twice communicates exactly the same thing both times.
☐	☐	2. The meaning of a symbol is the same regardless of the situation in which it occurs.
☐	☐	3. The audience for a message determines the effectiveness of the message.
☐	☐	4. Knowing the intent of the sender's message is important to understanding the communication process.
☐	☐	5. Communication reflects reality rather than creates it.
☐	☐	6. The most important function communication serves is to get something done.
☐	☐	7. High-quality communication must conform to the norms of the relationship or culture.
☐	☐	8. It is important to be consistent in the way you communicate.
☐	☐	9. Understanding one another and sharing meaning is the sole foundation for good communication.
☐	☐	10. To be effective, communication must be clear and unambiguous.

Answers: 1: F; 2: F; 3: T; 4: T; 5: F; 6: T; 7: F; 8: F; 9: F; 10: F

---

thousandth time it is said as it did the first time? Although the words may be the same, the meaning is different because the communicators, the situation, and the relationship—the entire communication process—are different. Although you may be able to say the same words twice, the words never mean the same thing. Statement 1 in the "Test Your Assumptions" box, then, is false.

The fact that communication is a process does not mean it must follow a specific series of steps to be effective. Rather, it suggests the meaning of an utterance depends on where it falls in the process—what has happened before the words are spoken and what happens afterward. To understand the process of communication, we must ask questions such as what was said, to whom, in what context, and how did they respond? The statement, "That's really bad" could be a criticism or a statement of how fun something was, depending on what it is referring to, who said it, and who the intended audience was. Thus, Statement 2 in the "Test Your Assumptions" box is false.

Understanding communication holistically means the speaker, the audience, and what they do together need to be viewed as complex sets of processes operating simultaneously. Taking a holistic approach is important, because focusing only on the speaker's intent or on the audience's perceptions of a message limits our understanding of the entire communication process. Can we understand the complete communication process if we focus on only the speaker's intention apart from the audience to whom he or she is speaking? Can we say a message is effective if the audience for that message views it as such, but the sender of the message does not? The simple answer is no. Understanding communication as a holistic process requires examining the past, looking to the future, and focusing on the situation itself. Statements 3 and 4, then, are both true.

COMMUNICATION CREATES OUR SOCIAL WORLDS.

Communication does have the unique ability to create our social worlds rather than just reflecting reality. Consider a common debate between the major political parties: Republicans tend to claim raising taxes on the rich "kills jobs." Democrats tend to argue that raising taxes on the rich reduces the deficit and funds programs that help the economy create jobs. Although politicians occasionally refer to studies to support such claims, most of the time they simply assert such claims because these claims fit with their broader beliefs about how the world works. These politicians reinterpret history, and the nature of society and the economy, in order to create a social world that matches their preconceived notions and views.

Communication does much more than simply say things to others about our internal states, such as thoughts and feelings. Rather, it creates and re-forms our understanding of those states, events, and people. It is communication that helps us create our own sense of reality and meaning about people and situations. Because the way we communicate is responsible to a large extent for creating our social worlds, Statement 5 in the "Test Your Assumptions" box is false.

COMMUNICATION IS FUNCTIONAL AND ADAPTIVE.

One of the central reasons for communicating is to accomplish something. People sometimes are reluctant to admit that everything they do or say is an attempt to do or get something. We often misinterpret this admission to imply that we are manipulative or selfish. Instead, it is a simple recognition that communication evolved because it was adaptive for thriving and surviving. Messages are **functional**, which means that they are enacted so as to accomplish preferred outcomes. They are also **adaptive**, which means that they are altered to fit particular situations in ways designed to produce better outcomes. So, Statement 6 in the "Test Your Assumptions" box is true.

FUNCTIONAL means messages are enacted so as to accomplish preferred outcomes.

ADAPTIVE means messages are altered to fit particular situations in ways designed to produce better outcomes.

When you think about communicating in a situation that is new to you, such as a first date or a new job, it is natural to think about adapting how you communicate to that situation. Indeed, there are times when acting in new or different ways opens up more possibilities. When you communicate in ways that are creative and liberating, you open up opportunities to reshape norms, values, and beliefs. However, you should do it in a way that others view as appropriate. Said a different way, human beings are able to both create and conform to expectations of any context. When we conform to a context, that context may limit or impose unnecessary constraints on our communication. Perhaps surprisingly, Statement 7, "High-quality communication must conform to the norms of the relationship or culture," is false.

Related to conformity is consistency. Many of us tend to place a high value on consistency. We expect others to maintain consistent attitudes, and an apparent contradiction between statements can seriously diminish a person's credibility. Yet, consistency implies an inability to adapt or change as circumstances change, and an inability to learn and grow from experience. The most competent communication is not the communication that is simply consistent for the sake of consistency, but rather is adapted to the situation. Thus, Statement 8, "You should always be consistent," is false.

Finally, most of us assume that for people to communicate well they must share precise meanings for events and words (Statement 9 in the "Test Your Assumptions" box), and that people always need to be clear and unambiguous to achieve good communication (Statement 10). Of course, we often need to share meaning and achieve clarity in how we communicate—but not all the time. There are times when we may need or want to be less than clear in our communication in order to adapt and be fully functional in the particular situation.

Being ambiguous can have two main benefits.[6] First, ambiguity helps people with diverse sets of opinions collaborate with each other. If there is ambiguity about what beliefs or values are important, people may assume that they share some of the same beliefs and values, and be willing to work together. When communication is clear, the differences between people become more distinct and may lead to excessive conflict. Second, ambiguous communication can promote creativity. For example, sometimes teachers may be ambiguous in their instructions about how to complete a particular assignment to encourage students to be creative in how they accomplish the task. So, Statements 9 and 10 are both false.

THE IMPORTANCE OF COMMUNICATION

This chapter began with the claim that communication and your communication competence are the most important factors in determining the quality of your life. Given how much time we devote to speaking, listening, writing, informing, persuading, and talking, human beings communicate almost constantly. Indeed, it is commonly accepted among communication scholars that "one cannot *not* communicate." Inaction is also an action. You are even communicating when just being silent— as you know if you have ever encountered someone giving you the "silent treatment."

In addition to the fact that we are constantly communicating whether we intend to or not, an analysis by two communication scholars of 93 journal and newspaper articles, reports, and national surveys also provided evidence of the importance of effective and appropriate communication.[10] The analysis found that communication and communication instruction are critical to your personal development, psychologically and socially; succeeding in school; becoming a responsible citizen and participant in the world; and succeeding in a career, in business, and in organizational life. In addition, good communication is considered necessary to our ability to address emerging social concerns in the 21st century, including health communication issues, crisis communication situations, and crime and policing problems.

As you can see by now, communication is much more complex than it first appears. Like Kathryn at the beginning of this chapter, you probably communicate every day with a large and diverse number of people, over a number of topics and issues, and in a wide variety of settings. Given this diversity and complexity, it is impossible to construct rules for communication that specifically detail what messages are required, permitted, or prohibited in any and all situations. Thus, building a comprehensive model of communication that can prescribe what people must do or say in all situations is impossible. So, what kind of model of communication can we create? It is possible to construct a model of communication for making informed choices about messages that will help you act in competent ways, so that your communication is perceived as appropriate and effective by others. Competent communication is the topic of Chapter Two.

CHAPTER SUMMARY

Communication is a pervasive force in our everyday life as we relate and connect to a wide variety of people through face-to-face and mediated channels in a large number of social and work contexts. Communication is a process of managing messages and media for the purpose of creating meaning. Messages are the words, sounds, actions, and gestures that people express to one another when they interact. Media are any means through which symbols are transmitted and meanings are represented. Meaning is the interpretation people assign to a message—how it is recognized or understood. Competent communication is both appropriate and effective. Appropriate communication means behaving in ways acceptable to the valued norms and expectations of a given context; and effective communication means achieving the most desirable objectives or outcomes possible in a given context.

There are various models by which the process of communication can be understood, such as communication as informing, communication as persuading, and communication as relating. All three models are useful when deciding how to communicate in different situations

Communication is a holistic process that unfolds over time and creates our social worlds. Communication is functional in that it helps us to accomplish preferred outcomes, and it is adaptive in that it can be altered to fit particular situations. Our ability to communicate creatively can open up opportunities to reshape norms, values, and beliefs, and create new ways of thinking and being.

KEY TERMS.

The key terms below are defined in this chapter and presented alphabetically with definitions in the Glossary at the end of the book.

- competent communication
- appropriate communication
- effective communication
- communication
- messages
- symbol
- referent
- language
- nonverbal communication
- nonverbal symbols

- media
- meaning
- managing
- communication as informing
- source
- channel
- receiver
- noise
- feedback loop

- persuasion
- communication as persuading
- communication as relating
- relationship
- community
- communication codes
- holistic
- functional
- adaptive

BUILDING MOTIVATION: SELF-ASSESSMENT TOOL.

Rate each of the eight communication situations described here, indicating your own typical level for communicating in that situation. Rate one situation all the way through for motivation, knowledge, and skills. Then rate the next situation. Use the 1–4 scale below, with 1 being minimal competence and 4 high competence.

Communication situations.

1. Meeting your future father-in-law for the first time.
2. Having dinner with an exchange student from a different culture.

3. Working on a team project using technology to communicate.
4. Working on a team project in a face-to-face meeting.
5. Facilitating a small-group discussion at a political meeting.
6. Presenting a speech in your entry-level public speaking class.
7. Presenting a training session to coworkers or fellow students on campus.
8. Attending a reception where you only know one or two other people.

Motivation.

1 = Distracted, disinterested, or simply little interest in appearing competent.
2 = Somewhat distracted or disinterested, but somewhat motivated to be competent.
3 = Moderately interested and motivated to be competent.
4 = Highly interested and motivated to be competent.

Knowledge.

1 = Often lacking a clear idea of what to say or do in situations.
2 = Occasionally lacking a clear idea of what to say or do in situations.
3 = Generally knowledgeable about what to say or do in situations.
4 = Highly knowledgeable about all aspects of what to say and do in situations.

Skills.

1 = Always seem to be saying and doing the wrong things when communicating.
2 = Often saying and doing the wrong things when communicating.
3 = Often saying and doing exactly the right things when communicating.
4 = Always saying and doing exactly the right things when communicating.

Interpreting your scores.

Total your score separately for each situation (motivation, knowledge, and skills). The possible range of the score for each situation is 3–12. If your total score for any of the situations is 6 or less, you see yourself as less competent in that situation than you should be. A score of 7–9 means that you are average at sending and receiving communication messages in the situation. A score of 10–12 indicates that you have a high level of communication competence in that situation.

BUILDING KNOWLEDGE: DISCUSSION QUESTIONS.

1. How are communication technologies such as e-mail, blogs, texting, tweeting, and video-conferencing influencing the communication process?
2. Identify three situations where it would make sense to use communication as informing, communication as persuading, and communication as relating. How else can you define and describe communication other than these three models?
3. Think of a time when you felt that a person was flexible in his or her communication, yet was not perceived as being wishy-washy or adapting just to meet someone else's needs. How did that person make his or her communication flexible?

4. Why is understanding communication important to our daily lives? Are there ever situations in which communication does not make a difference? Explain.

BUILDING SKILLS: STUDENT ACTIVITIES.

Individual activities.

1. Think of a recent conversation you would characterize as poor communication. On a piece of paper, draw a vertical line dividing the paper in two. In the left-hand column, write down the conversation. Note each speaker's turn on a separate line. In the right-hand column, next to each message write down what you think is the underlying reason for that message. Think about the key assumptions each conversational partner is making and the reasons that guided his or her interaction. How could you change the conversation to make the outcome better? How would the key assumptions need to change?
2. Find an opinion piece or an editorial in a magazine or a newspaper. Read the editorial and highlight the key words and phrases the author uses. Focusing on these key words and phrases, how would you describe the way the author perceives his or her community?
3. Write down all the major communication interactions you have had in the last 24 hours. Which would you consider effective and which not so effective? What could you have done to improve the quality of those interactions?

Group activities.

1. Form groups of four to five students. Take a blank piece of poster board and draw a picture of a model that captures your view of the communication process. As a group, discuss what features and components need to be included in the communication model and why. Compare your communication model with those created by other groups in the class.
2. As an individual, complete the following statement: "I dream of a community where. . . ." In groups of four to five students, share your dreams for your community. As a group, construct a vision for what an ideal community would look like. Then discuss the kinds of communication that need to happen to make that vision a reality. Who needs to talk to whom? About what? How?
3. Form groups of five to six students. The communication discipline has several national organizations, including the National Communication Association (http://www.natcom.org/) and the International Communication Association (http://www.icahdq.org/). Split up and visit each site, and write a one-page summary of the way that site portrays communication. Then compare each subgroup's finding on the sites. What is the purpose of communication according to each site? What kinds of issues are studied in communication?

NOTES

1. See Frey, Botan, & Kreps (2000).
2. See Littlejohn & Foss (2010).
3. See Spitzberg & Changnon (2009).
4. See Shannon & Weaver (1949).

5. See Lasswell (1964).

6. See Eisenberg & Goodall (2004).

7. See Harrison, Todd, & Lawton (2008).

8. See Pearce (1994).

9. See Bernstein (1971) and Steinfatt (2009).

10. See Morreale & Pearson (2008).

REFERENCES

Bernstein, B. (1971). *Class, codes, and control: Theoretical studies towards a sociology of language*. London, UK: Routledge & Kegan Paul.

Eisenberg, E. M., & Goodall, H. L. (2004). *Organizational communication: Balancing creativity and constraint* (4th ed.). Boston, MA: Bedford/St. Martin's.

Frey, L. R., Botan, C. H., & Kreps, G. L. (2000). *Investigating communication: An introduction to research methods* (2nd ed.). Boston, MA: Allyn and Bacon.

Harrison, S. J., Todd, Z., & Lawton, R. (2008). Talk about terrorism and the media: Communicating with the conduit metaphor. *Communication, Culture & Critique, 1*(4), 378–395.

Lasswell, H. D. (1964). The structure and function of communication in society. In L. Bryson (Ed.), *The communication of ideas: A series of addresses* (pp. 37–51). New York, NY: Cooper Square.

Littlejohn, S. W., & Foss, K. A. (2010). *Theories of human communication* (10th ed.). Belmont, CA: Wadsworth.

Morreale, S. P., & Pearson, J. C. (2008). Why communication education is important: The centrality of the discipline in the 21st century. *Communication Education, 57*(2), 224–240.

Pearce, W. B. (1994). *Interpersonal communication: Making social worlds*. New York, NY: HarperCollins.

Shannon, C. E., & Weaver, W. (1949). *The mathematical theory of communication*. Urbana, IL: University of Illinois Press.

Spitzberg, B. H., & Changnon, G. (2009). Conceptualizing intercultural competence. In D. K. Deardorff (Ed.), *The Sage handbook of intercultural competence* (pp. 2–52). Thousand Oaks, CA: Sage.

Steinfatt, T. M. (2009). Elaborated and restricted codes. In S. W. Littlejohn & K.A. Foss (Eds.), *Encyclopedia of Communication Theory* (pp. 329–330). Thousand Oaks, CA: Sage.

CHAPTER TWO

A MODEL OF COMMUNICATION COMPETENCE

The sign said, "This door to remain closed at all times." Correct me if I'm wrong, but doesn't that defeat the purpose of a door? —Danny McCrossan, Northern Irish Comedian, b. 1981

• • •

Cambria was a transfer student at a prestigious, small fine arts university where she had a little trouble opening the right doors. Shortly after leaving her hometown community college and moving into a small apartment, she was invited to a social for communication majors. She got back to her apartment from a day hike just in time to quickly clean up and get dressed. Upon arriving at the event, she saw she was dressed less formally than the others attending the social. The gathering was in a large carpeted room with marble columns and fine artwork on the walls. About 40 people were there, faculty and students from freshmen to seniors.

Cambria joined a small group of students conversing about the program, the courses, the professors, and the major. She repeatedly felt like she could not keep up with the conversation. She would occasionally make a general comment, but avoided saying much. About an hour into the social, the department chair asked everyone to form a large circle. After some introductory remarks, he asked everyone to take turns introducing themselves. As chance would have it, Cambria was asked to start, making her feel like there was a spotlight on her. She mumbled her name and that she was from California, and then blurted out the first thing that came to her mind: "I feel out of place here this evening." As the evening wore on, she felt nervous, unclear about what she was doing there, and simply unable to communicate well.

Your success or failure when communicating depends on many things. As Cambria's story suggests, three factors interact with one another and are especially important to communicating competently—motivation, knowledge, and skills. Cambria was tired, nervous, and at times unsure about why she was at the social, so her motivation was less than ideal. She was not very knowledgeable about some of the topics, the place, or the people, and could not contribute much to the conversations. Finally, she did not have the skills to overcome her tiredness and anxiety and then communicate in a way she would have liked. This chapter examines the motivation, knowledge, and skills that make up communication competence.

WHAT IS COMMUNICATION COMPETENCE?

Most of us do not communicate nearly as competently as we could. We think we communicate acceptably because we spend most of our waking hours communicating in one way or another—speaking, listening, reading, writing, or processing information of some sort. This fact is made more apparent in today's media-saturated society. A study by the Kaiser Family Foundation found that the average person between 8 and 18 years of age spends 45.5 hours a week interacting with or through electronic media, compared with an average of just more than 2 hours with parents and only 1.5 hours in physical activity (and only 50 minutes spent on homework)![1]

Research also shows that the more deficient a person is in communication skills, the more likely he or she is to experience problems with educational performance, loneliness, depression, divorce, drug abuse, dysfunctional conflicts with others, risky sexual activity, and even physical illness and premature death.[2] Furthermore, studies indicate that somewhere between 7% and 25% of the population experiences communication problems serious enough to interfere with their quality of life. In some areas, such as public speaking anxiety or shyness, this figure often reaches 40%.[2] So before you conclude that learning about communication is just common sense, it might be a good idea to consider how many of life's challenges and even problems could be addressed better by engaging in more competent communication. For you personally, think about how many important life goals would be better achieved through more competent communication.

As suggested in Chapter One, **communication competence** is the extent to which people achieve desired outcomes through behavior acceptable to a situation.[3] We will arrive at a more formal definition later, but for our current purposes, this definition already leads us to examine certain issues, such as "How do we know whether a desired outcome has been achieved?" and "How do we know whether a communication behavior fits a situation?" To better answer such questions, we first examine how people form impressions about whether some communication behavior is competent or not.

COMPETENCE AS AN IMPRESSION.

You have probably heard that first impressions are important. At the same time, we are often told to "just be ourselves." Ultimately, the impressions we create through communication become important to almost everything we do in life. However, how we actually behave in most instances is less important than how others *perceive* us to have behaved. You may "do everything right" in a situation (first date, job interview, etc.), and still the other person in that situation may form an undesirable impression of you. As a result, you may not achieve what you hoped to achieve in that relationship or encounter. Impressions matter, and favorable impressions result from communicating competently. In Chapter One, we introduced the idea of competent communication as being both appropriate and effective.

> **COMMUNICATION COMPETENCE** is the extent to which speakers achieve desired outcomes through communication behavior acceptable to a situation.

> **RULES** are prescriptions you can follow for what should or should not be done in a given type of situation.

As defined in Chapter One, appropriateness refers to communication that fits a given context, which means the behavior is considered legitimate, acceptable, or suitable to a situation. An important way of determining whether behavior fits is to ask whether it seems to follow the implicit or explicit rules or norms relevant to the situation. **Rules** are prescriptions for what should or should not be done in a given type of situation.[4] Sometimes they are explicit: "Don't call someone names when arguing." Sometimes they are more implicit: "You should arrive at parties 30 minutes to an hour after the stated beginning time." Despite the importance of being clear or understandable, some rules even call for ambiguous or somewhat unclear messages. For example, rules for polite behavior typically suggest in response to a question such as, "How do you like my new hair style?"

rather than saying, "It really sucks!" if you do not like it, you are better off saying something like, "Wow, that's a different look for you."

As defined in Chapter One, effectiveness is the extent to which communication accomplishes valued outcomes. We all pursue goals, objectives, intentions, and outcomes in our interactions with others. You may call someone to see whether you can borrow their notes, ask someone for a date, interview for a job, or speak to a group to persuade them to support a proposal. In this way, communication is functional when it serves to get things done (See Chapter One). Clearly, to be competent requires that a person be able to accomplish some basic communicative tasks and goals in life.[5] Culture, society, politics, religion, business, conflict, and relationships—all are accomplished through interaction and the behavior of communication. This is the only way these social activities can be done. In this sense, competence is the extent to which people are effective in accomplishing what they want through communication.

But how do you know when you have been effective? Usually you consider yourself effective when you obtain (a) something you value, (b) something you set as a goal to accomplish, or (c) something you expended some effort to obtain.[6] Unlike appropriateness, which is usually better judged by others, effectiveness is something generally only you determine for yourself. Only you really know when your communication results in an outcome you prefer.

THE COMPETENCE GRID.

Now we have considered two possible criteria or standards for competence: appropriateness and effectiveness. If we consider the possibility that someone can be perceived as inappropriate or appropriate, and ineffective or effective, there are four possible combinations for communication: A person can be inappropriate and ineffective, inappropriate and effective, appropriate and ineffective, or appropriate and effective. Each of these communication possibilities is examined next.

The first possible way to communicate is both inappropriate and ineffective. This represents **minimizing communication**, in which a person fails to achieve any desired outcomes in the interaction, and also alienates other people through his or her behavior. Consider someone frustrated by waiting in line and then yelling at the person working behind the counter, only to be told that nothing can be done. Indeed, by creating a scene this person may even be escorted out of the store by a security guard, forfeiting any chance to attain his or her goal. This person gets minimum results out of the interaction.

MINIMIZING COMMUNICATION is inappropriate and ineffective communication.

SUFFICING COMMUNICATION is appropriate but ineffective communication.

MAXIMIZING COMMUNICATION is effective but inappropriate communication.

The appropriate but ineffective person interacts with **sufficing communication**, which enables him or her merely to get by. This person's behavior is appropriate, but it does not accomplish much of anything. In our opening, Cambria spent most of the early part of the social merely standing silently in groups while other people talked. Her behavior did not break any rules or norms, but she probably did not make new friends, find out about upcoming activities, or get to know faculty members.

The inappropriate and effective type of communicator engages in **maximizing communication**. A person maximizes when he or she is assertive or aggressive without concern for other people's sense of appropriateness. From a maximizing perspective, winning is all that matters, and lying, cheating, coercing, or exploiting the other person are all fair game if the result is that you win. But the inappropriateness of such activities is destructive to any relationship. In fact, you may achieve a short-term goal using aggressive communication, but cut yourself off from achieving more important long-term goals. Consequently, maximizing communication behavior ultimately may move you toward an unsuccessful situation or relationship.

The communicator who achieves preferred outcomes in a way that preserves the relationship and respects the rules of the situation (i.e., who uses appropriate and effective communication) has chosen **optimizing communication**. This person

> OPTIMIZING COMMUNICATION is appropriate and effective communication.

achieves success through means others consider acceptable, and recognizes the importance of self-satisfaction in communication situations. He or she also understands that such satisfaction should not come at the expense of others' satisfaction.

Communication and communicators are judged on many characteristics, such as satisfaction, clarity, attractiveness, efficiency, and emotional warmth. However, such characteristics matter only to the extent that they contribute to the appropriateness and effectiveness of any encounter. The competence grid presented in Figure 2.1 allows you to analyze whether you have competently—effectively and appropriately—achieved your communication goals in any given situation.

Figure 2.1: The Communication Competence Grid

Using this competence grid, you can determine the extent to which your communication behavior in any situation is optimizing because it is characterized by both appropriateness and effectiveness.

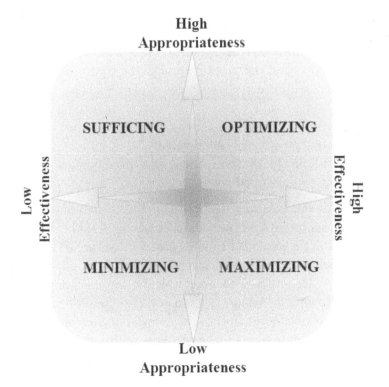

The key challenge to such competent communication in most situations is finding a delicate balance between the need for appropriateness and the desire for effectiveness.[2,7] Failure to attain such a balance is likely to call your competence into question. The ability to achieve such a balance of effectiveness and appropriateness results from understanding the ethics of your communication behavior. We examine this age-old question next.

ETHICS AND COMMUNICATION COMPETENCE.

At least since Plato and Aristotle, we have argued for ethical standards with which to evaluate communication. Ethical codes are sets of principles for guiding behavior in ways considered good or moral. Most ethical codes emphasize the nature of the behavior or conduct itself, the purpose the conduct serves, or aspects of the context where the conduct occurs.

The National Communication Association (NCA) developed a credo for ethical communication (see www.natcom.org). This credo outlines a set of beliefs in the values of freedom of expression, openness of access, accuracy of content, diversity of representation, and respect of persons and opinions. Here are nine big ideas for communicating ethically from the NCA Credo.

1. We advocate truthfulness, accuracy, honesty, and reason as essential to the integrity of communication.
2. We endorse freedom of expression, diversity of perspective, and tolerance of dissent to achieve the informed and responsible decision making fundamental to a civil society.
3. We strive to understand and respect other communicators before evaluating and responding to their messages.
4. We promote access to communication resources and opportunities as necessary to fulfill human potential and contribute to the well-being of families, communities, and society.
5. We promote communication climates of caring and mutual understanding that respect the unique needs and characteristics of individual communicators.
6. We condemn communication that degrades individuals and humanity through distortion, intimidation, coercion, and violence, and through the expression of intolerance and hatred.
7. We are committed to the courageous expression of personal convictions in pursuit of fairness and justice.
8. We advocate sharing information, opinions, and feelings when facing significant choices while also respecting privacy and confidentiality.
9. We accept responsibility for the short- and long-term consequences of our own communication and expect the same of others.

The concepts of appropriateness and effectiveness indirectly describe an ethical code for communication conduct. The appropriateness standard focuses on what behaviors tend to be considered ethical or unethical in the particular context, group, or cultures. The effectiveness standard focuses on whether the behaviors that accomplish the purpose for communicating are also ethical.

Applying the competence grid as a code for ethical communication conduct is not simple. Although the majority of people do not lie in a given day, a few people lie frequently.[8] Most of these lies, however, are motivated by a desire to make things easier or better for someone else. So the question becomes whether such lies are appropriate and therefore ethical. In any actual communication event, the participants need to determine how to balance and evaluate the importance of the two criteria or standards for competence. In general, you should keep ethical conduct in mind as you strive to balance appropriateness (honoring the rules and expected behaviors in the context) with effectiveness (accomplishing your goals while respecting the needs and concerns of others).

COMPONENTS OF A COMMUNICATION COMPETENCE MODEL

The competence grid illustrates what we need to accomplish as competent communicators, but it does not show us how. Learning how requires us to consider the factors that are likely to enhance our ability to communicate appropriately and effectively. These factors or components of competence are motivation, knowledge, skills, and context. They form the basic model of communication competence we will apply to the communication process throughout this book.[9]

MOTIVATION.

For you to communicate competently, it is important first to *want* to do so. That is, you must be motivated to be competent. **Motivation** has both positive and negative sides. **Negative motivation** is the experience of anxiety about a communication action or the perception of low potential reward, in a real or imagined communication situation. **Positive motivation**, in contrast, is the perception of high potential reward in pursuing a communication action.

People find the positive motivation to communicate competently from such sources as the situation itself and their own goals in it. These goals represent what you intend to bring about through your communication action. Goals are particularly relevant to communication competence because they are a way of assessing your effectiveness. A communicator who achieves his or her goals is effective and, therefore, more competent. Goals also help guide communication behavior. It is much easier to know what to do and how to do it if you are clear about the goals you want to accomplish.

Negative motivations exist as well. In particular, **communication apprehension** is the fear or anxiety an individual experiences as a result of either real or anticipated communication with another person or other persons.[10] Common signs of apprehension include shaky hands, sweaty palms, or just a squeamish feeling in the pit of your stomach. The result is a tendency to either avoid communication or suffer from feelings of yet more anxiety when you are expected to communicate. There are people who are generally apprehensive, but most people are anxious in particular types of situations. This **context apprehension** is anxiety about communicating in a particular context such as interpersonal, small groups, or public speaking. For example, many of us are fine talking with one other person, but we experience some anxiety about public speaking.

To be sure, one of the most problematic forms of context apprehension is public speaking anxiety. This stage fright is explored in detail in Chapter Twelve, including remedies for managing it. Although stage fright is perhaps the most common fear, anxiety in interpersonal situations, shy-

> **NEGATIVE MOTIVATION** refers to the experience of anxiety about a communication action or the perception of low reward potential, in a real or imagined communication situation.

> **POSITIVE MOTIVATION** refers to the perception of high potential reward in pursuing a communication action.

> **COMMUNICATION APPREHENSION** is the fear or anxiety an individual experiences as a result of either real or anticipated communication with another person or other persons.

> **CONTEXT APPREHENSION** is anxiety about communicating in a particular context such as interpersonal, small groups, or public speaking.

ness or **social anxiety**, is very common as well. Social anxiety is the real or imagined fear of interacting in an interpersonal encounter. Social situations can seem very threatening, because we derive so much of our self-concept from what we think others think of us. We refer to this in Chapter Three as the "looking-glass" self-concept, which suggests we are very concerned about how we look or appear to others.

Perhaps like Cambria in the opening story, you have found yourself at a social event in which you looked at people talking comfortably among themselves and thought, "I want to join in the conversation, but I don't know how to break in and capture the interest of people I don't know." You have the motivation to communicate, but you do not know what to say or do. Obviously, motivation is not enough—you also need knowledge to communicate competently. We now turn to this second component of the competence model.

KNOWLEDGE.

It is true that motivation alone is often not enough to make you a competent communicator. To be competent, you need to be knowledgeable about all the critical elements involved in the communication process. **Knowledge** consists of all the mental processes involved in awareness, ease of access, and organization of relevant information for enacting a communication behavior. Put simply, knowledge in communication guides us about what to say and do, and tells us the procedures by which we can do it.

So knowledge can be broadly separated into the what and the how of communication, known as content and procedural knowledge, respectively. **Content knowledge** is an understanding of the topics, words, meanings, and so forth, required in a situation. **Procedural knowledge** tells us how to assemble, plan, and perform content knowledge in a particular situation. Unfortunately for Cambria, she did not seem to know what to say at the social event, or how to say it. To illustrate further, you may know someone who can learn the lines of a joke (content) and even be aware of how (procedure) to tell it in a funny way, but when the joke is actually performed, it falls flat. In this case, competence depends on more than motivation and knowledge. Ultimately, it is the person's behavior, his or her verbal and nonverbal skills in joke telling, that we judge as competent or incompetent.

SKILLS.

You may have witnessed both terrible and terrific acting performances. Even the worst actors are usually motivated to perform well, and they probably know their scripts inside and out. So what makes some performances bad? The simple answer is that the actors lack the acting skills to apply their motivation and knowledge.

Skills, the third component of the communication competence model, are repeatable, goal-directed, proficient behaviors. They must be repeatable, because anyone could accomplish something by accident. But if it cannot be accomplished again, on demand, it is not a skill that the person possesses. You might give a very funny introduction to a speech, but if you cannot ever get a laugh again, you cannot say you have the skill of creating humorous introductions. Skills are also goal-directed,

SOCIAL ANXIETY is the real or imagined fear of interacting in interpersonal situations.

KNOWLEDGE consists of all the mental processes involved in awareness, ease of access, and organization of relevant information for enacting a communication behavior.

CONTENT KNOWLEDGE refers to understanding of the topics, words, meanings, and so forth, required in a communication situation.

PROCEDURAL KNOWLEDGE tells us how to assemble, plan, and perform content knowledge in a particular communication situation.

SKILLS are repeatable, goal-directed, proficient behaviors enacted in a given context.

because they must be designed to accomplish something. If they are not, they are just behaviors, rather than skills. Finally, skills must demonstrate some minimal level of proficiency in achieving the goals—otherwise, we consider someone lacking or deficient in a particular skill.

Communication skills can be understood along a continuum of abstraction, which we refer to as the macro, middle, and micro levels of communication.[2] At the *macro* level, for example, regardless of culture, people need to be able to display empathy, cooperation, engage in courtship, establish intimate relationships, and so forth. These are fundamental, *macro*-level activities involved in establishing and maintaining social relationships. At the *middle* level, also regardless of culture, people need to be able to engage in disagreements or agreements, greetings, promises, threats, requests, assertions, and various other communication acts that language enables. At the *micro* level, these macro- and middle-level actions are actually enacted through specific communication behaviors, such as asking questions, expressing intelligible statements, making eye contact, and displaying facial expressions like anger, sadness, or happiness. It is these micro-level behaviors that most people typically refer to as communication skills. All people in all cultures develop routines for all three levels and for how they will use micro communication skills. For example, every culture needs to express affection (macro level), but the specific social rituals (middle level), and the observable behaviors and skills (micro level) considered appropriate and effective for expressing affection may differ in any culture.[11]

The reason for distinguishing here among macro, middle, and micro skills is this: as you think about enhancing your own communication skills, you need to think about the skills level in need of enhancement. For instance, are you concerned with the macro-level skill of successful dating, the middle-level skill of initial greeting behaviors for a potential date, or the micro skills of making eye contact and saying the right thing when you approach an attractive person in the cafeteria or a book store? Obviously, these three levels interact and support one another, as do the three components of communication competence.

Without a doubt, the more motivated, knowledgeable, and skilled you are, the more likely it is that you can engage in competent communication interactions. However, the interrelationship of these three components is worth noting. A person may become aware of his or her lack of knowledge, for instance, and then develop a strong motivation to improve in the skills component. Motivation, as well, may be influenced by how accurately the communicator knows and understands constraints in the particular communication situation or **context**.

Definitely, we apply the three components in actual communication situations, which brings us to context, the fourth component of our model. Any communication behavior occurs in a particular place and time, and with some audience or receiver(s) in mind. Therefore, context becomes an essential part of the model of communication competence.

> CONTEXT is the frame within which the communication action occurs.
>
> CONTEXT TYPES are routine, socially negotiated understandings of what is going on in a communication encounter or event.

CONTEXT.

The context is the frame within which the communication action occurs. So far, we have been using the terms ***context*** and ***situation*** almost interchangeably. But context can be viewed in a number of different ways. We define ***context*** in two ways: by type and by level.

Context types are routine, socially agreed-to understandings of what is going on in a communication encounter or event. The most common context types are cultural, chronological, relational, situational, and functional.[6] Let us first discuss the five types of context, which you can think of as aspects or facets of the context that impact and shape communication.

Culture consists of the enduring patterns of thought, value, and behavior that define a group of people.[12] Culture represents a collection of the mental and behavioral patterns that give people a sense of belonging to a group or community viewed by its members as distinct from other groups. You are born into a culture, and your behavior constantly contributes to it and coevolves with it. Culture, as an aspect of context, clearly can impact communication in any interaction, so let us clarify culture a bit more.

> CULTURE consists of the enduring patterns of thought, value, and behavior that define a group of people.

Although culture is commonly thought of as the same as ethnicity, race, and nationality, it is not. *Ethnicity* refers "to a wide variety of groups who might share a language, historical origins, religion, and identification with a common nation-state or cultural system."[13] Similarly, *nationality* simply refers to people born, raised, or with citizenship in a given nation-state. In contrast, *race* implies a group of people with common genetic or physical characteristics. Many people also have expanded the notion of culture to include organizations, chat rooms, gender and sexual preference, and even eras—like the boomer generation. Given these expansive descriptions of culture, the impact on communication of this facet of context is apparent.

A second type of context is always with us, yet often unnoticed. Chronological aspects of communication involve the ways that time is experienced. If "time is money" in North America, then every minute that ticks by on the clock while a contract is not signed sends a message that money is lost. But if time is "all we have," and viewed as more natural and rhythmic, then there is less rush to push the natural order of things. Time is the collective and individual perception of the sequence and progression of events. Germanic cultures are known for their punctuality and precise organization of time. Other cultures, such as Mediterranean and Pacific Islander, are more relaxed when defining time and punctuality. Indeed, time is an aspect of context that weaves its way into everything we experience, as we make sense of both our own and others' chronological behavior. Interpersonally, for example, some people believe that rapid development of physical intimacy is appropriate in romantic relationships, whereas others believe physical intimacy should progress more slowly in relationships.

Definitely, context can be understood based on the nature of the relationship of the communicators—relational content is a third type of context. We can understand the relationship aspects of context according to two dimensions: power and affiliation.[14] Power refers to the status relationship of the people involved—who has the ability to influence whom? Most relationships contain some form of power that influences how people communicate—for example, relationships between boss and employee, parent and child, or professor and student. In any one of these pairs, however, interactions over time may redistribute the power to make the relationship quite different. Affiliation is the emotional and evaluative dimension of a relationship—the degree to which you like and are drawn toward someone or dislike and want to avoid the person. Determining whether you like or dislike someone, and in what way, is one of the most fundamental evaluations you can make about a person.

The fourth type of context consists of the situational aspects of the communication event, the environment or physical surroundings. This includes all the physical characteristics that are present—temperature, lighting, amount of space permitted for movement, objects in the space, and the media through which we communicate. Some public speakers discover the difficulty of keeping an audience's attention if there is background noise in the environment, or if the temperature is uncomfortable. Group leaders often find themselves challenged when their PowerPoint projectors or teleconference links fail to work. Surroundings can also help communication, for instance, choosing a quiet environment for an important conversation with a close friend.

The final type of context is about the functional aspects of communication. In Chapter One, we discussed that communication has many functions. The **function** of communication is what the communication behavior attempts to accomplish or actually accomplishes. A funeral is functionally different from a birthday party. The function of communication at home or on a date is different from that in a class lecture. Contexts in each of these situations are different, independent of the culture, time, relationship, and place in which they occur. Communicators are attempting to accomplish something different in each situation. These different communication goals or functions influence the types of behavior considered appropriate and effective.

In the opening story, Cambria's competence was challenged by each of the context types we just described. The mix of cultures was unfamiliar to her. She felt a little rushed and therefore somewhat anxious when she arrived. She did not know anyone well enough to have established a comfortable relationship. The situation was more formal than she anticipated, and she did not realize that one of the functions of the gathering would be to introduce herself to the entire group. In other words, had she been better informed and able to anticipate the context types, she could have communicated much more competently. We now turn our attention from the types of context to the levels of context.

Context levels refer to the number of communicators in the encounter or event, and the direction of communication among them. The number of people involved in any communication situation has implications for the complexity and formality of the interaction that takes place. The four most common levels of context are interpersonal, small group, public speaking, and mediated communication. They differ according to whether a person is communicating on a one-to-one, one-to-several, or one-to-many basis, and whether some technological medium is involved.

The levels are not entirely distinct, however. A communication event may fit more than one level of context. Is a family discussion an interpersonal or a group context? Is a weekly presentation by a department head to middle managers a group or public-speaking context? Is sending a tweet by a celebrity to a large fan base a form of group, public, or mediated communication? The answer in each case is that communication context is increasingly converging across these levels of communication. But although context levels frequently overlap, the levels do suggest the number of people involved does make a difference in your communication. For example, as the number of people increases, the potential number of meanings attributed to a message increases, and the number of audience characteristics to be considered also increases.

In this book, we concentrate on the most common levels of contexts. We discuss the **interpersonal context** as an informal interaction among people in social or personal relationships. Social relationships typically are those with family, friends, or lovers. However, other interactions, such as when you speak to a salesperson about a product, another student about an assignment, or another worker about a job, these are also considered interpersonal communication.

The complexity of connections among people differentiates interpersonal from the **group context.** When dealing with only one or two other people, you engage in fewer communication exchanges, and target messages to one particular person, rather than to a general group. Group contexts include a larger number of people, typically 3 to 12, and usually take place in a more formal, task-oriented

---

FUNCTIONS of communication are what the communication behavior attempts to accomplish or actually accomplishes.

CONTEXT LEVELS refer to the number of communicators in the encounter or event, and the direction of communication among them.

An **INTERPERSONAL CONTEXT** is an informal interaction among people in social or personal relationships.

GROUP CONTEXTS include a larger number of people, typically 3 to 12, and usually take place in a more formal, task-oriented context.

context. Although messages may sometimes be directed to specific individuals in the group, there is an understanding that the entire group is the appropriate audience, and other members of the group may respond to the messages.

In **public-speaking contexts**, typically one person or a small group of people will speak to a larger number of people who have little or no speaking role. But then audience members often may ask questions and provide feedback at the end of the speech, and their bodies and demeanors provide feedback, such as when they nod, laugh, look distracted, or make eye contact. All of these are forms of communication, even without a formally assigned speaking role.

> •
> PUBLIC-SPEAKING CONTEXTS include one person or a small group of people speaking to a larger number of people who have little or no speaking role.
>
> •
> The COMPUTER-MEDIATED CONTEXT is technologically facilitated communication.

Mediated contexts represent technologically facilitated communication. In such contexts, a person creates a message that is then distributed or transmitted through some technological medium. These contexts blur the distinctions between one-to-one and one-to-many. A tweet or email may go to a single person or to thousands (or millions). These media vary in the degree to which the message is immediately accessible to others, the extent to which both verbal and nonverbal message information is available, and the extent to which receivers can respond to the message.

People communicate in these context types and levels throughout their lives. As you can imagine, almost everyone communicates interpersonally practically every day. The success of educational systems, civic and religious organizations, private and public organizations, and even chat rooms, is based in large measure on group interactions. Finally, many people in business or politics, or attending community events, speak publicly with surprising frequency.

Before we describe communication competence as a process, take a look at the review and summary in Table 2.1 of the four components of communication competence. Then we will consider our model for competence and how it works.

THE PROCESS MODEL OF COMMUNICATION COMPETENCE

Models tend to be static—that is, they stop a process in the same way a photograph provides a still image of something that is ongoing. It is a limitation of models. However, it is important not to lose sight of how the ongoing aspects of the competence model work. The model of communication competence we have discussed so far consists of motivation, knowledge, skills, and context. The more motivated, knowledgeable, and skilled you are, in ways that are appropriate and effective to each type and level of context, the more likely that you will be perceived as a competent communicator. Each subsequent main part of this text examines the knowledge and skills relevant to a context level: interpersonal, small group, public speaking, and mediated. But before we get to those contexts, we want to call your attention briefly to several processes common to all contexts: verbal communication, nonverbal communication, impressions, and perceptions.

Communication in any context occurs in two basic forms: verbal and nonverbal. Verbal communication can be written, spoken, or otherwise behaviorally or visually transmitted, as in the case of American Sign Language (ASL). Nonverbal communication is all forms of communication not based on verbal language. It consists of physical behavior commonly referred to as body language, as well as gestures, use of space, and voice. We discuss verbal and nonverbal communication in more detail in Chapters Four and Five. The point here is that both of these forms of communica-

Table 2.1: Components of the Communication Competence Model

The model of communication competence consists of motivation, knowledge, skills, and context. The more motivated, knowledgeable, and skilled you are, in ways that are appropriate and effective to each type and level of context, the more likely you will be perceived as a competent communicator.

THE COMPONENT	DEFINITION OF THE COMPONENT	DESCRIPTION OF THE COMPONENT
MOTIVATION	Motivation to communicate is about *wanting* to communicate with competence. Motivation can be both positive and negative.	Negative motivation refers to the experience of anxiety about a communication action or the perception of low reward potential. Positive motivation refers to the perception of high potential reward in pursuing a communication action.
KNOWLEDGE	Knowledge consists of the mental processes of awareness, accessibility, and organization of information relevant to a communication behavior. Knowledge can be content or procedural.	Content knowledge refers to understanding the topics, words, meanings, and so forth, required in a communication situation. Procedural knowledge is about how to assemble, plan, and perform content knowledge in a communication situation.
SKILLS	Skills are repeatable, goal-directed, proficient behaviors. Communication skills can be understood along a continuum of abstraction from macro- to middle- to micro-level skills.	Macro-level skills are fundamental activities for extablishing and maintaining social relationships. Middle-level skills help people perform an array of speech acts that language enables. Micro-level skills help to enact the macro- and middle-level actions through specfic physical behaviors.
CONTEXT	Context is the frame within which the communication action occurs. Contexts in communication can be defined by type or by level.	The most common context types are cultural, chronological, relational, situational, and functional. The most common context levels are interpersonal, small-group, public, and mediated communication.

tion are critical to communication competence in any context. But, any behavior, whether verbal or nonverbal, must make an impression if it is to communicate a message. The behavior must be observed, interpreted, understood, and evaluated through a process called perception (see Chapter Three). Perception refers to the way we make sense of the infinite amount of information provided

Figure 2.2: The Communication Competence Model

Achieving competent communication requires the interplay of two or more communicators using their motivation, knowledge, and skills in a given context to create impressions of their appropriateness and effectiveness.

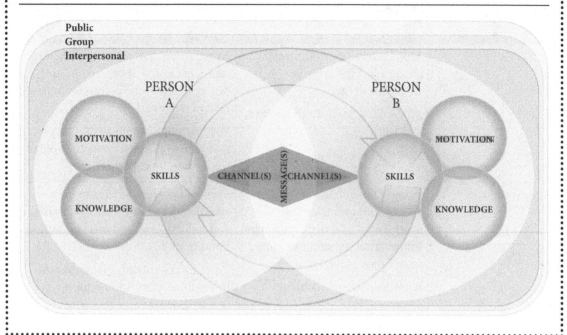

by the world around us. If any verbal or nonverbal behavior goes unobserved or unnoticed, then communication has not really occurred—perception and an impression must be part of the communication process.

Figure 2.2 displays the components of communication competence in action and as a process. It shows that motivation and knowledge are internal to individuals, but that both interact with and influence the individual's skills. These skills, or behaviors, are displayed in communication events with others, and each person forms an impression of the other person and the message based on the context and the process of perception. As we said, most of the remainder of this text is concerned with specific contexts. But although motivation, knowledge, and skills are important in all those contexts, each context may differ in terms of what constitutes motivation, or what knowledge is needed, and what skills are ideal or most appropriate and effective.

OVERCOMING CHALLENGES TO COMMUNICATION COMPETENCE

Given your solid understanding of what it means to communicate competently in various contexts, we conclude this chapter with a discussion of two significant challenges to competence. One of these challenges—communication apprehension—we already discussed and defined earlier in this chapter.

COMMUNICATION APPREHENSION.

The first step to addressing the challenge of communication apprehension is to understand the process of communication better—which you do now. The next step is to realize that not only is there room for improvement, but it is possible to *choose* to be a better, less apprehensive communicator. Any competent and confident communicator you observe has, at some point in time, experienced apprehension, and made a conscious choice to get a grip on it. Once you realize that everyone faces challenging communication situations from time to time, the question is how to go about improving one's communication and controlling any unreasonable apprehension.

Numerous approaches have shown moderate levels of success in treating communication apprehension and anxiety. Three such techniques, specifically for reducing public-peaking anxiety, are described in Chapter Twelve—systematic desensitization, cognitive modification, and skills training. Some of these are techniques that individuals can largely learn on their own. Most of them involve a process of managing the mind-body connection by getting the mind to better control the body, or getting the body to allow the mind to focus on something other than the anxiety.

One of the areas people are increasingly experiencing apprehension and anxiety about is the use and mastery of various new communication technologies. Even though most of us are very accustomed to using such technologies, there are almost always new devices and applications that outpace our ability to keep up with or master technology. If you do not skillfully use an iPhone, you are yesterday, not today. The key again is to manage the mind-body or knowledge and skills relationship and connection. Stop telling yourself that you cannot use a new application, and start telling yourself that you will become more skilled by enhancing your knowledge of it. This brings us to the second all-pervading challenge to communication competence in the 21st century.

GLOBALIZATION, TECHNOLOGY, AND MEDIA CONVERGENCE.

According to the website, **Internet World Stats** (http://www.internetworldstats.com/stats.htm), as of 2011, no country has a majority of its population using the Internet. Some regions (e.g., the Middle East and Africa) are still below 10% penetration of their population. By another estimate, only half of the world's population currently has cellular or mobile phone access (see http://www.reuters.com/article/2007/11/29/us-cellphones-world-idUSL2917209520071129). Yet in the United States, we turn these statistics upside down. Almost three-quarters of the American teen and young adult population has access to and engages in social network sites (see http://pewinternet.org/Reports/2010/Social-Media-and-Young-Adults.aspx). As social network sites increasingly include messaging options, and cell phones offer the ability to send instant messages and tweets, it is possible that traditional e-mail networks may lose much of their dominance. Clearly, the move to more mediated forms of communication seems inevitable, and these media appear to provide more options for how we can communicate with one another.[15]

This computer-mediated communication context of communication is distinguished from the other contexts by the fact that the medium through which communication occurs is technologically facilitated. During much of the 20th century, mediated communication was the same thing as mass communication. On television, for instance, one program was broadcast to a mass audience. However, with the development of the World Wide Web and the Internet, as well as the rapid evolution of digital and wireless technologies, the differences between interpersonal, group, and public-speaking contexts are dissolving. Is blogging a form of interpersonal, group, public, or mass communication? Are entries on a personal website or a personal advertisement on an online dating site forms of interpersonal, group, public, or mass communication?

Although most people use instant messaging (IM) for coordinating face-to-face contact, one study found that 24% reported using it to break up with someone.[16] There are likely to be very different impressions created by a breakup message on IM compared to face-to-face interaction. Definitely, the media we choose to send communication messages make a difference in how that communication is experienced, and how our competence as communicators is perceived and evaluated. These media also are rapidly experiencing **convergence**, which means that they are incorporating more and more of the capabilities of other forms of communication. So what once was just a mobile telephone for voice communication is now a multimedia platform that facilitates visual communication, global positioning guides, and instant access to the Internet.

Even though the medium clearly influences the ways in which messages are sent and received, it is important to understand that the fundamental aspects of communication do not change: the medium is really only one part of the message. That is, although the media we use to accomplish our goals have changed significantly, the functions we fulfill and the things we get done using everyday communication are essentially the same as they have always been. We may be using technology a lot more, but we are still using communication for making friends, deepening relationships, and exchanging messages about all kinds of activities and accomplishments. Regardless of the media we use to communicate, our competence in communicating will still depend significantly on our motivation, knowledge, and skills.

> CONVERGENCE is about the extent to which any given technology incorporates multiple or additional forms of communication.

CHAPTER SUMMARY

Communication competence involves the extent to which speakers achieve desired outcomes through communication acceptable to a situation. Rules prescribe what is deemed acceptable, and what should or should not be done in a given type of situation—what is appropriate and effective. The ability to balance these two standards of competence, using the competence grid, may result in communication being perceived as minimizing, sufficing, maximizing, or optimizing.

Achieving the perception of competence in communication is more likely if a person is motivated, knowledgeable, and skilled in a given context. Motivation can be negative, as in communication apprehension and context or social anxiety, or positive, as in recognizing the potential reward in pursuing a communication action. Knowledge can be content based, as in knowing what to say and do, or it can be procedurally based, as in knowing how to say and do something. The more motivated and knowledgeable a person is, the more likely he or she will be able to enact the appropriate verbal and nonverbal behaviors, the skills that will be judged as competent. Furthermore, motivation, knowledge, and skills occur in a context, and what is competent communication in one context is not necessarily competent in another.

The five context types are cultural, chronological, relational, situational, and functional aspects. Perception of the competence of a person's communication depends on what culture the behavior is enacted in, the timing of the behavior, the relationship and physical situation or space in which the behavior occurs, and the function or purpose the communication is intended to serve. The most common of context levels are: interpersonal, small group, public speaking, and mediated communication. These levels differ in the number of communicators involved and the direction of communication among them.

In addition to being motivated, knowledgeable, and skilled regarding communication in each type and level of context, you also need to be aware of these processes common to all contexts: verbal communication, nonverbal communication, impressions, and perceptions. Finally, you need to be able to overcome two significant challenges to competence regardless of context: communication apprehension, and the impact of globalization, technology, and convergence of media in the 21st century.

KEY TERMS.

The key terms below are defined in this chapter and presented alphabetically with definitions in the Glossary at the end of the book.

- communication competence
- rules
- minimizing communication
- sufficing communication
- maximizing communication
- optimizing communication
- negative motivation
- positive motivation

- communication apprehension
- context apprehension
- social anxiety
- knowledge
- content knowledge
- procedural knowledge
- skills
- context
- context types

- culture
- functions of communication
- context levels
- interpersonal context
- group contexts
- public-speaking contexts
- mediated context
- media convergence

BUILDING MOTIVATION: SELF-ASSESSMENT TOOL.

Rate each of the eight communication situations described here, indicating your own typical level of communication competence. Rate one situation all the way through for motivation, knowledge, and skills. Then rate the next situation. Use the 1–4 scale below, with 1 being minimal competence and 4 high competence.

Communication situations.

1. Telling someone that he or she interrupted you and should wait.
2. Reintroducing a topic you think is important after the conversation has moved on.
3. Correcting a group leader's minor error in summarizing the group's discussion.
4. Making an argument for what you believe in even though you know another is (or others are) against your position.
5. Explaining to a group that you have not prepared adequately for this meeting.
6. Preparing and presenting a technical report to a group of employees.
7. Giving a persuasive speech at a civic or political meeting.
8. Giving an interview on stage after being picked from a live television audience.

Motivation.

1 = Distracted, disinterested, or simply no motivation to be competent.
2 = Somewhat distracted or disinterested, but motivated to be competent.

3 = Somewhat interested and motivated to be competent.
4 = Highly interested and motivated to be competent.

Knowledge.

1 = Completely inexperienced and ignorant about what to do and how to do it.
2 = Minimal experience and sense of what to do and how to do it.
3 = Somewhat experienced and knowledgeable about what to do and how to do it.
4 = Highly knowledgeable about all aspects of what to do and how to do it.

Skills.

1 = Completely incapable of behaving competently.
2 = Barely capable of behaving minimally competently.
3 = Fairly capable of behaving competently.
4 = Highly capable of behaving competently.

Interpreting your scores.

Total your score separately for each situation (motivation, knowledge, and skills). The possible range of the score for each situation is 3–12. If your total score for any of the situations is 6 or less, you see yourself as less competent in that situation than you should be. A score of 7–9 means that you are average at sending and receiving communication messages in the situation. A score of 10–12 indicates that you have a high level of communication competence in that situation.

BUILDING KNOWLEDGE: DISCUSSION QUESTIONS.

1. Is clarity the best way of defining competent communication? If not, why?
2. What are the implications of defining competence as an impression rather than an ability?
3. Are there situations in which either appropriateness or effectiveness should be considered more important in determining a person's communication competence? If so, what are the circumstances?
4. How do the standards of appropriateness and effectiveness provide an ethical system for communication?
5. Provide an example of each type of competence and incompetence based on the competence grid (that is, minimizing, sufficing, maximizing, and optimizing).
6. Think back on your own communication experiences. Identify a difficult communication situation you have encountered. Describe how motivation, knowledge, skills, or all three helped your competence in the context.
7. Describe a communication situation in which the culture, time, relationship, place, function, or any mixture of these influenced your competence.

BUILDING SKILLS: STUDENT ACTIVITIES.

Individual activities.

1. Identify a recent communication encounter you feel did not go as well as it could have. Describe the situation in terms of who was involved, what you were hoping to get out of the encounter, what you might have said or done differently, and why you thought the encounter did not go well. Then analyze the encounter in terms of the communication competence model—motivation, knowledge, skills, and context.

2. Describe a recent communication encounter that went better than you expected, and then analyze it in terms of the communication competence model. Does the model provide a useful basis for understanding what happened? Why or why not?

3. Go to the websites for Coldstone Creamery(http://www.coldstonecreamery.com/main/index.asp) and Ben & Jerry's (http://www.benjerry.com/our_company/index.cfm). Assume you are applying for a job in the ice cream industry. Based on your research of these websites, how would you characterize the similarities and differences in the context of a job interview with these companies? For example, could you treat your relationship to the interviewer as more or less formal in both contexts? Would you expect one company to engage in more group rather than individual interviews? Knowing these differences in their contexts, how might this affect your communication behavior if you were to get a job interview?

4. Strike up a conversation with someone from a culture significantly different from your own. Afterward, identify the difficulties in communicating competently, such as any anxiety about approaching the person, engaging in the conversation, knowing what to talk about, and so forth. Reflect on how your understanding of communication competence could help you communicate in this situation.

Group activities.

1. Form groups of three to five students. Each group should identify a current event that all group members know about, and that involves one communicator who is making news. Analyze the event in terms of the person's communication competence and motivation, knowledge, and skills in the context. How applicable is the model?

2. Go to the National Communication Association's ethics credo website at www.natcom.org and read its ethical guidelines. Or, read the credo presented in this chapter. Individually, come up with an exception to one or more of the ethical principles in the credo. Then form groups of three to five students and share your exceptions. How do your exceptions differ from those of the other group members? What do the exceptions tell you about the relationship between appropriateness, effectiveness, and ethics?

3. Form groups of three to five students. As a group, brainstorm about the contexts in which you have the most difficulty communicating competently in terms of motivation. Repeat the process for knowledge, then for skills. As a group, rank the contexts from most to least difficult. To what extent did you find that others perceive the same or different types of contexts as most challenging? Speculate as a group as to why these similarities or differences exist, and how they might best be overcome from the perspective of the communication competence model.

NOTES

1. See Rideout, Foehr, & Roberts (2010).
2. See Spitzberg & Cupach (2011).
3. See Spitzberg (2000).
4. See Shimanoff (1980).
5. See Berger (2002).
6. See Spitzberg (2003).
7. See Spitzberg (2012).
8. See Serota, Levine, & Boster (2010).
9. See Spitzberg (2009).
10. See Beatty, McCroskey, & Heisel (1998).
11. See Spitzberg & Changnon (2009).
12. See Samovar, Porter, & McDaniel (2012).
13. See Lustig & Koester (2009).
14. See Dillard, Solomon, & Palmer (1999).
15. See Spitzberg (2011).
16. See Bryant, Sanders-Jackson, & Smallwood (2006).

REFERENCES

Beatty, M. J., McCroskey, J. C., & Heisel, A. D. (1998). Communication apprehension as temperamental expression: A communibiological paradigm. *Communication Monographs, 65*(3), 197–219.

Berger, C. R. (2002). Goals and knowledge structures in social interaction. In M. L. Knapp & J. A. Daly (Eds.), *Handbook of interpersonal communication* (pp. 181–212).Thousand Oaks, CA: Sage.

Bryant, J. A., Sanders-Jackson, A., & Smallwood, A. M. K. (2006). IMing, text messaging, and adolescent social networks. *Journal of Computer-Mediated Communication, 11*(2), 577–592.

Dillard, J. P., Solomon, D. H., & Palmer, M. T. (1999). Structuring the concept of relational communication. *Communication Monographs, 66*(1), 49–65.

Lustig, M. W., & Koester, J. (2009). *Intercultural competence: Interpersonal communication across cultures* (6th ed.). Boston, MA: Allyn and Bacon.

Rideout, V. J., Foehr, U. G., & Roberts, D. F. (2010, January). *Generation M2: Media in the lives of 8- to 18-year-olds.* Menlo Park, CA: Henry J. Kaiser Family Foundation. Retrieved from http://www.kff.org/entmedia/upload/8010.pdf

Samovar, L. A., Porter, R. E., & McDaniel, E. R. (Eds.). (2012). *Intercultural communication: A reader* (13th ed.). Belmont, CA: Cengage.

Serota, K. B., Levine, T. R., & Boster, F. J. (2010). The prevalence of lying in America: Three studies of self-reported lies. *Human Communication Research, 36*(1), 2–25.

Shimanoff, S. B. (1980). *Communication rules: Theory and research.* Beverly Hills, CA: Sage.

Spitzberg, B. H. (2000). What is good communication? *Journal of the Association for Communication Administration, 29*(1), 103–119.

Spitzberg, B. H. (2003). Methods of interpersonal skill assessment. In J. O. Greene & B. R. Burleson (Eds.), *Handbook of communication and social interaction skills* (pp. 93–134). Mahwah, NJ: Erlbaum.

Spitzberg, B. H. (2009). Axioms for a theory of intercultural communication competence [Japanese Association of Communication and English Teachers]. *Annual Review of English Learning and Teaching, 14,* 69–81.

Spitzberg, B. H. (2011). The Interactive Media Package for Assessment of Communication and Critical Thinking (IMPACCT©): Testing a programmatic online communication competence assessment system. *Communication Education, 60*(2), 145–173.

Spitzberg, B. H. (2012). Axioms for a theory of intercultural communication competence. In L. A. Samovar, R. E. Porter, & E. R. McDaniel, (Eds.), *Intercultural communication competence: A reader.* (13th ed., pp. 424–434). Belmont, CA: Cengage.

Spitzberg, B. H., & Changnon, G. (2009). Conceptualizing intercultural competence. In D. K. Deardorff (Ed.), *The Sage handbook of intercultural competence* (pp. 2–52). Thousand Oaks, CA: Sage.

Spitzberg, B. H., & Cupach, W. R. (2011). Interpersonal skills. In M. L. Knapp & J. A. Daly (Eds.), *The Sage Handbook of interpersonal communication* (4th ed., pp. 481–525). Thousand Oaks, CA: Sage.

CHAPTER THREE

PERCEPTION, CULTURE, AND THE SELF

This above all: To thine own self be true. And it must follow, as the night the day, thou canst not then be false to any man. —William Shakespeare, famous Elizabethan playwright, 1564–1616.

. .
● ● ●

Ann-Chinn and Loern are both enrolled in an introductory political science class. Ann-Chinn has noticed that Loern comes to class very well-prepared. She saw that he always highlighted sections of his text, and prepared two or three questions about the assigned reading that he asked in class. Ann-Chinn was surprised because she did the same thing and thought no one else did. When the instructor asked Loern questions, Ann-Chinn was impressed with how thoughtful and detailed his answers were. Although others in the class perceived Loern as trying to get on the professor's good side, Ann-Chinn thought of him as a serious and dedicated student.

One day, Ann-Chinn walked out of class with Loern, and they began talking. As they walked out into the parking lot, Ann-Chinn noticed several bumper stickers on Loern's truck. Two that stood out were "Earth first, we'll log the other planets later," and "A little nuke never hurt anyone." Ann-Chinn was startled by these messages, and asked Loern what those bumper stickers were doing on his truck.

Loern's eyes flashed with passion. "Well, honestly, I'm just sick of these fanatical environmentalists trying to halt our economic development. As for nukes, sure, nuclear energy has some problems, but it's an important energy source for the future."

"But what about our responsibility to the environment?" Ann-Chinn asked in shock. "If we log the old forests, people in the future will never have an opportunity to see a towering redwood tree or hike in a rain forest."

Loern responded, "But what about our responsibility to the economic well-being of future citizens? Sure, seeing old trees would be nice, but we need the lumber. Besides, trees are a renewable resource. If we just have a solid reforesting plan, we can keep the environment going."

Ann-Chinn was bewildered, "I feel I don't know who you are. You're not the same person I take political science with!"

Often we form an initial impression of a person only to have that perception disconfirmed later. Ann-Chinn noticed Loern's attention to detail and level of class preparation, and since she focused on her studies in the same way, she assumed he was similar to her in other ways—including attitudes about the environment. When her expectations were violated, she felt she did not really know the true Loern.

Like Ann-Chinn, our own sense of identity influences what we notice about others and how we perceive people and the world around us. Recall in Chapter Two, we introduced the idea that the perception process is a critical factor impacting communication. That being the case, this chapter begins with a discussion of perception and how it works.

WHAT IS PERCEPTION?

Perception is an active process by which all of us use our senses of touch, taste, sight, hearing, and smell to gather information from the external environment and our internal experiences. We then try to make sense of this information in ways that are meaningful and make sense to ourselves.

DEFINING PERCEPTION.

Specifically, **perception** is the process of noticing, organizing, and interpreting information and data about people, events, activities, and situations. Based on this definition, we now take a look at the three stages people go through as part of perception—noticing, organizing, and interpreting.

PERCEPTION AS NOTICING.

What moved Ann-Chinn to notice Loern's behavior in class? What caused her to notice and subsequently be surprised about his beliefs regarding the environment? Three major factors influence our ability to notice certain things within a situation:

1. Mindfulness,
2. The self-fulfilling prophecy, and
3. Language use.

Mindfulness involves paying close attention to the task at hand, and absorbing as much detail as you possibly can.[1] Typically, people become mindful of their own behavior and the situation in which they find themselves when the situation is somewhat novel. But the more others behave in routine ways and the more situations unfold predictably, the more people gloss over the details of the person or the situation. In a new job, we may hang on to every word that is uttered in a weekly staff meeting but lose such mindfulness when we experience the meetings as routine. When they become regular, we tend to gloss over the details.

> **PERCEPTION** is the process of noticing, organizing, and interpreting information and data about people, events, activities, and situations.

> **MINDFULNESS** involves paying close attention to the task at hand, and absorbing as much detail as you possibly can.

> A **SELF-FULFILLING PROPHECY** occurs when you make assumptions about yourself or another person and then behave or interact with the person as if these assumptions were true.

A **self-fulfilling prophecy** occurs when you make assumptions about yourself or another person and then behave or interact with the person as if these assumptions were true. Our assumptions guide how we act in a situation, as we seek out information and details that confirm our expectations. For instance, in employment interviews, as in many social situations, the interviewer forms an impression about the interviewee, and then may seek out information to confirm rather than disconfirm the first impression. Similarly, if you believe that you are unqualified for a job, or that you will botch the interview, often the interview will not go well, confirming your expectations. On the other hand, when our expectations are violated, we engage in a more extensive information search within the situation to understand what went wrong.[2]

Language, discussed in detail in Chapter Four, also influences what we notice and therefore our perceptions. Words act as pointers, directing our attention toward certain aspects of people and situations. Take, for example, the debate about whether to refer to a person as "Indian" or as "Native American." What do you notice when you call someone "Indian"? You notice ethnicity. What do you notice if you refer to someone as Native American? You notice that in the United States, Europeans are not native to North America, but that several tribal peoples were the first inhabitants of the country. Even though the terms *Indian* and *Native American* are similar in that they both gloss over differences between tribal nations, they point your attention to two different elements of the tribal experience in the United States.

Table 3.1 summarizes the factors that account for this first stage in the perception process—noticing.

Table 3.1: Perception as Noticing

The first stage in the perception process involves people noticing data and information in the environment. Three factors—mindfulness, the self-fulfilling prophecy, and language use—influence what we notice.

INFLUENCING FACTOR	DESCRIPTION OF THE FACTOR
MINDFULNESS	• Mindfulness involves paying attention and absorbing details. • We are more mindful in novel situations and less mindful in routine situations.
SELF-FULFILLING PROPHECY	• Self-fulfilling prophecy occurs when we make assumptions about ourselves or another person or other persons. • Our assumptions guide how we act in a situation as we seek more information.
LANGUAGE USE	• Language influences what we notice and therefore our perceptions. • Our words act as pointers directing our attention to certain aspects of people or the situation.

PERCEPTION AS ORGANIZING.

After noticing data in the external environment, the next stage in the perception process involves organizing those data and information in your own mind. Cognitive psychology suggests that people use schemas to make sense of and organize incoming information. We probably do this because the amount of incoming information would be overwhelming if we did not organize it somehow. A **schema** is a framework that helps people organize information and place it into a coherent and meaningful pattern. Imagine that you walked into an art museum and saw a painting by Picasso. Unless you had a schema in your mind that included information about cubism and surrealism, you might have difficulty recognizing the various elements in the painting, or even finding it beautiful. Three kinds of schemas help organize our impressions of people, events, situations, and activities:

1. Prototypes,
2. Stereotypes, and
3. Scripts.

A SCHEMA is a framework that helps people organize information and place it into a coherent and meaningful pattern.

The first kind of schema, a **prototype**, is the best example of some concept. These prototypes are perceptual schemas that provide a general example of any given category of people, things, and so forth. For instance, your prototype of a luxury car might be a Lexus, Corvette, or Mercedes sedan. Most people have developed a prototype for the competent communicator as someone who is intelligent, articulate, confident, outgoing, well-dressed, and a good listener.[3] And, in a recent research study, regardless of ethnic group, women reportedly bought into the prototypical ideal body image portrayed for them in magazine ads.[4]

Stereotypes, the second kind of schema, connect a variety of characteristics we believe to be true of a category, to a person or situation we see as an example of that category. For instance, we may develop stereotypes about tourists as people running around in tennis shoes, plaid shorts, and uneven sunburns, with cameras hung around their necks. You might predict that they will buy cheap trinkets to give as gifts to friends and family back home. Similarly, we may develop stereotypes about how people look or act on the basis of their ethnicity, sexual orientation, gender, age, religion, and level of education. Stereotypes tend to simplify complex situations. We cannot notice everything, so we seek to group as many things as possible into categories that make them understandable and familiar. However, we need to recognize that stereotypes do not ever capture the whole person or situation.

> A PROTOTYPE is the best example of some concept.

> STEREOTYPES are schemas that connect a variety of characteristics we believe to be true of a category, to a person or situation we see as an example of that category.

> A SCRIPT is an expected sequence of events that appears logical to the individual.

The third kind of schema, a **script**, is an expected sequence of events that appears logical to the individual. As schemas, scripts provide us with guides for interpreting events and organizing our communication. In a restaurant, if asked, "Would you like a little more time to make your selections?" we know that we are to answer either yes or no. But if a member of the wait staff came up to us and said, "I've had a lousy day—I don't even know why I came to work," we would be confused and would not know how to act. Such statements do not follow the typical script we have created for ordering food in a restaurant. We usually do not become aware that we are using scripts to guide our interpretations and actions until someone violates the storyline.

Table 3.2 summarizes how people make sense of and organize information—the second stage in the perception process.

PERCEPTION AS INTERPRETING.

Once we have noticed something and organized it according to a cognitive framework or schema using prototypes, stereotypes, or scripts, then we interpret what we have noticed. We attempt to make sense of the information in order to draw conclusions about the kind of person we are interacting with or the type of situation in which we find ourselves. At this final stage in the perception process, researchers tell us that variations in perception are quite likely. For example, in a medical study about the benefits and harms of taking two new drugs for heart disease, medical personnel and health consumers with heart disease interpreted the same medical evidence very differently.[5]

There are two ways to explain why and how we interpret information about others and draw conclusions: implicit personality theory and attribution theory.

Table 3.2: Perception as Organizing

The second stage in the perception process relates to how people organize data and information they gather from the environment. Three kinds of schema help us organize our impressions: prototypes, stereotypes, and scripts.

KIND OF SCHEMA	DESCRIPTION OF THE SCHEMA
PROTOTYPES	• A prototype is the best example of a concept. • Prototypes are schemas that provide a general example of a given category of people or things.
STEREOTYPES	• Stereotypes connect characteristics of a category to a person or situation we see as exemplary of that category. • Stereotypes are schemas that group as many things as possible into categories to make them understandable and familiar.
SCRIPTS	• Scripts are expected sequences of events that appear logical. • Scripts are schemas that provide guides for interpreting events.

Implicit personality theory suggests that we use one or a few personality traits to draw inferences about what people are like. We build general expectations about a person after we know something about a few of his or her traits. For example, we infer that a happy person is also friendly, or that a quiet person also is shy. Someone who appears unpredictable may be dangerous, or someone who speaks slowly may be slow-witted. Other observable traits or characteristics of a person also help us draw inferences, for example, the person's gender, age, or ethnicity. The problem in assuming that one particular trait is associated with other traits is that the association may or may not be true.

IMPLICIT PERSONALITY THEORY suggests that we use one or a few personality traits to draw inferences about what people are like.

ATTRIBUTION THEORY provides a framework for determining the motives underlying people's behavior, others and our own.

Implicit personality theory also examines how traits are clustered together, and how certain traits are assumed to be associated with other traits. For example, you may associate the construct of being college educated with being artistic and elitist. However, other people may associate the construct of a college education with prosperity and friendliness. In the opening story, Ann-Chinn wrongly associated the construct of "good student who is well prepared" with also placing a high value on environmental concerns. Ann-Chinn was wrong, and her faulty inference led to a negative communication encounter with Loern.

Our first impression of a person tends to set the mold by which later information we gather about the person is interpreted. For example, based on observing Ann-Chinn in class, Loern may first have viewed her as a stereotypical Asian woman, and assumed that she is quiet, hard-working, and unassertive—a stereotype, to be sure. Having reached these conclusions, rightly or wrongly, he now has a set of prototypes for understanding and interpreting Ann-Chinn's behaviors. When he notices her expressing disbelief over his selection of bumper stickers, he may simply dismiss it, or view it as an odd exception to her real nature, because it does not fit his existing prototype of her.

A second explanation of how we draw conclusions about others is attribution theory. While implicit personality theory considers how we make inferences about what people are like, attribution theory considers why people behave the way they do. **Attribution theory** provides a framework for determining the motives underlying people's behavior, others and our own. We tend to make such attributions about people based on four factors.

The first factor is the similarity of the person's characteristics or actions over time. If a student has a history in high school and college of getting teachers to accept late assignments, you are likely to attribute persuasiveness to this student. However, if you saw this student persuade only one professor to accept a late assignment, and she or he had no success in convincing two other professors, you would have no consistent pattern for attributing persuasiveness to this student.

The second factor we use to make attributions about people's behavior is whether their characteristics or actions that we observe are associated with unique outcomes in the situation. For example, if the student with the late assignments seems well-liked by professors but is clearly treated harshly by one of them, then the student seems to evoke a unique reaction from this professor. If the professor in question is consistently harsh with many other students, then the harsh behavior is not particular to the late-assignment student; and you will tend to consider the professor a harsh person.

The third factor used to make attributions relates to whether the cause of an outcome is internal or external to a person. Is the person responsible for the situation, or are external causes responsible? Is the student who asks permission to turn in assignments late working two jobs, a single parent, and taking six courses? If so, many would assume that the student is late with assignments not so much out of laziness—an internal condition—but out of the external demands of that student's life. In contrast, if you frequently see this student on campus throwing Frisbees and chatting with friends at the student union, you are more likely to attribute the student's late assignments to laziness, an internal characteristic.

Finally, we try to determine not only whether the cause of a particular action is internal or external, but also the extent to which a person is able to alter or change the outcome. Whether you feel sympathy or dislike for the late-assignment student depends in large part on whether your attribution is one of excessive external demands or internal laziness. But notice that even with the attribution of excessive demands, you could still blame the student for taking too much on or for failing to prioritize properly.

How do these four factors about attribution theory become important to us as communicators? The way we feel and act toward people—or companies and organizations, for that matter—depends on how we attribute outcomes to their actions in any situation. Researchers tested attribution theory in a national crisis situation with which you may be familiar.[6] The researchers examined the public's response to an oil company involved in an oil spill accident in the United States. They found that people made higher internal attributions—finding the oil company responsible for the spill—when they thought that the situation was not particularly unique, and they were not given information by the oil company about it being unique. Those attributions of responsibility for the spill resulted in greater negative opinions about the oil company. This case aside, a word of caution is needed here. Often we assume other people's behavior is due to internal characteristics such as their personality, whereas we view our own behavior as a result of external conditions in the situation. Stated simply, we see ourselves and our behaviors in a more favorable light than we see others—not a surprise.

Table 3.3 summarizes how we interpret and assign meaning to information—the third stage of the perception process. Review that table and the two tables that summarize stages one and two—noticing and organizing. Which of the three stages has the most effect on communication competence? The right answer is all three of them. Imagine that you are on a first date with someone, or meeting a new employer for the first time. If you notice one set of data and details, and not others, you may begin to form a faulty and inaccurate perception of the other person and her or his

Table 3.3: Perception as Interpreting

The third stage in the perception process is about how people interpret what they have noticed and then make sense of the information in order to draw conclusions. This table describes two of the more popular theoretical explanations of how people draw conclusions.

THETHEORY	DESCRIPTION OF THE THEORY
IMPLICIT PERSONALITY THEORY	• Implicit personality theory says that people use one or a few personality traits to draw inferences about what people are like. • People assume, rightly or wrongly, that some traits are automatically associated with other traits.

ATTRIBUTION THEORY	• Attribution theory provides a framework for determining people's motives for their behavior.
	• Four factors influence how we make attributions:
	  • Similarity of the person's characteristics or actions over time.
	  • Whether the person's characteristics or actions are associated with unique outcomes in the situation.
	  • Whether the cause of an outcome is internal or external to the person.
	  • Whether the person is able to alter or change the outcome.

comments and messages. You may organize that information in your own mind based on a faulty schema or stereotype of males or females or interviewers, making your inaccurate perception worse. If you assign meaning and interpret everything the other person says and does based on that stereotype, you will not be capable of communicating competently. What would a competent communicator do with regard to these three stages of perception? Based on our model of competence and its three components—motivation, knowledge, and skills—you now have the knowledge to avoid faulty impressions and perceptions of others. The key is to use skills and withhold judgement of what others say and do until you are sure you have enough accurate data to form fully informed perceptions.

Next we considerthis entire perception process as it is impacted by the cultures we are born into and in which we grow up.

CULTURE'S EFFECT ON PERCEPTION

We are born into preexisting and ongoing cultures. As we described in Chapter Two, a *culture* encompasses the enduring patterns of thought, value, and behavior that define a group of people. It includes their spirituality; their sense of status, hierarchy, and relationships; and even their use of time and physical space.[7] For example, in the West, silence is typically viewed as an empty space devoid of meaning, and people become uneasy when silence dominates a conversation. By comparison, in some Asian countries where silence is valued, people may sit side by side for long periods without talking, and they do not experience any discomfort.[8] That said, our understanding of culture is not limited to differences like these among nations or countries. Rather, culture can refer to any group or community of people, based on characteristics like gender,[9] physical ability, or disability.[10] And whether you use the term to refer to a nation, an organization, or a specific group of people, all cultures influence how we perceive other people, situations, and events. To put it simply, culture affects all of our perceptions, and variations and differences in perception significantly influence how we communicate.

CULTURE AND VARIATIONS IN PERCEPTION.

We are arguing that cultures are characterized by their own unique set of beliefs, attitudes, values, and behavioral patterns. In fact, one researcher found that people tend to value and want to buy what others in their culture want to buy. In this study, people's reactions to a product advertisement in the United States were enhanced by knowing what others consensually preferred.[11] Who among us has not bought a new pair of shoes or a certain tee shirt because others in our cultural peer group appear to value that product?

Since culture influences the way we perceive situations, events, and people, even how we perceive and handle honesty and deceit may vary based on culture. For example, is it sometimes appropriate to deceive others, and does our cultural identity affect what we think about deceptive communication? Researchers studying deception in Hong Kong, Hawaii, and the mainland United States say that culture matters when it comes to what we think about lying.[12] The study found that a higher degree of interdependence (Hong Kong) is related to greater motivation to deceive for the benefit of self and other. People in Hong Kong are more likely to perceive messages that depart from the truth as "not deceptive." Furthermore, a higher degree of independence (United States) results in perceiving any message that departs from the truth as highly deceptive.

Cultural variations can affect our perceptions—and thereby how we communicate—in two ways. First, culture influences our ability to understand and interpret how people from another culture communicate. For example, persons in individualistic, Western cultures view confrontational conflict styles as more appropriate than do people from collectivist, Eastern cultures. This difference in perception of how to engage in conflict can lead to misunderstandings between people from these two types of cultures, whether in interpersonal interactions or in business. Second, culture influences the attribution process, which we discussed earlier in this chapter. Of course, errors in attribution occur within all cultures. However, in collectivist cultures people tend to attribute behavior to factors in the situation or context rather than to the individual. In a study of U.S. college students compared to Chinese college students, the U.S. students attributed motivation to succeed as a personal achievement. On the contrary, the Chinese students considered success as a group achievement.[13]

As we consider culture's effect on perception and communication, we need to acknowledge the role of the "individual self" in these cultural and perceptual processes. At its core, communication is an individual experience that relates directly to how we see ourselves and our own self-concept.

DEVELOPING SELF-CONCEPT

Like culture, our self-concept influences our perceptions of people, situations, and events. The idea of having a self suggests that people are different from one another and, to understand others and their perceptions, you need to understand the uniqueness of each particular person. However, understanding one's self is a necessary first step to understanding others.

COMMUNICATION AND SENSE OF SELF.

How we feel about and perceive ourselves is largely based on messages others communicate to us. The meanings and interpretations we create for ourselves about ourselves result from our interactions with other people. The importance of the other in constructing a sense of the self was first noted by C. H. Cooley, who explicitly argued that the self is a **social self**.[14] According to Cooley, the self comes into being through interaction with others, and can be determined only through relationships with other people. Cooley coined the term, the *looking-glass self*, to demonstrate how our relationships with other people form the self. The **looking-glass self** assumes that people imagine the perception others hold of them, and this perceiving of the self through the eyes of others creates the sense of self.

Later on, Mead also argued that sense of self arises from communication with others but it comprises both an "I" and a "Me."[15] The "I" represents the impulsive and unpredictable part of the self. The "Me" represents the norms of a community and the expectations for what patterns of behavior are allowed within that community. The "I" serves as the driving force for wanting to do something, but is quickly controlled and guided by the "Me." For example, a mischievous aspect of the "I" may encourage you to shout, "Fire!" impulsively in a crowded movie theater; the "Me" controls this impulse because it knows that shouting such words in a crowded movie theater could not only injure people as they stampede for the exits, but could also lead to your arrest. For Mead, the "Me" serves an important function in regulating behavior in society.

In addition to messages from others, we also have conversations with ourselves, referred to as **self-talk**. Through these internal conversations we reflect on what we are doing well or what we are doing poorly; we ponder what we did in the past and what we anticipate doing in the future. The power of self-talk to help people accomplish their goals has been amply demonstrated. One sports psychologist wrote about the power of self-talk as a motivational and instructional tool to enhance athletic performance.[16] Some athletes do use self-talk to improve their performance and indirectly construct their identities and sense of self. When any of us thinks positive thoughts, such as "I can see what I need to do to improve," as opposed to negative thoughts such as "I hope I don't fail," we are more likely to perform the desired behavior.

> The SOCIAL SELF comes into being through interaction with others, and can be determined only through relationships with other people.

> The LOOKING-GLASS SELF assumes that people imagine the perception others hold of them, and this perceiving of the self through the eyes of others creates the sense of self.

> SELF-TALK denotes internal conversations in which we reflect on what we are doing well or what we are doing poorly.

> The MODERN SELF refers to the Western tradition of viewing people as having a core single self whose character and personality are stable over time.

THE 21st-CENTURY SELF.

The notion of the self as comprised of an "I" and a "Me" is the basis for the idea of the **modern self**. This Western tradition views people as having a core single self whose character and personality are stable over time.[17] The common expression, "just be yourself," reflects this philosophy, implying that there is a true self that others can perceive accurately or inaccurately. The goal of communication, then, is to become aware of that stable self and present it to others effectively (motivated by the "I") and appropriately (motivated by the "me").

Figure 3.1: The Looking-Glass Self

C. H. Cooley proposed the looking-glass self. Metaphorically, we look in a mirror and imagine the perception others hold of us. By perceiving ourselves through the eyes of others, we create our sense of self. This theory reinforces the old expression that we tend to see ourselves as others see us.

Source: http://anaisninblog.skybluepress.com/category/anais-nin-on-kindle/

The concept of a **postmodern self**, in contrast, rejects the notion of a single true self, and suggests instead that the self is actually made up of multiple personal constructions of self (**multiple self**).[18] As the world offers more and more opportunities and avenues for communication, the ways we can present ourselves to the world have become more complex. The postmodern self is a product of this increasing technological complexity. In truth, researchers now are debating and trying to understand the nature of your emerging "cyber self" in the digital age.[19] Are you the avatar you select to participate in an online game? The e-mailer or tweeter who sends messages to friends and family and even newscasters? Or are you the persona you present on your Facebook page? A postmodern perspective would say that you are all these selves and more—you also are a son or a daughter, a parent or a child, a student, a worker, or a teacher—the list of multiple selves seems almost endless.[20] This perspective seems to be a fitting description of the self for the 21st century.

THE POSTMODERN SELF suggests that the self is actually made up of multiple personal constructions of self.

THE MODERN SELF refers to the Western tradition of viewing people as having a core single self whose character and personality are stable over time.

Obviously, through our communication interactions with many different people and in different situations, we find ourselves adapting our "postmodern self" to these experiences, and to the expectations others have of us. Communication, therefore, is not just a situation in which you exchange messages with one another. Rather, it is a process in which you continually develop a sense of self and cocreate yourself with others. We now consider the pro-

Table 3.4: Developing Self-Concept

Scholars have conceptualized and described the self-concept very differently over time. This is a summary of the most important of these various approaches to thinking about the self-concept.

APPROACHES TO SELF-CONCEPT	DESCRIPTION OF THE APPROACH
SOCIAL SELF	• The self comes into being through interaction with others, and is determined only through relationships with other people.
LOOKING-GLASS SELF	• We imagine the perceptions others hold of us and, perceiving our self through the eyes of others, we create our sense of self.
MODERN SELF	• While the self may be comprised of an "I" and a "Me," we have a core single self, whose character and personality are stable over time.
POSTMODERN SELF	• Our self is made up of multiple constructions of self, and is a product of the increasing technological complexity of the 21st century.

cess by which we share and cocreate ourselves with others. But first, glance over the summary in Table 3.4 of how the self-concept is developed.

EXPRESSING SELF TO OTHERS

Every communication event gives us an opportunity to express ourselves. In doing so, we reveal something about who we are and who we view ourselves as being. If we reveal too much, we risk offending others or making ourselves vulnerable. If we reveal too little, others may not learn who we are or how to interact with us. Competent interaction means finding an appropriate and effective balance. The process by which we reveal ourselves to others is self-disclosure.

DEFINITION OF SELF-DISCLOSURE.

Self-disclosure is the process of intentionally and voluntarily providing others with information about yourself that you believe is honest and accurate and unlikely to be discovered elsewhere. To be considered self-disclosure, a message must be intentional. If Loern is staring at Ann-Chinn while she is talking about some vacations she took recently, and he responds, "What great lips, uh, I mean trips," Ann-Chinn may think he has self-disclosed. But if his comment was purely accidental and not intentional, then it is not self-disclosure. To be considered self-disclosure, a message must also be voluntary. It can hardly be considered self-disclosure if someone is brainwashed, tortured, or coerced to provide information. We come to know someone not only by what she or he chooses to tell us, but by the fact that she or he chooses to tell us at all.

Self-disclosure provides information about the self. If a student sitting next to you tells you that she thinks the class is

SELF-DISCLOSURE is the process of intentionally and voluntarily providing others with information about yourself that you believe is honest and accurate, and unlikely to be discovered elsewhere.

Figure 3.2. The Johari Window

The Johari Window is made up of four quadrants or panes, each of which contains some information about ourselves. For example, information in The Open Self pane is known to self and known to others.

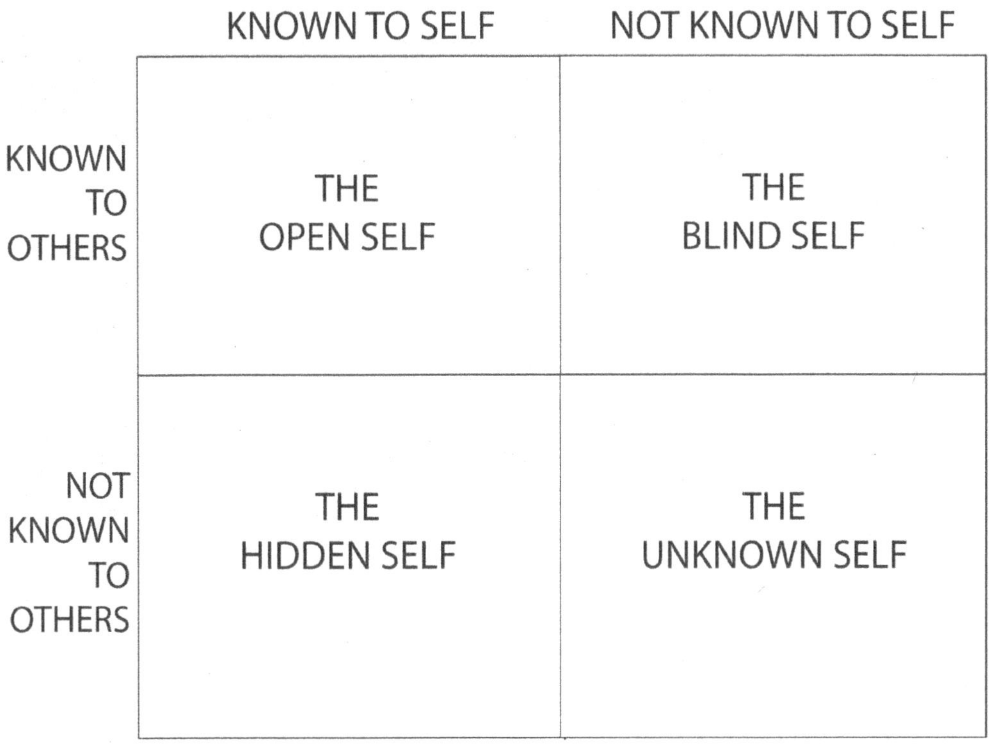

	KNOWN TO SELF	NOT KNOWN TO SELF
KNOWN TO OTHERS	THE OPEN SELF	THE BLIND SELF
NOT KNOWN TO OTHERS	THE HIDDEN SELF	THE UNKNOWN SELF

Source: Adapted from Wikimedia Commons

boring, you might not consider this information self-disclosure. But revealing her attitude about the class does give you some information about her. Attitudes, beliefs, and values make up a significant part of our self-concepts, and disclosing them, in effect, is disclosing who we think we are. Finally, self-disclosure reveals information that is unlikely to be discovered through other means. You are not revealing anything about yourself if you tell someone something he or she already knows. In contrast, if you tell someone something that can only be known because you say it, you have truly opened yourself up to that person.

DIMENSIONS OF SELF-DISCLOSURE.

We can better understand how self-disclosure works by taking a closer look at two more aspects of disclosure—the types of openness in which people can engage, and the appropriate type of disclosure for various situations.

A well-known model known as the **Johari Window** outlines four possible types of openness. Johari is pronounced "Joe Harry," after the scholars who first developed the ideas, Harry Ingham and Joseph Luft.[21] The window or model of self-disclosure is defined by two dimensions: the self-dimension and the other-dimension (See Figure 3.2). The self-dimension identifies what is or is not revealed or known to one's self. The other-dimension identifies information about the self that is or is not revealed or known to others. When these dimensions are crossed, they form a window with four quadrants, called the open, blind, hidden, and unknown selves.

....
THE JOHARI WINDOW outlines four possible types of openness, and is defined by two dimensions: the self-dimension and the other-dimension.

The *open self* is what is known to the self and to others, the part of you that you are aware of and show to people around you. Your hobbies, your major, your career objectives, whether or not you are married, all these often are very open. The *blind self* consists of those aspects of yourself that others know but you do not know yourself. You may not be aware that you come across as overly aggressive or critical, but others know this. The *hidden self* is known to you but not to others. This area represents those aspects of yourself that you intentionally keep to yourself. Perhaps you did something unkind or embarrassing when you were young that you choose not to reveal to others. Finally, the *unknown self* is the part of you that neither you nor those around you know. You may eventually want children, but may not realize it right now because the idea may simply not seem very relevant. However, once you experience something in the unknown self, it moves to either the hidden self or the open self.

In addition to understanding the four types of openness, a second important aspect of self-disclosure is determining the appropriate type of disclosure for the situation. Not only does this depend on how open or private you are as a person, it also depends on the nature of the disclosure process itself. The process of self-disclosure is more like a faucet than a light switch. With most light switches, the light is either on or off. But with a faucet, we can vary temperature, pressure, amount, and so forth. So it is with self-disclosure. We can vary what information we disclose and how we disclose it along several dimensions. In particular, we can alter our self-disclosure in terms of breadth, depth, valence, reciprocity, and relevance. Table 3.5 defines and clarifies these five dimensions. Think about a relationship you are in right now and a time when you disclosed something to the other person. Using Table 3.5, evaluate that self-disclosure based on the five dimensions.

The dimensions of self-disclosure described in Table 3.5 reveal that letting others get to know us is very complex. Even so, the more competently we disclose, the more comfortable people will be opening up to us, and the more satisfying the progress of the ongoing interaction is likely to be. In short, the better we are at letting others understand us, the better we become at understanding others and ourselves.

People vary considerably in their self-disclosure. Some people disclose very little, regardless of the person with whom they are communicating. Others seem to disclose almost everything. In *Test Your Self-Disclosure* in Box 3.1, you can assess your level of self-disclosure. Take a moment and complete the self-test before continuing on to our discussion of challenges to perception.

Table 3.5: Dimensions of Self-Disclosure

There are five dimensions along which information we could disclose can vary. By being aware of these dimensions, we can alter our self-disclosure appropriately for the communication situation and person with whom we are communicating.

THE DIMENSIONS	DESCRIPTION OF THE DIMENSION
BREADTH	• Breadth refers to the vast number of topics about which we may choose to disclose regarding ourselves. • Some people disclose a lot about a specific aspect of their life while others disclose less about more areas of their lives.
DEPTH	• Depth of disclosure is about the importance and relevance of the information to our core sense of self. • The closer the information is to your most intimate sense of who you are, the deeper the disclosure.
VALENCE	• Valence, derived from the same root as *value*, denotes whether the information casts the disclosing person in a positive or negative light. • Most people want to be viewed as attractive, and so we tend to disclose positive information more than negative.
RECIPROCITY	• Reciprocity means the degree to which the communicators match each other's levels of disclosure. • People tend to disclose at similar rates and levels of breadth and depth as others disclose to them.
RELEVANCE	• Relevance involves how closely related the information is to the topic being discussed. • Irrelevant disclosures knock conversations off track, and make you appear as if you are not listening or are not sensitive to the other person's concerns.

OVERCOMING CHALLENGES TO PERCEPTION

In an old *Peanuts* cartoon, Lucy asks Linus what he wants to be when he grows up. Linus simply replies, "Outrageously happy." Ultimately, people want to live lives that are meaningful and bring them joy. The challenge to creating meaningful lives depends, in part, on the choices we make every day about how we perceive the world and others; and it depends on understanding the impact of media and technology on perception and disclosure processes in the 21st century.

CHOICE MAKING AND PERCEPTION.

Three choices related to perception are particularly challenging, but can be overcome:

- Developing complete and more accurate perceptions.
- Managing the sense of self for the better.
- Using self-disclosures to share yourself with others most competently.

Box 3.1: Test Your Self-Disclosure

INSTRUCTIONS: Some of us are very open people, and have a big "open self" quadrant on the Johari Window. Some of us are very private, and have a big "hidden self" quadrant. Several situations in which you might find yourself communicating are described below. The five columns list people with whom you might be communicating in each situation. Rate how you would self-disclose in each situation with each person. Use a scale from 0 to 2, where 0 is, "I would never disclose something of a private or personal nature," 1 is, "I would occasionally disclose something of a private or personal nature," and 2 is, "I would usually disclose something of a private or personal nature."

THE SITUATION	BEST FRIEND	RECENT ACQUAINT- ANCE	ROMANTIC PARTNER	FAMILY MEMBER	COMPLETE STRANGER
In your dorm or apartment					
Over lunch in a restaurant					
In a class- room before the lecture					
In a study group at school					
In a speech to a volunteer group					
In a job inter- view or for a promotion at work					
On a long plane or train trip					

INTERPRETATION: Generally, a person who discloses everything to anyone (you chose almost all 2s here) is viewed with caution and distrust. If this person has no sense of privacy, perhaps he or she also has no sense of secrecy, and would tell others anything you reveal about yourself. Although you generally do not disclose everything to anyone (if you chose all 1s), consider a phenomenon known as the "stranger on the plane." On a plane, train, or bus you do not expect to see the person sitting next to you again, and so you may feel little risk in disclosing personal information. However, in most situations, if you think you may encounter a person again, you are concerned with what he or she might think of you, or do with the information you disclose. In contrast, people who never disclose (you answered almost all 0s here) are often viewed with distrust, but for another reason. Trust implies that we know what a person will do. If a person does not disclose anything to us, we may find it difficult to know this person and, thus, difficult to trust her or him.

1. The first choice we make relates to developing rich and detailed perceptions. People have a tendency to form judgments that are not only based on limited information, but also reflect certain biases. The key challenges to forming rich, detailed, and accurate perceptions are to guard against faulty attributions and biases. We all tend to have certain prejudices that shape the way we perceive people and events. One way to develop a richly detailed perception of a person or situation is to challenge our prejudices, and view a person or an event from a variety of different perspectives. Slow down the perception process and explore other ways to interpret the person's actions or the event. This may mean delaying or suspending judgment until later. Step outside yourself and explore your perceptions of people and events from different points of view.

2. The second choice relates to managing your sense of self. We have learned that significant others play an important role in the development of the self. Nonetheless, it is important to be proactive in developing the self, and not let others entirely dictate who we are to become. As you assess your behaviors, attitudes, and values, you may realize that you are acting in ways you would like to change. How can you change your attitudes and values—and, relatedly, your behaviors? First, focus on what you have done well in the past as well as on what you are currently doing well. By focusing positively on your successes, you can more quickly begin to enhance your sense of self. Also, manage any negative self-talk like athletes do. Second, set reasonable goals for change. If you make small changes in your behavior, these changes accumulate over time and yield bigger, more positive results.

3. The third choice is about engaging in appropriate and effective self-disclosure. What information should you disclose, and, equally important, when should you disclose it? The answer to these questions is that it all depends—on the person you are talking to and the situation. You first need to consider the short-term consequences of the disclosure. "Is the person ready for this type of disclosure? What will the person do with this information? Will he or she break off the relationship, or let it continue?" You also should consider the long-term consequences of this disclosure: "Will this disclosure strengthen our friendship or relationship over time? By being open and honest, can we build a trusting relationship, or will the disclosure make me appear too vulnerable in the eyes of the other person?" Often there are no clear answers to these types of questions. However, by thinking through the consequences of the disclosure, you can gain a better sense of whether it will help or hurt the development of a positive relationship.

IMPACT OF MEDIA AND TECHNOLOGY.

Understanding the impact of media and technology on perceptions and how people disclose and communicate in the 21st century is a necessity. We are constantly sending and receiving messages using texts, tweets, and all sorts of social media. When we say social media, we mean the use of any Web-based or mobile device to turn communication into interactive dialogue. Therein lies the problem. The potential for these interactive dialogues to result in misunderstandings and misperceptions when you self disclose, in a tweet for instance, cannot be overestimated. Fortunately, communication researchers are examining this challenge. Here is some of what they have learned so far.

One study looked at the long-term effects of online and offline (face-to-face) self-disclosure of boys and girls on the quality of their friendships.[22] The researchers examined if there were any differences based on sex/gender. The results of their study found that both online and offline self-disclosure had a positive effect on friendships. But boys, more often than girls, preferred online disclosure to offline, and the boys also benefitted more than girls from online disclosure to enhance the quality of their friendships. The advice here is to be aware of any gender differences, and adjust your self-disclosure accordingly.

Another study also examined online and offline self-disclosure, but in intercultural relationships.[23] These researchers were concerned about the effect of cultural differences when people engage in Internet-based communication. The findings of this study showed that communicators from collectivist (group-oriented) cultures engage in less self-disclosure in computer-mediated relatonships than they do in face-to-face interactions. By contrast, communicators from cultures high in individualism did not show the same preference for face-to-face disclosure over computer-mediated communication. The lesson here is to be aware of any cultural preferences when deciding how to communicate, online or offline, with someone from a collectivist or individualist culture.

Finally, one other researcher recently conducted a review of the seven leading research articles in scholarly journals on the topics of self-disclosure, disinhibition, and intimacy with regard to instant messaging.[24] As a point of information, disinhibition is a term used to describe a lack of restraint or self-control, including disregard for social norms, impulsiveness, and risk assessment. Displaying this type of communication behavior in an instant message obviously could cause misunderstandings and misperceptions. The author of this review outlined three findings about instant messaging:

1. Regarding self-disclosure: The use of instant messaging stimulates online self-disclosure.
2. Regarding disinhibition: The use of instant messaging occurs with some but not all users.
3. Regarding intimacy: The use of instant messaging is associated with increased intimacy and closeness in preexisiting friendships but not with strangers.

The takeaway from these results is to use instant messaging carefully, depending upon the level of intimacy or closeness in a relationship; and, do not instant message with strangers.

If you recall, we opened this chapter with a story about Ann-Chinn and Loern, and with a quotation from Shakespeare's play *Hamlet*:

"This above all: to thine own self be true. And it must follow, as the night the day, thou canst not then be false to any man."

This statement is Polonius's last piece of advice to his son, who is in a hurry to get on the next boat to Paris where he will be safe from his father's long-winded, Shakespearean speeches. By "to thine own self be true," Polonius means "be loyal to your own best interests." Take care of yourself first, he counsels, and you will be in a position to take care of others. By using the ideas about perception, self-concept, and self-disclosure outlined in this chapter, you will be taking care of yourself, and acting in ways that allow you to achieve desirable goals—for your "self," for others, and for your relationships.

In the next chapter, we explore language and its critical role in communicating competently with others.

CHAPTER SUMMARY

Perception is the process of noticing, organizing, and interpreting information and data about people, events, activities, and situations. Our ability to notice bits of data is directly influenced by how mindful we are within situations, the kinds of self-fulfilling prophecies we create for situations, and the way we use language. The way we organize the data depends on the kinds of schemas we use, such as prototypes, stereotypes, and scripts. When we interpret data and form impressions, we must be sensitive to whether we use one or a few personality traits to draw inferences about others, and whether we determine people's motives for their behaviors as internally or externally motivated.

We also need to be aware of culture's effect on perception. Culture affects all of our perceptions, and variations and differences in perception significantly influence how we communicate. Culture influences our ability to understand and interpret how people from another culture communicate, and it influences how we make attributions about others' behaviors.

A person's self-concept also influences perceptions of people, situations, and events. As we interact with others, we develop a sense of the social self. The looking-glass self is based on what we imagine to be the perception others hold of us. Through self-talk, we reflect on our sense of self and what we are doing well or poorly. Western tradition postulates the modern self, which is a core, single self whose character and personality are stable over time. More contemporary thought highlights the notion of a postmodern self, which is made up of multiple personal constructions of self. Our self-concept not only influences our perceptions but also what information we self-disclose to others. As the Johari Window illustrates, in any situation, parts of our self are open to others, such as the open and blind self, and parts of our self are not open to others, such as the hidden and unknown self. The degree to which we choose to self-disclose depends on the dimensions of breadth, depth, valence, reciprocity, and relevance.

The primary challenges to perception relate to developing complete and more accurate perceptions, managing the sense of self for the better, and using self-disclosures to share yourself with others most competently. In addition, we need to understand the impact of media and technology on perception and disclosure in the 21st century.

KEY TERMS.

The key terms below are defined in this chapter, and presented alphabetically with definitions in the Glossary at the end of the book.

- perception
- mindfulness
- self-fulfilling prophecy
- schema
- prototype
- stereotypes

- script
- implicit personality theory
- attribution theory
- social self
- looking-glass self
- self-talk

- modern self
- multiple self
- postmodern self
- self-disclosure
- Johari window

BUILDING MOTIVATION: SELF-ASSESSMENT TOOL.

Rate each of the eight communication situations described here, indicating your own typical level of competence with regard to perception and self-disclosure in the particular situation. Rate one situation all the way through for motivation, knowledge, and skills. Then rate the next situation. Use the 1–4 scale below, with 1 being minimal competence and 4 high competence.

Communication situations.

1. Meeting a member of the opposite sex at a party.
2. Going out to dinner with a group of people from a different culture.
3. Sitting at a bus stop with a homeless person and chatting for a few minutes.

4. Going door-to-door to promote a political candidate or worthy cause.
5. Communicating with a significant other by e-mail.
6. Communicating with a significant other using text messaging.
7. Discussing a problem at work with your immediate supervisor.
8. Traveling in a foreign country and needing information from a stranger on the street.

Motivation.

1 = Distracted, disinterested, or simply no motivation to be competent.
2 = Somewhat distracted or disinterested, but motivated to be competent.
3 = Somewhat interested and motivated to be competent.
4 = Highly interested and motivated to be competent.

Knowledge.

1 = Completely inexperienced and ignorant about what to do and how to do it.
2 = Minimal experience and sense of what to do and how to do it.
3 = Somewhat experienced and knowledgeable about what to do and how to do it.
4 = Highly knowledgeable about all aspects of what to do and how to do it.

Skills.

1 = Completely incapable of behaving competently.
2 = Barely capable of behaving minimally competently.
3 = Fairly capable of behaving competently.
4 = Highly capable of behaving competently.

Interpreting your scores.

Total your score separately for each situation (motivation, knowledge, and skills). The possible range of the score for each situation is 3–12. If your total score for any of the situations is 6 or less, you see yourself as less competent in that situation than you should be. A score of 7–9 means that you are average at sending and receiving communication messages in the situation. A score of 10–12 indicates that you have a high level of communication competence in that situation.

BUILDING KNOWLEDGE: DISCUSSION QUESTIONS.

1. What is the role of perception in understanding people and situations?
2. How do you see the relationships among noticing, organizing, and interpreting data about people and events? Does noticing influence how we organize data or vice versa? Do the interpretations we draw about people and events at one time influence what we notice at a later time?
3. In what kinds of situations are people more likely to become mindful of their surroundings?
4. Think of a recent argument you had with someone. How might that argument be better informed by an understanding of variations in perception?
5. When you meet someone new, how can you guard against the negative effect of implicit personality theory?

6. When you observe a friend engaging in a behavior you question, how can you guard against the negative effect of attribution theory?

7. Do you think there is a single self or multiple selves? Why? What influences how you create your own sense of self? What influences how you disclose about yourself to others?

BUILDING SKILLS: STUDENT ACTIVITIES.

Individual activities.

1. How well do you know yourself? Review the following two scenarios and put yourself in the situation described, and then answer the following questions.

   - Situation A: Your best friend tells you that he or she is having an affair, and then asks you not to tell his or her spouse about it, even though you consider yourself a close friend to the spouse as well. What do you do?
   - Situation B: You have been waiting in line for 35 minutes to get tickets to a hot concert, and three people cut in front of you when they see someone they know in line ahead of you. What do you do?

   Reflect on how easy or difficult it was to respond to the situations. What role did your self-concept play in your responses? What role did others' possible impressions of your behavior play in your responses?

2. Return to the situations in question 1, and predict what a good friend of yours would do. Is it easier to predict your behavior or your friend's? Why?

3. Think of yourself as a postmodern, multiple self. Identify and list as many versions of yourself as you can.

4. Think back on an occasion when you were unsure about disclosing a piece of information about yourself to somebody else. Review the information on self-disclosure in this chapter and reflect on the occasion and what you could have done differently or better.

Group activities.

1. Pair off with another person. Each person in your dyad should write down a common emotion or adjective on each of five separate note cards, such as happy, sad, boring, angry, intelligent, and so on. Collect the ten cards and shuffle them. Each person should select a card without revealing the card to the other person. Have a conversation acting in ways that are consistent with the emotion or adjective provided on the card. After the conversation, each person should guess the emotion or adjective the other person is acting out. After guessing, reveal the emotions that were being performed. Discuss what cues or information were used to make judgments about the emotions performed. How accurate were the guesses? Discuss what ideas about perception might have influenced your ability to assess each other's emotion.

2. Form a group of four to five students. Each group member should write a brief personal advertisement describing themselves to a prospective date or employer, and then share the personal advertisement with the group. Each person should answer the following questions: "Why did you decide to feature certain aspects of yourself and not others?" "How similar was what each person chose to disclose to what she or he typically discloses in relationships?"

3. Form a group of four to five students and have each person write down on a sheet of paper the best thing and the worst thing about the class you are now in. Compare your perceptions of the class and think about why there are any variations in perception.

4. In a group of several students, have each person reflect on a challenge she or he faces on a regular basis with regard to self-disclosure. Discuss each person's challenge and how to overcome it. Reflect on the fact that this activity in and of itself is an exercise in self-disclosure.

NOTES

1. See Ucok (2007).
2. See Campo, Cameron, Brossard, & Frazer (2004).
3. See Morreale (2008).
4. See Tajima, Ong, & Chia (2006).
5. See Workman (2010).
6. See Jeong (2009).
7. See Samovar, Porter, & McDaniel (2012).
8. See Lim (2002).
9. See Wood & Reich (2010).
10. See Braithwaite & Braithwaite (2011).
11. See Chang (2010).
12. See Min-Sun, Kam, Sharkey, & Singelis (2008).
13. See Feeny & Qi (2010).
14. See Cooley (1922).
15. See Mead (1934).
16. See Tovares (2010).
17. See Giddens (2007).
18. See Gould (2010).
19. See Robinson (2007).
20. See Gergen (2001).
21. See Luft (1969).
22. See Valkenburg & Peter (2009).
23. See Tokunaga (2009).
24. See Fogel (2011).

REFERENCES

Braithwaite, D. O., & Braithwaite, C. A. (2011). 'Which is my good leg?' Cultural communication of persons with disabilities. In L. A. Samovar, R. E. Porter, & E.R. McDaniel (Eds.), *Intercultural communication: A reader* (13th ed., pp. 241–253). Belmont, CA: Cengage.

Campo, S., Cameron, K. A., Brossard, D., & Frazer, M. S. (2004). Social norms and expectancy violation theories: Assessing the effectiveness of health communication campaigns. *Communication Monographs, 71*(4), 448–470.

Chang, C. (2010). Making unique choices or being like others: How priming self-concepts influences advertising effectiveness. *Psychology & Marketing, 27*(4), 399–415.

Cooley, C. H. (1922). *Human nature and the social order* (Rev. ed.). New York, NY: Scribner's.

Feeny, K., & Qi, W. (2010). Success through a cultural lens: Perceptions, motivations, and attributions. *China Media Research, 6*(2), 56–66.

Fogel, J. (2011). Instant messaging communication: Self-disclosure, intimacy, and disinhibition. *Journal of Communications Research*, 2(1), 13–19.

Gergen, K. J. (2001). *The saturated self: Dilemmas of identity in contemporary life* (2nd ed.). New York, NY: Basic Books.

Giddens, A. (2007). *The consequences of modernity*. Boston, MA: Polity Press.

Gould, S. J. (2010). 'To thine own self(ves) be true': Reflexive insights for etic self theory from consumers' emic constructions of the self. *Consumption, Markets & Culture*, 13(2), 181–219.

Jeong, S. (2009). Public's responses to an oil spill accident: A test of the attribution theory and situational crisis communication theory. *Public Relations Review*, 35(3), 307–309.

Lim, T-S. (2002). Language and verbal communication across cultures. In W. B. Gudykunst & B. Mody (Eds.), *Handbook of international and intercultural communication* (2nd ed., pp. 69–88). Thousand Oaks, CA: Sage.

Luft, J. (1969). *Of human interaction*. Palo Alto, CA: National Press Books.

Mead, G. H. (1934). *Mind, self, and society*. Chicago, IL: University of Chicago Press.

Min-Sun, K., Kam, K. Y., Sharkey, W. F., & Singelis, T. M. (2008). Deception: Moral transgression or social necessity? Cultural-relativity of deception motivations and perceptions of deceptive communication. *Journal of International & Intercultural Communication*, 1(1), 23–50.

Morreale, S.P. (2008). Competent and incompetent communication. In W. F. Eadie, (Ed.), *21st century communication: A reference handbook* (pp. 444–453). Thousand Oaks, CA: Sage.

Robinson, L. (2007). The cyberself: The selfing project goes online, symbolic interaction in the digital age. *New Media & Society*, 9(1), 93–110.

Samovar, L. A., Porter, R. E., & McDaniel, E. R. (Eds.). (2012). *Intercultural communication: A reader* (13th ed.). Belmont, CA: Cengage.

Tajima, A., Ong, M., & Chia, S. (2006). A Cross-national examination of third-person perception about ideal body image. Paper presented at the International Communication Association Conference. Retrieved from EBSCO *host*, www.ebscohost.com

Tokunaga, R. S. (2009). High-speed Internet access to the other: The influence of cultural orientations on self-disclosures in offline and online relationships. *Journal of Intercultural Communication Research*, 38(3), 133–147.

Tovares, A. V. (2010). Managing the voices: Athlete self-talk as a dialogic process. *Journal of Language & Social Psychology*, 29(3), 261–277.

Ucok, I. (2007). *'Dropping into being': Exploring mindfulness as lived experience*. Paper presented at the National Communication Association Conference. Retrieved from EBSCO *host*, www.ebscohost.com

Valkenburg, P., & Peter, J. (2009). The development of online and offline self-disclosure in preadolescence and adolescence and their longitudinal effects on the quality of friendships. Paper presented at the International Communication Association Conference. Retrieved from EBSCO *host*, www.ebscohost.com

Wood, J. T., & Reich, N. M. (2010). Gendered speech communities. In L. A. Samovar, R. E. Porter, & E. R. McDaniel (Eds.). *Communication between cultures* (7th ed.). Belmont, CA: Cengage.

Workman, T. (2010). The reluctant consumption of evidence-based decision making. *Health Communication*, 25(5), 480–482.

CHAPTER FOUR

LANGUAGE COMPETENCE

- **What Is Language?**
  Defining Language
  Language as a Set of Symbols
  Language as a Set of Rules
  Valuing Language

- **Functions of Language**
  Noticing Things
  Creating Opportunities *and* Constraints
  Facilitating Interactions

- **Overcoming Challenges to Language Competence**
  Language Communities
  Impact of Media and Technology

- **Chapter Summary**
  Key Terms
  Building Motivation: Self-Assessment Tool
  Building Knowledge: Discussion Questions
  Building Skills: Student Activities

The difference between the right word and the almost right word is the difference between lightning and the lightning bug. —Mark Twain, American novelist, 1835–1910

.:
• • •

Ernesto is enrolled in an introductory communication course. Prior to each class, the communication professor emails a discussion question to all the students, and has them post their responses on the class website. Ernesto downloads this message Monday evening when he opens up his mailbox.

Ernesto scratches his head and asks himself, "What in the world is Professor Bateux asking for?" He calls one of his classmates for assistance.

"Sylvia? Hi, this is Ernesto. Did you get the discussion question from Professor Bateux?"

"Yeah, I did. It looks pretty easy."

> Date: 3 October 2012 09:12 AM
> From: Professor Bateux <bateux@univ.edu>
> Subj: ASSIGNMENT FOR OCTOBER 5, 2012
> To: Comm 101<comm101@univ.edu>
>
> Please consider the following question on language for Wednesday's class discussion:
> How can language marginalize certain groups of people and perpetuate their minority status?
> Please send me your responses by Thursday night no later than 9 p.m.

"Easy? I didn't see it that way. What did you write about?"

"What I said is that sometimes minority groups like African Americans, Hispanics, or gays and lesbians develop their own jargon and use it to talk among themselves. Because they are the only ones who use the language, they set themselves up as different and exclude others from participating in their discussion. I mean, if you don't know the slang, how can you talk with them?"

"So you think when the professor uses the term minority he means a minority like an ethnic group?"

"Of course. Isn't it obvious?"

"I don't know, Sylvia. In my psychology class we talked about 'minority opinion.' That's when a small number of people in a large group have opinions different from the majority of the group. I think Professor Bateux wants us to talk about how people who are in the minority according to their opinions use language—not ethnic minorities."

"Well, go ahead and send your answer in—but I think you're going down the wrong track." In the next class, Ernesto and Sylvia sit together to find out who's right. Professor Bateux opens the lecture by saying, "What really pleased me was how each of you picked up on the notion that there are multiple meanings for the term minority. So let's start there and discuss how you all used the term minority." Ernesto and Sylvia looked at each other in confusion. Why wasn't the professor going to give them the correct definition and meaning of the word minority?

How we make sense of the meaning of words influences how we respond to others in conversations. Until Ernesto could grasp what the word, *minority*, meant to him, he was unable to formulate a response to the professor's question. Words do mean different things to different people. For Sylvia, the word, *minority*, referred to minority status based on ethnicity, religion, or sexual orientation. For Ernesto, the word, *minority*, referred to a small group of people with a set of opinions different from those of the majority group.

Competent communicators recognize that words take on different meanings depending on how they are used in specific contexts. They are able to spot the unique meaning of a word, and determine the most appropriate and effective use of language to respond. We begin this chapter with a description of language and its complexity, and then we look at the functions language serves for us.

WHAT IS LANGUAGE?

Language is complex, with its meaning depending on where, when, and how it is used. But this complexity does not prevent us from making decisions about what people mean by what they say, and anticipating the effect our language has on others. The following discussion relates to what we discussed in Chapter Three about how perceptions vary from one person to the next.

DEFINING LANGUAGE.

As you saw in Chapter One, language is defined as a verbal symbol system that allows us to take messages and utterances, in the form of words, and translate them into meaning. Competent communicators accomplish this complex task by understanding the symbols and the rules people use to interpret the meaning of words.

LANGUAGE AS A SET OF SYMBOLS.

In Chapter One, we said that a symbol is a word, sound, action, or gesture that refers to something else. We also said that the symbols we use in everyday speech are arbitrary—they are not inherently connected to the things they represent. The things to which the symbols refer are called referents. For example, we could just as easily refer to your cellular phone as a hand-held communicator; however, we have arbitrarily decided to call it a cell phone.

Over time, people in a community create a set of agreements that specify the arbitrary relationship between symbols and referents. New speakers entering into the community are socialized into that set of agreements. Language and words as symbols play an integral role in this socialization process.[1] Part of understanding a language, therefore, is grasping the set of arbitrary connections between symbols and referents. For example, in English-speaking cultures we use the symbol, *bear*, to describe "any of various usually omnivorous mammals of the family Ursidae, having a shaggy coat and short tail."[2] Depending on the particular culture we belong to and the language we speak, we could easily have developed another word to describe this animal. For *bears*, Arabic speakers use *dubab*, Danish speakers use *bjorne*, Finnish speakers use *karhu*, Mandarin Chinese speakers use *xíong*, and Spanish speakers use *oso*. While the relationships between the symbols and referents are arbitrary, competent communicators must learn these relationships if they are to communicate effectively and appropriately.

Learning a language requires more, however, than simply understanding the set of connections among symbols and referents. You also need to understand the entire symbol system, which includes the set of relationships among symbols themselves. Philosophers such as Jacques Derrida used the term **signifier** for symbol, and **signified** for referent.[3] If you are to understand what a signifier (a symbol) means, you also need to look at other signifiers associated with it at a specific time and place. If we stopped our understanding of the meaning of the word *bear* with the relationship between the signifier (the word itself) and the signified (the animal itself), we would know only

> **SIGNIFIER** is a term used for symbol.
>
> **SIGNIFIED** is a term used for referent.

that the word *bear* is associated with a specific kind of animal. However, much more is associated with the word *bear*—perceptions, feelings, and attitudes—that we can grasp only if we explore the other words linked to it. Figure 4.1 illustrates how different signifiers associated with *bear* are inter-related. In the United States, the signifier, *bear*, has become linked with the words, *wild animal*, and *ferocious*. Other English speakers associate the word *bear* with strong and protective, because bears often attack humans and other animals if they perceive them as threatening their cubs. Finally, we

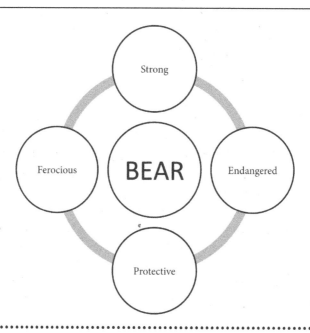

Figure 4.1: The Relationship Among Signifiers

Many words, including wild animal, strong, ferocious, protective, and endangered species, are signifiers that may be related to the word we use in the United States to signify the animal we call a bear. The signifier, bear, takes on slightly different meanings when associated with each of the words.

may also think of bears as endangered species, such as pandas, and North American grizzlies that are in danger of becoming extinct.

Figure 4.1 illustrates the important relationship among signifers. But even when people within a community agree on some of the arbitrary relationships between a signifier (the word, *bear*) and what it signifies (a ferocious bear), they may differ on other associations (a cub bear can be cute or cuddly). This is the reason that people use a system by which they can agree about the denotative meaning of symbols but do not agree as much about their connotative meaning. **Denotative meaning** refers to the "dictionary definition" of words; for example, the signified symbol, *chair*, typically means a seat, especially for one person, usually having four legs for support and a rest for the back. **Connotative meaning** refers to the personal associations people make with a signified symbol. Depending on the web of relationships among the signifiers, they may have different meanings. *Chair* may connote punishment or restricted behavior, if you were told to sit in a "time out" chair as a child. It also could connote comfort, if you have a favorite "easy chair" for reading or watching TV.

> DENOTATIVE MEANING refers to the "dictionary definition" of words.
>
> CONNOTATIVE MEANING refers to the personal associations people make with a signified symbol.
>
> CONSTITUTIVE RULES take the basic content of the message, its words, and tell us what they mean, and how we are to make sense of them.

Since there is less agreement about the connotative meaning of symbols, obviously it is the connotations we assign to words that can cause misunderstandings. In Chapter Three, we discussed how variations in perceptions of situations, events, and people represent a challenge to communicating competently with others. Now take that notion a step further. Variations in our perceptions of the *connotative* meaning of symbols (words) often are the cause of misunderstandings. Professor Bateux's use of the word, *minority*, resulted in Ernesto's and Sylvia's confusion about the connotative meaning of that symbol.

In addition to understanding language as a set of symbols, we also need to think about the unconscious rules people use for interpreting the symbols.

LANGUAGE AS A SET OF RULES.

In Chapter One, we introduced the idea of communication codes, and defined codes as the set of principles and meanings that guide how members of any social group use language. These codes also are referred to as the "rules" for how we use language, and there are two types—constitutive rules and regulative rules. People use constitutive rules to help sort out what certain words or phrases mean, and regulative rules to determine what they should say next in an ongoing conversation.[4]

Constitutive rules take the basic content of the message, its words, and tell us what they mean, and how we are to make sense of them. They connect signifiers (words) and signifieds (the things referred to) to one another. Consider, for example, the following words and phrases. What do they have in common?

- "Hi!"
- "How are you doing?"
- "Hello!"
- "What's happening?"
- "Haven't seen you in a while."
- "It's good to see you!"

You probably have heard these words and phrases millions of times, and you correctly interpret them as greetings. Whether consciously or unconsciously, you apply constitutive rules to them in order to determine their meaning and function in conversation. Of course, the context in which the phrase is said will affect the meaning you assign to it. Suppose you see a friend on campus and the person says, "Hey, what's happening?" You probably will assume the phrase to be a simple greeting. But suppose you are in an emergency room of a hospital with the friend, and a doctor asks, "What's happening?" You will assume that the phrase constitutes a real inquiry into what has happened. Then, as a result of how you make sense of the constitutive meaning of the phrase, you will reply appropriately, which leads us to regulative rules for language.

Regulative rules help you determine the appropriate response, given your interpretation of a message. Regulative rules are moral, in the sense that they tell you what you should or should not do during an interaction. They create opportunities for action—what you can do—as well as constraints for your actions—what you cannot do. Using our previous example, if you have assigned the meaning, *greeting*, to the words, in most cases, regulative rules obligate you to respond. Additionally, you are prohibited from insulting or ignoring the person after the initial greeting. To illustrate, have you ever had the experience of nearing the end of a phone conversation, and the other person hangs up without somehow saying goodbye? A simple "see yuh," or "later" would do. That person, probably unknowingly and unintentionally violated a regulative rule for ending conversations.

> •••••••••••••••••••••••••••••••••••
> REGULATIVE RULES help you determine the appropriate response given your interpretation of a message.

An American philosopher, John Searle, was one of the early writers to explore the distinction between constitutive and regulative rules for language.[5] He simply stated that all speech acts we engage in are based on our understanding of the rules of language. To this day, communication researchers continue to investigate these rules. One study explored the rules that reporters use to choose which stories to report and how to report them.[6] According to this study, constitutive rules say what the news is, and regulative rules say how the news ought to be produced and presented. Another study looked at regulative rules for how military personnel use language to communicate with superiors and subordinates in different types of situations.[7] By comparison with combat, military personnel in noncombat office situations have a set of rules for the polite use of language, regulative rules for how to engage in workplace talk when not on the battlefield. The regulative rules for communicating on the battlefield call for very different use of language. Obviously, the lesson here is that we need to pay attention to what words mean (constitutive rules), and what is appropriate to say in the flow of any conversation or situation (regulative rules).

VALUING LANGUAGE.

People have traditionally viewed language as important, because it is our primary vehicle for getting a point across and expressing thoughts and ideas to others. This is why lawyers use concrete and specific language in their legal briefs for judges. It is also why effective public speakers devote attention to using clear, vivid, and appropriate language to make their points understood but also memorable. Chapter Twelve discusses the effective use of language in public speaking in more detail. However, language does more than make messages clear and memorable, or transfer information. Language plays another important role in our lives, in that it helps us put labels on what we perceive and see, and, thereby, it helps to create our social worlds. This role is so important that, over time, several significant theories about it have been put forward.

In the 1950s, Edward Sapir and Benjamin Lee Whorf developed the **Sapir-Whorf hypothesis**.[8] This theory was based on a form of **linguistic determinism**, which means that language determines what we see or notice in the world, and what we think about what we see. Take the word, *key*, as an example. In German, *key* is masculine, and when German speakers are asked to describe a key, they tend to use words like *hard*, *heavy*, and *jagged*. In Spanish, *key* is feminine, and Spanish speakers choose words like *golden*, *intricate*, and *lovely* when describing a key. German and Spanish speakers see *key* differently as a function of whether their language conceives of *key* as a masculine or feminine term or word.[9] The Sapir-Whorf hypothesis maintains that reality is already embedded in the structure of our language, and that this structure determines how we perceive our world.

> The SAPIR-WHORF HYPOTHESIS maintains that reality is already embedded in the structure of our language, and that this structure determines how we perceive our world.

Other theorists and researchers take a different approach to the way language creates our reality; this approach is called **social constructionism**.[10] Rather than assume that reality is already embedded in our language, social constructionists say that people create their reality through the process of interacting with one another. Think about what happens when you label the emotions you experience during an interaction by saying, "I'm angry!" Labeling your emotion as "anger" not only helps you make sense of your emotions, it also provides you and the other person with clues about how to perceive the

> LINGUISTIC DETERMINISM says that language determines what we see or notice in the world, and how and what we think about what we see.

> SOCIAL CONSTRUCTIONISM states that people create their reality and relationships through the process of interaction with others.

situtation you find yourselves in. For example, angry people may be expected to show their anger through yelling and saying things in the heat of the moment that they normally would not say. The labels, words, and language we choose to characterize our experiences help us make sense of a situation, and tell us how to act and what to do.

Whether we subscribe to the Sapir-Whorf theory of linguistic determinism or social constructionist theory, both emphasize that language and how we use it are critical to creating our perceptions of our social worlds. That said, let us now consider several other ways that language is useful to all of us.

FUNCTIONS OF LANGUAGE

Language is an active force in our lives that shapes the way we live together as human beings, and the kinds of communities in which we live. Language performs three key functions for us as individuals:

1. It helps us notice things.
2. It creates opportunities and constraints in our daily lives.
3. It facilitates social interaction.

NOTICING THINGS.

Language organizes our perceptions of people, events, and issues, and directs our attention to certain aspects of things and situations. It also informs our understanding of what those aspects of things and situations mean. Moreover, the words we use to label a situation highlight certain possible actions that are appropriate to take in the future. Words and language not only tell us how to make sense of a situation (what we view as important), but also how to act now and in the future (what to do).

Imagine that you are a consultant called in by a hotel to solve the problem of guest complaints about slow elevators. What would you recommend? Instead of reducing the long wait time by replacing the elevators' motors with faster ones or installing more elevators, the consultant in this situation diagnosed it as a "people problem," not a mechanical one, and recommended simply placing mirrors on each floor by the elevators.[11] Although the wait was just as long, guests stopped complaining, because the mirrors gave them something useful to do as they waited, checking out their appearance. Labeling the situation as a mechanical problem would not have led to such a quick and simple solution, which demonstrates the power of language to make us notice certain things more than others.

As another example of the ability of language to direct our attention to some things rather than others, think about the term, **politically correct language**. Its proponents argue that we can rid our minds of discriminatory thoughts by removing from our language any words or phrases that could offend people by the way they reference differences among us. Out of concern for cultural sensitivity, Los Angeles County in California asked suppliers to stop using the terms "master" and "slave" on computer equipment, even though these are commonly used to refer to primary and secondary hard disk drives.[12] Other substitutions, such as police officer for policeman, are intended to highlight that such positions may be held by both men and women. Whether you agree or disagree with using politically correct language, the intention clearly is to minimize social and institutional offense based on occupation, gender, race, sexual orientation, or any other differences among people or groups.[13]

> **POLITICALLY CORRECT LANGUAGE** intends to rid our minds of discriminatory thoughts by removing from our language any words or phrases that could offend people by the way they reference differences among us.

CREATING OPPORTUNITIES *AND* CONSTRAINTS.

Because of its ability to provide regulative rules, language does create opportunities for and constraints on interactions and relationships. Take the example of what it means to be "just friends." Let us say that you have developed a close relationship with someone. When people ask you about your relationship, you both reply, "We're just friends." If you label your relationship as "just friends," what opportunities does that create in terms of what you can say and do with one another? Some of the regulative rules that offer opportunities might look like this:

- If we are "just friends," we can talk about our personal lives, including our love lives.
- If we are "just friends," we can offer advice and counsel to the other person when he or she is having difficulties.
- If we are "just friends," we can do things together like go to a party or have dinner.

Though the status of "just friends" creates certain opportunities, it also prohibits certain actions. Some of the regulative rules that impose constraints may look like this:

- If we are "just friends," we should not make any sexual advances.
- If we are "just friends," we should not go out on what appears to be an official date.
- If we are "just friends," we should not share a room with only one bed, if we go on vacation.

Indeed, the language we use to characterize relationships influences what we can say and do with one another, as well as what we cannot say and do. In addition, language creates opportunity and constraints, because it plays a critical role in shaping our identities. We see this connection between language and social identities in two types of biased communication: gender-biased language and hate speech.

Language is **gender-biased** if it tends to favor one gender over another. In the case of the English language, the bias is usually a preference for masculine over feminine. The basic idea underlying gender-bias in language is that it shapes the way girls and boys perceive themselves as part of a feminine or masculine culture. Girls are socialized to emphasize building harmonious relationships and being cooperative, while boys are socialized to be more individualistic, focused on the self, assertive, and competitive.[14] These gender roles encourage women and men to use certain patterns of language use.[15] For example, some researchers have found:

> GENDER-BIASED LANGUAGE tends to favor one sex over another.

> HATE SPEECH has been defined as "speech that (1) has a message of racial inferiority, (2) is directed against a member of a historically oppressed group, and (3) is persecutory, hateful, and degrading" (Nielsen, 2002).

1. Men use more direct language styles, including directive statements ("Write that down."), while women are more indirect and tend to use uncertainty verbs ("It seems to me . . . ."), questions ("What do you think?"), and hedges ("kind of").

2. Men are more succinct in their use of language, as they use more abbreviated sentences ("Great posture."), while women are more elaborate in their language use, including adverbs that intensify feeling and emotion ("really," "so"), and women begin sentences with adverbs ("Actually, it's. . . ."), and use longer sentences.

Obviously, the use of gender-biased language shapes the identity of both males and females, and exercises constraints on how members of both sexes can communicate.

Another type of language that shapes the identity is hate speech. Whether it is radio shock jocks making racist and sexist remarks, White supremacist groups verbally attacking ethnic minorities, or rap music artists advocating the killing of cops or the rape and brutalization of women, hate speech, unfortunately, has become part of our social fabric. **Hate speech** has been defined as "speech that (1) has a message of racial inferiority, (2) is directed against a member of a historically oppressed group, and (3) is persecutory, hateful, and degrading."[16] Although many people believe that freedom of speech is a civil liberty guaranteed by the Constitution, hate speech is viewed negatively, and as an exception to the Bill of Rights. One reason is that the effects of hate speech are overwhelmingly negative. Hate speech can produce negative emotions in the aggressor, hurt feelings in those targeted, and changes in the victims, ranging from psychological to physical, brought on by severe emotional distress.

Language plays an important role in shaping people's identities. Your use of language should ensure that individuals and groups are treated fairly and respectfully. Consider both the way you speak to others and how you speak about them when they are not present. Here are four useful reminders to help you avoid bias or hateful language of any kind.

1. Describe individuals and groups precisely and appropriately: To describe all human beings as man or mankind is not as precise as using the phrase men and women. When describing the sexual orientation of a group of men and women, the term, *gay*, can be interpreted to refer to men and women or only men. To provide greater preciseness, use the phrase gay men and lesbians.

2. Avoid labeling people: Using labels deprives people of their individuality and objectifies them. When you make statements about the handicapped, the elderly, youth, and so on, your language labels them

in terms of only one characteristic they possess. Counter the use of labels by placing the descriptive adjective in front of a noun (handicapped people, elderly man, young woman), or "put the person first" followed by a descriptive phrase (people with AIDS). You thus suggest that these people have other characteristics other than just the disease of AIDS.

3. Avoid using one group as a standard against which others are judged: When you portray one group as superior or "normal," and use this group as the standard to judge others, your language creates bias and possibly justifies discrimination. Avoid any level of judgment and bias that suggests that one group is inherently better than another.

4. Use gender-neutral language and gender-inclusive language: Rather than gender-biased language, try to eliminate (or neutralize) reference to gender in terms that describe people. For example, the words, *chairman*, *fireman*, and *stewardess* are gender-specific; the corresponding gender-neutral terms are *chairperson* (or *chair*), *firefighter*, and *flight attendant*. If you have flown recently, you probably have noticed airlines now use the gender-neutral term, *flight attendant*.

FACILITATING INTERACTIONS.

The way you use language can either enhance or hurt your ability to effectively and appropriately engage in interactions and work with others. Obviously, language that promotes coordination does not insult or demean others, or place them in a defensive position. But your ability to work together also depends on the level of abstraction in your language and word choice. Most of the time, facilitating interactions with others requires you to select language that is clear and direct, so that others can easily understand what you have to say.

One tool for selecting language that is appropriately clear and direct is Hayakawa's Ladder of Abstraction.[17] Samuel. I. Hayakawa, a noted linguist and language scholar, placed language on a continuum from the very concrete to the more abstract. He devised a **ladder of abstraction** on which he placed the most concrete words or concepts on the lower rungs, and arranged words on the upper rungs as they increased in abstraction. Table 4.1 provides three examples of the ladder of abstraction. Low-level abstractions, or descriptions of concrete things or

> The LADDER OF ABSTRACTION places the most concrete words on the lower rungs, and arranges words on the upper rungs as they increase in abstraction.

Table 4.1: Hayakawa's Ladder of Abstraction

The Ladder of Abstraction moves from concrete language at the bottom to abstract language at the top. Here are three examples of ladders of abstraction for the concepts of society, human endeavors, and the economy.

HIGHEST LEVEL OF ABSTRACTION	SOCIETY	HUMAN ENDEAVORS	THE ECONOMY
Next to Highest	Most People	Manufacturers	Financial Assets
Next to Lowest	A Sibling	Cosmetic Company	Stock Portfolio
Lowest Level of Abstraction	My Sister, Tracy	Revlon	Enron Holdings

occurrences on the lowest rung of the ladder, are the most descriptive and clear, because they refer to specific instances and behaviors. The middle rungs of the ladder are more abstract because they include words that draw general inferences about a person or situation. Finally, the highest level includes abstract generalizations about a person, issue, or event.

Can we assume that concrete, specific language is always the best and most competent way to use language? In some situations, using concrete language is very useful for facilitating interactions with others. In other cases, using more abstract language may be best. A recent study applied the ladder of abstraction to help music journalists face the challenge of how to describe music.[18] The researcher, an expert in semantics and the study of meaning, decided that it is important in music journalism to include descriptions of technical or concrete aspects of music, as well as aesthetic or abstract aspects. This example illustrates that people need to make conscious choices regarding the level of abstraction of their words and language, if they are to facilitate interactions and communicate with others most effectively and appropriately.

Now review the summary of the three functions of language in Table 4.2. Then we will conclude this chapter with advice on overcoming challenges to using language competently.

OVERCOMING CHALLENGES TO LANGUAGE COMPETENCE

Language is challenging to speakers and listeners for many reasons, some of which were already explored in this chapter. Whether a sender or receiver, you need to be aware of the arbitrary nature

Table 4.2: Functions of Language

Because language is so pervasive in our daily lives, you may not be aware of these three key functions language serves: noticing things, creating opportunities and constraints, and facilitating our interactions with others. Think about any language encounter you had today, and determine which of these three functions it served for you.

FUNCTION OF LANGUAGE	DESCRIPTION OF THE FUNCTION
Noticing Things	• Language organizes our perceptions, directs our attention to certain aspects of things and situations, and tells us what those things and situations mean. • Words and language tell us how to make sense of a situation and how to act, what actions are appropriate.
Creating Opportunities and Constraints	• Language creates opportunities for interactions and relationships by influencing what we *can* say and do with one another, and it puts constraints by influencing what we *cannot* say and do. • Language and words play a critical role in shaping our identities.
Facilitating Interactions	• Language enhances or hurts our ability to engage in interactions and work with others. • Words and language, when at an appropriate level of abstraction, facilitate communication interactions.

of symbols and signifiers, and the constitutive and regulative rules governing their use. You also need to avoid using biased language and hate speech. Two other challenges are worth mentioning in closing our discussion of language—the nature of language communities, and the impact of media and technology on language in the 21st century—a critical challenge we already mentioned in previous chapters.

LANGUAGE COMMUNITIES.

In Chapter One, we defined a community as a group of people who come together in the same physical, mental, or virtual space to interact or pursue a common goal. Now we would like to extend that definition and apply it to language. A **language community** is a group of people who have developed a common set of constitutive and regulative rules, which guide the meaning of words and the appropriate reactions, based on interpreting those words. We all belong to different language communities, and that can make it difficult to communicate, because there is no shared understanding of what words mean. Some of your language communities may be based on your type of work, gender, religion, race, ethnicity, political affiliation, and so on. In truth, some communication theorists and educators say that we now live in plurilingual (multilingual) speech communities, because of the divisive and partisan political culture in the United States.[19] To be sure, political conservatives and liberals seem to use the same language and words to mean very different things. To the contrary, another group of theorists think that having a shared language is not important, and plays only a limited role in communication.[20] Understandably, these theorists think that there is no need to make English the national language in the United States.

> **A LANGUAGE COMMUNITY** is a group of people who have developed a common set of constitutive and regulative rules, which guide the meaning of words and the appropriate reactions, based on interpreting those words.

> **ETHNOCENTRIC COMMUNICATORS** recognize as valid only their own meanings for words, and reject alternative meanings as wrong.

> **COSMOPOLITAN COMMUNICATORS** recognize that the meanings they have created for certain words are unique to them, and are not shared by others.

This political argument aside, the language we use may be understandable within a particular language community, but it may be incomprehensible to those outside—and those outside people may interpret our messages in ways other than we intend. This is a real challenge to language use because it makes it difficult to predict how other people will interpret your language.

To overcome this challenge, simply realize that different words have different meanings in different language communities. For a musician a gig is positive, but for a frog a gig means having a metal spike inserted into the brain stem to scramble the brain. We develop these personal meanings for words that differ from others' meanings, based on our unique background and experiences in language communities. Yet we sometimes forget this simple fact and assume that others have the same meaning for words. This leads to ethnocentric communication.

Ethnocentric communicators recognize as valid only their own meanings for words, and reject alternative meanings as wrong. In contrast, when we acknowledge the existence of a number of different, equally valid meanings for words, we become cosmopolitan communicators. **Cosmopolitan communicators** recognize that the meanings they have created for certain words are unique to them, and are not shared by others. They are curious about the unique meanings other people have for words, and they know if you have a closed and rigid opinion about the "right" meaning, you might miss the distinctive meaning of the other person's message, and fail to engage in productive dialogue.[21]

Table 4.3: Overcoming Challenges to Language Competence

These recommendations and strategies for using language will help you address any challenges you may encounter personally, at work, and face-to-face or in technology-mediated situations.

RECOMMENDED STRATEGY	DESCRIPTION OF THE STRATEGY
Ask any of these three types of questions to clarify your interpretation of words and language.	• *Clarifying questions* invite the other person to elaborate on his or her meaning. "What exactly do you mean by that?" • *Showing questions* invite the other person to focus on specific actions or activities that they associate with the word. "Exactly what does it look like to you when that happens?" • *Comparison questions* invite the other person to point to words that are similar in meaning to the word in question. "What other phrases could you use to describe what you're feeling?"
Use these three strategies to anticipate how others may interpret your message.	• A *first strategy* calls for examining your wording before you say it, from the multiple perspectives of different audiences. "Who are the different people to whom you are presenting your message, and how might each of them interpret your language?" • A *second strategy* is to examine the larger context in which the message occurs. "What is the meaning of a word or phrase in the context, relationship, and culture in which it will be uttered?" • A *third strategy* involves anticipating possible interpretations based on any historical background to your message. "What happened in the past before you spoke, and how might these events influence the language you choose to use?"
Play with phrasing of your messages by experimenting with how you use pronouns.	• A *you-message* is a statement that labels another person, and involves some evaluation of that person's behavior. "You are very angry." This phrasing locates responsibility for the anger in the other person, and could put her or him on the defensive. • An *I-message* is a statement that labels a behavior or perception as your own. "I think you are very angry." This phrasing identifies the anger as your perception, so you can clarify if the perception is accurate or not. • A *we-message* is a statement that labels and describes the common behaviors of two or more people. "We are angry with one another." This phrasing places responsibility for the anger in the relationship, and is the most constructive of the three types of messages or ways of using pronouns. Both people can deal with the situation instead of debating the label of anger or their perceptions of it.

IMPACT OF MEDIA AND TECHNOLOGY.

As already mentioned in Chapter Three, communicating in the 21st century is significantly influenced by the use of media and technology, and this impact is equally significant regarding language. Interpersonal relationships develop and are maintained using cell phones, e-mail, texting, tweeting, and all forms of social media. Small groups are making decisions and solving problems in virtual environments using webcasting and webinar technologies. Public speakers are using the Internet and World Wide Web to communicate with remote and sometimes unseen audiences around the globe.

Predictably, communication researchers are on the job, and examining this new challenge to language, sometimes in the light of older theories. One researcher is applying John Searle's notion of constitutive and regulative rules to how readers follow hyperlinks in online messages, and how the hyperlinks shape interpretations of messages.[22] The hyperlinks themselves are considered constitutive rules used by the online reader to make sense of what the message means. Guided by the rules (the hyperlinks), the reader's attention is linked to other places, and she or he engages in rapid retrieval of information by following trails of hyperlinks.

Another researcher is concerned with a more tangible challenge to language and media use in the global society of the 21st century.[23] The challenge is using language effectively and appropriately in light of the substantial increase in international mobility, professionally and personally. Not only are we communicating with different language communities, these communities frequently are located around the world, and we communicate with them using all kinds of mediated technologies. A typical question becomes whether members of your work team in other countries, or even other language communities in the United States, understand what you mean by LOL (laugh out loud), OMG (oh my god), NNTR (no need to reply), TTYL (talk to you later), or LMAO (go look this one up!).

Addressing all these challenges requires developing abilities that allow us to make sense of the unique characteristics of a situation and determine the most useful language choices. Such abilities include being sensitive to the situation, including the people involved and their expectations, and adjusting your language to fit the opportunities and constraints of the situation.

Review Table 4.3, which summarizes recommendations and strategies for overcoming challenges to using language competently in today's society. Then you will be ready to learn about using nonverbal communication competently, the topic of Chapter Five.

CHAPTER SUMMARY

Language is a complex, verbal symbol system that allows us to take messages and utterances, in the form of words, and translate them into meaning. The meaning of a symbol is determined by the arbitrary relationship between a signifier (the symbol) and the signified (the referent to which it refers), as well as the signifier's relationship with numerous other signifiers (symbols). People agree about the denotative or dictionary meaning of words as symbols, whereas the connotative meaning is based on the personal associations people make with a signified symbol. In addition, we use constitutive rules to help sort out what certain words or phrases mean, and regulative rules to determine what to say next in response, given your interpretation of a message.

In addition to making messages clear and memorable and transferring information, language also helps us put labels on what we perceive, and thereby helps create our social worlds. The Sapir-Whorf hypothesis suggests that our world is linguistically determined, that is, that language determines what we see or notice in the world and what we think about what we see. While emphasizing the connection between language and social reality, social constructionists believe that people create their reality through the process of interacting with one another.

Language performs three key functions for us as individuals. First, it helps us notice things and directs our attention to certain aspects of situations. Politically correct language, for example, proposes that we can rid our minds of discriminatory thoughts by removing from our language any offensive words or phrases that could offend people by how they reference differences among us. Second, language creates opportunities but also some constraints in our daily lives. For example, the language we use to characterize relationships influences what we can say and do with one another, but also what we cannot say and do. Forms of communication, such as gender-biased language favoring one gender over another, and hate speech with its messages of racial inferiority and oppression, can play a critical role in shaping our identities. Third, language facilitates interactions when we use it to promote coordination and avoid insulting or demeaning others. We also should make conscious choices about the level of abstraction of our language.

Two contemporary challenges to language competence are the nature of language communities, and the impact of media and technology in the 21st century. First of all, each language community may have a unique way of using language, which may make it difficult to communicate. Ethnocentric communicators ignore these differences, whereas cosmopolitan communicators recognize that their meanings for certain words are unique to them, and are not shared by others. A second challenge to using language in today's society is the influence of media and technology in interpersonal relationships, small groups, and when speaking publicly using the Internet and the World Wide Web.

Strategies for using language competently in today's society include: clarifying your interpretation of words and language, anticipating how others may interpret your message, and using phrasing possibilities, such as experimenting with pronouns.

KEY TERMS.

The key terms below are defined in this chapter, and presented alphabetically with definitions in the Glossary at the end of the book.

- signifier
- signified
- denotative meaning
- connotative meaning
- constitutive rules
- regulative rules
- Sapir-Whorf hypothesis

- linguistic determinism
- social constructionism
- politically correct language
- gender-biased language
- hate speech
- ladder of abstraction
- language community

- ethnocentric communicators
- cosmopolitan communicators

BUILDING MOTIVATION: SELF-ASSESSMENT TOOL.

Rate each of the eight communication situations described here, indicating your own typical level of language competence. Rate one situation all the way through for motivation, knowledge, and skills. Then rate the next situation. Use the 1–4 scale below, with 1 being minimal competence and 4 high competence.

Communication situations.

1. Having dinner with people from another country but who do not speak English.
2. Going on a date with a person whose job and line of work differ from yours.
3. Meeting a person online and getting acquainted electronically.
4. Participating in a group discussion at school about a class project.
5. Describing a project at work on a topic with which your coworkers are not familiar.
6. Presenting the convocation address to open the school year on campus.
7. Discussing a problem using texts and tweets with a person of the opposite sex.
8. Attending a formal reception where you do not know anyone.

Motivation.

1 = Distracted, disinterested, or simply no motivation to be competent.
2 = Somewhat distracted or disinterested, but motivated to be competent.
3 = Somewhat interested and motivated to be competent.
4 = Highly interested and motivated to be competent.

Knowledge.

1 = Completely inexperienced and ignorant about what to do and how to do it.
2 = Minimal experience and sense of what to do and how to do it.
3 = Somewhat experienced and knowledgeable about what to do and how to do it.
4 = Highly knowledgeable about all aspects of what to do and how to do it.

Skills.

1 = Completely incapable of behaving competently.
2 = Barely capable of behaving minimally competently.
3 = Fairly capable of behaving competently.
4 = Highly capable of behaving competently.

Interpreting your scores.

Total your score separately for each situation (motivation, knowledge, and skills). The possible range of the score for each situation is 3–12. If your total score for any of the situations is 6 or less, you see yourself as less competent in that situation than you should be. A score of 7–9 means that you are average at sending and receiving communication messages in the situation. A score of 10–12 indicates that you have a high level of communication competence in that situation.

BUILDING KNOWLEDGE: DISCUSSION QUESTIONS.

1. Why is it important to see how words or signifiers relate to other words or signifiers? For example, why is it important to know whether the word, *execute*, relates to words like *computer* and *software program*, as opposed to *prison* and *justice*?

2. Describe a situation in which the language someone used caused you to notice something about the situation that you might not normally have noticed. What language did the person use to focus your attention on that aspect of the situation?

3. In what ways does language create opportunities or constraints? Give an example of language that does both.

4. Under what conditions is it competent to use concrete language? Under what conditions might it be better to use abstract language?

5. If you are not sure of the meaning of what a person is saying, what kinds of questions would you ask to help make sense of his or her meaning?

6. Consider a situation in which you felt your language was misunderstood when you communicated electronically with another person. How should you have communicated to be better understood?

BUILDING SKILLS: STUDENT ACTIVITIES.

Individual activities.

1. Write down as many bumper sticker messages as you can recall. Next write a list of the different kinds of people you know. How would each of them interpret the meaning of each bumper sticker?

2. Consider the following kinds of conversations: job interview, greeting a friend, greeting a professor, and asking someone out for a date. For each conversation write down as many constitutive and regulative rules as you can.

3. The two major national political parties in the United States have websites: The Democratic Party (http://www.democrats.org/) and the Republican National Committee (http://www.gop.com/index.php). Look at each website and examine the language used to describe the party that sponsors the website. What kind of language is used to describe the views of the other party? How do the words and phrases used on each website differ?

4. Take a word and place it in the center of the first diagram below; it can be a noun, a concept, an event, whatever you want. List four words you associate with that word. For each of the four words associated with the main word, list several other words that come to mind. What does your diagram tell you about the related or associative nature of words?

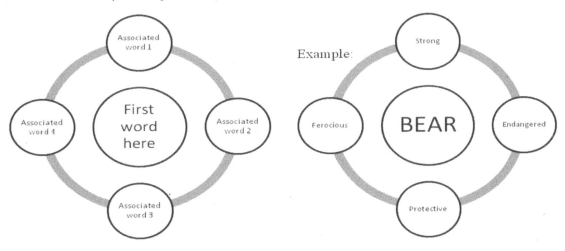

Group activities.

1. Form groups of four to five students. Using the following list of words, compare what the words mean to each member of the group. Discuss how the meaning of a word changes depending on the language community to which a group member belongs.

family values	welfare
happiness	freedom
liberal	conservative
religious	spiritual
intellectual	practical

2. Form groups of four to five students. Have one of the group members answer the following question: "What does it mean to be a good friend?" Each group member then asks a question of the first person that adds to the understanding of the meaning the first person has for "good friend." After each question has been asked and answered, go to the next person. Repeat this process for each person in the group. Discuss the kinds of questions that help you understand the meanings people have for words.

3. Form groups of four to five students. Each person should describe his or her daily use of technology and media to communicate. Analyze each person's description in regard to any possible constraints on communication interactions and relationships.

NOTES

1. See Landry, Allard, & Deveau (2007).
2. See *The American Heritage Dictionary of the English Language* (2006).
3. See Derrida (1978).
4. See Cronen (1999).
5. See Searle (1969).
6. See Ryfe (2006).
7. See Halbe (2011).
8. See Joseph (1996).
9. See "Continental Divide" (2002).
10. See Vygotsky (1934/1986).
11. See Mitroff (1978).
12. See "'master' and 'slave' computer labels unacceptable" (2005).
13. See Banning (2004).
14. See Eagly & Koenig (2006).
15. See Mulac (2006).
16. See Nielsen (2002).
17. See Hayakawa (1964).
18. See Bongiovanni (2008).
19. See Silverstein (2010).
20. See Rönnström (2011).
21. See Barge (2006).
22. See Mazzali-Lurati (2007).
23. See Kenning (2005).

REFERENCES

The American heritage dictionary of the English language (4th ed.). (2006). Boston, MA: Houghton Mifflin.

Banning, M. E. (2004). The limits of PC discourse: Linking language use to social practice. *Pedagogy: Critical Approaches to Teaching Literature, Language, Composition, and Culture, 4*(2),191–214.

Barge, J. K. (2006). Dialogue, conflict, and community. In J. Oetzel & S. Ting-Toomey (Eds.), *The Sage handbook of conflict communication: Integrating theory, research, and practice* (pp. 517–544). Thousand Oaks, CA: Sage.

Bongiovanni, D. (2008). Arts reporting and the gradation of abstraction. *ETC: A Review of General Semantics, 65*(2), 165–167.

'Continental Divide.' (2002, March 18). *Report/News Magazine* (Alberta Edition), *29*(6), p. 4.

Cronen, V. E. (1999). Coordinated management of meaning: Practical theory for the complexities and contradictions of everyday life. In J. Siegfried (Ed.), *The status of common sense in psychology* (pp. 185–207). Norwood, NJ: Ablex.

Derrida. J. (1978). *Writing and difference.* London, UK: Routledge & Kegan Paul.

Eagly, A. H., & Koenig, A. M. (2006). Social role theory of sex differences and similarities: Implication for prosocial behavior. In K. Dindia & D. J. Canary (Eds.), *Sex differences and similarities in communication* (2nd ed., pp. 156–172). Mahwah, NJ: Erlbaum.

Halbe, D. (2011). Language in the military workplace—Between hierarchy and politeness. *Text & Talk, 31*(3), 315–334.

Hayakawa, S. I. (1964*). Language in thought and action* (2nd ed.). New York, NY: Harcourt, Brace, & World.

Joseph, J.D. (1996). The immediate sources of the Sapir-Whorf hypothesis. *Historiographia Linguistica, 23*(3), 365–404.

Kenning, M. (2005). Language, media use, and mobility in contemporary society. *Communications: The European Journal of Communication Research, 30*(4), 445–457.

Landry, R., Allard, R., & Deveau, K. (2007). A macroscopic intergroup approach to the study of ethnolinguistic development. *International Journal of the Sociology of Language, 185*(1), 225–253.

"'Master' and 'slave' computer labels unacceptable, officials say." (2005). Retrieved from www.cnn.com.

Mazzali-Lurati, S. (2007). Here is the author! Hyperlinks as constitutive rules of hypertextual communication. *Semiotica, 167*(1–4), 135–168.

Mitroff, I. I. (1978). Systemic problem solving. In M. M. Lombardo & M. W. McCall, Jr. (Eds.), *Leadership: Where else can we go?* (pp. 129–144). Durham, NC: Duke University Press.

Mulac, A. (2006). The gender-linked language effect: Do language differences really make a difference? In K. Dindia & D. J. Canary (Eds.), *Sex differences and similarities in communication* (2nd ed., pp. 211–231). Mahwah, NJ: Erlbaum.

Nielsen, L. B. (2002). Subtle, pervasive, harmful: Racist and sexist remarks in public as hate speech. *Journal of Social Issues, 58*(2), 265–280.

Rönnström, N. (2011). Cosmopolitan communication and the broken dream of a common language. *Educational Philosophy & Theory, 43*(3), 260–282.

Ryfe, D. (2006). The nature of news rules. *Political Communication, 23*(2), 203–214.

Searle, J. (1969). *Speech acts.* Cambridge, UK: Cambridge University Press.

Silverstein, M. (2010). Society, polity, and language community: An enlightenment trinity in anthropological perspective. *Journal of Language & Politics, 9*(3), 339–363.

Vygotsky, L. S. (1934/1986). *Thought and language* (A. Kozulin, Ed.; Rev. ed.). Boston, MA: MIT Press.

CHAPTER FIVE

NONVERBAL COMMUNICATION COMPETENCE

The most important thing in communication is hearing what isn't said. —Peter F. Drucker, Author and Columnist, 1909–2005

. .
. . .

Bookstore cafés are popular meeting places for college students. One Saturday afternoon, right before the beginning of fall semester, Samantha drove to campus to visit the bookstore and pick up books for her classes. She also hoped that she might meet a few other students taking the same classes that fall.

Samantha was wearing a tweed jacket and turtleneck with a nice pair of jeans. On entering the bookstore café, Samantha spotted Steve having a cup of coffee at a small table. Steve's clothes, hairstyle, and even personal mannerisms looked awesome. At a glance, Samantha decided that she liked how he looked, so she grabbed a latte and sat down at a table near him. Finding Samantha attractive despite her tweedy appearance, Steve moved over to her table and struck up a conversation.

As Samantha got to know Steve, she changed the way she communicated very slightly without even realizing it. Her voice became a little softer and lower, and she leaned toward Steve, smiling and making direct eye contact. As their conversation continued, Steve sat up taller, and spoke with a little more authority in his voice.

After an hour of conversation, Samantha glanced nervously at her watch. Noticing that nonverbal cue, Steve leaned across the table, touched Samantha lightly on the arm, and asked if she would like to see him again. She agreed to a date the next Friday, and Steve said he would pick her up at her apartment at 7:00 p.m. sharp. As she left the bookstore, Samantha wondered how she could control her tendency to arrive late. She was about to miss a movie date with a friend, and she was already worried about being ready at 7:00 p.m. on Friday when Steve arrived.

During this first meeting, Steve and Samantha reacted to an array of nonverbal cues that play a critical role in shaping people's first impressions of one another. At first glance, Samantha appeared conservative, and Steve more casual and cool. However, both students overcame these differences in appearance by using nonverbal communication to help them get better acquainted. Whenever people communicate, in addition to using words, they send, receive, and react to nonverbal cues. The effectiveness and appropriateness of nonverbal communication, in addition to what is said verbally, add to the competence of communication.

Let us begin this chapter by defining nonverbal communication, and considering its importance to you as a communicator.

WHAT IS NONVERBAL COMMUNICATION?

Scholars' opinions differ about what constitutes nonverbal communication. Some describe it as all communication other than words. Others prefer to distinguish between nonverbal behaviors, which contain no meaning, and **nonverbal cues**, which are nonverbal behaviors or objects to which meaning is assigned. For instance, if you wear a unique piece of jewelry or a tweed jacket, as Samantha did, that may become a nonverbal cue when someone notices it and assigns meaning to it. When Steve reached across the table and touched Samantha on the arm, that nonverbal cue communicated that he wanted to get better acquainted.

NONVERBAL CUES are nonverbal behaviors or objects to which meaning is assigned.

NONVERBAL COMMUNICATION includes all behaviors, attributes, and objects of humans—other than words—that communicate messages and have shared social meaning.

DEFINING NONVERBAL COMMUNICATION.

In Chapter One, we introduced the idea of nonverbal communication as consisting of communicative symbols to which people attribute meaning. We now can define **nonverbal communication** as all behaviors, attributes, and objects of humans—other than words—that communicate messages and have shared social meaning. This definition includes any aspect of physical appearance, body movements, gestures, facial expressions, eye movements, touching behaviors, the voice,

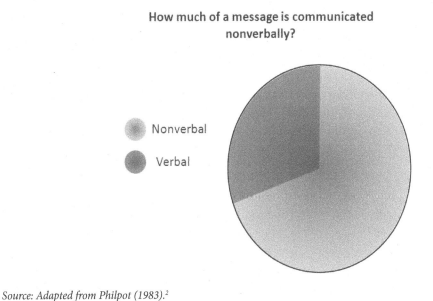

Figure 5.1: The Dominance of Nonverbal Communication

A summary of research studies finds that a surprising 65% of the meaning of conversational messages is communicated using nonverbal cues.

How much of a message is communicated nonverbally?

- Nonverbal
- Verbal

Source: Adapted from Philpot (1983).[2]

and the way people use objects, time, and space to communicate. And as we said in Chapter Two, communication competence relates to how effectively and appropriately a person uses any of these nonverbal cues in the given context.[1]

VALUING NONVERBAL COMMUNICATION.

An early summary of various studies on the importance of nonverbal communication found that 65% of the conversational meaning in most interpersonal interactions comes from nonverbal cues.[2] Figure 5.1 highlights this summary. While this precise percentage has been challenged by some scholars, numerous other recent studies attest to the importance of nonverbal communication competence.

For example, teachers expressed stronger liking for students who were effective nonverbally.[3] For married couples, accuracy in interpreting the nonverbal messages of a partner is associated with greater marital satisfaction.[4] In the business world, nonverbal cues have a positive effect on interviewers' perceptions of job candidates.[5] In a study on persuasion, an eager but appropriate nonverbal style resulted in more positive attitudes toward the persuasive message, and greater intention to follow the recommendations.[6] In the news media, the effective use by politicians of active rather than passive nonverbal behaviors influenced perceptions of the politicians' images in TV talk shows.[7] Other researchers confirm that extroverted individuals make very effective use of expressive forms of nonverbal communication.[8] More contemporarily, a study of nonverbal communication in computer-mediated interactions identified a strong potential for the effective use of nonverbal cues to enhance online interactions.[9]

Given the importance of nonverbal communication, let us now consider how we all use nonverbal cues to accomplish various communication goals and functions in our everyday lives.

FUNCTIONS OF NONVERBAL COMMUNICATION

A well-respected authority on nonverbal communication, Judee Burgoon, provided a worthwhile way to think about how we use nonverbal cues.[10] Burgoon and her fellow researchers talked about how people relate to one another. In essence, they said that people use communication and relational messages to indicate how they regard each other, their relationship, and themselves in the context of the relationship. Burgoon asserted that a lot of this relating happens nonverbally, and that nonverbal cues are crucial to effectively communicating in relationships. We agree with Judee Burgoon. Without being aware of it, we all use nonverbal cues to complement what we say verbally, to regulate our interactions with others, and to define the nature of our relationships. Let us take a closer look at these functions.

COMPLEMENTING VERBAL MESSAGES.

People use nonverbal cues to take the place of a word or a spoken message. The cue, which has meaning for a particular cultural group, translates into a word or phrase and substitutes for the word. For example, in North America, people hold up a hand with the palm turned outward to say "stop where you are." Although the meaning is agreed to by a majority of people in North America, the same gesture is considered an insult in Greece. In addition to substituting for a word, nonverbal cues also are used to repeat and reinforce a spoken word or verbal message. If you are giving some-one directions, you would use words to say that a street is three blocks away, and point toward the street or hold up three fingers.

Nonverbal cues do significantly enhance and accent verbal messages. People use tone of voice and rate of speech, facial expressions, and gestures to bring their spoken words to life. Good public speakers use gestures to add excitement to speeches, though some cultures use gestures more frequently than others. Most Americans, for example, make extensive use of gestures when they are excited, or when they need to explain a difficult concept or idea. In our everyday conversations, Americans often use facial expressions to heighten the drama of a story they are telling, or the significance of their recounting of a personal experience.

On some occasions, a nonverbal message may contradict the verbal message. Interestingly, when nonverbal and verbal messages contradict one another, most of us tend to believe the nonverbal message. For instance, in interpersonal situations, when you are already suspicious about what some-one might say, you are more likely to rely on the person's nonverbal cues to determine what they really mean. But surprisingly, when relying on nonverbal cues to detect deception, most people are not very effective. A meta-analysis of 253 studies of people distinguishing truths from lies revealed overall accuracy was just 53%, not much better than flipping a coin.[11]

REGULATING INTERACTIONS AND DEFINING RELATIONSHIPS.

People often use nonverbal cues to manage the flow of conversations, and to help coordinate communication interactions with others. For example, we use nonverbal cues when we want to ask for a turn in a conversation, or yield a turn to the other person. If you want to ask for a turn to speak, you might lean forward toward the speaker and use direct eye contact. If someone is about to interrupt you, you might suppress the interruption by speaking faster and avoiding pauses. In the chapter's opening story, Samantha's glance at her watch sent the message, "I need to end this con-versation." Steve responded verbally by setting a date for their next meeting.

As Burgoon suggested, people also use nonverbal cues to define and make statements about the social and emotional quality of their relationships with others. For instance, nonverbal cues are used to indicate a turning point or a change in a relationship.[12] As Samantha and Steve became better acquainted, she changed how she communicated nonverbally. Her voice became a little softer and lower, and she leaned toward Steve, smiling and making direct eye contact. In addition, researchers have found that as romantic relationships mature over time and go through different stages of rela-tional development, perceptions of the importance of nonverbal communication tend to change.[13] Casual dating partners reported lower levels of the importance of nonverbal communication than individuals in an engaged or married relationship. These results tell us that the more involved roman-tic partners become, the more important nonverbal cues are in their relationship.

As you now can see, people use nonverbal cues to accomplish many different communication functions. Actually, the functions we are trying to accomplish tend to dictate whether we use non-verbal or verbal channels. In sum, we tend to use verbal channels when we want to transmit fac-tual information. We rely on nonverbal channels to manage our interactions and relationships. As a result, we assign meaning to all sorts of human behaviors and objects, sending and receiving the following types of nonverbal messages.

TYPES OF NONVERBAL MESSAGES

Nonverbal communication makes use of physical appearance, body language (including movement and posture, gestures, facial expression, and eye contact), touch, voice, and time and space. As you learn more about these types of nonverbal messages, you will understand how fundamental they are to your communication competence.

PHYSICAL APPEARANCE AND FIRST IMPRESSIONS.

Physical appearance consists of everything you notice about a person, including how attractive or unattractive the person is to you, the person's race and ethnicity, age, gender, height, weight, body shape, clothing, and even how the person smells. Based on this physical appearance, you quickly form a first impression about a person's education level, social status, economic background, trustworthiness, and moral character. When Samantha noticed Steve in the bookstore café, her initial reaction to him was typical of how quickly people form first impressions. Indeed, your clothing and any decorative items of personal choice, make immediate nonverbal statements about you and your status, position in life, and even beliefs and values. So if you are giving a speech or interviewing for a job, remember how quickly you may be judged based on nonverbal cues and personal appearance. Furthermore, when judging others, be sensitive to how their physical appearance may be affecting your reactions to them.

To wrap up this discussion of physical appearance, take a quick look at Box 5.1 and the results of a study of "bad hair days."

PHYSICAL APPEARANCE includes everything you notice about a person, including degree of attractiveness, race and ethnicity, age, gender, height, weight, body shape, clothing, and even how the person smells.

BODY LANGUAGE, or KINESICS, focuses on how people communicate through movement and posture, gestures, and expressions of the face and eyes.

BODY MOVEMENT and POSTURE can communicate three things in any situation: how people see power operating, how they feel about themselves in the situation, and how they feel about the topic of discussion.

BODY LANGUAGE, GESTURES, FACE, AND EYE CONTACT.

In addition to appearance, the human body itself sends strong nonverbal cues. **Body language**, sometimes called kinesics, focuses on how people communicate through movement and posture, gestures, and expressions of the face and eyes.

Whether you intend to send a message or not, the way you stand, sit, and walk communicates strong nonverbal messages to others. **Body movement and posture** can communicate three things in any situation: how people see power operating, how they feel about themselves in the situation, and how they feel about the topic of discussion. If you feel powerful, you may communicate that power nonverbally by expanding your body into the space around you, or gesturing more expansively. When you feel self-confident, you communicate a sense of confidence by facing people directly, and sitting in an erect but relaxed and open body posture. You communicate positive feelings about the topic of discussion by sitting up fairly straight, and looking at or leaning toward the speaker. As with most types of nonverbal messages, researchers have identified gender differences in the use of body language.[14] An open body posture, using

Box 5.1: What does it mean to have a "Bad Hair" day?

Physical appearance is important—including your hair! A new study conducted at Yale University concluded that "bad hair days" affect more than just your appearance.

According to a study conducted at Yale University, bad hair days are very real—the perception of bad hair actually produces negative consequences beyond not feeling good about how we look. Dr. Marianne LaFrance, Professor of Psychology and of Women's and Gender Studies at Yale University, directed the study and said: "Bad hair days affect individuals' self-esteem, increasing self-doubt, intensifying social insecurities, and becoming more self-critical in general. Both women and men are negatively affected by the phenomenon of bad hair days," says Professor LaFrance. LaFrance's recent study uncovered important findings about bad hair resulting in reduced self-esteem; increased social insecurity; and a diminished sense of being a worthwhile person. The perception of bad hair leads both men and women to doubt their capabilities and, on such a day, may even result in performing below their real level of competence. Most notably, just the thought of a bad hair day caused both men and women to feel they are not as smart as others. The study further found bad hair intensifies feelings of social insecurity and self-consciousness. Women tend to feel more disgraced, embarrassed, ashamed or self-conscious when experiencing bad hair. Men on the other hand, feel more nervous, less confident and are more inclined to be unsociable. And a bad hair day leads individuals to find personal character flaws that go beyond their appearance. When asked to complete a list of statements about who they are, bad hair caused people to mention significantly more negative traits and attributes.

Obviously, the lesson we can take away from this study is to avoid the "bad hair day!"

Source: Adapted from the January 26, 2000, Procter & Gamble article, "New Study Conducted at Yale University Concludes That 'Bad Hair Days' Affect More Than Your Appearance." Retrieved from http://www.super-hair.net/yale-hair.html

both the arms and legs, is often used unconsciously by men to communicate power. By comparison, when women feel that they have less power, they tend to be less expansive, and restrict the amount of space their bodies take up. Nonverbal cues indicating weakness for women include slouching, sitting with stooped shoulders, and clutching their arms around the torso. How you stand, sit, and move says a lot about you to others.

You can send a powerful message about your level of self-confidence by how you use these simple nonverbal cues. Here are four suggestions for using body movement and posture to communicate competently.

1. Be aware of how you stand, sit, walk, and take up space to make statements about power relationships with others.
2. Be aware of the nonverbal messages your body movement and posture send about your personal sense of self-esteem.
3. Be mindful of how other people use these subtle cues, both consciously and unconsciously.
4. When appropriate, modify your body language to be sure you are sending the message you intend.

Another key aspect of body language is **gestures**—large and small movements of the hands and arms that commu-

GESTURES are the large and small movements of the hands and arms that communicate meaning.

nicate meaning. Typically, bigger gestures communicate greater involvement and more of a sense of immediacy on the part of the speaker, and smaller gestures communicate less involvement and immediacy. However, as with most nonverbal cues, gestures are used differently depending on the culture.[15] For example, people from Mediterranean cultures tend to use large gestures that are more animated than the gestures of people from the British Isles and eastern Asia.

Used appropriately, gestures can enhance the verbal message, but they also can detract from it. A speaker who fiddles with a pencil or plays with the buttons on a jacket communicates nervousness or a lack of confidence. Limited gesturing may communicate a lack of enthusiasm or involvement in a conversation. Public speakers who do not gesture at all—who keep their hands in their pockets or clasped together in front or back—seem insecure and nervous. Speech instructors sometimes tell students that this clasping of the hands in front of the body is referred to as the "fig leaf." This fig leaf posture by either sex is considered a closed body position. It blocks the private midsection from view. It shows insecurity, and occurs when someone is in a novel environment—like giving a speech—or around people they do not know and are not familiar with.

How you move your hands and arms enhances or distracts from what you say verbally. Using this nonverbal cue, you can communicate enthusiasm and involvement in any communication interaction or presentation. Here are three suggestions for using gestures to communicate competently.

1. Be sure that your gestures match your verbal message. If you are talking about an expansive or important topic, use bigger gestures. If you are involved in a quiet discussion, avoid such large gestures.
2. When speaking, gesture freely and naturally with both hands. Do not clasp your hands together nervously or leave them in your pockets while speaking.
3. Do not allow another person's gestures to divert your attention from the message.

In contrast to gestures, movements of the face convey feelings, and the emotional meaning of messages. These **facial expressions**, also called "affect displays," communicate six basic, universal emotions that the human face is capable of displaying: sadness, anger, disgust, fear, surprise, and happiness.[16] Frequently, people blend two or more of the facial expressions into one affect display, resulting in what is called an **affect blend**. Typical affect blends are fear/anger and surprise/happiness, and judging which of the two emotions is being displayed may be difficult.

Researchers have studied the kinds of judgments people make about others based on facial expressions. Not only do we judge emotions, but we also form opinions about a person's interpersonal traits. For example, we think that "baby-faced" people, whose faces resemble those of children, are more truthful than other people.[17] Preschoolers think that adults who smile more when reading to them are more trustworthy and likable.[18]

Accurately identifying emotions and other aspects of a person, based on facial expressions alone, is not always easy. Although we usually know when we are reacting to someone's expressions, we sometimes react to a **micro-momentary facial flash**—an expression that flashes across the face so quickly that it is imperceptible. In the blink of an eye, in about two seconds, your mind jumps to a conclusion about what was observed.[19]

FACIAL EXPRESSIONS, also called "AFFECT DISPLAYS," communicate six basic, universal emotions that the human face is capable of displaying: sadness, anger, disgust, fear, surprise, and happiness.

AN AFFECT BLEND occurs when a person blends two or more facial expressions into one affect display. Typical affect blends are fear/anger and surprise/happiness.

A MICRO-MOMENTARY FACIAL FLASH is an expression that flashes across the face so quickly that it is imperceptible.

When you have an intuitive sense during a conversation that something is wrong and you are not sure why, you may be reacting to a micro-momentary facial flash.

To complicate matters, the way people use facial expressions varies based on gender and cultural background. In North America, women tend to be more facially expressive, and smile more than men, even when they are not genuinely happy. Men tend to display less emotion on the face, and smile less. The Chinese and Japanese do not show emotion freely on their faces in public. In fact, in these cultures, the face is sometimes used to conceal rather than reveal feelings. By contrast, people from Latin American and Mediterranean cultures often display emotions on the face more freely.

You send revealing messages to others using six basic displays of affect or emotion—sadness, anger, disgust, fear, surprise, and happiness. Let others know your feelings—or conceal them—by how you use these nonverbal cues. Here are three suggestions for using facial expressions to communicate competently.

1. Be aware of what your face is communicating, particularly in a heated or emotional discussion.
2. Avoid a deadpan expression, which can happen when you are involved in a situation of little interest to you.
3. Be alert and sensitive to differences in the way people use facial expressions as a result of individual, gender, or culturally based differences. Although the basic facial expressions are universal across cultures, timing and appropriateness for different facial expressions vary by culture.

The eyes also send powerful nonverbal messages. **Eye contact,** also called oculesics, helps you to appear credible, dynamic, believable, likable, and persuasive. People generally use eye contact—or the lack thereof—to accomplish two goals: to communicate interest and intimacy, or to express dominance, power, and control. The person with the most power often engages in less eye contact, and looks away from the other person. The person with less power maintains eye contact, and watches the dominant person more closely to figure out what that person is thinking and feeling.

Like other nonverbal cues, the use of eye contact varies based on gender and culture. Women engage in more frequent and sustained eye contact than men, and are generally more visually attentive than men. Both sexes communicate interest and involvement with others using eye contact, but men also use it to challenge others or to assert their status and power. In Western cultures, such as North America and Western Europe, direct eye contact communicates interest and respect, and indicates that channels of communication are open. In contrast, people in many Asian, Native American, and Latin cultures are made uncomfortable by too much eye contact. In Japan, people may look away from one another almost completely, and in China, Indonesia, and rural Mexico, the eyes are lowered to communicate deference.

EYE CONTACT, OR OCULESICS, is a tool you can use to promote a sense of involvement with audience members that helps you to be seen as credible, dynamic, believable, likable, and persuasive.

An old Western song refers to another person's "Lyin' Eyes." Indeed, your use or lack of eye contact makes a powerful statement to others. Here are three suggestions for using eye contact to communicate competently.

1. Use eye contact to communicate interest and attention, but remember, some people are comfortable with direct eye contact whereas others are not.
2. Eye contact can be misunderstood, so be sensitive to the other person's reactions to avoid miscommunication.

3. Pay attention to any unspoken cultural rules for eye contact, and adapt your behaviors accordingly to communicate competently.

TOUCH.

Touch, physical contact between people, is another potent form of nonverbal communication, which social scientists refer to as haptics. Touch, when used appropriately, communicates support, power, and the intimacy level of a relationship. If you recall from the opening story, Steve leaned across the table and touched Samantha lightly on the arm when he asked her for a date, a nonverbal cue that marked the beginning of their relationship. In the same way, a defense lawyer in court might purposefully touch a client to send a message to the jury that the person is likable enough to touch. People also use touch as a social ritual, saying hello and goodbye with handshakes, hugs, and kisses. Social and cultural groups have unique forms of ritualistic touching. In Europe, for example, a social greeting involves kissing the other person on both cheeks. In North America, a hand shake, hug, or kiss on one cheek will suffice.

The amount of touching that occurs among people varies culturally. Italians and Greeks involved in casual conversations touch far more than the English, French, and Dutch, and people of a Jewish cultural background touch a great deal. In addition to knowing how much touch is appropriate in any culture, it is essential to be aware of culturally based touching taboos. Muslims in Arab cultures, for example, eat and engage in socially acceptable touching with the right hand, reserving the left hand for use in the toilet. To touch an Arab Muslim with the left hand is considered a social insult. Gender differences in touching behaviors also exist. Women are more likely to hug and use touch to express support and affiliation. Men use touch to assert power or express sexual desires, and men tend to touch females more than females touch males. By the same token, higher status individuals, regardless of gender, touch lower status individuals more than vice versa.

> TOUCH, which social scientists call haptics, involves physical contact between people, and communicates support, power, and the intimacy level of a relationship.

> VOCALICS, OR PARALANGUAGE, includes all the nonverbal elements of the voice that contribute to communication competence.

How you use touch or physical contact in any relationship or situation sends messages about support, power, and intimacy. Pay attention to how you use this powerful nonverbal cue in your daily interactions. Here are four suggestions for using touch to communicate competently.

1. Be sure the touching behavior is appropriate to the relationship and the situation.
2. Realize that your intention in touching someone could be misunderstood, not just by the person being touched, but by others watching you.
3. Pay attention to how the other person reacts to being touched. If a person reacts negatively, acknowledge his or her feelings and apologize.
4. Be respectful of any cultural norms and rules for touching others in the particular situation.

VOICE.

The human voice itself adds a significant nonverbal dimension to communication. **Vocalics**, also termed paralanguage, includes all the nonverbal elements of the voice that contribute to communication competence. These elements are rate, or the speed at which you talk; pitch, or the highness or lowness of your voice; and intensity, or your volume. Most communication instructors agree that variety in the use of these three elements is essential to being perceived as persuasive, competent, and dynamic.

The absence of voice, or silence, also communicates a nonverbal message. In an age where we are surrounded by constant sound and stimulation, strategic silence can send a powerful message. A silent pause can underscore the importance of a remark, and allow listeners to reflect on what was said. Furthermore, using silence effectively will help you avoid **filled pauses**, the nonfluencies and distracters that slip out when you speak, particularly when you are nervous (*uh, um, y'know,* and *OK*).

Men and women use their voices differently. In general, women use a softer voice, less volume, and more vocalic inflection when they speak, as Samantha did in the café when talking with Steve. Men use their voices to be assertive and take command of a conversation, which results in a lower pitch, more volume, and somewhat less inflection.

Not surprisingly, culture affects the use of vocalics. Members of cultures that have strong oral traditions, such as African Americans and Jews, tend to speak with more gusto and enthusiasm. Italians and Greeks also are noted for using more volume, whereas the Thai and Japanese may speak with quieter voices. In many Asian cultures, people talk less and appreciate silence more.

The rate or speed of your voice, its highness or lowness, and its volume or loudness, all three affect whether others see you as persuasive, competent, and dynamic. Try to become a little more aware of how you use your voice to enhance what you say verbally. Here are three suggestions for using the voice to communicate competently.

1. Use vocal variety to reinforce meaning and add emotion to what you say to hold listeners' attention.
2. Incorporate silent pauses at strategic points in conversations, and control filled pauses that distract listeners from your message.
3. Anticipate cultural differences in paralanguage, and modify your vocalics appropriately.

TIME AND SPACE.

"Time is money." "Don't keep me waiting." "Give me some space." "I feel crowded by this relationship." These expressions illustrate a final set of nonverbal cues that you may not at first consider to be nonverbal communication. People exchange meaningful messages with one another using time and space.

Time, nonverbally referred to as chronemics, involves the intentional and unintentional use of time to communicate. The way people structure and use time in a society communicates messages about their evaluation of the importance of time itself, whether they value each other, and the status and power of those communicating. In a society where a high value is placed on time, such as North America, people try to accomplish as much as possible within a given amount of time. When time is highly valued, respect for others is communicated by not "wasting" their time, by arriving promptly for appointments, and replying to phone calls or e-mail or text messages promptly.[20] Finally, in such time-sensitive cultures, people with higher status and power often control the use of time by deciding whether and when meetings take place.

FILLED PAUSES are the nonfluencies or distracters that slip out when you speak, particularly when you are nervous (uh, um, y'know, and OK).

TIME, nonverbally referred to as CHRONEMICS, involves the intentional and unintentional use of time to communicate.

How people use and feel about time varies significantly from one culture to the next and one person to the next. In the opening story, Samantha was immediately aware that her tendency to be late could have a negative impact on her relationship with Steve, who mentioned arriving at 7:00 p.m. *sharp*. When people from cultures with different orientations to time interact, problems can arise. People from the United States, Germany, and Switzerland place a high value on time, and avoid "wasting" it, which often results in rushing, multitasking, impulsiveness, and making quicker decisions. By contrast, people from Mexico, Japan, China, and Korea favor a slower pace, giving fuller attention to the moment, which results in more reflection and less impulsiveness. As a result, people from clock-bound societies and backgrounds may move more quickly to solve a problem, whereas those who are less clock-bound may favor a slower, more deliberative approach to interacting and solving problems.

Indeed, how you structure and use time sends powerful messages about whether you value time itself and the other person(s) with whom you are communicating. If you often arrive late to meet someone, realize the message you may be sending with this nonverbal cue. Here are three suggestions for using time to communicate competently.

1. Make sure that your use of time matches your intentions. If a friend values promptness, the message you send by arriving late or not returning phone calls or e-mails is a negative one.
2. When communicating with someone whose culture values and uses time differently, respect his or her behaviors and preferences.
3. If a person of higher status, such as a supervisor, appears to control or take advantage of your time, try to understand that it may be a result of some of our unspoken cultural rules.

In addition to time, people send nonverbal messages through their use of space. One important aspect of space is the physical environment in which communication occurs. Physical environments affect how people feel, and therefore how they communicate. Architects and home builders are well aware of how the physical structure of an environment affects communication. Designed communities and public buildings contain gathering spots such as club rooms and recreation facilities. Private homes often have conversation pits or large, open living and dining rooms that bring families together to encourage conversation.

Two elements in any physical environment significantly affect communication—spatial arrangement, and the use of artifacts and objects. **Spatial arrangement** is the way spaces are laid out and relate to one another, as well as how objects and furniture are placed in the spaces. The arranging of furniture in rooms can promote or hinder communication. For example, in homes, communication can be encouraged by positioning couches and chairs at slight angles to one another, and at a comfortable distance apart for easy conversation. In the workplace, spatial arrangement sends a message about the power of various employees. Upper-level executives often get corner offices with walls of windows.

Artifacts are the objects in the environment that make non-verbal statements about the identity and personality of their owner. These include furniture, wall hangings, books, houseplants, art, or any other items used for practical or decorative purposes. Artifacts make statements about status and position in life, and reveal what the room's owner thinks is important or attractive. Of course, money affects what a person has, so artifacts are not always accurate indicators of personal taste.

SPATIAL ARRANGEMENT is the way spaces are laid out and relate to one another, as well as how objects and furniture are placed in the spaces.

ARTIFACTS are the objects in the environment that make nonverbal statements about the identity and personality of their owner.

In the United States, there is continuing interest in a practice that suggests that artifacts have unique powers when arranged in a certain way in a room. **Feng shui** (pronounced, fung shway), a 3,000-year-old Chinese approach to spatial arrangement and the use of artifacts, is gaining popularity in North America and around the world. Practitioners of feng shui claim to be able to affect many facets of people's lives simply by rearranging their homes and offices.[21] They believe that blessings and good fortune result from the correct positioning and use of artifacts such as furniture, plants, mirrors, or lighting.

> FENG SHUI is a 3,000-year-old Chinese approach to spatial arrangement and the use of artifacts in homes and offices.

In addition to spatial arrangement and artifacts, how people physically use space often communicates as loudly as words. Use of **space**, also called proxemics, is the study of how people move around in and use space to communicate. **Personal space** focuses on how people distance themselves from one another, and **territoriality** is concerned with how people stake out space for themselves. A well-respected anthropologist, Edward T. Hall, said that people prefer to maintain a comfortable, personal distance from others based on how they feel about them, the situation they are in, and their goal for communicating.[22] According to Hall, each of us is at the center of a space bubble

> SPACE, also called PROXEMICS, is the study of how people move around in and use space to communicate.

> PERSONAL SPACE involves how people distance themselves from one another.

> TERRITORIALITY refers to how people stake out space for themselves.

Figure 5.2: E. T. Hall's Concept of a Personal Space Bubble

We live at the center of a space bubble that extends outward from our bodies starting with intimate, personal, social, and then public space.

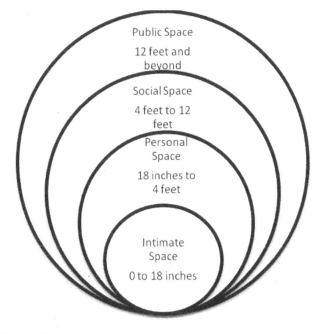

Public Space
12 feet and beyond

Social Space
4 feet to 12 feet

Personal Space
18 inches to 4 feet

Intimate Space
0 to 18 inches

Source: Adapted from Hall (1969).[22]

that extends outward from our bodies. We are surrounded by intimate, personal, social, and then public space. When someone invades our intimate or personal space, it makes us uncomfortable. But in the opening story, when Steve moved from a social distance into Samantha's personal space, she did not mind at all. Figure 5.2 illustrates Hall's concept of personal space and the space bubble.

Along with personal preferences for distance, as described by Hall, unspoken cultural norms and rules dictate the amount of space people need, and how closely they interact. In Eastern European, Middle Eastern, and Latin cultures, people tend to sit and stand closer together than in North America or northern Europe. In the United States, people feel comfortable with more personal space, and when this distance is intruded on, cultural norms are violated. Not surprisingly, powerful people are usually given more personal space, and allowed to encroach on the personal space of those lower in status. Nevertheless, invading a person's personal or intimate space may be considered intrusive, and therefore not appropriate, regardless of status.

Closely linked to the idea of personal space is the concept of territoriality. Whereas personal space refers to the space around you and your body, territoriality relates to a fixed space, such as a room, a house, a yard, a city, or even a country and its borders. Because people become uncomfortable when their space is invaded, they stake out and mark what they consider their territory using fixed or movable markers. Fixed markers include fences around houses, or even a regular seat at the dinner table, as well as the borders that mark where one country ends and another begins. Movable markers are the things you take with you into public spaces, such as clothing or books that you use to stake out your territory. You might leave your jacket on the seat at a movie, or a water bottle on the floor at your aerobics class. At the extreme, invading others' territory can result in a fight or even a war.

How you arrange space and objects in space can make powerful statements to others. For instance, think about the nonverbal cues others may react to, when they walk into your home for the first time. Here are three suggestions for using the environment and space to communicate competently.

1. Be sensitive to the way physical environments, spatial arrangement, and artifacts affect the way you and others communicate.
2. Recognize any unspoken rules for using personal space, and respect other people's personal and cultural preferences.
3. Respect the territory of others, and understand when others unintentionally invade your territory.

Given the many types of nonverbal messages all of us are exposed to regularly, the chance for miscommunication is unlimited. And differences in the meaning of these many nonverbal cues results in significant challenges to communicating competently.

OVERCOMING CHALLENGES TO NONVERBAL COMPETENCE

As you can see, nonverbal communication can be an effective way to communicate, but it also presents some challenges to communication competence. Throughout this chapter, we referenced these challenges. Now let us summarize the three biggest challenges, and how to overcome them.

QUANTITY, CONSTANCY, AND AWARENESS OF NONVERBAL CUES.

The sheer quantity of nonverbal messages people send and receive every day makes accurate interpretation difficult, and increases the potential for misunderstanding. Nonverbal communication takes place constantly, even when we try not to communicate. This constant flow of nonverbal cues creates even more potential for misinterpretation. To make matters worse, nonverbal communication operates at a low level of awareness. We are well aware of the verbal message, what someone is saying to us; but we are far less aware of the subtle nonverbal cue we are picking up on at the same time. Without awareness of the nonverbal cues, the potential to misunderstand others and be misunderstood or viewed as less competent is great.

Decoding nonverbal cues involves skills such as understanding emotions and the complexity of relationships.[22] Try to become more mindful of the nonverbal cues you receive from others, but without overreacting or giving too much weight to any one message. Instead, look for similar messages that are expressed in various ways nonverbally. Avoid jumping to conclusions, ask for clarification, and listen to what the speaker is saying with an open mind.

INDIVIDUAL, GENDER, AND CULTURAL DIFFERENCES.

Each of us sends and receives nonverbal messages in a unique way. We also attribute meaning to nonverbal messages differently. When you try to determine a friend's reason for behaving in some way, if you base your interpretation solely on nonverbal cues, you are more likely to make a mistake. As we pointed out repeatedly in this chapter, gender plays an influential role in the way people send and interpret nonverbal messages. For example, men pay more attention to verbal information, whereas women attend to both verbal and nonverbal cues in conversations.[23] All the gender-based, nonverbal differences we have discussed represent challenges to competent communication, and can lead to misunderstandings. Culture also is a challenge, because few of us are aware of all of the rules and expectations for nonverbal communication in cultures other than our own. The inability to communicate nonverbally with persons of other cultural backgrounds can limit how well people coordinate their activities, from something as simple as getting directions in a foreign country to determining appropriate seating arrangements at an international meeting.

You need to become as knowledgeable as possible about how other people communicate nonverbally based on individual, gender, and cultural differences. As you learn about these differences, avoid judging other people's nonverbal cues as wrong, and do not expect the other person's nonverbal messages to mirror yours. If you are uncertain about what nonverbal cues are appropriate, exercise restraint and avoid nonverbal behavior that could be misinterpreted. If you anticipate an interaction with someone from a social group or culture different from yours, educate yourself about their customs, including nonverbal behavior. Most important, give everybody respect, regardless of any nonverbal behavior they exhibit that may be new to you.

IMPACT OF MEDIA AND TECHNOLOGY.

In the chapter on language, we discussed how media and technology are affecting interpersonal, small group, and even public speaking. When we communicate using technology in these contexts—sending texts or tweets, communicating on *Facebook*, or conducting a nonsynchronous webinar—it first may appear that nonverbal communication is completely missing. But that is not true. For example, e-mail messages and cell phone text messages include automatic time stamps displaying when the message was sent. A message may be perceived as more intimate if sent out at night, as opposed to during the day.[25]

To this point, one study examined whether computer-mediated communication is devoid of emotional cues and interpersonal expression.[26] Perhaps surprisingly, participants in face-to-face interactions and synchronous computer chats rated the emotion expressed as the same in both settings. Research studies aside, it is intuitively obvious that with technology-mediated communication, all the nonverbal cues described in this chapter are not fully available. If you are to communicate competently, it is essential to be aware of any misunderstanding as the result of a misleading verbal message sent or received electronically. Ask the speaker to clarify the message instead of guessing what it means. This process of seeking clarity will introduce mindfulness and respect for the communicators, and enhance your competence in the use of today's and tomorrow's communication technologies.

In the opening story to this chapter, Steve and Samantha used nonverbal cues effectively and appropriately to communicate their interest in one another. When Samantha realized that she found Steve attractive, she sat at a table near him. When they began to talk, she lowered her voice, leaned toward Steve, smiled, and made direct eye contact. In response to Samantha's quick glance at her watch, Steve leaned forward, touched Samantha gently on the arm, and asked her for a date. Steve and Samantha used nonverbal cues to send and receive subtle messages to one another and accomplish their communication goals. Like them, you can improve how you communicate by the mindful use of nonverbal cues, and by respecting differences in how people communicate nonverbally. By skillfully using both nonverbal and verbal cues, separately and in concert, you too will achieve nonverbal communicative competence.[26]

Building on your knowledge of verbal and nonverbal communication, we turn our attention in Chapter Six to a neglected but important skill—competent listening.

CHAPTER SUMMARY

Nonverbal cues are nonverbal behaviors or objects to which meaning is assigned. Nonverbal communication includes all behaviors, attributes, and objects of humans—other than words—that communicate messages and have shared meaning. Nonverbal cues provide 65% of the meaning of conversational messages, signaling that nonverbal communication is crucial to communication competence.

People use nonverbal cues to complement verbal messages, to regulate interactions, and to define the socio-emotional quality of relationships. Specifically, we use nonverbal cues to replace words, and to enhance and accent verbal messages. We also use nonverbal cues to manage the flow of conversations and coordinate interactions. We often define and make statements about the social and emotional quality of our relationships with others nonverbally.

The types of nonverbal messages that achieve these functions are physical appearance, body language (including body movement and posture, gestures, facial expressions, and eye contact), touch, voice, and time and space.

Physical appearance, which includes everything you notice about a person, significantly impacts first impressions. Body movement and posture communicate how people see power operating, how they feel about themselves, and how they feel about a discussion topic. Gestures can enhance the verbal message, but gestures such as fidgeting or limited gesturing detract from the message. Facial expressions, including the basic, universal affect displays of sadness, anger, disgust, fear, surprise, and happiness, convey feelings and the emotional meaning of messages.

Eye contact is used to communicate interest and intimacy, or to express dominance, power, and control. Touch is used to communicate support, power, and the intimacy level of the relationship. Variety in the rate, pitch, and intensity of the voice results in being perceived as persuasive, competent, and dynamic. The way people use time communicates messages about their value of time itself, whether they value one another, and the status and power of the people communicating. Physical environments affect how people feel and communicate. Two elements in any physical environment that affect communication are spatial arrangement and the use of artifacts and objects. Challenges to nonverbal communication include the quantity and constancy of nonverbal messages; the low level of awareness of nonverbal cues; individual, gender, and cultural differences in how people communicate nonverbally; and the impact of media and technology. These challenges can be overcome by being more mindful of nonverbal messages, learning about and respecting differences in nonverbal communication, and integrating verbal and nonverbal messages skillfully.

KEY TERMS.

The key terms below are defined in this chapter, and presented alphabetically with definitions in the Glossary at the end of the book.

- nonverbal cues
- nonverbal communication
- physical appearance
- body language
- body movement and posture
- gestures
- facial expressions

- affect blend
- micro-momentary facial flash
- eye contact
- touch
- vocalics
- filled pauses
- time

- spatial arrangement
- artifacts
- feng shui
- space
- personal space
- territoriality

BUILDING MOTIVATION: SELF-ASSESSMENT TOOL.

Rate each of the eight communication situations described here, indicating your own typical level of nonverbal competence. Rate one situation all the way through for motivation, knowledge, and skills. Then rate the next situation. Use the 1–4 scale below, with 1 being minimal competence and 4 high competence.

Communication situations.

1. Visiting a foreign country for the first time.
2. Going on a blind date with a person from a different culture.
3. Developing a plan for a vacation with your significant other or life partner.
4. Accompanying a close friend to a therapy group discussion about drug abuse.
5. Presenting a project to a work team at your job, or to your class at school.
6. Presenting a speech of endorsement of a candidate at a political rally.
7. Discussing a problem with your boss who is of the opposite sex.
8. Attending a party by yourself where you know hardly anyone.

Motivation.

   1 = Distracted, disinterested, or simply no motivation to be competent.
   2 = Somewhat distracted or disinterested, but motivated to be competent.
   3 = Somewhat interested and motivated to be competent.
   4 = Highly interested and motivated to be competent.

Knowledge.

   1 = Completely inexperienced and ignorant about what to do and how to do it.
   2 = Minimal experience and sense of what to do and how to do it.
   3 = Somewhat experienced and knowledgeable about what to do and how to do it.
   4 = Highly knowledgeable about all aspects of what to do and how to do it.

Skills.

   1 = Completely incapable of behaving competently in the situation.
   2 = Barely capable of behaving minimally competently.
   3 = Fairly capable of behaving competently.
   4 = Highly capable of behaving competently.

Interpreting your scores.

Total your score separately for each situation (motivation, knowledge, and skills). The possible range of the score for each situation is 3–12. If your total score for any of the situations is 6 or less, you see yourself as less competent in that situation than you should be. A score of 7–9 means that you are average at sending and receiving communication messages in the situation. A score of 10–12 indicates that you have a high level of communication competence in that situation.

Building knowledge: Discussion questions.

   1. Discuss the functions of nonverbal communication as they relate to the three levels of communication (interpersonal, group, public speaking). For each level of communication, which function do you think is most important and why?
   2. Explain to someone from another planet, who just landed on Earth, why humans have two communication systems, verbal and nonverbal.
   3. Discuss what could have been done to change a misunderstanding, resulting from nonverbal differences between individuals from different cultures, into a positive experience.
   4. Of the various types of nonverbal messages, which is the most powerful and meaningful in North American culture? Offer a description and examples to support your choice. If you are familiar with another culture, describe which types of nonverbal messages are important in that culture.
   5. If you had to choose only one type of nonverbal communication to use, which type would it be and why?
   6. Knowing how to use nonverbal cues effectively could give people an unfair advantage, and help them manipulate, mislead, or deceive others. What are the ethical implications of becoming a better nonverbal communicator?

BUILDING SKILLS: STUDENT ACTIVITIES.

Individual activities.

1. On a single sheet of paper, list the types of nonverbal messages described in this chapter. Next to each type of message, describe how competently you use it, and how you could improve.
2. Go to http://www.cio.com/article/facial-expressions-test. Using the photos displayed on the site, determine how good you are at identifying emotions displayed on the face. What steps might you take to correct any weak areas?
3. Observe several environments in which you communicate: at school, work, and home. How does the spatial arrangement in those environments affect communication? Are there unspoken rules about the way space is used?

Group activities.

1. Form small groups of four to six students. Select two students to act out either of the following scenarios for about five minutes using both verbal and nonverbal communication. Others in the group observe the role play, and take notes about how the two actors use nonverbal cues to substitute, repeat, complement, accent, or contradict words; and to regulate their interactions. Discuss the role play with the student actors.

    •   Scenario 1: A student asks a professor to change a grade on an essay exam. The student first approaches the professor right after class, and a second discussion takes place during the professor's office hours.
    •   Scenario 2: An employee approaches his or her boss to ask for a day off to attend to a personal matter not covered by the sick leave or vacation policy of the company.

2. Form a group of six students. Write each of the basic emotions and affect blends identified in this chapter on a piece of paper. Have each student choose a slip of paper from a hat. Each student should demonstrate the selected emotion, and other group members should guess which emotion is portrayed, and identify parts of the face used to display it. Discuss which basic emotions and affect blends are the most difficult to identify and why.
3. With a partner, visit The Nonverbal Dictionary of Gestures, Signs, & Body Language Cues website at http://www.center-for-nonverbal-studies.org/6101.html. Test each other to see how many of the definitions of different nonverbal cues you know.

NOTES

1. See Weger Jr., Seiter, Jacobs, & Akbulut (2010).
2. See Philpot (1983).
3. See Baringer & McCroskey (2000).
4. See Koerner & Fitzpatrick (2002).
5. See DeGroot & Gooty (2009).
6. See Cesario & Higgins (2008).
7. See Haumer & Donsbach (2009).
8. See LaFrance, Heisel, & Beatty (2004).
9. See Antonijevic (2008).

10. See Burgoon & Hale (1984) and Burgoon, Guerrero, & Floyd (2010).
11. See Adelson (2004).
12. See Manusov, Docan-Morgan, & Harvey (2008).
13. See Prinsen & Punyanunt-Carter (2010).
14. See Wood (2010).
15. See Samovar (2000).
16. See Ekman & Friesen (1975).
17. See Masip, Garrido, & Herrero (2004).
18. See Rotenberg et al. (2003).
19. See Gladwell (2005).
20. See Kalman & Rafaeli (2011).
21. For more information, access http://fengshui.about.com/
22. See Hall (1969).
23. See Phillips, Tunstall, & Channon (2007).
24. See Gore (2009).
25. See Doering & Poeschl (2007).
26. See Walther, Loh, & Granka (2005).
27. See Puccinelli (2008).

REFERENCES

Adelson, R. (July 2004). Detecting deception. *Monitor on Psychology, 35*(7), p. 70 in print version. Retrieved from http://www.apa.org/monitor/julaug04/detecting.aspx

Antonijevic, S. (2008). From text to gesture online: A microethnographic analysis of nonverbal communication in the second life virtual environment. *Information, Communication & Society, 11*(2), 221–238.

Baringer, D. K., & McCroskey, J. C. (2000). Immediacy in the classroom: Student immediacy. *Communication Education, 49*(2), 178–186.

Burgoon, J. K., Guerrero, L. K., & Floyd, K. (2010). *Nonverbal communication.* Boston, MA: Allyn & Bacon.

Burgoon, J. K., & Hale, J. L. (1984). The fundamental topoi of relational communication. *Communication Monographs, 51*(3), 193–214.

Cesario, J., & Higgins, E. (2008). Making message recipients 'feel right': How nonverbal cues can increase persuasion. *Psychological Science, 19*(5), 415–420.

DeGroot, T., & Gooty, J. (2009). Can nonverbal cues be used to make meaningful personality attributions in employment interviews? *Journal of Business & Psychology, 24*(2), 179–192.

Doering, N., & Poeschl, S. (2007). Nonverbal cues in mobile phone text messages: The effects of chronemics and proxemics. Paper presented at the International Communication Association Conference.

Ekman, P., & Friesen, W. (1975). *Unmasking the face.* Englewood Cliffs, NJ: Prentice-Hall.

Gladwell, M. (2005). *Blink: The power of thinking without thinking.* New York, NY: Little, Brown.

Gore, J. (2009). The interaction of sex, verbal, and nonverbal cues in same-sex first encounters. *Journal of Nonverbal Behavior, 33*(4), 279–299.

Hall, E. T. (1969). *The hidden dimension.* Garden City, NY: Doubleday.

Haumer, F., & Donsbach, W. (2009). The rivalry of nonverbal cues on the perception of politicians by television viewers. *Journal of Broadcasting & Electronic Media, 53*(2), 262–279.

Kalman, Y. M., & Rafaeli, S. (2011). Online pauses and silence: Chronemic expectancy violations in written computer-mediated communication. *Communication Research, 38*(1), 54–69.

Koerner, A. F., & Fitzpatrick, M. A. (2002). Nonverbal communication and marital adjustment and satisfaction: The role of decoding relationship relevant and relationship irrelevant affect. *Communication Monographs, 69*(1), 33–51.

LaFrance, B. H., Heisel, A. D., & Beatty, M. J. (2004). Is there empirical evidence for a nonverbal profile of extraversion? A meta-analysis and critique of the literature. *Communication Monographs, 71*(1), 28–48.

Manusov, V., Docan-Morgan, T., & Harvey, J. (2008). When a small thing means so much: Nonverbal cues as turning points in relationships. Paper presented at the National Communication Association Conference.

Masip, J., Garrido, E., & Herrero, C. (2004). Facial appearance and impressions of credibility: The effects of facial babyishness and age on person perception. *International Journal of Psychology, 30*(4), 276–289.

Phillips, L., Tunstall, M., & Channon, S. (2007). Exploring the role of working memory in dynamic social cue decoding using dual task methodology. *Journal of Nonverbal Behavior, 31*(2), 137–152.

Philpot, J. S. (1983). *The relative contribution to meaning of verbal and nonverbal channels of communication: A meta-analysis*. (Unpublished master's thesis). University of Nebraska, Lincoln, Nebraska.

Prinsen, T., & Punyanunt-Carter, N. M. (2010). The difference in nonverbal behaviors and how it changes in different stages of a relationship. *Texas Speech Communication Journal, 35*(1), 1–7.

Puccinelli, N. M. (2008). Nonverbal communicative competence. In G. Rickheit & H. Strohner (Eds.), *Handbook of communication competence* (pp. 257–275). New York, NY: Mouton de Gruyter.

Rotenberg, K., Eisenberg, N., Cumming, C., Smith, A., Singh, M., & Terlicher, E. (2003). The contribution of adults' nonverbal cues and children's shyness to the development of rapport between adults and preschool children. *International Journal of Behavioral Development, 27*(1), 21–30.

Samovar, L. A. (2000). *Oral communication: Speaking across cultures* (11th ed.). New York, NY: Oxford University Press.

Walther, J. B., Loh, T., & Granka, L. (2005). Let me count the ways: The interchange of verbal and nonverbal cues in computer-mediated and face-to-face affinity. *Journal of Language & Social Psychology, 24*(1), 36–65.

Weger Jr., H., Seiter, J. S., Jacobs, K. A., & Akbulut, V. (2010). Perceptions of debater effectiveness and appropriateness as a function of decreasingly polite strategies for responding to nonverbal disparagement in televised political debates. *Argumentation & Advocacy, 47*(1), 39–54.

Wood, J. T. (2010). *Gendered lives: Communication, gender and culture* (9th ed.). Belmont, CA: Cengage.

CHAPTER SIX

LISTENING COMPETENCE

The most basic of all human needs is the need to understand and be understood. The best way to understand people is to listen to them. —Ralph Nichols, Historian and famous listening expert, 1910–2006

. : .
• • •

Carrie and Jesse met at the computer lab where they both worked while going to school. They went on a date the first day they met, and spent plenty of time together from then on. Because they worked at the same place and were students on the same campus, they had a great deal in common. When they first met, they were curious to learn more about each other. They would listen attentively and tune in to each other's verbal and nonverbal messages. Even though Carrie talked rather fast and sometimes left out important details, this was not a problem for Jesse. After listening closely to what Carrie said, he would try to figure out exactly what she meant. Then he would describe what he thought he had heard and ask whether he was right. Likewise, when Jesse told Carrie what happened during his shift in the computer lab, she would listen attentively and express genuine interest in his daily activities.

However, as time went on, Carrie and Jesse began to take each other for granted, and their excellent listening skills began to fade. In contrast to the early days, now there were times when they did not listen to each other at all. When Jesse complained about a tough assignment in his calculus class, Carrie found her attention wandering from Jesse's problem to matters of more importance to her. When Jesse asked for advice on how to approach the calculus professor about the difficult assignment, Carrie faced a typical listening dilemma— she had no answer to his question because she had not even listened to Jesse's problem. Over time, poor listening skills began to have a negative influence on their relationship.

Have you ever found yourself in a similar situation? Your friend or partner or coworker is talking away, and suddenly looks to you for a response. You have nothing to say because you were not really listening. Your mind was far away, and you have not a clue about what was just said. Or you are multitasking—talking on your cell phone and processing e-mail at the same time—and the person on the phone asks you a pointed question. Such listening dilemmas are not unusual in today's busy world. Although bad listening habits are the norm, most people, including college students like Carrie and Jesse, spend more time listening than using any other communication skill. Some teachers of listening say that people spend more time every day listening than reading and writing combined![1] Take a look at the pie chart illustrating this statistic in Figure 6.1.

Given the dominance of listening, we begin our discussion in this chapter by considering what listening is, how it works, and why it is important.

WHAT IS LISTENING?

Often we confuse listening, which is a very active process, with simply hearing the sounds that emanate from the other person. Hearing and listening are *not* the same thing, so we start by clarifying the difference.

DEFINING LISTENING.

The following definition reflects the best thinking of leading researchers and experts in the field who describe listening as an active, three-step process: "**Listening** is the process of receiving, constructing meaning from, and responding to spoken and/or nonverbal messages."[2]

1. **Receiving** means tuning in to the speaker's entire message, including both its verbal and nonverbal aspects, and consciously paying attention to it. This means making critical choices about paying attention to some things and ignoring others.

LISTENING is the process of receiving, constructing meaning from, and responding to spoken and/or nonverbal messages" (International Listening Association, 2011).

RECEIVING means tuning in to the speaker's entire message, including both its verbal and nonverbal aspects, and consciously paying attention to it.

Figure 6.1: Dominance of Listening

Most people spend more time listening to others than they spend on reading and writing combined.

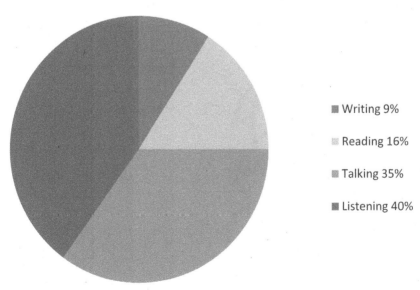

Types of Communication

- Writing 9%
- Reading 16%
- Talking 35%
- Listening 40%

Source: http://articles.webraydian.com/article4793-How_Much_Time_Do_You_Spend_Listening.html[1]

2. **Constructing meaning** involves assigning meaning to a speaker's message, and mentally clarifying your understanding of it. This step is made more difficult because listeners often do not construct the same meaning as the speaker intends.

3. **Responding** completes the interaction between the listener and speaker, and is the step in which the listener lets the speaker know the message, its verbal and nonverbal aspects, has been received and understood. This step, if overlooked or poorly done, leads to misunderstandings between the listener and speaker.

> CONSTRUCTING MEANING involves assigning meaning to a speaker's message, and mentally clarifying your understanding of it.

> RESPONDING completes the interaction between the listener and speaker, and is the step in which the listener lets the speaker know the message has been received and understood.

In the opening vignette, Carrie followed a process opposite of these three steps. She failed to receive the message and pay attention to Jesse, so she could not construct any meaning out of his message. She found herself with only bad choices for responding: guess what Jesse probably said and fake a response, or admit to not listening. Figure 6.2 illustrates these three steps in the listening process. At each of the three steps, listening involves really paying attention to the speaker's verbal and nonverbal messages. As you consider these three steps for competent listening, think back to Chapter Three and the three stages people go through as part of perception—noticing, organizing, and interpreting. The listening steps of receiving the message and constructing meaning from it are very similar to those three stages in the perception process.

Figure 6.2: Listening: A Three-Step Process

The listener receives the message in Step 1 of this process. During Step 2, the listener constructs meaning out of the message that is received. In Step 3, the listener responds to the speaker.

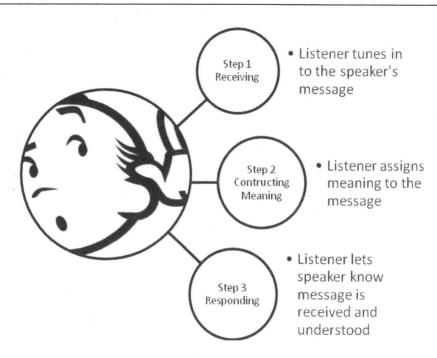

Step 1 Receiving
• Listener tunes in to the speaker's message

Step 2 Contructing Meaning
• Listener assigns meaning to the message

Step 3 Responding
• Listener lets speaker know message is received and understood

VALUING LISTENING.

In interpersonal relationships, if we fail to listen, we do not understand one another, and communication satisfaction with the relationship is lower.[3] In small groups, we sometimes fail to listen to other group members. Instead we listen for an opening in the discussion to present the best idea: ours! In public-speaking situations, like lectures or training sessions, our attention often wanders. In fact, you have probably sat through more than your share of dense lectures and failed to listen to what was being said.

Listening is also important at work, particularly in the technology-rich communication environment of the 21st century.[4] Leaders in a variety of fields, for example, engineering,[5] accounting,[6] and business,[7] all need effective, on-the-job listening skills. In helping professions, listening is equally important. Researchers find that good listening skills are crucial for help-line volunteers,[8] mental health care providers,[9] and even workers in crisis negotiation situations.[10] Clients in a welfare-to-work, job-training program also found that learning basic communication competencies, including listening skills, is a good antidote for their welfare dependence.[11]

Given how important these studies say listening is, you would expect listening education to be state-of-the-art. That is not the case. In a recent analysis of communication textbooks, two communication scholars found listening to be included only to a slight degree.[12] And some communication teachers think that people only learn about listening when they find themselves in complex or demanding communication situations that require a lot of them. Then they quickly reflect on the need to listen and how to do it in order to cooperate and collaborate, which requires listening. To correct this shortcoming for you, let us now learn about some different types of listening, as well as how you can integrate them effectively in different situations.

TYPES OF LISTENING

We can categorize types of listening by their purpose. We listen for any one of three reasons: to learn and comprehend, to evaluate and critique messages, and to empathize with and understand others (See Table 6.1). To listen competently in any communication situation, you need to figure out which type of listening will be most helpful.

TO LEARN AND COMPREHEND.

Listening to learn and comprehend includes a search for facts and ideas, and a quest for information. This type of listening often occurs during public presentations, when technical subjects are explained, or new information is presented. The listener's purpose is to receive a message that is as similar as possible to the speaker's intended message. Here people listen because they need to know something, such as the meaning of ideas or events, or because they want to keep up with the world. A good example of listening to learn is the classroom lecture.

> LISTENING TO LEARN AND COMPREHEND includes a search for facts and ideas, and a quest for information.

A challenge to listening to learn and comprehend is the vast amount and complexity of information that bombards us every day through broadcast, print, and electronic media. Although you might not think of reading computer-mediated messages as a form of listening, the steps of receiv-

Table 6.1: Types of Listening

Each of the three types of listening encompasses a particular set of problems. Solutions to each problem are shown in the right-hand column.

LISTENING TYPES	DESCRIPTION	PROBLEMS	SOLUTIONS
To learn and comprehend	• Involves searching for facts, ideas, and information.	• Vast amount of information available. • Complexity of information.	• Discriminate among available messages. • Attend to message carefully.
To evaluate and critique	• Focuses on critically analyzing the speaker's message.	• Speaker biases. • Listener biases.	• Be open-minded. • Postpone judgment.
To empathize and understand	• Entails concentrating on the speaker's feelings and attitudes.	• Disagreement with speaker. • Discomfort talking about feelings.	• Suppress desire to argue or jump in with solutions. • Let speaker know you understand.

ing, constructing meaning, and responding apply to e-mail, text messaging, tweets, and even conversations on blogs and social networking sites. By carefully selecting which messages to attend to and then giving them your full attention, you can listen to learn and comprehend more competently, both in traditional settings and online.

TO EVALUATE AND CRITIQUE.

In addition to comprehending a message, **listening to evaluate and critique** calls for critically analyzing the meaning and merit of a speaker's message. The purpose of this evaluative listening is to critique the speaker's facts, opinions, and assumptions. When Jesse told Carrie about the problem he was experiencing in his calculus class, he might have been looking for her to listen in an evaluative manner, and give him some advice about managing the workload in the course.

LISTENING TO EVALUATE AND CRITIQUE calls for critically analyzing the meaning and merit of a speaker's message.

The main challenge to evaluative and critical listening is biases, both your own and the speaker's. These biases affect the way you perceive a message, as well as the way the speaker presents it. Interestingly, we all tend to critique a message more severely when we disagree with the speaker, and less severely when we agree with what is said. So when listening to evaluate, listen with an open mind, and postpone judgment of the message, even when you disagree with the speaker's opinions and biases on the topic.

TO EMPATHIZE AND UNDERSTAND.

Listening to learn and listening to evaluate concentrate our attention on the *content* of the message. By contrast, in **listening to empathize and understand** we focus more on the speaker's *feelings and attitudes* while gaining information. You are not trying to gain information for your own purposes or to form judgments of what is said. Rather, the interests, opinions, and feelings of the other person override your own. The empathic listener's purpose is to see and feel the world as the other person does, which is beneficial to both the individuals involved and to the relationship.[13]

There are two types of empathic responses. A **nonjudgmental empathic response** from a listener helps both people better understand and probe what is going on. A **judgmental empathic response** provides support but also helps to interpret and evaluate the speaker's situation. At the beginning of this chapter, when Jesse shared his worries about the calculus class, he might have wanted Carrie to listen empathically, understand his frustration with the course and professor, and provide a judgmental empathic response.

> **LISTENING TO EMPATHIZE AND UNDERSTAND** focuses on the speaker's feelings and attitudes while gaining information.

> A **NONJUDGMENTAL EMPATHIC RESPONSE** helps both people better understand and probe what is going on.

> A **JUDGMENTAL EMPATHIC RESPONSE** provides support but also helps to interpret and evaluate the speaker's situation.

One of the main challenges to empathic listening is to avoid criticizing even when you disagree with the speaker. Overcoming this challenge requires us to suppress the desire to argue about what the person is saying, or jump in to offer solutions too soon. Instead, try to just listen to all the speaker has to say, and use nonverbal and verbal feedback to communicate that you understand and respect the message.

Another challenge to empathic listening is finding your own level of comfort in talking about feelings and emotions. For example, if you find yourself in a situation where you need to listen to someone who is dying, you might use a new type of empathic listening that two researchers referred to as perspective-taking listening.[14] They said that the key element of effective perspective-taking listening is actively trying to understand how the situation looks from the other person's point of view. While this may sound hard to do in the case of listening to someone who is dying, it certainly is the kindest and most supportive thing to be able to do.

INTEGRATING TYPES OF LISTENING.

For the sake of clarity, we have discussed the three types of listening separately. However, thinking about them as if they were unconnected to one another is misleading. There are times when you want to use more than one type of listening during the same conversation. Suppose you are talking with a good friend about an important life decision, such as deciding whether to change careers, get married, or even get a divorce. In addition to empathizing with how difficult some decisions in life can be, you also want to listen critically to evaluate your friend's choices and offer advice if asked. If you are participating in a group discussion about a new project at work, listening both to learn and to critically evaluate others' ideas are equally important. But if your coworkers start worrying aloud about not liking the task, or how much time it will take, listening to empathize may be helpful, followed by a nonjudgmental empathic response.

OVERCOMING CHALLENGES TO LISTENING COMPETENCE

We have seen that integrating the three types of listening has many benefits. If that is true, why have not we all become better listeners? The reason is that every day we encounter challenges to competent listening: physical barriers, psychological barriers, interaction barriers, and a somewhat new set of barriers related to online and electronic communication.

PHYSICAL, PSYCHOLOGICAL, AND INTERACTION BARRIERS.

The world in which we live and communicate is full of **physical barriers** to listening, including interferences from the physical environment, and distracting characteristics or behaviors of the speaker, the listener, or both. An environment does not have to be loud to be distracting. Any interfering sounds or noises, however minor, can become obstacles to competent listening. Even mild distractions such as voices from a nearby discussion or traffic in the street outside can become barriers. An uncomfortable chair, a bad view of the speaker, or a hot and stuffy room can easily distract you from listening.

PHYSICAL BARRIERS TO LISTENING include interferences from the physical environment, and distracting characteristics or behaviors of the speaker, the listener, or both.

PSYCHOLOGICAL BARRIERS to listening reside within the listener, and include mental and emotional distractions to listening such as boredom, daydreaming, and thinking about personal concerns.

Physical characteristics or behaviors of a speaker can also serve as barriers to listening. A slight accent, a lisp, or even nervous pacing or the clothing of a speaker may be enough to distract a well-intentioned listener. Physical barriers sometimes also exist in listeners. Feelings of physical fatigue, hunger, or thirst can easily distract any of us from listening. Other physiological limitations, such as hearing problems, also act as physical barriers.

Because physical barriers to listening are common, in some cases you may need to plan ahead to be ready to listen. For example, arrive early and take a seat near the front of the class in any course that you find challenging or unappealing. At an interpersonal level, if you and a friend need to have an important conversation, choose a quiet restaurant, not a noisy bar. And if you need to attend an important training or meeting at work, be as well rested as possible.

Closely linked to physical barriers are **psychological barriers** to listening. This set of barriers resides within the listener, and includes mental and emotional distractions to listening such as boredom, daydreaming, and thinking about personal concerns. If you are not interested in the topic of a message, or if some aspect of it offends you, you may succumb to psychological distractions.

These psychological distractions to competent listening may occur as a result of several factors: the difference in speaking and listening rate, message overload, and message complexity. The difference between how fast people speak and how fast they can listen causes a psychological distraction. Some researchers say people in today's world speak at approximately 200 words per minute, but can listen at about 500 to 600 words per minute, a vast difference.[15] This discrepancy leaves mental downtime during which your mind wanders and psychological barriers such as daydreaming occur. In one study, in fact, the barrier most frequently cited as hindering effective listening to radio commercials was daydreaming.[16]

Two other causes of psychological distractions are **message overload**—the sheer quantity of messages—and **message complexity**—the extent to which messages are detailed and complicated.

A remedy for overcoming the psychological obstacles of message overload and complexity is to listen more selectively and attentively. Consider your typical day. As a college student, you probably attend several lectures a day. At work, you spend plenty of time listening to your coworkers. Outside school and work, you listen to your friends and family. Among all these messages, you need to make decisions about which are most important. Once you consciously decide to listen to a message, give it your full attention and concentration.

Although physical and psychological barriers primarily occur within us, other obstacles to listening result from our interactions with other people. **Interaction barriers** may arise as a result of engaging in verbal battles and using inflammatory language, or because of individual and cultural differences between the speaker and listener.

> MESSAGE OVERLOAD refers to the sheer quantity of the message.
>
> MESSAGE COMPLEXITY refers to the amount of detail, density, and integration of information in a message, i.e., how complicated it is.
>
> INTERACTION BARRIERS arise from engaging in verbal battles and using inflammatory language, or because of individual and cultural differences between the speaker and listener.

When people become entangled in heated arguments, they often fail to listen to one another. In a variety of situations—at home, school, or work—discussions that begin as conversations about opinions and preferences sometimes spiral into disagreements and verbal battles; people react emotionally, and little or no listening occurs. While one person is speaking, the other is preoccupied with planning a counterattack, rather than listening. You can address this obstacle to listening by making a conscious effort to control verbal battles and your own use of inflammatory language. You also have to learn to handle such language when you are on the receiving end. When a verbal battle is intensifying, refocus the discussion on how you and the other person can communicate more competently. Counselors often use this method of stepping outside the conversation and focusing on the process of communication to diffuse and deal with conflict situations.

A last interaction barrier to listening can occur when communicating with people from other cultures and cultural subgroups.[17] The general rules for communicating in any culture may predispose members of that culture to favor particular listening styles. Think about how you tend to listen. You probably have a style or approach to listening that you use in most situations. Two leading authorities on listening pointed to these four possible listening styles, depending on your personal preference or the style your culture tends to favor.[18] Some listeners are people-oriented, and typically show a strong concern for others and their feelings. Other more content-oriented listeners are interested more in what is said than who is saying it, or what they are feeling. Action-oriented listeners are interested in what will be done, what actions will happen and when, and who will do them. Time-oriented listeners have their eyes constantly on the clock and organizing their day into neat compartments; they will allocate time for listening in one of those compartments.

These four styles become more a function of habit than conscious choice. But other people you interact with may favor a listening style unlike yours or not to your liking. Since individual and cultural differences in listening styles do exist, you need to recognize and respect them. To listen competently, be patient with the way the other person seems to be listening, and avoid being distracted by individual or cultural differences in listening style.

ONLINE AND ELECTRONIC BARRIERS.

We said earlier that listening is affected by a somewhat new set of 21st-century barriers. **Online and electronic barriers** involve any communication messages that are sent or received using blogs, wikis, social networking, computers, and the like.[19] So far, most of the research in this area has focused on communicators as senders of electronic messages. Now, some researchers are trying to understand the online receivers of messages, the listeners.[20]

How we listen and pay attention online is being scrutinized, partly to help individuals, but also politicians and corporations. For example, this information is potentially useful to public relations and advertising people who want to understand our online listening habits in order to communicate with us most effectively. One researcher moved away from the traditional types of listening described earlier in this chapter. This newer model suggests that we engage in three different types of online listening:[21]

- **Reciprocal listening**: "The act of hearing and responding meaningfully to comments and direct messages." You may engage in this type when involved in a synchronous discussion on a blog of high interest to you.
- **Background listening**: "Scanning and skimming tweets and online commentary with little focus, attention, or response." If you are doing something else at the time, like attending a lecture or out for dinner, you may scan Twitter for a few minutes, but not pay much attention.
- **Delegated listening**: "Giving the responsibility of tracking and responding to tweets to a third party." A company executive may delegate responsibility to another staff member to monitor online discussions about certain products or issues affecting the company.

This model for listening in online and electronic environments suggests a need for all of us to examine our own social media listening habits. Here are four simple tips from the experts for addressing any challenges, and honing your online listening skills:

1. **Know your own online listening habits.** Think about the types of information you need to be better at what you do—professionally and personally. Target where that information comes from (*Google News*, *Reuters*, *Twitter*, etc.) and determine when, where, and whether you need to engage in reciprocal, background, or delegated listening.
2. **Filter what you listen and attend to.** Use tools like *TweetML*, *Twitter Search*, *Google Alerts*, and *Gmail Priority Inbox* to prioritize what you will actually listen and pay attention to.
3. **Think about what you are seeing and hearing.** Before re-tweeting or giving a "Like," take a minute to examine what you read in a tweet or *Facebook* update. Connect what you have read to what you know from other sources. Ask a follow-up question. Basic critical-thinking skills need to be applied to listening online.
4. **Track your online listening habits.** Keep a record of what you learn from social media. If you are listening to social media for your company, create a spreadsheet to track trends, clicks, responses, and other relevant data. If your online listening is for personal reasons, track how much time and energy goes into this form of listening. Determine if some of that time could be better spent on other activities.

Before closing our overall discussion of challenges to listening, several suggestions from communication experts may prove helpful—the first relates to ethical listening. In 2009, the International Listening Association published a special issue of its journal devoted entirely to the topic of ethics

Table 6.2: Challenges to Listening

Becoming aware of the challenges and barriers to listening and their causes will help you become a far more competent listener.

CHALLENGES TO LISTENING	DESCRIPTION OF THE BARRIER	CAUSES AND RESULTS OF THE BARRIER
Physical barriers	• Environment and noise.	• Peripheral conversations, uncomfortable furniture, bad view, crowds, heat, cold, noise.
	• Distracting speaker characteristics or behaviors.	• Accent, lisp, pacing, unusual clothing.
	• Distracting listener characteristics or behaviors.	• Fatigue, hunger, thirst, hearing problems.
Psychological barriers	• Speaking versus listening rate.	• Boredom. • Daydreaming. • Worry about personal concerns.
	• Message overload and complexity	• Inability to listen and pay attention.
Interaction barriers	• Verbal battles and inflammatory language.	• Emotional reactions and no listening occurs.
	• Individual and cultural differences.	• Individual and cultural listening styles negatively affect listening.
Online and electronic barriers	• Amount and complexity of electronic messages.	• Scanning and skimming of messages.
	• Messages in blogs, wikis, social media, and e-mail lists.	• Delegation of listening to others.

and listening. In the introduction to the special issue, the author identified five choices we all make every day regarding ethical listening.[22] We choose whether we as individuals will listen. We also can choose not to listen. We choose if we will listen selectively. Or we can choose to listen collaboratively to each other. Making this last choice is the best, and clearly relates to the motivation component of our communication competence model. The point is that we have an ethical responsibility to be motivated, and to make a choice to listen to one another.

To live up to this responsibility, another listening expert found that we sometimes need to listen more patiently.[23] Four simple steps are provided to help with this slowing down: Observe, React, Judge, and Intervene. First, we perceive what is happening (observe); next, the emotional brain reacts positively or negatively (react); then the rational brain makes a judgment about the situation (judge); and finally, we intervene by taking some action. Four listening traps are associated with this model that a patient listener should avoid: Misperception, Emotional Response, Faulty Thinking, and Acting Incorrectly. The point here is that by slowing down and listening patiently, more ethical listening can occur.

Finally, to integrate these two ideas of ethical and patient listening, we harken back to this recommendation about ethics from the National Communication Association's Credo on Ethical Communication presented in Chapter Two: "promote communication climates of caring and mutual understanding that respect the unique needs and characteristics of individual communicators."

Table 6.3: Competent Listening Skills

The challenges to listening may seem to be just that . . . a real challenge! You can overcome the challenges by using these specific skills at each step in the listening process.

STEP ONE: RECEIVING SKILLS FOR BECOMING A MORE COMPETENT LISTENER

- Prepare yourself to listen mentally, physically, and emotionally.
- Be well rested and well fed (but not too well fed!).
- Clarify your purpose for listening—to learn, evaluate, or empathize.
- Set a specific but flexible listening goal for yourself in the situation.
- Identify barriers to listening, and eliminate any distractions that you can.
- Focus your attention on listening in the moment.
- Concentrate on the speaker and the message, not on your own thoughts and feelings.
- Postpone evaluation of the message until the speaker has finished.

STEP TWO: CONSTRUCTING MEANING SKILLS FOR LISTENING COMPETENTLY

- Set aside personal biases and prejudices as you attribute meaning to the message.
- Listen as impartially as possible before you decide what the message means.
- Repress responding emotionally or negatively to the message.
- Do not overreact or listen for flaws in the message.
- Analyze objectively what the speaker is saying.
- Listen for the global meaning of the message and the speaker's evidence or argument.
- Mentally construct a picture of the speaker's message, and examine and evaluate its meaning and worth.

STEP THREE: RESPONDING SKILLS FOR COMPETENT LISTENING

- Identify and remember the main points of the message.
- Take notes to help you accurately recall what was said.
- Try to understand and clarify the meaning of the message by asking questions about anything you do not understand.
- Demonstrate interest in the speaker's message by providing appropriate verbal and nonverbal feedback.
- Feedback is the process a listener uses to communicate to the speaker his or her understanding of the message, reactions to it, and any effects it might have had on the listener.
- Paraphrase the message to achieve full understanding and clarity.
- Paraphrasing is a technique a listener uses to provide verbal feedback to the speaker by summarizing and restating the meaning of the speaker's message.

Communication climate refers to the tone, general mood, or feeling that colors any interpersonal relationship. Communication climates are characterized by either supportive or defensive communication.[24] Supportive communication climates foster better listening, whereas defensive communication climates foster just the opposite—poor communication. People can change their communication climates, and that has a direct effect on how comfortable and willing we are to listen to one another ethically and patiently. Creating a supportive climate for listening, using the strategies outlined in this chapter, is an important part of communication competence.

COMMUNICATION CLIMATE refers to the tone, general mood, or feeling that colors any interpersonal relationship, and is characterized by either supportive or defensive communication.

Table 6.2 summarizes the challenges to listening just discussed. Table 6.3 provides a summary of listening skills to address the challenges at each step in the listening process. Review these two tables in order to lock in the learning, and enhance your own listening competence.

The next three main parts of this book focus on interpersonal communication, small group communication, and public speaking. The motivation, knowledge, and skills necessary for competent listening discussed in this chapter are essential to competence in each of these three communication contexts.

CHAPTER SUMMARY

Listening is the process of receiving, constructing meaning from, and responding to spoken and/or nonverbal messages. Receiving means tuning in to the speaker's verbal and nonverbal message; constructing meaning involves assigning meaning to the message, and clarifying your understanding of it; and responding completes the interaction, and lets the speaker know the message is received and understood. Achieving competence in listening is crucial in interpersonal relationships, small groups, public speaking situations, and at work.

Types of listening are categorized by their purpose. Listening to learn and comprehend requires a search for facts and ideas, and a quest for information. Listening to evaluate and critique focuses on critically analyzing the meaning and merit of a speaker's message. Listening to empathize and understand entails concentrating on the speaker's feelings and attitudes. When listening with empathy, a listener can respond nonjudgmentally or judgmentally.

Challenges to listening competence result from physical, psychological, and interaction barriers, and from online and electronic barriers. Physical barriers include interferences from the physical environment, and distracting characteristics or behaviors of the speaker or the listener. Psychological barriers include mental and emotional distractions to listening and can result from the difference between speaking and listening rates, and from message overload and complexity. Interaction barriers arise when people engage in verbal battles and use inflammatory language, or because of individual or culturally based differences in listening styles. There are people-oriented, content-oriented, action-oriented, and time-oriented listening styles. Online listening includes three types: reciprocal listening, background listening, and delegated listening. You can hone your online listening skills by knowing your own habits, filtering what you listen and attend to, thinking about what you see and hear, and tracking your online listening habits. Competent listeners have an ethical responsibility to choose to listen to one another, to listen more patiently, and to encourage a supportive communication climate for listening competently.

KEY TERMS.

The key terms below are defined in this chapter, and presented alphabetically with definitions in the Glossary at the end of the book.

- listening
- receiving
- constructing meaning
- responding
- listening to learn and comprehend
- listening to evaluate and critique

- listening to empathize and understand
- nonjudgmental empathic response
- judgmental empathic response
- physical barriers
- psychological barriers

- message overload
- message complexity
- interaction barriers
- online and electronic barriers
- communication climate

BUILDING MOTIVATION: SELF-ASSESSMENT TOOL.

Rate each of the eight communication situations described here, indicating your own typical level of listening competence. Rate one situation all the way through for motivation, knowledge, and skills. Then rate the next situation. Use the 1–4 scale below, with 1 being minimal competence and 4 high competence.

Communication situations.

1. Listening to a person from a culture very different from your own.
2. Listening at a family wedding to a distant relative whom you have not met before.
3. Visiting your elderly grandmother and spending the afternoon with her and her friends.
4. Attending a training session at work to learn about a new software program you will not use frequently.
5. Attending a public lecture with a friend on a topic you do not find very interesting.
6. Attending a class taught by a lecturer who overestimates what you know about the complex topic.
7. Participating in a lengthy team meeting about a new project at work.
8. Becoming part of a guided tour of a gallery displaying art you find unappealing.

Motivation.

1 = Distracted, disinterested, or simply no motivation to be competent.
2 = Somewhat distracted or disinterested, but motivated to be competent.
3 = Somewhat interested and motivated to be competent.
4 = Highly interested and motivated to be competent.

Knowledge.

1 = Completely inexperienced and ignorant about what to do and how to do it.
2 = Minimal experience and sense of what to do and how to do it.
3 = Somewhat experienced and knowledgeable about what to do and how to do it.
4 = Highly knowledgeable about all aspects of what to do and how to do it.

Skills.

1 = Completely incapable of behaving competently.
2 = Barely capable of behaving minimally competently.
3 = Fairly capable of behaving competently.
4 = Highly capable of behaving competently.

Interpreting your scores.

Total your score separately for each situation (motivation, knowledge, and skills). The possible range of the score for each situation is 3–12. If your total score for any of the situations is 6 or less, you see yourself as less competent in that situation than you should be. A score of 7–9 means that you are average at sending and receiving communication messages in the situation. A score of 10–12 indicates that you have a high level of communication competence in that situation.

BUILDING KNOWLEDGE: DISCUSSION QUESTIONS.

1. If listening competently would improve the quality of life in society, what can you do to encourage more people to listen better?
2. Which of the three steps in the listening process (receiving, constructing meaning, responding) is most important and why? Which step causes the most misunderstandings? Explain.
3. Of the three types of listening (to learn, to evaluate, and to empathize), which do you find most difficult to do and why? How can you address that personal challenge?
4. Of the three types of barriers to listening (physical, psychological, and interaction), which causes you the most problems as a listener? Why, and what can you do about it?
5. If you had to choose one, which of the listening styles do you tend to favor most of the time—people-oriented, content-oriented, action-oriented, or time-oriented? Should you expand your style choices for use in different listening situations?
6. Motivation to listen in a variety of communication situations is important to competent listening. What can you do to become more motivated in less appealing situations?
7. Research suggests that paraphrasing and feedback in intimate conversations can be annoying, but we know that it helps prevent misunderstandings. How can we provide feedback in the most acceptable way in intimate discussions?

BUILDING SKILLS: STUDENT ACTIVITIES.

Individual activities.

1. Ralph Nichols, a notable scholar of listening, constructed a list, Top 10 Bad Listening Habits. Evaluate yourself based on the list. Go to http://www.dartmouth.edu/~acskills/docs/10_bad_listening habits.doc.
2. Identify a communication situation in which it is important to listen to learn. List the reasons for that importance. Then identify communication situations in which listening to evaluate and listening to empathize are crucial, and list the reasons why.
3. On the Internet, go to http://thinkexist.com/quotations/listening/, a site containing many quotations about listening. Choose several quotations that particularly appeal to you, and write a short explanation of why they are meaningful.

4. Watch an interview on television, perhaps one of the late-night or Sunday morning talk shows. Observe the listening skills of the interviewee and interviewer. Critique each person's listening, feedback, and paraphrasing skills. Who is the better listener and why?

5. Analyze a listening situation in which you were recently involved, and develop an action plan to develop and refine your listening skills.

6. Analyze your online listening habits as described in the challenges section of this chapter. Develop a plan to improve those habits.

Group activities.

1. Form a small group of four to five students, and have each group member think of a person who is a good listener. Each member then writes a description of what that person actually does, and why he or she is a good listener. Compare the descriptions, and produce a summary list of characteristics and behaviors of good listeners.

2. In a small group, have each group member describe a recent communication situation involving one of the three types of listening. Determine how communication in each situation could be enhanced by more competent listening.

3. In a small group, have each member identify his or her greatest strength as a listener and greatest challenge. Discuss a plan for addressing each of the challenges.

4. In a small group, have each member describe her or his typical online communication day. Decide with each student if that typical day needs any modification.

NOTES

1. See Watkins(2011).
2. See International Listening Association (2011).
3. See Weger, Castle, Emmett, & Minei (2008).
4. See Bentley (2000).
5. See Darling & Dannels (2003).
6. See Tan, Fowler, & Hawkes (2004).
7. See Flynn, Valikoski, & Grau (2008).
8. See Paukert, Stagner, & Kerry (2004).
9. See Rea & Rea (2000).
10. See Agne (2008).
11. See Waldron & Lavitt (2001).
12. See Adams & Cox (2010).
13. See Bodie (2011).
14. See Vora & Vora (2008).
15. See Wolvin (2010).
16. See Goby (2008).
17. See Dragan & Sherblom (2008).
18. See Watson& Barker (1995).
19. See Wolvin (2010).
20. See Crawford (2009).
21. See *Listening to the Web* (2011).

22. See Beard (2009).
23. See Bartholomew (2005).
24. See Gibb (2006).

REFERENCES

Adams, W., & Cox, E. (2010). The teaching of listening as an integral part of an oral activity: An examination of public-speaking texts. *International Journal of Listening, 24*(2), 89–105.

Agne, R. (2008). Listening discourse in an unconventional crisis negotiation: The FBI and the Branch Davidians at Waco. Paper presented at the National Communication Association Conference. Retrieved from EBSCOhost, www.ebsco.com

Bartholomew, P. T. (2005). Slowing down to go fast. *Listening Professional, 4*(1), 10–16.

Beard, D. (2009). A broader understanding of the ethics of listening: Philosophy, cultural studies, media studies and the ethical listening subject. *International Journal of Listening, 23*(1), 7–20.

Bentley, S. (2000). Listening in the 21st century. *International Journal of Listening, 14*(1), 129–142.

Bodie, G. D. (2011). The Active-Empathic Listening Scale (AELS): Conceptualization and evidence of validity within the interpersonal domain. *Communication Quarterly, 59*(3), 277–295.

Crawford, K. (2009). Following you: Disciplines of listening in social media. *Continuum: Journal of Media & Cultural Studies, 23*(4), 525–535.

Darling, A., & Dannels, D. (2003). Practicing engineers talk about the importance of talk: A report on the role of oral communication in the workplace. *Communication Education, 52*(1), 1–16.

Dragan, N., & Sherblom, J. C. (2008). The influence of cultural individualism and collectivism on US and post-Soviet listening styles. *Human Communication, 11*(2), 177–192.

Flynn, J., Valikoski, T., & Grau, J. (2008). Listening in the business context: Reviewing the state of research. *International Journal of Listening, 22*(2), 141–151.

Gibb, J.R. (2006). Defensive communication. *Journal of Communication, 1*(3), 141–148.

Goby, V. (2008). Radio commercial listening behaviour: Barriers and avoidance. *Australian Journal of Communication, 35*(1), 27–39.

International Listening Association. (2011). *An ILA definition of listening.* Retrieved from http://www.listen.org/Legend?emulatemode=2

Listening to the Web. (2011). Retrieved from http://dotlearnt.com/2010/09/21/listening-to-the-web/

Paukert, A., Stagner, B., & Kerry, H. (2004). The assessment of active listening skills in helpline volunteers. *Stress, Trauma, and Crisis: An International Journal, 7*(1), 61–76.

Rea, C., & Rea, D. (2000). Responding to user views of service performance. *Journal of Mental Health, 9*(4), 351–363.

Tan, L., Fowler, M., & Hawkes, L. (2004). Management accounting curricula: Striking a balance between the views of educators and practitioners. *Accounting Education, 13*(1), 51–67.

Vora, E., & Vora, A. (2008). A contingency framework for listening to the dying. *International Journal of Listening, 22*(1), 59–72.

Waldron, V., & Lavitt, M. (2001). "Welfare-to-work": An analysis of the communication competencies taught in a job training program. *Communication Education, 50*(1), 15–33.

Watkins, K. (2011). How much time do you spend listening? Retrieved from http://articles.webraydian.com/article4793-How_Much_Time_Do_You_Spend_Listening.html

Watson, K. W. & Barker, L. L. (1995). *Listening styles profile.* Amsterdam, The Netherlands: Pfeiffer.

Weger, H., Castle, G., Emmett, M., & Minei, E. (2008). Active listening in initial interactions: Perceptions of perceived understanding, social attraction, and conversational satisfaction. Paper presented at the National Communication Association Conference. Retrieved from EBSCOhost, www.ebsco.com.

Wolvin, A.D. (2010). *Listening and human communication in the 21st century.* Malden, MA: Wiley-Blackwell.

PART TWO

INTERPERSONAL COMMUNICATION

CHAPTER SEVEN

INTERPERSONAL COMMUNICATION: BUILDING KNOWLEDGE

- **What Is Interpersonal Communication?**
  Interpersonal Communication as Interaction
  Interpersonal Communication as Relationship

- **Content Knowledge and Interpersonal Communication**
  Repertoires and Roles
  Scripts and Stories
  Rules and Norms

- **Overcoming Challenges to Interpersonal Relationships**
  Planning
  Empathy and Perspective Taking
  Knowledge-Gaining Strategies

- **Chapter Summary**
  Key Terms
  Building Motivation: Self-Assessment Tool
  Building Knowledge: Discussion Questions
  Building Skills: Student Activities

The greatest problem in communication is the illusion that it has been accomplished. —George Bernard Shaw, Irish Playwright, 1856–1950

.:
• • •

Eliah was an attractive, young college student tending bar in the campus pub. Preston, a recent graduate, was chatting with his friends, Greg and Jeff, who had decided to meet him at the pub to discuss their job-finding experiences and catch up with each other. After some discussion, one of them mentioned how attractive he found Eliah. All three agreed, and their conversation turned to the awkwardness of asking someone out for a date. They talked about various ways of introducing themselves to women, and the general strategies of directness versus indirectness, and serious versus humorous approaches. After some heated discussion about their respective "theories," Preston excused himself for a moment. A few minutes later, he returned to the table and announced that he had gotten Eliah's number, and that she was expecting a call from him next week!

Thoroughly surprised, Greg and Jeff asked how he had managed to get her number. Preston explained that he had approached the bar with a big smile on his face, placed his cell phone on the bar, and asked her to look at what day she would like him to call her. At first she seemed flustered, but regaining her composure, she gave him the excuse of a busy schedule. Preston realized that Eliah had experienced some embarrassment about being put on the spot. He made small talk about how busy the bar looked, sympathizing that she must have a lot of responsibility at work. He then suggested that he could adapt his schedule to hers, and again asked what time on his schedule would work for her. She looked over his calendar of appointments, took out a paper napkin, and wrote her number and a date on which Preston had nothing scheduled. Greg and Jeff looked at each other in disbelief, and after a long silence, Jeff simply said, "There goes my theory."

This situation illustrates several important features about the role of knowledge in interpersonal communication. First, people often have implicit theories about how communication is supposed to work, and what actions work better than others. In the story, Preston, Greg, and Jeff were operating on the assumption that men are supposed to do the asking. Greg and Jeff assumed further that the asking should be planned out as some sort of a strategy.

Second, people's theories are not always correct in all situations. In fact, any of Greg's, Jeff's, or Preston's strategies could have worked equally well depending on several other possibilities. Eliah may already be in an exclusive relationship. She may only go out with people of a given religion or ethnic group. Or, she might even prefer to do the selecting and asking herself, rather than letting the man do it. In short, people's working theories of communication are just that: theories. They may do a fair job of accounting for things most of the time, but they are rarely right in all cases.

Third, sometimes people overanalyze. Preston had the same chance of being right as Greg or Jeff. But he took the chance, and acted creatively on his instinct and perhaps his experience in a similar situation. Then he changed his action plan when his initial move of putting his cell phone on the bar did not work. Sometimes it is good to analyze what to say or do, but in some situations the best plan is to follow your instincts. In order to make the best choices, you need to know more about interpersonal communication and how it works.

WHAT IS INTERPERSONAL COMMUNICATION?

To understand how we develop knowledge in interpersonal communication, it is important first to understand what interpersonal communication is. It can be understood in many ways, but it comes down to two central concepts: interaction and relationship.

INTERPERSONAL COMMUNICATION AS INTERACTION.

In Chapter One, communication was defined as the process of managing messages and media for the purpose of creating meaning. In Chapter Two, the interpersonal context of communication was described as an interaction among people in social or personal relationships. Combining these two definitions, **interpersonal communication** is the process of managing messages and media for the purpose of creating meaning in interactions among people in social or personal relationships.

Interaction means that there is interdependence among the behaviors or moves made by the communicators in a situation. One of the most essential aspects of conversation is that it tends to consist of paired types of speech.[1] For example, questions tend to elicit answers. Disclosures tend to elicit other disclosures. Greetings tend to elicit other greetings. Any statement on one topic tends to elicit a response that is relevant to that topic. So interaction means that one person's actions influence the actions of the other, and this interdependence of action is core to all relationships.

INTERPERSONAL COMMUNICATION AS RELATIONSHIP.

Even though many interactions may not feel like a relationship is being formed, all interpersonal communication is, at some level, about developing a relationship, even if that relationship is temporary or fleeting. Recall in Chapter One, we said that a relationship is formed when some sense of interdependence occurs among communicators. We now expand that understanding of interdependence characterizing relationships. A **relationship** is the sense of positioning of one person to another, that is, how you orient yourself or connect to one another. I relate to you as my friend or as my parent, or as my professor. In any of these relationships, every message exchanged occurs at two levels of information: content and relationship.[2] The **content level** of a message is what the words mean in a literal or denotative sense. The **relationship level** of a mes-

> **INTERPERSONAL COMMUNICATION** is the process of managing messages and media for the purpose of creating meaning in interactions among people in social or personal relationships.
>
> **INTERACTION** refers to the interdependence among sequential behaviors or moves made by communicators in a situation.
>
> **A RELATIONSHIP** is the sense of relative positioning to one another, that is, how you orient yourself or connect to one another.
>
> **THE CONTENT LEVEL** of a message is what the words mean in a literal or denotative sense.
>
> **THE RELATIONSHIP LEVEL** is what a message implies about the relationship.

Box 7.1: Content and Relationship Levels in an Interpersonal Relationship

In this conversation from the movie *The Break-Up*, Gary continually seems focused on the content of the message—the question of the desirability of washing dishes. Brooke, in contrast, is focused on the relational level of the message—Gary's disinterest in sharing equally in a household chore. Brooke sees Gary's disinterest as disrespect for their relationship.

Brooke:	"... You know I don't like waking up to a dirty kitchen."
Gary:	"Who cares?"
Brooke:	"I care. Alright! I care! I busted my ass all day cleaning this house and cooking that meal and I worked today, and it would be nice if you said 'thank you,' and helped me with the dishes."
Gary:	"Fine [with disdain]! I'll help you with the damn dishes."
Brooke:	"Oh come on. You know what? No, that's . . . see, that's not what I want."
Gary:	"You just said you want me to help you do the dishes."
Brooke:	"I want you to want to do the dishes."
Gary:	[in disbelief] "Why would I want to do dishes. Why?!"
Brooke:	"See! That's my whole point."
Gary:	"Let's see if I'm following this, okay. Are you telling me you're upset because I don't have a strong desire to clean dishes?"
Brooke:	"No I'm upset because you don't have a strong desire to offer to do the dishes."
Gary:	"I just did!"
Brooke:	"After I asked you!"

Source: The Break-Up (Besser, S. M., et al., & Reed, 2006)

sage is what the message implies about the relationship. These two levels of information in an interpersonal conversation are clearly illustrated in an excerpt from the movie, *The Break-Up*, presented in Box 7.1. As you read that conversation, the two levels of messages will become quite clear and meaningful to you.

To summarize, interpersonal communication is about interactions in which relationships develop, and messages are exchanged at a content level and a relationship level. When Preston approached Eliah to get her phone number, a relationship began to develop. The content level of the messages they exchanged focused simply on finding a time for a phone call. But at a relationship level, what they said to each other implied that a new relationship was a possibility. How any relationship develops and unfolds, whether it is successful or unsuccessful, brief or enduring, depends on how you use your knowledge of communication. As we said in Chapter Two and in the competence model, knowledge underlies communication in all contexts and situations. We now consider what you need to know and understand about interpersonal communication.

CONTENT KNOWLEDGE AND INTERPERSONAL COMMUNICATION

Most of us take pride in what we have learned to do in our lifetime. When it comes to your communication competence, you probably assume you have acquired it by being a keen observer of life, and by developing social intelligence through careful attention to the effects of your communication behaviors. Certainly, much of what we know about communicating is learned by observing the world around us.[3] You misuse a word and are corrected, and you learn to not use it that way again. You crack a joke and others laugh, and you learn you can achieve social rewards through humor, so you are more likely to seize opportunities to make jokes in the future. But if your joke is responded to with nervous or embarrassed laughter, you are less likely to tell a joke again. While we do learn how to communicate through observation, a surprising amount of our communication knowledge also is based on our genetic inheritance. For example, studies of twins suggest that a third to half of our communication anxiety, general friendliness, and interpersonal aggressiveness is genetic.[4] That said, it is likely that our inherited tendencies to communicate in one way or another also are shaped and influenced by our experiences and what we learn throughout our lifetimes.

To the extent that we have learned bad communication habits, we may fail to recognize them in ourselves, and we are unaware of how to change them. For instance, research shows that highly competent people tend to underestimate their competence, whereas incompetent people tend to significantly overestimate their competence. Further, overestimation of one's own competence is one of the very things that makes the person incompetent.[5] To avoid this problem, what do you need to know about interpersonal communication? As illustrated by performance activities like speeches in your communication courses, deliberate practice is one good way to expand your knowledge. As your knowledge and understanding of public speaking improve, the speed, accuracy, and flexibility of your skills increase, and you can better apply those skills.[6] By giving speeches repeatedly in class, you develop more knowledge of the skills you need to give a good speech. In addition to performing and practicing, there are three other categories of knowledge you need to be aware of and understand that are essential to interpersonal communication competence: repertoires and roles, scripts and stories, and rules and norms.

REPERTOIRES AND ROLES.

A **repertoire** is the set of roles a person is capable of playing or enacting, along with behaviors or actions that comprise those roles. **Roles** are the patterns and the style of statements and behaviors a person is able to perform across contexts. Thus, you may have a large repertoire of roles for how you communicate with members of the opposite sex. And those roles govern how you act and interact with the opposite sex, whether you know it or not.

Repertoires vary in both breadth and depth. If you recall, we discussed breadth and depth in regard to self-disclosure in Chapter Three. **Breadth** relates to the number of different types of roles you can play. The actors Johnny Depp and Kate Winslet have played many different types of roles. Most Elvis impersonators, in contrast, probably only know the role of Elvis. **Depth** refers to the level of familiarity you have with any given role in a repertoire. A typical singer may know only a few Elvis songs, but a professional Elvis impersonator is likely to know many of them in depth. In general, the broader and deeper a communicator's repertoires are, the higher the competence level. Broader repertoires allow you to select from a wider set of roles and achieve competent communication in more situations. Greater depth in a repertoire results from more experience and expertise in performing any given role. Obviously,

REPERTOIRE is the set of roles a person is capable of playing or enacting, along with behaviors or actions that comprise those roles.

ROLES are the patterns and the style of statements and behaviors a person is able to perform across contexts.

BREADTH relates to the number of different types of roles a person can play.

DEPTH refers to the level of familiarity a person has with any given role in a repertoire.

Table 7.1: Repertoires of Behaviors in Different Types of Roles

Different roles require different types (breadth) and amounts (depth) of behavior, as illustrated by the roles of friendly, flirtatious, and seductive communication.

CHANNEL	FRIENDLY	FLIRTATIOUS	SEDUCTIVE
Use of body language	Small amount of smiling; body relaxed	Moderate amount of smiling; head tilted; open mouth/pout	Frequent amount of smiling; body relaxed, exposed skin
Use of touch	Little/no touch	Moderate touch (arm, shoulder)	Touch hand/leg
Use of space	Farther away from each other while talking	Moderately close; cross legs, face/lean toward each other	Orient bodies close to each other
Use of eye contact	Little/moderate eye contact	Moderate eye contact with occasional glances downward	Frequent eye contact with occasional gaze
Use of voice	Neutral voice tone; less fluency/more silences	Animated voice tone; decreased silences	Intimate voice tone; greater fluency/fewer silences

Source: Adapted from Koeppel, Montagne-Miller, O'Hair, & Cody (1993).[7]

most people prefer to have more rather than less roles in their repertoires, and to be competent communicators in all of them. In our opening story, Preston demonstrated the ability to use an appropriate role from his repertoire to effectively get Eliah's phone number.

Roles are characterized by a particular set of appropriate behaviors, as well as prohibited or inappropriate behaviors. For example, consider the repertoire of nonverbal behaviors for different roles listed in Table 7.1. The entries in the second through fourth columns reveal that appropriate behaviors differ slightly from one role to another, depending on whether the person intends to play the role of a flirt, a friend, or a seducer. In sum, a repertoire is a set of the various roles you are able to perform in various communication situations. The roles imply that there are scripts that guide and shape how you communicate in particular situations.

SCRIPTS AND STORIES.

In Chapter Three, we said that a script is an expected sequence of events that appears logical to the communicators, and guides how we interpret events and communicate. A script is like a **story** or a narrative of what is expected or needs to occur in the given communication situation. If any actions or communication behaviors occur out of sequence, the story may fall apart. For instance, if another person engages in premature self-disclosure when you first meet, you may feel uncomfortable, because the disclosure is not what you expected.

Most scripts do take the form of general sequences of actions. Wedding vows and greeting rituals typically are highly scripted—we know what to say and approximately what others probably will say. Table 7.2 illustrates typical scripts for the

A SCRIPT or STORY is a narrative of what is expected or needs to occur in the given situation.

Table 7.2: Scripting the Story of Romantic Relationships

Research has shown in the relatively recent past (1970s to 1990s) that different stages of heterosexual romantic relationships were represented by different scripts for the behavior that should occur and in what sequence. In this table, when sex differences were found, these are noted by italics. In the last two stages of the relationship, few differences were found based on sex.

GETTING AND GOING OUT ON A DATE

WOMAN'S SCRIPT	MAN'S SCRIPT
• Notices the other	• Notices the other
• Get caught staring at each other	• Get caught staring at each other
• Smile	• Smile
• Find out about the other person from friends	• Find out about the other person from friends
• Find ways to "accidentally" encounter/meet	• Find ways to "accidentally" encounter/meet
• Get introduced by friend	• Get introduced by friend
• *Say "Hello" or "Hi"*	• *Initiate conversation*
• Attempt to find common interests in casual conversation	• Attempt to find common interests in casual conversation
	• Ask for phone number
	• Phone later to ask for date
	• Make small talk

DEVELOPING THE DATING RELATIONSHIP

• Groom and dress	• Pick up date
• Man picks up	• Leave to pick up date
• Introduce to parents or roommate	• Meet parents or roommate
• "Courtly behavior" (e.g., open doors)	• Pick up friends
• Discuss specific plans for the date	• Discuss specific plans for the date
• Talk, joke, laugh	• Talk, joke, laugh
• Go to destination (movie, club, party, etc.)	• Go to destination (movie, club, party, etc.)
• Eat and/or drink	• Eat and/or drink
• Talk to friends	• Initiate sexual contact
• Have something go wrong	• Make out
• Be taken home	• Take date home
• Be asked for another date	• Ask for another date
• Man says he'll call	• Says he'll call
• Respond to (attempted) goodnight kiss	• Initiate (attempt at) goodnight kiss
• Go home	• Go home

(CONTINUED ON NEXT PAGE)

Table 7.2: Scripting the Story of Romantic Relationships (CONTINUED FROM PREVIOUS PAGE)

BECOMING MORE INTIMATE (SCRIPT FOR BOTH SEXES)

• Meet for the first time (party, class, bar, and so on)	• Other-oriented statements (stating interest in each other's goals)
• Small talk (discuss weather, school, and so on)	• Verbal expression of love
• Show physical affection (kiss, hug, touch, and so on)	• Bonding rituals (give gifts of flowers, gifts, jewelry)
• Formal/planned dating activities (dinner, movie, and so on)	• Verbal commitment (stating a desire for an exclusive relationship)
• Self-disclosure of intimate information	• Sexual intercourse
• Overcome relational crisis (jealousy, uncertainty)	• Cohabitation (living together)
• Meet parents	• Marriage
• Talk about future plans as a couple	

DECLINE AND DISENGAGEMENT (SCRIPT FOR BOTH SEXES)

• Display lack of interest	• Try to work things out
• Notice other people	• Date other people
• Act distant/display lack of interest	• Get back together
• Try to work things out	• Consider/discuss breaking up
• Increase physical distance/avoidance	• Move on and recover
• Communicate feelings	• Break up

Sources: Adapted from Battaglia, Richard, Datteri, & Lord (1998); Honeycutt, Cantrill, & Greene (1991); Pryor & Merluzzi (1985); and Rose & Frieze (1993).[8]

stages through which romantic relationships progress. These scripts were derived from studies of college students over the past few decades. What you may encounter in your life today, as the typical sequence of communication behaviors in relationships, may differ from the script in Table 7.2. Regardless, three characteristics of scripts become apparent from examining the communication stages outlined in the table.

First, scripts vary in their complexity and detail. As shown in Table 7.2, some steps in developing a romantic relationship, such as getting to know one another, rely on a wide variety of communication activities. These activities may include self-disclosure, asking questions, storytelling, and so on. Second, scripts can vary based on the roles communicators are playing in the particular context. In the acquaintance and development stages shown in the table, some sex differences are obvious, because dating in our culture is influenced by traditional gender expectations like who should initiate the first date. In the developing and dissolution stages, gender is less relevant to the roles men and women take on. Third, scripts are very flexible. In the table, the breakup script reveals several times when the partners might be able to rekindle the relationship and then leave it again. Apparently, interpersonal relationships, and therefore their scripts, are relatively fluid, and often get several chances to revive.[9]

Scripts give coherence and meaning to what would otherwise be illogical sequences of actions. In general, your actions and communication behavior should not violate the expected story line of any situation. This is because the scripts you follow, like virtually all communication, are constrained by social preferences known as rules and norms.

RULES AND NORMS.

In Chapter Two, we defined rules as prescriptions for what should or should not be done in a given type of situation. **Social norms** are the explicit or implicit *rules* specifying what behaviors are acceptable within a society or group. In other words, social norms are patterns for rule-governed, followable behaviors. Rules specify society's general expectations of what communication behavior is called for, or is not allowable. "Be nice" is advice many people give, but it is not a useful rule because its meaning in any particular situation is not clear. In contrast, "When having an argument, let the other person finish what he or she is saying before starting to speak," is a specific prescription or rule about what is socially expected. The prescriptions can indicate what to do or what *not* to do, and sometimes both. For example, the rule just stated about interruptions is really another way of saying, "Don't interrupt the other person when having an argument." In both

> SOCIAL NORMS are the explicit or implicit rules specifying what behaviors are acceptable within a society or group.

Table 7.3: Content Knowledge for Interpersonal Communicators

To communicate competently in interpersonal relationships, you need to be aware of three categories of knowledge: repertoires and roles, scripts and stories, and rules and norms. That knowledge will inform and guide how you should communicate in most interpersonal situations.

KNOWLEDGE CATEGORY	DEFINITION OF THE CATEGORY	DESCRIPTION OF THE CATEGORY
REPERTOIRES AND ROLES	Repertoire is the set of roles a person is capable of playing or enacting, along with behaviors or actions that comprise those roles. Roles are the patterns and the style of statements and behaviors a person is able to perform across contexts.	Breadth is the number of different types of roles you can play. Depth is the level of familiarity you have with any given role in a repertoire. The broader and deeper your repertoires and the more roles you have access to, the higher your competence level.
SCRIPTS AND STORIES	A script or story is a narrative of what is expected or needs to occur sequentially in the given situation.	Scripts vary in complexity and detail. Scripts vary based on the roles communicators are playing in the particular context. Scripts vary in flexibility for the communicators.
RULES AND NORMS	Rules are prescriptions for what should or should not be done in a given type of situation. Social norms are the explicit or implicit rules specifying what behaviors are acceptable within a society or group.	Rules specify society's general expectations for communication behavior. Prescriptions indicate what to do or what not to do, and sometimes both. Rules are context specific.

instances the rule specifies what is allowable, not allowable, or expected in the situation or context of having an argument.

Indeed, rules are context specific. "Don't interrupt" is in fact not a very useful rule in all communication contexts. Some interruptions are actually appropriate. They can signal involvement, such as when you excitedly give reinforcing feedback in the form of "yeah," "OK," or "no kidding." Other interruptions help the speaker, such as filling in a desired word when the speaker cannot think of the right phrase.

Together, repertoires and roles, scripts and stories, and rules and norms constitute the content knowledge of interpersonal communication. They provide you as a communicator with a sense of what can and should be communicated in any situation. Think back to our opening story when Greg, Jeff, and Preston strategized about getting to know Eliah in the bar. They talked over the repertoire of roles and communication behaviors they thought they might be able to put into action—what they called their strategies. They were aware of the scripts that say what is expected or needs to occur in the bar setting. Even Preston, who managed to get Eliah's phone number, communicated with her in a way that conformed to the rules and social norms for communication behavior when trying to get acquainted with someone in a bar.

Before we talk about the main challenges to interpersonal relationships, look over Table 7.3 that summarizes content knowledge for you as a competent interpersonal communicator.

OVERCOMING CHALLENGES TO INTERPERSONAL RELATIONSHIPS

Competent interpersonal communication does not appear out of thin air as though conjured by a magic trick. As we said earlier, people learn how to be competent over long periods of time, and that learning is represented in the communicator's knowledge. But knowledge is not always as useful or as accessible as we need it to be. We now examine some of the challenges to knowledge about interpersonal communication. Overcoming these challenges involves planning on your part, empathy and perspective taking, and effective knowledge-gaining strategies.

PLANNING.

Planning is the process of anticipating and formulating possible strategies for achieving a communication goal or goals.[10] The resulting **plan** is an intentional description of the actions and means needed to achieve a communication goal. In most situations, your plan does not have to be entirely conscious. Rather, you anticipate an interpersonal discussion, what will happen, and what will be said. Most of us do this anyway on occasion, when an interpersonal encounter is of some importance to us. We anticipate what the other person may say or do, and plan how we will act or react. So this suggestion is simply to bring the planning and anticipating process to a more conscious level.

PLANNING is the process of anticipating and formulating possible strategies for achieving some communication goal or goals.

A PLAN is an intentional description of the actions and means needed to achieve a communication goal.

When you flirt with someone, you may be fulfilling a plan to initiate a romantic relationship, but you may also be facilitating a larger plan to get married someday. For example, in the opening story, Preston's first goal was getting Eliah's phone number, which in turn was a step in getting a first date, and a step in a plan to achieve an intimate relationship. At first glance, this planning process may seem a little pointless. But the importance of developing and adapting somewhat complex communication plans is illustrated by the fact that students who were found to have simpler plans tended to be higher in loneliness than those with more complex or complete plans.[11]

Several principles can guide us through the process of competent communication planning. First of all, you should select plans based on how adequately they will help in achieving your goals. While most communicators want to accomplish their goals, often they fail to choose the most effective plan. The lesson here is to consider your possible options carefully, and choose the plan with the greatest potential for success.

Second, most communicators choose a new plan based on previous plans that seemed to work well for them. As a communicator, you could spend an enormous amount of energy analyzing the roles, rules, and script options present in a given situation. "I could do or say this. . . then again, maybe I should not say that. . . ." Or you can realize that you may have faced at least a similar situation before, and you were able to achieve your goal by using a certain type of plan. For example, a question interviewers often ask during a job interview is, "What are your weaknesses?" You can think back to an answer you used for that question, and stick with it in future interviews.

Third, all things being equal, most communicators tend to simplify their plans or make only slight alterations, rather than complicate them. If you can think of two plans to achieve a goal, the simpler plan is what you probably will choose. Furthermore, once you begin on a plan, you typically may stick to it, and only make changes sparingly as you go along. By comparison, competent communicators are likely to develop more complex plans, because they understand all the factors in a situation. For such knowledgeable communicators, producing more involved plans is efficient, because they do not need to put much effort into analyzing the possibilities. "I have several options for approaching this problem with my work team. Based on what works, I'll keep my options open, and change to Plan B if Plan A doesn't seem to work."

Indeed, competence in interpersonal relationships depends on having knowledge, and planning for its effective use in challenging and difficult communication situations. You need to consider several possible options, start with the option that has the most potential to achieve your communication goal, and be ready to shift or change it as needed. In addition to such thoughtful planning, you also need to be able to empathize and take the perspective of the other communicators.

EMPATHY AND PERSPECTIVE TAKING.

Few characteristics have so consistently challenged interpersonal communication competence as self-centeredness. Self-centered communicators think primarily of their own goals, needs, communication behaviors, and ways of doing things. In its more extreme forms, self-centeredness is revealed in a narcissistic style of interaction. As a personality trait, **narcissism** is a tendency to be outgoing, self-absorbed, but also arrogant.[12] Narcissists are more likely to pursue topics of conversation they find interesting, direct the conversation to their own topics of interest, and interrupt others during the conversation. Furthermore, narcissistic communicators tend not to see things from the other person's perspective, resulting in simplistic ways of thinking about the world.

Self-centeredness and narcissism weaken your interpersonal communication competence in several ways. Narcissists are often viewed as strong leaders or charismatic to begin with, but over time their self-centered style of interaction wears on others, and impressions of competence diminish. If a narcissist wants to get another person to do something, that person is less likely to comply, as he or she begins to view the narcissist as self-absorbed. Finally, a large part of what makes for a satisfying relationship is sharing. If you are self-centered

> NARCISSISM is a tendency to be outgoing, self-absorbed, but also arrogant.

Box 7.2: Empathy and Perspective Taking in an Interpersonal Relationship

Notice in this conversation that empathy and perspective taking did not take the form of preaching, advising, evaluating, or trying to change what the other person is feeling. In response to Person A, Person B did not say: "Hey, don't feel down—there's so much to feel good about"; or, "I felt down last week, but I got over it pretty fast." Sometimes people just want to have their feelings validated or allowed to be.

Person A offers an opportunity for empathic recognition: "I'm feeling really down today."

Person B moves to imagine and recognize Person A's experience, cognitively and affectively (emotionally): "You do seem a little depressed today. It makes me sad to see you like this. Do you want to talk about it?"

Person A confirms Person B's response: "I don't think so, but I appreciate your understanding."

---

in your communication, you do not get the benefit of what the other person has to offer to you and the relationship.

In contrast to narcissism, **empathy** is the ability to experience feelings similar to or related to those of another person. It is often confused with sympathy, but is quite different. **Sympathy** is a desire to offer support to another, generally when that person is in a difficult situation. Empathy and sympathy do not necessarily occur at the same time. If you see a person on the news who just lost a loved one in a home fire, you may sympathize by feeling sorry for that person, but not be able to empathize and feel what that person is feeling. If you see an expectant father in a hospital waiting or delivery room, you may feel empathy for him even if you have never been a father, but there may be little reason for you to feel sympathy for him.

> EMPATHY is the ability to experience feelings similar to or related to those of another person.

> SYMPATHY is a desire to offer support to another, generally when that person is in a difficult situation.

> PERSPECTIVE TAKING means seeing the world cognitively as the other person sees it.

Empathy and sympathy are affective or emotional reactions, whereas **perspective taking** means seeing the world cognitively as the other person sees it. In the examples just described, you may not feel the loss of a loved one or the excitement of a birth, but you can visualize and imagine what the people are experiencing, and the thoughts they might be thinking. So empathy primarily elicits emotions, whereas perspective taking primarily elicits thoughts and perceptions. Box 7.2 contains a short conversation in which empathy and perspective taking are combined in an interaction that otherwise could have become a challenge in an interpersonal relationship.[13] Read over the conversation to clarify for yourself how empathy and perspective taking can work together.

Competent empathy and perspective taking help you to adjust communication plans by having a better understanding of what the other person is feeling and thinking. Another way to get more information is to use any of several knowledge-gaining strategies.

KNOWLEDGE-GAINING STRATEGIES.

A critical challenge to any interpersonal relationship is simply not having enough information about what is going on in the relationship. One of the ways people acquire such knowledge is through active and interactive **knowledge-gaining strategies**, which are behaviors we use to obtain information about others or about situations.[14] Active strategies involve solitary behaviors, such as imagining something and trying it out mentally, or reading up on a situation. For example, if you were asked to go on a date to an art auction, you could do a little research on what happens and what people do at these auctions, or you could imagine what you have seen or heard about auctions. Interactive strategies involve obtaining information from others through communication. The most common interactive strategies for gaining information relevant to interpersonal communication are questioning and self-disclosure. Sticking with the art auction example, you could call the gallery, disclose that you have not been there before, and ask for a little information.

> **KNOWLEDGE-GAINING STRATEGIES** are behaviors people use to obtain information about others or about situations.

If you need more information about another person, one of the best ways to get it is to ask the person directly. Instead of assuming that Patricia would like to be called "Pat" or "Patty," you can simply ask her. You can also apply this strategy less directly, such as when you ask someone else for information about a particular person or a relationship in which you are involved. For example, you can ask a friend or associate of Patricia's whether she likes to be referred to by a nickname. You also could ask if Patricia's use of nicknames with you suggests a possible interest in going on a date or starting a relationship with you.

One last knowledge-gaining strategy actually involves self-disclosure. In Chapter Three, we described self-disclosure as the process of intentionally and voluntarily providing others with information about you. We generally use self-disclosure as a strategy for making ourselves known to others. But by making yourself known to someone else, you also make it easier to get to know the other person. Especially in the early stages of a relationship, people tend to engage in reciprocal self-disclosure.[15] As any relationship progresses, the two people engage in mutual self-disclosure, as they increasingly feel safer sharing personal information.

Acquiring knowledge of communication involves more than simply reading about it in a book—improving your communication competence also comes from trying out what you learn. What you know and what you are able to do often are quite different. In addition to the knowledge you acquired in this chapter, Chapter Eight covers the interpersonal skills critical to communication competence.

CHAPTER SUMMARY

Interpersonal communication is the process of managing messages and media to create meaning in interactions among people in social or personal relationships. Interaction refers to interdependence among the behaviors or moves of communicators in a situation. The resulting relationship is the sense of relative positioning to one another; that is, how you orient yourself or connect to one another. Every message that is communicated in any relationship occurs at a content level and a relationship level. The content level of a message is what the words mean in a literal or denotative sense. The relationship level is what a message implies about the relationship.

We store content knowledge about relationships in the form of repertoires and roles, scripts and stories, and rules and norms. A repertoire is the set of roles we can play or enact in interactions, and roles are the patterns and style of statements and behaviors we can perform across contexts. Breadth refers to the number of roles you can play, and depth to the level of familiarity you have with any role. Scripts or stories are narratives of what is expected or needs to occur in a given situation. Social norms are the explicit or implicit rules specifying what behaviors are acceptable within a society or group.

Overcoming challenges to knowledge about interpersonal communication involves planning, empathy and perspective taking, and the use of effective knowledge-gaining strategies. Planning includes anticipating and formulating possible strategies for achieving a communication goal, and using a plan to achieve the goal. In this sense, a plan is an intentional description of the actions and means needed to achieve a communication goal. To overcome the challenge of narcissism—the tendency to be outgoing, self-absorbed, but also arrogant—a communicator should demonstrate empathy, the ability to experience feelings similar to or related to those of another person. Empathy is not the same as sympathy, which involves offering support to another person, usually someone in a difficult situation. Empathy and sympathy are affective or emotional reactions, whereas perspective taking means seeing the world cognitively as the other person sees it. Knowledge-gaining strategies are behaviors people use to obtain information about others or about situations. Active strategies include imagining something and trying it out mentally, or reading about a particular situation. Interactive strategies for gaining information include questioning and self-disclosure.

KEY TERMS.

The key terms below are defined in this chapter, and presented alphabetically with definitions in the Glossary at the end of the book.

- interpersonal communication
- interaction
- relationship
- content level
- relationship level
- repertoire

- roles
- breadth
- depth
- story
- social norms
- planning
- plan

- narcissism
- empathy
- sympathy
- perspective taking
- knowledge-gaining strategies

BUILDING MOTIVATION: SELF-ASSESSMENT TOOL.

Rate each of the eight communication situations described here, indicating your own typical level of knowledge about interpersonal communication. Rate one situation all the way through for motivation, knowledge, and skills. Then rate the next situation. Use the 1–4 scale below, with 1 being minimal competence and 4 high competence.

Communication situations.

1. Interacting with a police officer who is giving you a ticket for speeding.
2. Having a dispute with your professor when you do not feel that you have received an appropriate grade in a course.
3. Discussing feeling betrayed by a good (but not your best) friend, who told others something about you that you had shared with the friend confidentially.
4. Talking with someone you are attracted to while on a first date.
5. Handling embarrassment when you say or do something really humiliating in a public setting.
6. Negotiating the purchase of your first new car with an aggressive salesperson.
7. Supporting a friend who tells you her or his mother just died unexpectedly.
8. Receiving a high compliment in a public setting, such as a comment on your attractiveness.

Motivation.

    1 =Distracted, disinterested, or simply no motivation to be competent.

    2 = Somewhat distracted or disinterested, but motivated to be competent.

    3 = Somewhat interested and motivated to be competent.

    4 = Highly interested and motivated to be competent.

Knowledge.

    1 = Completely inexperienced and ignorant about what to do and how to do it.

    2 = Minimal experience and sense of what to do and how to do it.

    3 = Somewhat experienced and knowledgeable about what to do and how to do it.

    4 = Highly knowledgeable about all aspects of what to do and how to do it.

Skills.

    1 = Completely incapable of behaving competently.

    2 = Barely capable of behaving minimally competently.

    3 = Fairly capable of behaving competently.

    4 = Highly capable of behaving competently.

Interpreting your scores.

Total your score separately for each situation (motivation, knowledge, and skills). The possible range of the score for each situation is 3–12. If your total score for any of the situations is 6 or less, you see yourself as less competent in that situation than you should be. A score of 7–9 means that you are average at sending and receiving communication messages in the situation. A score of 10–12 indicates that you have a high level of communication competence in that situation.

BUILDING KNOWLEDGE: DISCUSSION QUESTIONS.

1. Of the two levels of messages, content and relationship, which one are you least likely to be aware of? Why?

2. Identify an interpersonal situation that you think is relatively well scripted. How flexible is that script? What factors might influence changes in that script? Why?

3. Identify an interpersonal situation that you think has a lot of rules and norms associated with it, and a situation that has very few rules associated with it. What is different about these situations, and in which would you prefer to communicate? Why?

4. Think of a recent interpersonal communication encounter you found particularly challenging. How could you have used better planning to improve the outcome of the encounter?

5. Think of a recent interpersonal communication encounter you found particularly challenging. How could you have used empathy and perspective taking to improve the outcome of the encounter?

6. Think of a recent interpersonal communication encounter you found particularly challenging. How could you have used knowledge-gaining strategies to improve the outcome of the encounter?

BUILDING SKILLS: STUDENT ACTIVITIES.

Individual activities.

1. The following five problems are about familiar or everyday scripts. Answer each of them, and do not read any farther until you do so.

   a. If you had only one match, and entered a room in which there was a kerosene lamp, a wood-burning stove, and a gas fireplace, which would you light first?
   b. How many outs are in an inning of baseball?
   c. A patient is wheeled into the emergency room, and the surgeon, looking at the patient, says, "I can't operate on this patient—he's my son!" The surgeon is not the patient's father. How is this possible?
   d. You have a dime in an otherwise empty wine bottle. The bottle is corked. How do you get the dime out without removing the cork or damaging the bottle in any way?
   e. Connect the following nine dots using only straight lines, without removing your pen from the paper.

   These questions seem simple enough, but people often answer them incorrectly, or cannot answer them at all. This is in part because each of them leads you to expect a script that is not actually the appropriate script, or because each leads you to focus on the wrong part of the script. In each case, discuss what led you to apply the wrong script. In what everyday communication encounters might you apply the wrong script?

   Answers:

   a. The match. We are led to think of lighting the sources of warmth, rather than the item we use to light these sources.
   b. Six. We tend to think of baseball in terms of how many outs there are for our team. But there are two teams.
   c. The surgeon is the patient's mother. We still tend to think of surgeons as men.
   d. Push the cork in. We tend to think of wine bottles only in terms of removing the cork.
   e. Follow along as illustrated on next page. This problem tends to frustrate people because they think the nine dots form a square. We are accustomed to seeing squares, and therefore think "inside the box." The only way to solve the problem is to think "outside the box."

2. Think about the many interpersonal communication interactions you engaged in during the last 24 hours. List these interactions, and identify the role you enacted in each. Then reflect on the repertoire of communication skills you had available for enacting each of the roles.

3. One of the indirect ways we learn how to communicate is by playing roles. We often look to others to tell us what role we should play. These persons are role models. Our role models include mothers, fathers, movie stars, rock stars, and historical figures. One way of devel-

oping your knowledge in any given situation is to imagine what your role models would do in that situation. List three problematic communication situations you have experienced recently, and list the role model you would most want to follow as an example for how to behave in that situation. What would the model's response have been in each situation?

4. Think through some of the challenging interpersonal situations you have experienced (student-professor discussion about a grade, job interview, negotiating the price of a car, and so on). Choose one, and write out the script for this situation. How might you have communicated in order to change the predictability of that script?

5. For a full day, keep an interpersonal interaction diary. After each conversation of more than ten minutes, whether face-to-face or mediated, take notes on the following aspects: When did it occur? Where did it occur? How long did it last? What was your relationship with the other person? What were the main themes or topics of the conversation? What were your goals in the conversation? How competent were you and the other person? What might either of you have done to enhance the outcomes of each of the interactions?

6. Think of an important conflict you recently had with another person. Reflect on how empathy and perspective taking, and knowledge-gaining strategies may have facilitated more productive management of the conflict.

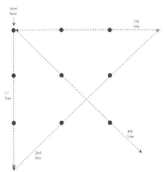

Group activities.

1. Form groups of four students. Each member should write down three strategies for gaining information on a first date. Compare your list with those generated by the other members in the group. How competent do you think these strategies would be? Would any of them violate the rules or the scripts of the first-date situation? Why?

2. Form groups of three to five students. Identify an interpersonal communication context of interest to the group. For example, your group might select an intimacy situation in which you ask someone to marry you, a confrontation situation in which you try to get a roommate to change a personal habit, a negotiation situation in which you are bargaining for a better deal on a car or computer system. Each member of your group should then individually construct his or her plan for accomplishing the communication goal. As a group, compare, discuss, and combine your plans to construct an effective script and set of rules for achieving the communication goal.

3. Form a dyad (two people) with someone you do not know very well in your class. The chart below lists several questions. Engage in a get-acquainted conversation, but do not directly ask the other person any of the questions listed in the chart. After the conversation, each member of the pair should try to answer the questions right below, even if they are guesses. Quietly write down your guesses in the space provided below.

After the conversation and the quiet writing down, compare your answers about your partner to see how accurate they are. What kinds of information can you reasonably expect to get about a person from casual conversation? What knowledge-gaining strategies would work best for you had this been a real attempt to get to know someone?

1. What is the person's religious affiliation, if any?	2. Is the person in a satisfying intimate relationship?
3. Does the person have or want to have children?	4. Is this person a political liberal, conservative, independent, or politically disinterested?
5. Is the person basically happy most of the time?	6. What is this person's favorite food or cuisine?
7. Would the person rather go to a formal ball or a casual party?	8. What career does this person want after college?
9. Where would the person most like to visit or travel to?	10. Are or were the person's parents divorced?

NOTES

1. See Robinson (2004).
2. See Watzlawick, Bavelas, & Jackson (1967).
3. See Bandura (1977).
4. See Beatty, Heisel, Hall, Levine, & La France (2002).
5. See Kruger & Dunning (1999).
6. See Afifi & Weiner (2004).
7. See Koeppel, Montagne-Miller, O'Hair, & Cody (1993).

8. See Battaglia, Richard, Datteri, & Lord (1998); Honeycutt, Cantrill, & Greene (1991); Pryor & Merluzzi (1985); and Rose & Frieze (1993).

9. See Dailey, Pfiester, Jin, Beck, & Clark (2009).

10. See Duran & Spitzberg (1995).

11. See Berger (2003).

12. See Foster & Twenge (2011).

13. See Wynn & Wynn (2006).

14. See Berger & Bradac (1982).

15. See Ignatius & Kokkonen (2007).

REFERENCES

Afifi, W. A., & Weiner, J. L. (2004). Toward a theory of motivated information management. *Communication Theory*, *14*(2), 167–190.

Bandura, A. (1977). *Social learning theory*. Englewood Cliffs, NJ: Prentice-Hall.

Battaglia, D. M., Richard, F. D., Datteri, D. L., & Lord, C. G. (1998). Breaking up is (relatively) easy to do: A script for the dissolution of close relationships. *Journal of Social and Personal Relationships*, *15*(6), 829–845.

Beatty, M. J., Heisel, A. D., Hall, A. E., Levine, T. R., & La France, B. H. (2002). What can we learn from the study of twins about genetic and environmental influences on interpersonal affiliation, aggressiveness, and social anxiety? A meta-analytic study. *Communication Monographs*, *69*(1), 1–18.

Berger, C. R. (2003). Message production skill in social interaction. In J. O. Greene & B. R. Burleson (Eds.), *Handbook of communication and social interaction skills* (pp. 257–290). Mahwah, NJ: Erlbaum.

Berger, C. R., & Bradac, J. J. (1982). *Language and social knowledge: Uncertainty in interpersonal relations*. London, UK: Edward Arnold.

Besser, S. M., et al. (Producers) & Reed, P. (Director). (2006). *The break-up* [Motion picture]. U.S.: Universal Pictures.

Dailey, R. M., Pfiester, A., Jin, B., Beck, G., & Clark, G. (2009). On-again/off-again dating relationships: How are they different from other dating relationships. *Personal Relationships*, *16*(1), 23–47.

Duran, R. L., & Spitzberg, B. H. (1995). Toward the development and validation of a measure of cognitive communication competence. *Communication Quarterly*, *43*(3), 259–275.

Foster, J. D., & Twenge, J. M. (2011). Narcissism and relationships: From light to dark. In W. R. Cupach & B. H. Spitzberg (Eds.), *The dark side of close relationships* (2nd ed., pp. 381–407). New York, NY: Routledge/Taylor & Francis.

Honeycutt, J. M., Cantrill, J. G., & Greene, R. W. (1991). Memory structures for relational escalation: A cognitive test of the sequencing of relational actions and strategies. *Human Communication Research*, *16*(1), 62–90.

Ignatius, E., & Kokkonen, M. (2007). Factors contributing to verbal self-disclosure. *Nordic Psychology*, *59*(4), 362–391.

Koeppel, L. B., Montagne-Miller, Y., O'Hair, D., & Cody, M. J. (1993). Friendly? Flirting? Wrong? In P. J. Kalbfleisch (Ed.), *Interpersonal communication: Evolving interpersonal relationships* (pp. 13–32). Hillsdale, NJ: Erlbaum.

Kruger, J., & Dunning, D. (1999). Unskilled and unaware of it: How difficulties in recognizing one's own incompetence lead to inflated self-assessments. *Journal of Personality and Social Psychology*, *77*(6), 1121–1134.

Pryor, J. B., & Merluzzi, T. V. (1985). The role of expertise in processing social interaction scripts. *Journal of Experimental Social Psychology*, *21*(4), 362–379.

Robinson, J. D. (2004). The sequential organization of "explicit" apologies in naturally occurring English. *Research on Language and Social Interaction*, *37*(3), 291–330.

Rose, S., & Frieze, I. H. (1993). Young singles' contemporary dating scripts. *Sex Roles*, *28*(9–10), 499–509.

Watzlawick, P., Bavelas, J. B., & Jackson, D. D. (1967). *Pragmatics of human communication: A study of interactional patterns, pathologies, and paradoxes*. New York, NY: W.W. Norton.

Wynn, R., & Wynn, M. (2006). Empathy as an interactionally achieved phenomenon in psychotherapy: Characteristics of some conversational resources. *Journal of Pragmatics*, *38*(9), 1385–1397.

CHAPTER EIGHT

INTERPERSONAL COMMUNICATION

DEVELOPING SKILLS

The genius of communication is the ability to be both totally honest and totally kind at the same time. —John Joseph Powell, S. J., Jesuit Priest and Author (1925–2009)

.
. .

Nancy and Don have been living together for a few months, after dating for a year. They met and then graduated from the same college together. Nancy works as a paralegal at a downtown law firm, and Don works largely from home as a sales manager for an event planning firm. Nancy comes home from work to find Don focused on a computer screen, busily clicking through scheduled items on his calendar.

D: Hey, Hon, you're home . . . how was your day?

N: Exhausting. What's for dinner?

D: We'll figure something. Listen, what are you doing tomorrow afternoon?

N: Why, what's up?

D: My staff is playing our rival company in a corporate softball tournament. We're playing them at two.

N: [sarcastically] Wow. Sounds really thrilling. . . . No, I should work on a draft of a brief that's due to my boss on Monday.

D: You never seem to have time for my corporate events.

N: This isn't a corporate event—it's a bunch of wannabe jocks with an excuse to drink.

D: I wish you would be a little more enthusiastic about what I do.

N: [exasperated] Fine. I'll go to your little game.

D: Forget it! Stay here and I'll make excuses to the guys for you again.

N: What's the big deal—it's not like it really matters.

D: You know, I wish you would take a little more interest in my career. These games are a way of maintaining morale and making contacts. Besides, I always go to your office events.

N: My events serve catered food! Look, why would I want to watch a bunch of people running around bases all day.

D: You just don't get it.

N: What's not to get? I just don't find the idea of going to your game a good use of my time.

D: I suppose you also don't think this relationship is a good use of your time.

N: I'm beginning to have my doubts.

.

Conflicts and arguments often bring out the worst in people.[1] One reason is that many of us have never learned, or had the opportunity, to refine competent interpersonal skills for managing conflict. Don and Nancy's conflict seems to be about a game and a schedule conflict, but clearly it is about other things, such as whether or not they value one another's careers, and ultimately, whether they value their relationship. Neither attempts to take the other's position, and they seem to have difficulty getting to the underlying issues. They may have the skills to manage the conflict, but neither seems to be using their motivation or knowledge to enact those skills.

Ultimately, most of what we know about any communicator is what we observe through her or his behavior, or what we learn through conversations. Because we cannot know exactly what other people are thinking or feeling, we often infer things from their actions and behavior. The behavior we observe in conversations, like Nancy and Don's, reflects the competence of their communication skills. This chapter examines communication skills in conversations. It is primarily through such conversations that people create, maintain, cause problems for, and end relationships. Of course, sometimes these conversations happen online, or use cell phones, which are discussed at the end of this chapter. We begin now with a description of the nature of communication skills as they relate to interpersonal communication.

UNDERSTANDING INTERPERSONAL SKILLS

Much practical information about communication competence comes across as intuitive or common sense. And as we pointed out in Chapter Seven, people generally believe they are more communicatively skilled than they actually are. This overestimation is actually part of their problem, as it contributes to their inability to communicate competently.[2, 3] In job settings, for example, your own view of your skills is less predictive of your career success than other people's view of your skills.[4] Yet most people continue to assume that they are competent communicators. To be blunt, most of us are probably not as good at using communication skills as we think we are, and this is especially true the higher your self-confidence and self-esteem.[5] Even though most of us can get through everyday conversations using common sense and intuition, we may not really understand the principles and general communication skills critical to competence in everyday interactions and conversations.

CHARACTERISTICS OF SKILLS.

As defined in Chapter Two, a skill is a repeatable, goal-oriented sequence of actions enacted in a given context.[6] To clarify, **skills** are behaviors directed toward the achievement of preferred outcomes in a context. Several key concepts help explain this simple notion.

Actions are the behaviors performed by a person. They are not the same thing as motivation, knowledge, or ability. You do not enact all the behaviors you are able to perform in every conversation. You select which behaviors to enact on the basis of motivation and knowledge, and the characteristics of message needed to achieve the particular goal.[7] The more motivated you are, the more consciously you search your knowledge for the best possible behaviors to select. The more knowledgeable you are, the broader and deeper your repertoire of behaviors from which to select. Finally, when we speak of skills, it refers to the actions you enact as a result of these motivation and knowledge processes.

SKILLS are behaviors directed toward the achievement of preferred outcomes in a context.

ACTIONS are the behaviors performed by a person.

Since a skill is a set of behaviors directed toward achieving a goal, the more of your goals you achieve through communication, the more effective you are. Goals generally define the skill itself. The goal of managing conflict relates to *conflict skills*. *Assertiveness skills* refer to the goal of asserting your rights. *Argumentation skills* refer to the goal of constructing arguments. So all communication skills achieve some outcome. The effectiveness with which they achieve these outcomes determines the quality of the skill itself, and, in large part, your effectiveness. In our opening story, Don and Nancy displayed rather poor conflict management skills because neither seemed to achieve their desired goals.

Skills are repeatable. As mentioned in Chapter Seven, you might tell a joke with all the right inflections and delivery one time, but not the next time. Such subtleties can make all the difference in telling a joke, and the skill of telling it is in the ability to perform it similarly, or better, as called for in new situations. Skills are also related to the context. Smiling after telling a joke is different than smiling in response to someone else's joke. Given that different contexts involve different goals, clearly skills that will be effective vary according to the context.

Skills exist at many different levels of abstraction, as mentioned in Chapter Two. The **level of abstraction** for communication behaviors ranges from micro skills to macro skills. **Micro-level** skills include such behaviors as gestures, eye contact, smiling, vocabulary, articulation, and vocal variety. **Macro-level** skills represent the assembly of micro-level skills to create the performance of general skills such as assertiveness, self-disclosure, social support, conflict management, deception, and wit or use of humor. If micro-level skills are the bricks and mortar of communication, macro-level skills are the actual rooms built from the bricks and mortar. And selecting the right micro-level interpersonal skill for the relevant macro-level interpersonal skill you want to carry out affects whether you are perceived as competent.

> **LEVEL OF ABSTRACTION** refers to the range of communication behaviors from specific or micro-level skills to general or macro-level skills.

> **MICRO-LEVEL SKILLS** include such behaviors as gestures, eye contact, smiling, vocabulary, articulation, vocal variety, and so forth.

> **MACRO-LEVEL SKILLS** represent the assembly of specific- or micro-level skills to create the performance of general skills such as assertiveness, self-disclosure, social support, conflict management, deception, and wit.

Most of us at some point have had a job interview in which we used a variety of micro-level communication skills—we made eye contact, used humor, answered questions, avoided interruptions, and so forth—but we did not get the job. There was just something the interviewer did not like about us. That reaction may have related to using micro-level skills that did not work effectively with the macro-level skills of assertiveness and confidence we wanted to showcase for the interviewer. This illustrates one of the most important lessons about communication skills—*they are not the same thing as competence.* Skills are behaviors, but any given behaviors can be viewed as competent by some and incompetent by others. As noted in Chapter Two, motivation, knowledge, and skills make it more *likely* you will be perceived as competent, but they do not guarantee your competence.[8] Competence rests in the *perception* that skills have been performed appropriately and effectively.

This distinction between impressions and behaviors is central to interpersonal competence. A given set of behaviors comprises a skill. But the competence of the skill still depends on how it is perceived, interpreted, and evaluated. Fortunately, such impressions are rarely arbitrary. In any given culture, certain types of skills and behaviors are more likely to be viewed as more competent than others. The question, then, is which skills are most likely to be viewed as competent? The following section addresses this question.

TYPES OF INTERPERSONAL SKILLS.

If competence varies from context to context, how can you hope to develop a set of skills that helps you communicate competently across contexts? Consider that the rules of sports differ widely, but most still require eye-hand coordination, fast reflexes, and endurance. Similarly, even though communication contexts vary considerably, certain interpersonal skills are important across these contexts.

The communication skills we discuss here represent four general or macro-level skills useful in all interpersonal contexts—the skills of attentiveness, composure, coordination, and expressiveness. Micro-level or specific skills are the building blocks of these four general skills.[9,6] But any given specific skill can help support more than one of the general skills. Figure 8.1 shows how some of the specific skills support more than one general skill. Expression of personal opinions, for example, is clearly an aspect of a communicator's expressiveness. In addition, expressing personal opinions also reveals a person's sense of composure and confidence in speaking up for himself or herself. Seeing these four skills displayed in a straightforward way may make them seem simple. However, there are many challenges to their competent use that we discuss later in this chapter, after looking at each of the skills in more detail.

Figure 8.1: Macro Skills Comprised of Micro Skills

The four general macro-level skills of interpersonal communication are made up of smaller, specific microskills, some of which support more than one general skill.

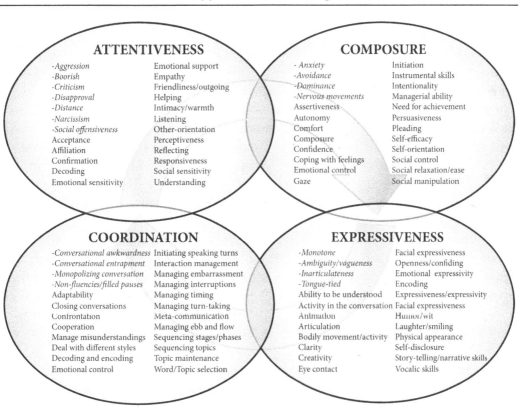

Attentiveness is the general interpersonal skill of showing interest in, concern for, and attention to the other person or persons in the interaction. It is the ability to involve the person with whom you are communicating in the interaction, and to demonstrate your own involvement with that person's contribution to the conversation. Attentiveness significantly overlaps with listening, the topic of Chapter Six, but it is also distinct in many ways. The goal of attentiveness is not to understand exactly what the other person is saying; rather it is to behave in ways that support and involve the other person in the interaction. Such attentiveness can take many forms, only some of which include listening skills.

Two closely related aspects of attentiveness that can greatly improve or impair this skill are topic development and time management. **Topic development** is the management of the subject under discussion in a conversation. Topic development progresses in two basic ways, using topic shifts and questions. A **topic shift** is a move of the conversation away from one subject of discussion to another. This skill, when used carefully, can show competence, because it requires careful attention to the other person's topic in order to make a transition to another topic smoothly. However, most people want to talk about a topic of interest to themselves, and this is where the second skill of topic development is relevant: questioning.

Questions, by verbally soliciting information, alert the other person as to where the topic and discussion are going. You can influence topic development using two types of questions. **Open-ended questions** permit the other person wide discretion in how to answer. They contrast with **closed-ended questions**, which give the other person very limited options in answering. For example, "What's your major?" and "Where were you born?" are closed-ended as they generally call for one-word answers. In contrast, consider the following questions: "What got you interested in your major?" and "What, if anything, do you miss about where you were born?" These concern the same topics as the closed-ended questions, but they encourage the other person to become much more involved in the process of developing the topic.

The second aspect of topic development that can improve or impair attentiveness is **time management**, the skill of balancing the amount of time each communicator gets to speak during a conversation. Achieving the right balance in speaking time is crucial to attentiveness and therefore competent communication. Research shows that people are perceived as more competent the more time they spend speaking, but only up to a point. When someone begins talking 70%, 80%, or 90% of the time, rather than letting others take their turn, this person tends to be viewed as egotistical and manipulative, and thus less competent.[10]

Composure, the second general interpersonal skill, relates to appearing in control of one's communication behavior. The main reason people fail to manage their composure is anxiety. Virtually everyone has experienced communication anxiety in public-speaking contexts. However, anxiety in interpersonal situations is very common as well. **Social anxiety** is the real or imagined fear of

ATTENTIVENESS is the skill of showing interest in, concern for, and attention to the other person or persons in the interaction.

TOPIC DEVELOPMENT is the management of the subject under discussion in a conversation.

A TOPIC SHIFT is a move of the conversation away from one subject of discussion to another.

OPEN-ENDED QUESTIONS permit the other person wide discretion in how to answer.

CLOSED-ENDED QUESTIONS give the respondent very limited options in answering.

TIME MANAGEMENT refers to the skill of balancing the amount of time each communicator gets to speak during a conversation.

COMPOSURE is the skill of appearing in control of one's communication behavior.

interacting in an interpersonal encounter. Social situations can seem threatening, because we derive so much of our self-concept from what we think others think of us. Generally speaking, the more formal the situation, the more unfamiliar, and the more important the goals, the more nervous people become.

When someone experiences anxiety across a wide variety of social situations over an extended period of time, it generally is known as **shyness**, a tendency to withdraw from social activities. Shy people may not appear very different from others in a given situation, but they are less likely to initiate or actively participate in conversations. That said, some cultures, such as many Asian cultures, value more unassertive communication styles, and their members may seem shyer than others. In these cultures, conversational shyness does not necessarily reflect incompetence.[11] However, it is possible to be shy even by the standards of a relatively unassertive culture.

Social anxiety and shyness make it more difficult for people to meet their needs and goals in interactions. Generally speaking, you do not get a date if you do not ask or accept, you do not get a job if you do not interview for it, and your partner does not know how much you love him or her if you do not communicate it. The specific behaviors resulting from social anxiety and a deficit of composure are probably familiar. Avoiding eye contact, fidgeting, tripping over words, speaking quietly with a quavering voice, initiating speaking turns less often, and displaying an impression of nervousness are all behaviors that result from a deficit in composure skills. In comparison, positive composure skills are associated with confidence, dynamism, and charisma. Such skills tend to result in more fluent speech, a steadier vocal tone and louder volume, more confident and expressive gestures, and greater eye contact.

SOCIAL ANXIETY is the real or imagined fear of interacting in an interpersonal encounter.

SHYNESS is a tendency to withdraw from social activities.

ASSERTIVENESS is the skill of expressing one's rights or views without violating another's rights or views.

AGGRESSIVE COMMUNICATION refers to the expression of your rights or views in a way that violates other's rights or views.

PASSIVE COMMUNICATION is the avoidance of self-expression, or the accommodation to others' concerns over your own.

Composed communicators initiate more speaking turns, spend more time talking, and appear more in control of the course the conversation takes. These specific skills result in the appearance of assertiveness. **Assertiveness** is the skill of expressing one's rights or views without violating another's rights or views. It is the ability to give voice to your interests, position, needs, desires, and opinions in a way that is appropriate to the context. Assertiveness is different from its alternatives, aggression and passivity. **Aggressive communication** is the expression of your rights or views in a way that violates other's rights or views. It generally represents an excess of composure, in that all you care about are your own motives. Finally, **passive communication** is the **avoidance** of self-expression, or the accommodation to others' concerns over your own.

Interestingly, research shows that most people "think" a better game than they actually enact or perform.[12] That is, in the abstract, it is easy to believe you would say something competently in most situations, but sometimes people do not. Most of us often are nervous about causing trouble, disrupting a situation, or drawing attention to ourselves. Others think that if they assert themselves, they will be seen as rude or aggressive. Indeed, when assertiveness is performed with abruptness and intensity, it is often interpreted as aggressive. Some of the distinctions among assertive, aggressive, and passive communication are discussed in Box 8.1 on conflict, assertiveness, and competence.

Coordination, the third general interpersonal skill, involves managing the ebb and flow of the interaction. Coordination regulates whose turn it is to speak, development of topics for discussion,

Box 8.1: Conflict, Assertiveness, and Competence

Conflict tends to bring out the worst in people for an array of complex reasons that we need to be aware of and understand.

Conflict is difficult to manage in part because it pits the competence dimensions of effectiveness and appropriateness against one another. You are trying to be effective by achieving your goals. However, in your attempt to pursue effectiveness, you are likely to be perceived as inappropriate. Plus, the other person's attempts at keeping you from achieving your goals will in turn seem inappropriate to you.

Research on competence in conflict has identified three general conflict skills: avoidance, distributive, and integrative skills. **Avoidance skills** function to displace conflict. You postpone the conflict to another time or place to avoid dealing with the issue, or you sidetrack the interaction so that it is forgotten or redirected. Avoidance often means shifting the topic of discussion, postponing the discussion until later, or simply leaving the situation when the conflict seems ready to get out of hand. In the opening vignette, Don could have asked to talk with Nancy at a later time, or he might have started talking about what to do about dinner. Avoidance is commonly assumed to be an incompetent approach to conflict, but sometimes it helps communicators avoid escalating a destructive conflict.[13]

The second conflict skill is distributive interaction. **Distributive skills** attempt to divide, that is, distribute, the outcomes of the conflict so that you win more than the other person. It is a maximizing and aggressive approach to communication. Deception, competition, persistent arguing, yelling, criticizing, complaining, and refusing to admit fault are all forms of distributive communication. There are times when we need to behave in very competitive ways, and some communicators are clearly better at it than others. However, generally speaking, the more that communicators use these skills, the more incompetent they are perceived to be.[14] Certainly, Don and Nancy engaged in their share of distributive communication in the opening story, and viewed each other's approaches to the disagreement as incompetent.

The final conflict skill is integrative communication. Whereas distributive skills attempt to divide the outcomes of the conflict, **integrative skills** attempt to bring your goals and the other person's goals together, so that both of you can achieve what you want. It requires careful interaction that uncovers both persons' goals, clarifies the importance of these goals, identifies possible options, and develops a plan to achieve everyone's interests. Had Don and Nancy calmed down and discussed ways in which Don might be able to help around the home to give Nancy more time to work on her brief, it would have illustrated an integrative approach to the conflict.

Research on conflict has made several things clear about these skills.[15] For example, in any given situation or context, any one of these skills can be competent.[16] Sometimes, it is best to avoid a conflict rather than let your anger loose.[17] Sometimes, distributive skills are the only way to escape being exploited by someone who is determined to be distributive, such as in negotiating for the best price on a car. In fact, any of these skills *can* be perceived as competent, and linked to relational satisfaction in some situations.[18] However, competing behavior, particularly aggressive competitive behavior, tends to be viewed as relatively less competent most of the time. Conversely, across most situations, collaborative behavior tends to be viewed as the most competent.[16]

AVOIDANCE SKILLS function to displace conflict.

DISTRIBUTIVE SKILLS attempt to divide, that is, distribute, the outcomes of the conflict so that you win more than the other person.

INTEGRATIVE SKILLS attempt to bring your goals and the other person's goals together so both of you can achieve what you want.

Table 8.1: General Interpersonal Skills

These four general skills—attentiveness, composure, coordination, and expressiveness—are made up of many specific skills. All are critical to communication competence in any interpersonal interaction or conversation.

GENERAL MACRO-LEVEL SKILL	DEFINITION OF THE SKILL	DESCRIPTION OF THE SKILL
ATTENTIVENESS	The skill of showing interest in, concern for, and attention to the other person or persons in the interaction.	Involves the competent use of topic development, topic shifting, open-ended and closed-ended questions, and time management.
COMPOSURE	The skill of appearing in control of one's communication behavior.	Is negatively affected by social anxiety and shyness, aggressive and passive communication. Benefits from assertiveness and integrative skills rather than avoidance skills or distributive skills.
COORDINATION	The skill of managing the ebb and flow of the interaction.	Includes the use of talkovers, deep interruptions, and topic initiation.
EXPRESSIVENESS	The skill of animating verbal and nonverbal communication.	Calls for adaptability and consistency, and the avoidance of conversational narcissism.

and entering, maintaining, and exiting conversations. The skill of coordination generally is considered competent when people engage in a conversation that is viewed as smooth rather than awkward.

Smooth conversation also implies that communicators do not interfere excessively with each other's efforts to contribute to the interaction. Like most people, you might think this means avoiding interrupting others, which most of us believe to be a general rule of conversation. However, this rule's inaccuracy illustrates just how imperfect our intuition about communication can be. When we study everyday conversations word by word and turn by turn, we find that interruptions are both complex and common. They also tend not to be disruptive; on the contrary, most of the time, they are even considered competent forms of helping to manage conversations.[19] The two most common forms of interruptions are talkovers and deep interruptions.

Talkovers are instances in which you say something during someone else's turn to talk, usually during natural pauses or near the end of the other speaker's sentences. Most of these interruptions provide feedback to the speaker that his or her words are understood or need clarification. As you saw in Chapter Six in the discussion on responding skills, expressions such as "Hm-hm," "yeah,"

COORDINATION is the skill of managing the ebb and flow of the interaction.

TALKOVERS are instances in which you say something during someone else's turn to talk.

"uh-huh," "Really?" "You're kidding," and so on, are common expressions inserted while another person is speaking to display listener involvement.

Deep interruptions are interruptions that take over a speaker's turn in the middle of that person's statement. This is what most people mean when they warn us not to interrupt others. However, even deep interruptions are not always disruptive or incompetent. In lively groups, members often are so excited about working toward their common goal that they build on each other's thoughts before the speaker is finished talking. These deep interrupters sometimes are perceived as less appropriate but more dynamic, and they tend to be effective in gaining a turn at talk.[20]

DEEP INTERRUPTIONS are interruptions that take over a speaker's turn in the middle of that person's statement.

TOPIC INITIATION refers to introducing topics for discussion.

EXPRESSIVENESS is the skill of animating verbal and nonverbal communication.

One of the reasons for interruptions is that silences and pauses, even extremely short silences, are the doorways through which people generally get a turn in a conversation. Any pause of one second or more is typically seen as representing some kind of problem in the conversation.[21] Most of the time, a second is all most of us need to pick up on the next turn to talk.

Avoiding silences reflects another coordination skill, **topic initiation**, which involves introducing topics for discussion. Competent topic initiation typically means introducing topics of interest to all the communicators, as well as relevant to the conversation at hand. It also can mean continuing threads of topics from previous conversations, which adds a dimension of cohesiveness. This cohesiveness of topics over the course of a conversation is highly flexible. You may frequently wonder how you got from the beginning topic of a conversation to the topic you are currently discussing. Yet, if you were to trace the turn-by-turn shift of topics, you would see that each turn represents a reasonable and relevant extension of the previous topics.

Expressiveness, the fourth general interpersonal skill, is about animating verbal and nonverbal communication. Expressiveness makes communication behavior lively, varied, and colorful. It serves as the primary avenue for displaying emotion in interactions, as well as getting across your meaning and intentions. As described in Chapter Five on nonverbal communication, this skill relies heavily on an array of observable nonverbal cues.

If you have experienced a conversation with someone with an emotionally flat vocal tone, you quickly realize that such a voice detracts from communication competence. The skill of expressiveness is also evident in nonverbal messages sent though facial expressions and eyes. In most contexts, people who are more facially expressive are perceived as more competent and attractive,[22] and the resulting interactions are judged as more satisfying.[23] Even something as simple as a smile can positively affect people's impressions of a communicator.[24] In short, facial expressiveness generally enhances perceptions of a communicator's competence.[25]

Collectively, expressiveness skills have a great influence on whether or not people find you interesting. One way of thinking about the value of expressiveness is to think of how you might describe a boring communicator. Boring communicators are passive, tedious, sometimes unemotional and self-focused, and they seem to engage only in small talk or the use of trite sayings.[26] Obviously, the opposite characteristics and related skills are the goal of a competent communicator.

The four general or macro-level skills—attentiveness, composure, coordination, and expressiveness—are summarized for you in Table 8.1. Review that list, and then we close this chapter with a discussion of three major challenges to interpersonal communication.

OVERCOMING CHALLENGES TO INTERPERSONAL COMMUNICATION SKILLS

We use the four general communication skills in all our interpersonal interactions. Each one of these skills is made up of many more specific skills. In every instance of interpersonal communication, we attempt to manage these skills to effectively achieve our goals in a way appropriate to the context. Given the number, subtlety, and complexity of these interpersonal communication skills, it is not surprising that we face several challenges to our competence. The major challenges are balancing adaptability and consistency, balancing self-interests versus other-interests, and enhancing our computer-mediated competence.

ADAPTABILITY AND CONSISTENCY.

Our tendency to rely on habit and routine creates a related challenge we can refer to as excessive consistency. If we become too consistent and predictable, we may become boring. To overcome this challenge, people need to balance adaptability with consistency in their communication skills.[27] **Adaptability** is the ability to alter skills appropriately as contexts and conversations evolve and change. **Consistency** means maintaining similar or predictable ways of behaving across contexts and conversations. Although these skills are the opposite of one another, a balance of the two is essential to interpersonal communication competence.

ADAPTABILITY is the ability to alter skills appropriately as contexts and conversations evolve and change.

CONSISTENCY means maintaining similar ways of behaving across contexts and conversations.

CONVERSATIONAL NARCISSISM is the appearance in your communication of caring only about yourself.

We rely on others to be at least somewhat predictable. For instance, we trust most people to speak the truth as they know it most of the time. We expect others to respond to what we say in a relatively appropriate manner. This consistency in our conversational partner's communication skills permits us to concentrate on conversational goals without second-guessing every aspect of the encounter. If nothing were predictable, every interaction would require a huge amount of effort just to coordinate basic communication activities.

To a large extent, each new communication interaction does bring with it a variety of predictable behaviors, but also a variety of new behaviors and experiences. Competence in these interactions requires a skillful balancing of adaptability and consistency. The communicators need to be somewhat consistent in their behaviors, but simultaneously able to adapt or alter what they say and do as needed in the situation. If the person you are talking with veers off in a direction you did not expect, or introduces a new topic you did not anticipate to the discussion, you need to be able to "go with the flow," so to speak. In short, competence means changing your communication behaviors, but against a backdrop of consistency and dependability.

SELF-INTERESTS AND OTHER-INTERESTS.

When communicating, most of us have something we want to achieve, and, in the process, we often pay little attention to what others are trying to achieve. Balancing this pursuit of your own goals with the other person's goals is a key challenge to competent interaction. Too much self-satisfaction becomes narcissistic, whereas too much satisfaction of others' goals becomes submissive or passive. Extremes of self-satisfying behaviors can result in **conversational narcissism**, which is the appearance in your communication of caring only about yourself.[28] Recall that we already introduced the notion of narcissism in Chapter Seven. Conversational narcissism is displayed through self-praising or defensive statements, interruptions and other attempts to control a conversation, uninvolved responses to others' statements, lengthy and frequent speaking turns, excessive self-disclosure, and showy or exhibitionist behavior.[29] Surely, this type of conversationalist is to be avoided whenever possible. However, research suggests that the average U.S. college student today is about 30% more narcissistic and 30% less empathic than three decades ago.[30, 31] This implies that in the United States at least, conversations may be increasingly self-focused and inattentive, and that we may be communicating within a very "me" generation and culture.

Some interpersonal skills are directed toward satisfying your goals, whereas other skills are directed toward satisfying others' goals. Composure and expressiveness are largely self-focused skills. Composure is about controlling your own behavior, and expressiveness is about giving voice to your own experiences, feelings, and thoughts. But if you concentrate too much on expressiveness and composure, you may appear narcissistic or self-focused. And if you display the skills of coordination and attentiveness too much, you may be perceived as lacking individuality. But think back now to the unproductive discussion of Don and Nancy in our opening story. They were unable to balance their self-interests versus the interests of the other person. The result was a stalemate about a question as simple as attending a softball tournament for a couple hours.

We now examine a final challenge to interpersonal communication that is truly omnipresent in 21st-century relationships.

IMPACT OF COMPUTER-MEDIATED COMMUNICATION ON INTERPERSONAL SKILLS.

The world is increasingly experiencing rapid diffusion of new communication technologies that present new challenges as well as opportunities. As an example of the opportunities, consider the breadth and scope of *Facebook* as a communication medium. Box 8.2 shows that *Facebook* is global, and extensively adopted and used. Over half of the U.S. population uses a social media site, and for the most part, that is *Facebook*. Although *Twitter* is as familiar as *Facebook*, only 8% of people in the United States over the age of 12 use it. About a quarter of U.S. *Facebook* users check their site or services multiple times a day, and about half of this checking occurs through mobile access.[32] Yet, substantial percentages of *Facebook* users are experiencing interpersonal communication problems, such as being denied or ignored for a friend request, disparate friend rankings, excessive intrusion or surveillance, jealousy because of posts on others' sites, ignored questions or remarks, detrimental or uncontrollable gossip, disparaging remarks, restricted access to another's page, being excluded from groups, and being dropped or removed as a friend.[33]

In other words, *Facebook* may be a different medium than face-to-face interaction, but it is still subject to many of the same forms of incompetence as face-to-face interactions.

As we think about the extent to which people are communicating using computers and the Internet, the macro-level interpersonal skills of attentiveness, composure, coordination, and expressiveness appear to have their counterparts in these new media.[34]

Attentiveness on the computer consists of adding a personal touch to the message. For example, in an online business letter you can still direct questions to the recipient, and show an awareness of past correspondence and messages. To show interest, you might begin a business e-mail memo with a question or pleasant comment of some kind. As with natural media, responding rapidly and rel-

Box 8.2: Facebook Statistics

As a form of social media, Facebook has experienced amazing growth since its launch in February, 2004.

PEOPLE ON FACEBOOK

- As of March 2012, there were 901 million active users per month
- On average, there are 526 million active users per day (as of March 2012)
- The average U.S. Facebook user has 200-250 friends (Hampton, Goulet, Marlow, & Rainie, 2012; Ugander, Karrer, Backstrom, & Marlow, 2011)
- The average person on Facebook is 3 to 5 degrees of separation from any other user (Backstrom, Boldi, Rosa, Ugander, & Vigna, 2012; Ugander et al., 2011)

ACTIVITY ON FACEBOOK

- Approximately 500 million mobile users of Facebook
- Approximately 400 million Facebook users access it at a minimum of 6 of the last 7 days
- The average U.S. Facebook user sends a friend request, receives a friend request, and accepts a friend request approximately 4 times in a typical month (Hampton et al., 2012)
- Approximately 300 million photos were uploaded on an average day
- Over 3 billion "Likes" and "Comments" messages per day

GLOBAL REACH

- Over three-quarters of active monthly users are outside North America
- Accessible in over 70 languages worldwide
- A Facebook user who has 100 friends will also have "27,500 unique friends of friends and 40,300 non-unique friends of friends" (Ugander et al., 2011, p. 8)

Source: *All information from the following source unless noted otherwise: http://newsroom.fb.com/content/default.aspx?NewsAreaId=22

evantly to someone's message shows attention. The medium alters the way in which attentiveness is shown, but not its importance.

Composure in a mediated environment is reflected in your knowledge of and mastery of both the medium and your communication behavior using that medium. A person who knows more about a medium and how to use it is generally going to come across as more composed. A person who meets the challenges of using new software programs and technologies displays more confidence than a technophobe. Some people go out of their way to learn how to set up their own Web pages. Others may only enter online environments "lurking" rather than contributing, and they will appear less composed and confident.

Coordination in the computer-mediated environment involves managing time and relevance. Senders who manage their time competently send and respond to messages when they should, and with messages that are neither too long nor too dense. Some people send e-mail messages that are too long for people to read, whereas others are so brief that their messages appear terse, and often need more elaboration. Some studies also suggest that people become too personal when communicating by computer, disclosing too much too fast.[35] If such rapid escalation of intimacy seems inappropriate to one of the communicators, it suggests a lack of sensitivity and coordination. Knowing what is acceptable to talk about and what is *not* acceptable is critical to competent online communication.

Expressiveness in the computer-mediated environment relates to the richness of the message. Richness describes how alive and animated a message seems to be. When e-mail first became popular, people realized the limited extent to which it could convey emotions. They began to invent emoticons, or icons that conveyed the emotion underlying a verbal statement, and acronyms and abbreviations to make messages more efficient. By 2011, there were over 2,000 recognized acronyms (see http://www.netlingo.com/acronyms.php), although for most of us, the "top 50" listed on this website would be sufficient for most of our everyday interactions (http://www.netlingo.com/top50/popular-text-terms.php). Emoticons are not the only way to enhance the expressiveness of a cold medium. Using colorful word choices, creating interesting avatars, including visual information such as photos or videos, and creating more rather than less interactive forms of media all reflect greater richness.

Now, think back again to the negative interaction between Nancy and Don in our opening story. Despite the fact that they were communicating face-to-face, they obviously did not use the interpersonal skills of attentiveness, composure, coordination, and expressiveness in their brief conversation about Don's corporate event. They did not adapt their communication behavior to one another, and both appeared more concerned about self-interests than other-interests. Were they in class with you, and had they read this chapter on interpersonal skills, they may have solved their problems more competently, and been better off as a result.

CHAPTER SUMMARY

Communication competence appears intuitive or commonsense, when in fact it depends on our effective and appropriate use of communication skills. A skill is a repeatable, goal-oriented sequence of actions or behaviors performed by a person. Skills vary along a level of abstraction, from micro-level, specific skills, such as gesturing or making eye contact, to macro-level, general skills, such as being assertive, self-disclosing, or providing social support. The more skilled you are, generally the more likely it is that you are perceived, by yourself and others, as a competent communicator.

We adapt our skills to various contexts, but certain sets of macro or general skills are used across most interpersonal communication situations. The four macro-level skills most common across communication encounters are attentiveness, composure, coordination, and expressiveness. The macro-level skill of attentiveness consists of behaviors that display interest in and concern for others. To use this skill competently, you need to know how to develop topics, shift topics, use open-ended and closed-ended questions, and manage time in conversations. The macro-level skill of composure relates to appearing in control of one's communication behavior. Composure is negatively affected by social anxiety, shyness, and aggressive or passive behaviors, whereas it is enhanced by the competent use of assertive behaviors and integrative skills, rather than avoidance or distributive skills. The macro-level skill of coordination involves managing the ebb and flow of interactions. Talkovers and deep interruptions are allowable, and topic initiation is a recommended coordination skill. The macro-level skill of expressiveness is about animation in verbal and nonverbal behaviors.

The three challenges to using all of these skills effectively and appropriately are: balancing adaptability with consistency, balancing self- with other-interests, and enhancing our interpersonal skills when we use mediated forms of communication.

KEY TERMS.

The key terms below are defined in this chapter, and presented alphabetically with definitions in the Glossary at the end of the book.

- skills
- actions
- level of abstraction
- micro-level skills
- macro-level skills
- attentiveness
- topic development
- topic shift
- open-ended questions
- closed-ended questions

- time management
- composure
- social anxiety
- shyness
- assertiveness
- aggressive communication
- passive communication
- avoidance skills
- distributive skills
- integrative skills

- coordination
- talkovers
- deep interruptions
- topic initiation
- expressiveness
- adaptability
- consistency
- conversational narcissism

BUILDING MOTIVATION: SELF-ASSESSMENT TOOL.

Rate each of the eight communication situations described here, indicating your own typical level of competence with regard to interpersonal communication skills. Rate one situation all the way through for motivation, knowledge, and skills. Then rate the next situation. Use the 1–4 scale below, with 1 being minimal competence and 4 high competence.

Communication situations.

1. Meeting new people in a social situation like at a party.
2. Meeting new people in a professional situation at work.
3. Paying attention to the other person when you think you know more than they know about the topic of a conversation.
4. Maintaining your composure despite feeling a little anxious in the particular situation.
5. Controlling a desire to become a little bit aggressive in an argument with your significant other.
6. Waiting your turn to talk in a heated debate of an important issue.
7. Expressing your opinion about the topic of conversation in an animated manner.
8. Adapting what you say in a conversation to the needs and concerns of the other person.

Motivation.

1 = Distracted, disinterested, or simply no motivation to be competent.
2 = Somewhat distracted or disinterested, but motivated to be competent.
3 = Somewhat interested and motivated to be competent.
4 = Highly interested and motivated to be competent.

Knowledge.

1 = Completely inexperienced and ignorant about what to do and how to do it.
2 = Minimal experience and sense of what to do and how to do it.

3 = Somewhat experienced and knowledgeable about what to do and how to do it.

4 = Highly knowledgeable about all aspects of what to do and how to do it.

Skills.

1 = Completely incapable of behaving competently.

2 = Barely capable of behaving minimally competent.

3 = Fairly capable of behaving competently.

4 = Highly capable of behaving competently.

Interpreting your scores.

Total your score separately for each situation (motivation, knowledge, and skills). The possible range of the score for each situation is 3–12. If your total score for any of the situations is 6 or less, you see yourself as less competent in that situation than you should be. A score of 7–9 means that you are average at sending and receiving communication messages in the situation. A score of 10–12 indicates that you have a high level of communication competence in that situation.

Building knowledge: Discussion questions.

1. What is the relationship of interpersonal skills and impressions of competence?
2. How are general, macro-level skills (empathy, assertiveness, and so on) related to specific, micro-level skills (facial expressiveness, asking questions, and so on)?
3. How can conversational interruptions be competent?
4. What are the four general skill areas of interpersonal communication competence? How do they differ from one another? Give examples for each type of skill.
5. Distinguish among assertive, aggressive, and passive communication behavior.
6. Describe the process of balancing adaptability with consistency.
7. How can you as a communicator balance the need to serve your own interests with others' needs to serve their interests?
8. How can challenges to interpersonal communication, resulting from the increased use of computer-mediated communication media, be overcome?

BUILDING SKILLS: STUDENT ACTIVITIES.

Individual activities.

1. Go to the Conflict Resolution Network and their component on the twelve skills of conflict management (http://crnhq.org/twelveskills.html). Think of two communication situations you have faced recently, one in which you responded too aggressively, and one in which you responded too passively. As accurately as you can remember the conversation, write down a statement or response you provided that was too aggressive in the first situation, and too passive in the second situation. Now, using the information in this website's description of "I statements," reformulate your statements to be more appropriately assertive. How could such "I statements" help resolve conflicts in which you find yourself in everyday encounters?

2. Following are several potentially problematic situations. For each situation, describe an aggressive, a passive, and an assertive response.

    a. A week ago, you and your steady dating partner of a year broke up. You still have strong feelings for this person, but you need to move on. A week later, your best friend calls and says, "Guess what? I'm going to a party with your ex-partner. I hope you don't mind."

    b. Despite having agreed to buy food separately to avoid disputes over who can eat which snacks, you come home to find your roommate eating the last of your microwave popcorn.

3. Here are several situations in which you might find yourself. For each situation, write three possible statements you might use to open up a conversation—a topic initiator.

    a. You are at the veterinarian, and you see another person with a pet like yours.

    b. You see your professor in the hallway, and want to talk about a recent assignment and the grade you got.

    c. You are at the park watching people throw a Frisbee, and an elderly person sits next to you on the bench.

    e. You are at a party and an attractive person asks you what time it is.

4. Here are some examples of closed-ended questions. For each question, write three open-ended questions that are related to the same topic area.

    a. Where are you from?

    b. How long have you been in or out of school?

    c. What is or was your major?

    d. Where do you work? What is your position?

    e. What are your hobbies?

    f. Where do you live?

Group activities.

1. Here is a list of terms and topics. In this activity you will be asked to show creativity in topic development. Choose a partner. The first person should select a topic from the list and make a comment related to the topic. For example, if the first topic selected is gun control, you might start by saying something like, "I can't believe the government hasn't banned assault rifles yet." The other person will then select another topic from the list, and make a statement that is relevant to both the topics selected. Thus, following our example, if the next topic was abortion, the second person's statement might be something like, "Yeah, if they don't start controlling guns better, they'll keep having these nuts go out and attack abortion clinics or whatever else they disagree with." Each person continues by making a comment that is topically relevant to both the previous comments provided. Continue with the conversation to examine how hard it is to stay on topic. When you have exhausted the conversation, start at the beginning with a new set of two statements about two new topics.

Equal rights	Immigration
Terrorism	The economy
Welfare	AIDS and HIV
Drunk driving	Foreign language education
Hunting and poaching	Media violence
Sports	Genetic engineering

Separation of church and state	Sex education
Right to die	Taxes
Family values	The environment

When the conversations end, discuss the skill of topic maintenance and development. What distinguished competent from incompetent follow-up comments?

2. Choose a partner in class whom you do not know very well. Conduct a get-acquainted conversation. Throughout the conversation, both parties should wait five seconds before responding to the other's previous statement. You can do this by mentally counting off the seconds before saying anything. After about ten minutes, discuss the effects of the delays in managing the flow of the conversation.

3. Form a group of three to four students. Below is a list of the macro-level general skills. For each general skill, have the group develop a list of what you all think are the most competent and incompetent micro-level specific skills—what people should do and what they should not do. Then discuss which specific skills are most characteristic of you in most conversations.

MACRO-LEVEL (GENERAL SKILL)	COMPETENT SPECIFIC SKILLS	INCOMPETENT SPECIFIC SKILLS
ATTENTIVENESS		
COMPOSURE		
COORDINATION		
EXPRESSIVENESS		

NOTES

1. See Spitzberg, Canary, & Cupach (1994).
2. See Chang, Arora, Lev-Ari, D'Arcy, & Keysar (2010).
3. See Fay, Page, & Serfaty (2010).
4. See Jaramillo, Carrillat, & Locander (2005).
5. See Baumeister, Campbell, Krueger, & Vohs (2005).
6. See Spitzberg & Cupach (2011).
7. See Samp & Solomon (2005).
8. See Canary & Spitzberg (1990).
9. See Spitzberg (2007).
10. See Wheeless, Frymier, & Thompson (1992).
11. See Kim (1999).
12. See Spitzberg & Cupach (1984).
13. See Raush, Barry, Hertel, & Swain (1974).
14. See Olson (2002).
15. See Spitzberg (1994).
16. See Gross, Guerrero, & Alberts (2004).
17. See Canary, Spitzberg, & Semic (1998).
18. See Cramer (2002).

19. See Kennedy & Camden (1983).

20. See Hawkins (1991).

21. See Jefferson (1989).

22. See Sabatelli & Rubin (1986).

23. See Friedman, DiMatteo, & Taranta (1980).

24. See Harwood & Williams (1998).

25. See Norton (1984).

26. See Leary, Rogers, Canfield, & Coe (1986).

27. See Spitzberg (1993).

28. See Vangelisti, Knapp, & Daly (1990).

29. See Leary, Bednarski, Hammon, & Duncan (1997).

30. See Twenge, Konrath, Foster, Campbell, & Bushman (2008).

31. See Konrath, O'Brien, & Hsing (2011).

32. See Edison Research (2011).

33. See Tokunaga (2011).

34. See Spitzberg (2006).

35. See Walther (1996).

REFERENCES

Backstrom, L., Boldi, P., Rosa, M., Ugander, J., & Vigna, S. (2012, Jan. 5). *Four degrees of separation.* Retrieved from: http://arxiv.org/pdf/1111.4570v3.pdf

Baumeister, R. F., Campbell, J. D., Krueger, J. I., & Vohs, K. D. (2005, January). Exploding the self-esteem myth. *Scientific American, 292*(1), 84–91.

Canary, D. J., & Spitzberg, B. H. (1990). Attribution biases and associations between conflict strategies and competence outcomes. *Communication Monographs, 57*(2), 139–151.

Canary, D. J., Spitzberg, B. H., & Semic, B. A. (1998). The experience and expression of anger in interpersonal settings. In P. A. Andersen & L. K. Guerrero (Eds.), *Handbook of communication and emotion: Theory, research, and applications* (pp. 189–213). San Diego, CA: Academic Press.

Chang, V. Y., Arora, V. M., Lev-Ari, S., D'Arcy, M., & Keysar, B. (2010). Interns overestimate the effectiveness of their hand-off communication. *Pediatrics, 125*(3), 491–496.

Cramer, D. (2002). Linking conflict management behaviors and relational satisfaction: The intervening role of conflict outcome satisfaction. *Journal of Social and Personal Relationships, 19,* 425–432.

Edison Research. (2011). *The social habit 2011.* Edison Research. Retrieved from http://www.edisonresearch.com/home/archives/2011/05/the_social_habit_2011.php

Fay, N., Page, A. C., & Serfaty, C. (2010). Listeners influence speakers' perceived communication effectiveness. *Journal of Experimental Social Psychology, 46*(4), 689–692.

Friedman, H. S., DiMatteo, M. R., & Taranta, A. (1980). A study of the relationship between individual differences in nonverbal expressiveness and factors of personality and social interaction. *Journal of Research in Personality, 14*(3), 351–364.

Gross, M. A., Guerrero, L. K., & Alberts, J. K. (2004). Perceptions of conflict strategies and communication competence in task-oriented dyads. *Journal of Applied Communication Research, 32*(3), 249–270.

Hampton, K. N., Goulet, L. S., Marlow, C., & Rainie, L. (2012, Feb. 3). *Why most Facebook users get more than they give: The effect of Facebook 'power users' on everybody else.* Washington DC: Pew Research Center's Internet & American Life Project. Retrieved from: http://www.pewinternet.org/~/media//Files/Reports/2012/PIP_Facebook%20users_2.3.12.pdf

Harwood, J., & Williams, A. (1998). Expectations for communication with positive and negative subtypes of older adults. *International Journal of Aging & Human Development, 47*(1), 11–33.

Hawkins, K. (1991). Some consequences of deep interruption in task-oriented communication. *Journal of Language and Social Psychology, 10*(3), 185–203.doi:10.1177/0261927X91103003

Jaramillo, F., Carrillat, F. A., & Locander, W. B. (2005). A meta-analytic comparison of managerial ratings and self-evaluations. *Journal of Personal Selling & Sales Management, 25*(4), 315–328.

Jefferson, G. (1989). Preliminary notes on a possible metric which provides for a "standard maximum" silence of approximately one second in conversation. In D. Roger & P. Bull (Eds.), *Conversation: An interdisciplinary perspective* (pp. 166–196). Philadelphia, PA: Multilingual Matters.

Kennedy, C. W., & Camden, C. T. (1983). A new look at interruptions. *Western Journal of Speech Communication, 47*(1), 45–58.

Kim, M-S. (1999). Cross-cultural perspectives on motivations of verbal communication: Review, critique, and a theoretical framework. In M. E. Roloff & G. D. Paulson (Eds.), *Communication yearbook 22* (pp. 50–89). Thousand Oaks, CA: Sage.

Konrath, S. H., O'Brien, E. H., & Hsing, C. (2011). Changes in dispositional empathy in American college students over time: A meta-analysis. *Personality and Social Psychology Review, 15*(2), 180–198.

Leary, M. R., Bednarski, R., Hammon, D., & Duncan, T. (1997). Blowhards, snobs, and narcissists: Interpersonal reactions to excessive egotism. In R. Kowalski (Ed.), *Aversive interpersonal behavior* (pp. 111–131). New York, NY: Plenum.

Leary, M. R., Rogers, P. A., Canfield, R. W., & Coe, C. (1986). Boredom in interpersonal encounters: Antecedents and social implications. *Journal of Personality and Social Psychology, 51*(5), 968–975.

Norton, R. (1984). *Communicator style: Theory, applications, and measures.* Beverly Hills, CA: Sage.

Olson, L. N. (2002). "As ugly and painful as it was, it was effective": Individuals' unique assessment of communication competence during aggressive conflict episodes. *Communication Studies, 53*(2), 171–188.

Raush, H. L., Barry, W. A., Hertel, R. J., & Swain, M. A. (1974). *Communication, conflict, and marriage.* San Francisco, CA: Jossey-Bass.

Sabatelli, R. M., & Rubin, M. (1986). Nonverbal expressiveness and physical attractiveness as mediators of interpersonal perceptions. *Journal of Nonverbal Behavior, 10*(2), 120–133.

Samp, J. A., & Solomon, D. H. (2005). Toward a theoretical account of goal characteristics in micro-level message features. *Communication Monographs, 72*(1), 22–45.

Spitzberg, B. H. (1993). The dialectics of (in)competence. *Journal of Social and Personal Relationships, 10*(1), 137–158.

Spitzberg, B. H. (1994). The dark side of (in)competence. In W. R. Cupach & B. H. Spitzberg (Eds.), *The dark side of interpersonal communication* (pp. 25–49). Hillsdale, NJ: Erlbaum.

Spitzberg, B. H. (2006). Preliminary development of a model and measure of computer-mediated communication (CMC) competence. *Journal of Computer-Mediated Communication, 11*(2), 629–666. Retrieved from http://jcmc.indiana.edu/vol11/issue2/spitzberg.html

Spitzberg, B. H. (2007). *CSRS: The conversational skills rating scale—An instructional assessment of interpersonal competence* [NCA Diagnostic Series, 2nd ed.]. Annandale, VA: National Communication Association.

Spitzberg, B. H., Canary, D. J., & Cupach, W. R. (1994). A competence-based approach to the study of interpersonal conflict. In D. D. Cahn (Ed.), *Intimates in conflict* (pp. 183–202). Hillsdale, NJ: Erlbaum.

Spitzberg, B. H., & Cupach, W. R. (1984). *Interpersonal communication competence.* Beverly Hills, CA: Sage.

Spitzberg, B. H., & Cupach, W. R. (2011). Interpersonal skills. In M. L. Knapp & J. R. Daly (Eds.), *Handbook of interpersonal communication* (4th ed., pp. 481–524). Thousand Oaks, CA: Sage.

Tokunaga, R. S. (2011). Friend me or you'll strain us: Understanding negative events that occur over social networking sites. *CyberPsychology, Behavior, and Social Networking, 14*(7–8), 425–432.

Twenge, J. M., Konrath, S. H., Foster, J. D., Campbell, W. K., & Bushman, B. J. (2008). Egos inflating over time: A cross-temporal meta-analysis of the narcissistic personality inventory. *Journal of Personality, 76*(4), 875–902.

Ugander, J., Karrer, B., Backstrom, L., & Marlo, C. (2011, Nov. 18). *The anatomy of the Facebook social graph.* Retrieved from: http://arxiv.org/pdf/1111.4503v1.pdf

Vangelisti, A. L., Knapp, M. L., & Daly, J. (1990). Conversational narcissism. *Communication Monographs, 57*(4), 251–274.

Walther, J. B. (1996). Computer-mediated communication: Impersonal, interpersonal, and hyperpersonal interaction. *Communication Research, 23*(1), 3-43.

Wheeless, L. R., Frymier, A. B., & Thompson, C. A. (1992). A comparison of verbal output and receptivity in relation to attraction and communication satisfaction in interpersonal relationships. *Communication Quarterly, 40*(2), 102–115.

PART THREE

SMALL-GROUP COMMUNICATION AND LEADERSHIP

CHAPTER NINE

SMALL GROUPS
AND DECISION MAKING

KNOWLEDGE AND SKILLS

Players win games, teams win championships. —William C. Taylor, Writer, Speaker, and Entrepreneur, b. 1959

.
. . .

Student enrollment at National University has risen dramatically, provoking concerns about the faculty's ability to provide high-quality instruction, and conduct cutting-edge research. National University's President has appointed a task force comprised of students, faculty, and administrators to generate recommendations for managing the student enrollment problem. She appointed Eva, a faculty member, to chair the task force.

Eva began the first meeting by providing an overview of the President's charge to the task force: "The committee's charge is to make a recommendation to the President on how to manage future student enrollment. There is a concern that our recent growth is causing problems."

Bob, the Vice President for Finance, immediately responded, "As far as I'm concerned, this isn't a problem. More students mean more tuition dollars and revenue for the university. We should continue to enroll more students each year."

Sally, the President of the Faculty Senate, jumped in. "What I hear from faculty is that they are seeing 20% more students in every class. The overall quality of students has gone down, and faculty find that they are having to spend a lot more time covering basic material in their classes. This is a huge problem!"

Nilam, President of the student body, said, "I know there is a lot of overcrowding in the classes and the students don't feel they're receiving enough attention from the faculty." Eduardo, the Alumni Association President, chipped in, "Our alumni have also been quite vocal in their opinions. If we decrease the number of students we admit each year by raising entrance requirements, they worry some of their kids won't be able to get in."

The discussion quickly erupted into a heated debate while Eva, the task force chair, sat quietly, trying to figure out what to do. There were so many different issues to manage before the task force could make a decision. When another task force member mused out loud that perhaps this was a time to reconsider the university's mission, since the size of the university depended on its mission, Eva sighed heavily, and knew it was going to be a long afternoon.

Small groups are increasingly being used to make decisions and solve problems. The issues confronting organizations, governments, and societies, such as the environment, health care, globalization, and terrorism, are growing in complexity, and require the coordinated efforts of many people to make wise decisions. When issues grow more complex, knowledge and information become fragmented, as some people possess unique facts regarding issues that others do not have. For example, National University's enrollment task force faces a very complicated issue, with students, faculty, administrators, and alumni each having a different understanding of what the enrollment crisis means, and different ideas about how to manage it.

The key to effectiveness in groups such as the task force is competent communication. In this chapter, we first describe what a small group is, and then the role communication plays in promoting high-quality, small-group decision making and problem solving.

WHAT IS A SMALL GROUP?

In our opening story, Eva was placed in charge of the enrollment management task force. Do you view this task force as a small group? Although many criteria exist for classifying a collection of people as a group, only four determine a small group:

1. The collection must be made up of three or more people.
2. Every group member must have the perception of belonging to the particular group.
3. Each group member's behaviors and goals must be interdependent, and the group must be interdependent with its larger context or environment.
4. There must be communication among group members.

DEFINING A SMALL GROUP.

Using these criteria, a **small group** can be defined as three or more people who perceive themselves to be a group, who are interdependent, and who communicate with one another. These criteria also help distinguish small-group communication from interpersonal and public communication. Based on the criteria and the definition of communication in Chapter One, **small-group communication** is the process of managing messages and media for the purpose of creating meaning in groups of three or more people who perceive themselves to be a group, are interdependent, and who communicate with one another.

If the lower bound for any small group is three people you may wonder, "How large can a group be and still be called a small group?" For instance, do you consider a large lecture class of 250 people a small group? One way to distinguish a small group from a large group is the ability to be aware of all the other people in the group, and to recall what a particular group member was like or what he or she did.[1] In addition, the three or more people are interdependent, which means that they are related to and mutually affect one another, and they need to communicate with one another. In Eva's task force, the primary communication channel was face-to-face. But the explosion of information technologies such as e-mail, videoconferencing, and audioconferencing now allows group members to communicate using all kinds of mediated channels. If we knew the rest of Eva's story, we might see that she chose to use some other mediated communication channels to effectively address the task of the group.

Table 9.1 further clarifies what a small group is by providing a list of many different types of small groups.[2] Look over the list to identify the many different small groups to which you may

> A SMALL GROUP is three or more people who perceive themselves to be a group, who are interdependent, and who communicate with one another.
>
> SMALL-GROUP COMMUNICATION is the process of managing messages and media for the purpose of creating meaning in groups of three or more people who perceive themselves to be a group, are interdependent, and who communicate with one another.

Table 9.1: Types of Groups by Activity and Goal

Groups can be categorized according to the activities in which they engage and the goals they aim to achieve. A person can belong to many different groups. How many do you belong to?

ACTIVITY AND GOAL	TYPES OF GROUPS
Commercial	Consumer groups, food cooperatives, investment groups, real estate boards.
Educational	Work groups in preschool, ability-level groups in elementary and secondary school, study groups in college and graduate school, occupational training groups.
Familial	Immediate family, extended family, orphanages, foster-care groups, day-care groups, communal-living groups, assisted-living home groups, senior residential facility groups, convents, rectories, abbeys.
Health and Welfare	Therapy groups, support groups, rehabilitation groups, residential care facility groups.
Occupational	Quality circles, management teams, research and development teams, committees, corporate boards of directors, work teams.
Political/Civic	Zoning boards, planning boards, political party committees, protest groups, boards of directors for charities, civic leagues.
Recreational	Sports teams, fraternal associations, lodges, scout troops, musical bands, choirs.
Social	Friendship groups, groups of acquaintances, gangs, clubs.
Spiritual	Church groups, Sunday school classes, synagogues, mosque congregations, cults, covens.

Source: Adapted from Socha (1996).

belong. The groups on the list are categorized according to the goals each group tries to accomplish. In order to accomplish their goals, one of the most critical challenges most small groups face is making good decisions. In the small-group context, decisions can only be made through a process of communication.

DETERMINING WHEN GROUPS SHOULD MAKE DECISIONS.

Using groups to make decisions within the public and private sector has increased dramatically over the last 20 years. Given this increase, when is it appropriate and effective to use groups to make decisions? Leaders and managers sometimes set up committees to make unpopular decisions, so they can blame the committee for the decision, and avoid taking the blame. When a group devotes time and energy to making a decision that has no chance of being implemented or adopted, we are inclined to say that using groups to make decisions in these circumstances is not appropriate.

Group leaders should explore their motivation for using groups to make decisions and address problems, based on these five considerations and responsibilities.

1. *Motive:* Explore your motivation for using a group to make a decision or develop a recommendation. Use groups when you need a diversity of opinions on a particular issue. Conversely, if the motivation for assembling a group is simply to avoid accountability for a decision, it is not appropriate to use groups.

2. *Scope:* Determine the scope of the group's responsibility, and clearly specify the scope of the group's task. It is not alright to hold a group accountable if members do not have the authority to implement their recommendations.

3. *Task:* Clearly communicate the task to the group. When groups meet for the first time, it is critical for the manager or leader creating the group to provide a clear orientation to the task. As long as the group knows what its responsibilities are, who will accept or reject its final decision, and how it will be implemented, the manager has ethically appointed this group to the task.

4. *Process feedback:* Provide periodic feedback to the group as it performs the task. Keep in close contact with group members as they are working. A common mistake is to assign the group a task, and then never check back with the group until it has come to a decision or completed the task. This can create difficulties for the group if it has gone in a different direction than intended by the manager.

5. *Decision fedback:* Provide feedback on the implementation of the group's decision. Many times, group members make decisions, but never find out what has been done with their work. Providing feedback on how the work has been used is an important part of the group decision-making process. Not only does this provide the group closure on a project, it also communicates valuable information about what members may need to consider the next time they are given a group task.

Certainly, the use of groups to make decisions is a trend that will continue in the 21st century. The question, therefore, is not "Will we use groups to make decisions?" but rather, "*How* do we use groups to make decisions?" The following information answers that question for you.

MAKING GROUP DECISIONS

What are some of the major decisions being made in your local community? In your state? In your country? In the world? In your local community, perhaps people are trying to make decisions about how to create affordable housing for low-income families. At the state level, perhaps groups of people are trying to decide the best way to manage the competing needs of economic development while conserving the environment. At a national level, political parties may be struggling with issues related to providing access to health care, and developing stronger schools. At an international level, groups such as the United Nations or the Red Cross may be making decisions about how to provide assistance to countries where natural disasters like hurricanes or earthquakes have decimated the country, and denied people basic needs such as food or water. Regardless of where you look, groups of people are making important decisions that influence and impact others.

Competent small-group communicators need to be knowledgeable in four areas:

1. The relationship between problem solving and decision making.
2. Types of group decision-making tasks.

3. The process of communication in decision making.
4. The criteria for high-quality decisions.

DISTINGUISHING PROBLEM SOLVING AND DECISION MAKING.

A **problem** exists when there is a gap between an ideal state and the current state of events. For example, community leaders may need to develop a plan for affordable housing because there is a gap between the number of low-income families that own a home and the national average of home ownership. At a national level, the need for health care may be outpacing the services and facilities presently available. In these examples, a gap exists between an ideal state, where the group would like to be, and the current state of events, where the group is presently.

> A PROBLEM exists when there is a gap between an ideal state and the current state of events.

Therefore, **problem solving** is a group process in which members assess problems, and formulate solutions to resolve the problems. Central to the notion of assessing problems is Kurt Lewin's idea of a **force field analysis**, a process for analyzing the reasons for a problem, as well as what is preventing the problem from being eliminated.[3] Figure 9.1 illustrates a force field analysis. The problem—the gap between an ideal and current state of affairs—is at the center of a force field analysis. The key questions a group must ask are: (1) What is causing this problem? and (2) What is preventing the resolution or management of the problem? The first question focuses on the **drivers**, or the causes of a particular problem, or the sources that create the problem, and the second question introduces the idea of **restraining forces**, or forces that prevent the resolution of the problem.

> PROBLEM SOLVING involves a group process in which members assess problems, and formulate solutions to resolve the problems.

> FORCE FIELD ANALYSIS is a process for analyzing the reasons for a problem as well as what is preventing the problem from being eliminated.

> DRIVERS are the causes of a particular problem, or the sources that create the problem.

In order to understand a problem fully, it is important to assess the drivers and restraining forces. Then you can solve the problem and close the gap by addressing the drivers, and removing restraining forces. How might the enrollment task force manage the gap between the current enrollment of National University and where it needs to be? Task force members might begin by asking, "What is driving this gap?" Some possible drivers may include the university's need for tuition revenue dollars, a lack of rigorous admissions policies, and a low student-to-faculty ratio. They may also ask, "What is preventing the problem from being solved?" Possible restraining forces could include the alumni's resistance to making National more selective, a university mission that emphasizes giving access to a wide variety of students, and financial issues. Using this analysis, the task force members could propose two solutions: (a) hiring additional faculty to meet student demand, or (b) establishing more selective enrollment policies. The former solution removes a significant driver for the problem (low student-to-faculty ratio), and the latter removes a key restraining force (resistance to becoming more selective in admissions policies).

> RESTRAINING FORCES are forces that prevent the resolution of the problem.

> A DECISION is the selection among alternative explanations or proposals.

Decisions are somewhat distinct from this problem-solving process. A **decision** is the selection among alternative explanations or proposals. These alternatives may be competing explanations for what causes a problem. For instance, Eva's task force members do have alternative explanations for

Figure 9.1: Force Field Analysis

A gap is the disparity between the actual and ideal state of affairs. Drivers are the reasons the gap exists in the first place, and restraining forces limit people's abilities to reduce the gap.

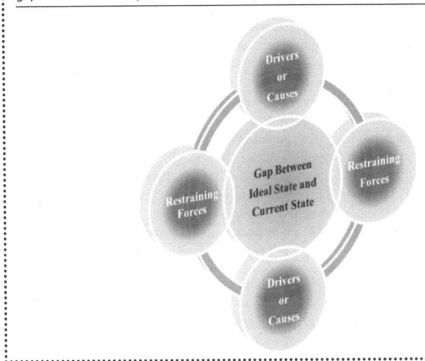

what is causing the problem they are asked to address. Alternatives may also include competing proposals or plans for solving a problem. Which alternative is better—hiring more faculty, or creating more selective enrollment policies? Is there some way of integrating alternatives to make a new, preferable alternative? Decision making may be used to solve problems, but it is not the same as problem solving. For example, suppose Congress agreed to extend health care benefits to all uninsured citizens of the United States. Then they would need to decide on the best way to create this program, choosing among a variety of possible alternative proposals. At this stage of discussion, they are not solving a problem; they are making a decision by selecting among alternative proposals.

DEFINING GROUP DECISION-MAKING TASKS.

Groups perform a wide variety of tasks, such as manufacturing products, providing services, creating strategic plans, developing marketing campaigns, and so on. Each of these tasks requires making decisions and choices among various alternatives for action. One way to understand decision-making tasks is to identify the particular types of question the group is trying to answer. There are four kinds of questions small groups most frequently consider:

1. Questions of fact.
2. Questions of conjecture.
3. Questions of value.
4. Questions of policy.[4]

To put it simply, a group needs to know the types of questions being considered before it can begin to evaluate the best alternative or answer to the question. Table 9.2 describes these four types of questions, and illustrates how the task force in our opening story could use these questions to examine the enrollment management task they are considering.

Groups rarely make a decision based on the answer to only one question of fact, conjecture, value, or policy. Making decisions about most tasks usually involves a variety of related issues. This is called **nested decision making**, which requires decision makers to prioritize the interdependent questions they ask. Questions they ask earlier in the process serve as the foundation for subsequent questions, which, in turn, lead to the answer of the major question. In making a nested decision, it is difficult to answer the central question that the group is responsible for without answering those questions that serve as the foundation.

NESTED DECISION MAKING
involves prioritizing interdependent questions and issues the group faces.

For example, to answer the central policy question, "What should the university's policy be regarding enrollment?" the enrollment management committee must answer a number of other questions of fact, conjecture, and value. If the committee is not clear on the factual economic impact of varying levels of student enrollment, it will make a poor policy decision. If the committee has not explored the possible consequences of varying levels of student enrollment on facility issues, again,

Table 9.2: Types of Questions for Small Groups

This table demonstrates how the four kinds of questions for small groups could be used to explore the problem that the enrollment management task force is addressing in our opening story.

TYPE OF QUESTION	APPLICATION TO ENROLLMENT MANAGEMENT TASK
• Questions of conjecture are questions that ask what might happen in the future, projections about events or possibilities that might occur.	• What will happen to the university if we raise enrollment? • How will faculty respond to increased numbers of students? • What are the possible positive or negative consequences of increasing enrollment? Decreasing enrollment? • How will the culture of the university be influenced if we raise entrance requirements, such as minimum ACT or SAT scores? Lower entrance requirements?
• Questions of value are moral and ethical questions that explore issues of intrinsic importance, worth, utility, and desirability of objects, attitudes, and beliefs.	• What kind of university community do we desire? What kinds of students best fit the kind of community we would like to create? • How important is limiting enrollment to us? • What is most important to us—quantity of students or quality of students? • Are we serving our community if we limit our enrollment?
• Questions of policy focus on actions that need to or should be taken to solve a problem.	• What actions should the university take regarding enrollment?

the decision may be a poor one. Finally, if the committee has not clarified the values of the university and key stakeholder groups, the decision may be inappropriate. The ultimate quality of the policy decision and actions to be taken depends on the ability of the group to identify and answer the questions nested beneath the major question of what to do. Those nested questions are clearly spelled out for the task force committee in Table 9.2.

USING COMMUNICATION IN GROUP DECISION MAKING.

If a group wants to make effective and appropriate decisions, then it is important for small-group members to be aware of the communication processes associated with high-quality decision making. In the early 1900s, John Dewey, a scholar in philosophy, interviewed hundreds of students, and asked them to describe the processes they used to make decisions.[5] From the information he gathered in these interviews, he created the **reflective thinking model**, which profiles a series of six steps decision makers follow in order to make high-quality decisions. This model assumes each of the steps needs to be followed in the prescribed sequence in order to analyze problems logically and make decisions. The six steps are presented in Table 9.3.

Dewey's seminal ideas about reflective thinking became the basis for a contemporary perspective on decision making called the **functionalist approach**.[6, 7] This approach argues that four key decision-making functions need to be performed if a group is to make a high-quality decision. These four functions also are presented in Table 9.3.

> THE REFLECTIVE THINKING MODEL profiles a series of steps that decision makers follow in order to make high-quality decisions.
>
> A FUNCTIONALIST APPROACH assumes that particular decision-making functions can be identified that, when performed, will lead to high-quality decision making.

Table 9.3: Models for Using Communication in Group Decision Making

These two approaches to communicating about decisions in small groups appear very similar. The six steps in the Dewey Model from the early 1900s served as the foundation for the four decision-making functions in the more contemporary functionalist approach.

REFLECTIVE THINKING MODEL	FUNCTIONALIST APPROACH TO GROUP DECISION MAKING
1. Recognize that a problem exists.	1. Assess the problem situation.
2. Define the scope and nature of the problem, and identify factors that cause the problem.	2. Establish evaluation criteria.
3. Generate a number of solutions that may solve the problem.	3. Generate a range of alternatives.
4. Develop criteria for choosing among alternative solutions, and evaluate those solutions using those criteria.	4. Evaluate the alternatives in light of positive and negative consequences.
5. Select the best solution.	
6. Assess solution to see if it is the best one.	

Early versions of the functional approach said groups that fail to fulfill these key functions will make poor decisions.[8] For example, if a group fails to assess the problem accurately, it may generate solutions which do not address that particular problem. Similarly, if group members do not identify a wide

> A TASK SKILL is any communication message or behavior a person sends that helps a group make a decision.

range of alternatives, the most appropriate alternative may be overlooked. Some research also suggests that certain functions are more important to high-quality decision making than others, and that importance may vary depending on the task and situation.[9] For example, communication that assesses the problem and evaluates the risks and negative consequences of alternative solutions is a stronger predictor of high-quality decisions than communication that only generates alternatives.[10] So if a group wants to make a good decision, group members need to evaluate the kind of question they are discussing, the context or situation in which the group finds itself, and any potential disadvantages of the possible decision alternatives.

How does a functional approach to decision making relate to the task force in this chapter's opening story? Their task is challenging, because many possible solutions exist, and the evaluation criteria for solutions are unclear. It is not surprising that the task force members would spend much of their time analyzing the task they were given and the causes for the student enrollment problem. Given that the task force is a mix of students, faculty, and administrators, they likely had differing perspectives on the problem they were charged to resolve. Therefore, they will need to spend more time sharing the unique knowledge and information each of them possesses. To make an optimal choice, functional theory suggests that the task force should also devote a good amount of time to assessing the negative consequences of any decisions they make. And finally, Eva and the task force members need to be aware of and able to use the following task skills related to the four decision-making functions of the functionalist approach.

TASK SKILLS FOR MAKING DECISIONS

A **task skill** is any communication message or behavior that helps a group make a decision. The three primary task skills for making effective decisions are:

1. Defining and analyzing the problem.
2. Identifying criteria for solving the problem.
3. Generating and evaluating solutions or alternatives.

Using the story that opened the chapter, let us explore these kinds of communication messages that help groups make high-quality decisions.

DEFINING AND ANALYZING THE PROBLEM.

Developing an answer to the question, "What appears to be the problem?" can be difficult. Group members often see the situation differently, but they assume that others see it as they do. That assumption results in groups often skipping this task because they fail to realize its importance. The result is that well-intended group members all try to solve very different problems. However, group members can send messages to facilitate defining and clarifying the problem. The purpose of this task skill is to ensure that all group members clearly understand the problem in the same way.

Each of the following four messages could help a group to collaborate and define the problem:

1. Problem statement: Messages that propose a specific definition of the problem.
2. Modifying the problem statement: Messages that combine competing definitions of the problem, or slightly alter an existing problem statement.
3. Detailing assumptions: Messages that examine the assumptions made about the nature of the problem, and the people who are either involved in the decision-making process or who will be affected by the group's decision.
4. Changing perspectives: Messages that highlight how different people or stakeholders perceive the problem.

As task force chair, if Eva had sent the types of messages listed above, what might she have said during the board meeting? She might have stated the problem this way: "I think our problem is that we don't have enough faculty and staff to meet the increased enrollment." Or she might have asked each member of the task force for their problem statement: "What do you see as the problem facing National University?" She may have detailed the assumptions regarding the problem statement: "One of the assumptions I make when looking at enrollment trends is that providing high-quality instruction to our students is key to our future success." She may have used other people's perspectives to explore the problem statement: "What do you think our alumni would view as the problem?" Or "If some of the town's community leaders were here at this meeting, what might they say is our problem?" In the event that multiple problem statements surfaced during the discussion, Eva might have modified the problem statements: "It sounds as if the problem is both declining revenues and limited faculty resources." Group members and leaders who want to facilitate constructing a useful problem definition need to be skilled at using these kinds of messages.

The next skill for effective decision making is analyzing the problem confronting the group. These statements help analyze the causes, obstacles, history, symptoms, and significance of the problem that the group is attempting to solve. The purpose of this task skill is to be sure that all group members share their perceptions of the problem, and the group comes to agreement as to the problem's symptoms and drivers.

Five questions, like those listed below, help flush out the rich detail inherent in any problem:

1. Symptoms: How do we know there is a problem? What signs point to this?
2. Drivers: What is driving the problem? What is the basis for the problem?
3. Restraining forces: What is preventing us from solving the problem? What forces are restraining our ability to manage the problem?
4. Significance: How important is the problem? To whom?
5. History: What is the history of this problem? When did it begin? Who was the first to determine it was a problem?

To lead the task force, Eva could have asked several questions to analyze the problem: "How do we know there is a problem?" "Who was the first person to notice the problem?" Or "When did the problem start?" Asking about the symptoms of the problem would allow Eva to guide the discussion toward exploring the problem's significance and history. For example, she could offer a statement of the significance of the problem: "If we're unable to raise money through increased grant writing by our faculty, we'll have to explore other means of generating revenue, including raising enrollment." She may offer an account of what led to the problem: "This problem really began five years ago when we lost our Vice President for Development. Since then we have not been able to raise enough contributions from alumni and businesses and industries."

In order to set up the discussion for generating solutions, Eva could guide the meeting into a discussion of drivers and restraining forces. She may have articulated a driver for the problem, such as: "The reason we've enrolled too many students is that we're not selective enough in our admissions policy." Or she could solicit board members' opinions regarding possible drivers: "What do you think are the major reasons for too much enrollment?" Then, she could ask a question such as: "What's preventing us from solving these problems?" That would help the task force identify the restraining forces that prevent finding a solution for the problem.

IDENTIFYING CRITERIA FOR SOLVING THE PROBLEM.

The task skill of identifying criteria for solving a problem involves statements to help assess the quality of possible alternatives for the problem. Before a small group can choose among possible solutions for a problem, they need to develop criteria based on which alternative solutions may be evaluated. The purpose of this task skill is to provide the group with the criteria they will need later when they generate and evaluate solutions.

The two questions listed below facilitate a group's establishment of criteria, and their modification of those criteria:

1. Propose criteria: What are the criteria or standards we need to use when evaluating solutions?
2. Modify criteria: How can these criteria be combined to create a useful standard for evaluation? How can we alter a criterion to make it more appropriate in light of the group's task?

For example, the task force members could identify criteria by asking questions or making comments such as: "What criteria do we need to use when selecting among plans for raising tuition?" Or "Any action that helps provide quality student instruction must take faculty resources into account." Questions and comments that help modify criteria include: "I agree that any proposal we put forth must recommend a decrease in admissions, but it also needs to suggest that the Development Office be more involved in generating revenue." Or "I understand that we need to decrease student enrollment significantly, but could you quantify what you consider to be an acceptable decrease?" Proposing and modifying decision criteria in this way will enable any group to make higher-quality decisions.

GENERATING AND EVALUATING SOLUTIONS.

Two types of messages that generate alternatives to address a problem are solution-soliciting messages and solution-proposing messages. Leaders of small groups should solicit solutions from other group members, as well as propose possible solutions for the problem. The purpose of this task skill and these messages is to help group members consider the consequences and appropriateness of each alternative they generate.

The four questions listed below will facilitate a well-rounded analysis of the strengths and weaknesses of various alternatives, as they are proposed by the group:

1. Positive consequences: What advantages are gained from adopting this solution?
2. Negative consequences: What disadvantages are created from adopting this solution?
3. Problem-solution fit: Does the solution meet the criterion established at the beginning?
4. Reality testing: Does the solution make sense? Is the solution possible? Will people support the solution?

To assist the task force in generating solutions, Eva could have solicited solution proposals by asking, "What can we do to resolve this problem?" She also could have proposed solutions by providing the group a possible list of recommendations. When a solution is proposed, however, it often is modified by other group members. For example, Eva may have proposed higher admissions requirements as a strategy for reducing student enrollment. During the group discussion, another committee member may have introduced exceptions for the children of alumni. This committee member may have offered the rationale that a higher enrollment of children of alumni will encourage their parents to make more donations.

After generating and modifying various alternatives, the last task skill calls for evaluating the solutions. Rather than making quick decisions about which solution is best, small-group members need to evaluate each solution or proposal using the criteria they already developed for a good solution. This task skill allows the group to assess each alternative carefully, and thereby choose the most viable solution.

The following five questions will help any group evaluate and test the potential success of their solutions to a problem:

1. *Progression:* If we adopted this alternative, what would be the next step?
2. *Delegation:* Who would be in charge of the next step?
3. *Contingencies:* What would we do if the next step failed?
4. *Support:* Who would be supportive of this alternative? Who would oppose it?
5. *Prospects:* Given the level of support and opposition, can we realistically expect this solution to work?

How might Eva have encouraged the committee to look more closely at the advantages and disadvantages of each proposed solution? Certainly, she could have asked broad, open-ended questions: "What do we gain or lose if we adopt this alternative?" Or she might have made statements to communicate her assessment of the various alternatives: "If we adopt X, what I am afraid will happen is. . . ." Then again, she could have tied the discussion of alternatives back to the criteria set by the group, and discussed how each solution would work in real life: "How well does this alternative meet our goal of managing student enrollment?"

In the final analysis, using messages and questions like these allows any group to anticipate and overcome the following challenges all groups face when making decisions.

OVERCOMING CHALLENGESTO DECISION MAKING

Many groups are not vigilant about using the task skills just described. They become involved in talking about their assignment, and fail to think about the group processes necessary to accomplishing the assignment. One of the main reasons for this shortcoming and for poor decision making is referred to as groupthink. As a challenge, groupthink can be managed using divergent and convergent thinking. Let us first consider what groupthink is and why it happens.[11, 12]

GROUPTHINK.

Groupthink occurs when group members establish a norm that makes consensus the highest priority, thereby diminishing the vigilant appraisal of possible alternatives

GROUPTHINK occurs when group members establish a norm that makes consensus the highest priority, and that diminishes the vigilant appraisal of possible alternatives to a final decision.

Figure 9.2. Janis's Model of Groupthink

Three preexisting conditions propel groups to seek concurrence regarding an issue: (a) group cohesiveness, (b) structural factors, and (c) a provocative situational context. The concurrence-seeking tendency of groups can lead to symptoms of groupthink that ultimately cause defective decision making and a decision fiasco—a failure to reach the true goal.

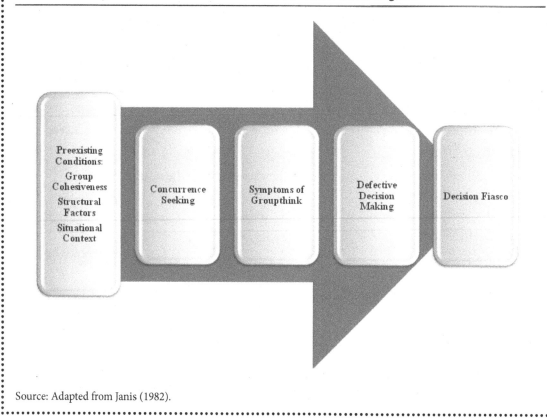

Source: Adapted from Janis (1982).

to a final decision.[13] Simply stated, the group members seek consensus too early. Groupthink results from preexisting conditions that lead to ineffective decision-making behavior, as shown in Figure 9.2.

As the groupthink model in Figure 9.2 illustrates, three major preexisting conditions lead to groupthink. First, groups that are moderately or highly cohesive tend to suffer from groupthink. As group members become more cohesive and share similar values, there is a danger that each individual will be so similar in their orientations to a problem that they stop thinking critically, in order to maintain group spirit and a strong sense of affiliation with other group members.

Second, several structural factors may influence a group's likelihood to engage in groupthink. These factors include the following:

- *Member similarity:* The more people share attitudes, values, and beliefs, the more likely they are to engage in groupthink. Group members may take certain things for granted, and neglect to evaluate alternatives.
- *Leader bias:* When group leaders express strong opinions about solutions to problems, the group members may be more prone to engage in groupthink. Group members may try to please the leader by following his or her opinions without evaluating alternatives.

- *Procedural void:* Groupthink is more likely to occur when the group does not have procedures in place to encourage rigorous analysis of the problem and possible solutions.
- *Group insulation:* When groups begin to feel cut off from their larger environment, they are more likely to engage in groupthink. A classic example of insulated groups are cults that are isolated from society at large. Sometimes, close-knit groups simply avoid seeking input or influence from others outside the group.

Third, the situational context may propel groups toward groupthink. Two situational factors are often a problem: stress and self-esteem. High stress is positively linked to groupthink. When group members are placed under pressure, they tend to short-circuit the decision-making process out of a sense of urgency. They may conclude that they do not have enough time to analyze the problem, generate solutions, or evaluate alternatives. Similarly, when group members have low self-esteem, they are more likely to engage in groupthink. Members suffering from low self-esteem lack the confidence to articulate an individual viewpoint, particularly one that challenges the larger group.

CONCURRENCE SEEKING occurs when groups try to achieve a consensus regarding their decision.

DIVERGENT THINKING involves generating multiple ideas and alternatives about issues, problems, and solutions.

As illustrated in Figure 9.2, the preexisting conditions lead to premature **concurrence seeking**, which is when groups try to achieve a consensus regarding their decision. The tendency for concurrence seeking is not inherently problematic; after all, most groups try to come to a consensus on the actions that need to be taken regarding a problem. However, when this tendency overrides critical thinking, it produces the following symptoms of groupthink:

- Group members possess an illusion of invulnerability.
- There is an unquestioned belief in the group's inherent morality and sense of rightness.
- Group members tend to provide collective rationalizations or justifications for their decisions.
- Group members who disagree, raise concerns, or oppose the decision are negatively stereotyped or characterized as wrong, weak, unintelligent, or unimportant compared with those in the majority.
- Direct pressure is applied to group members who dissent from the majority opinion. Their opinions are attacked and their positions in the group threatened.
- As direct pressure is leveled against dissenters, other group members may not even voice minority opinions. As a result, an illusion of unanimity and agreement is created.
- Some group members assume the role of protecting the group from dissenting opinions, and maintaining and defending the majority argument.

These symptoms of groupthink lead to defective decision making (again, see Figure 9.2). The group suffers from informational problems, because groupthink prevents it from collecting relevant and necessary information, and seeking expert opinions on the issue under consideration. The group also is hurt by an inability to engage in rigorous and open analysis of the decision. Finally, in the event the decision is defective, the group does not create contingency plans.

How can groups overcome these challenges and make high-quality decisions? One answer is that competent small-group members need to intentionally employ effective group procedures in order to (a) stimulate divergent thinking, and (b) initiate convergent thinking.

Table 9.4: Encouraging Divergent Thinking

Two effective procedures for encouraging divergent thinking are brainstorming and brainwriting.

	BRAINSTORMING AND BRAINWRITING
Three rules for brainstorming and brainwriting	• The "no criticism rule": Group members are not allowed to evaluate the quality of other group members' ideas. • The "hitchhiking rule": Group members are allowed to develop their ideas based on other ideas from the group. • The "quantity breeds quality rule": By generating lots of ideas, the chances that high-quality and creative ideas will emerge is increased.
How to's for brainstorming and brainwriting	• Brainstorming is done orally with one group member recording ideas on a computer or flip chart. • Brainwriting is used in groups whose communication is not face-to-face, such as geo-dispersed teams that communicate electronically. • Group leaders using either procedure should monitor and encourage all group members to participate. • Group leaders and members using either procedure should take responsibility to ensure they focus on multiple ideas, not only one idea.

DIVERGENT AND CONVERGENT THINKING.

The first description of any problem or the first solution to it often is not the most effective or creative. Yet, small-group members tend to latch on to their first problem description or the first solution suggested. By contrast, **divergent thinking** involves generating multiple ideas and alternatives about issues, problems, and solutions. Divergent thinking is particularly useful for examining the possible causes of and solutions to a problem.

Brainstorming and brainwriting, described in Table 9.4, are two group procedures that can be used to enhance divergent thinking. **Brainstorming** is a group procedure in which each individual in a group generates ideas, and adds them to the group discussion. In **brainwriting**, a written method for brainstorming, a grid is created and passed along for each member to contribute an idea while reviewing what previous group members have written.

To use brainstorming or brainwriting effectively, group leaders need to pay close attention to two procedural issues.[14] First, is every group member participating? Group brainstorming works best when each member feels free to contribute ideas. Yet some group members do not feel comfortable volunteering their ideas in large group settings, and need more encouragement. A second issue is the degree to which the group as a whole focuses on only one idea, as opposed to multiple ideas. One of the drawbacks to brainstorming is that one idea may

BRAINSTORMING is a group procedure in which each individual in a group generates ideas, and adds them to the group discussion.

BRAINWRITING is a written method for brainstorming, in which a grid is created and passed along for each member to contribute new ideas while reviewing what previous group members have written.

CONVERGENT THINKING involves evaluating the ideas, narrowing a wide range of alternatives, and selecting the one most appropriate to the task at hand.

become the base for all subsequent ideas. Group members may be so heavily influenced by one idea that the subsequent ideas they generate are simply variations on the initial idea. These issues can be addressed, if each individual silently generates and writes down a few ideas before sharing them with the group. This method prevents group members from being influenced by others in their initial thinking about the problem.

Whereas divergent thinking generates many ideas, **convergent thinking** is concerned with evaluating the ideas, narrowing a wide range of alternatives, and selecting the one most appropriate to the task at hand.[15] Procedures that narrow the range of alternatives and explore the strengths and weaknesses of each alternative help promote convergent thinking. A procedure particularly useful in stimulating convergent thinking is the nominal group technique.

Nominal group technique is a procedure in which group members generate ideas individually, share these ideas with the group, and then evaluate them as a group. This popular technique assumes that idea generation is best done individually, and idea evaluation is best done as a group.

Here are the six steps of this technique for encouraging convergent thinking:

1. Each group member silently generates and writes down as many ideas as possible on the selected topic.
2. Each person volunteers one idea, which is recorded on a flip chart set before the large group. This process is repeated until each member has volunteered all of his or her ideas.
3. Using the list of ideas written on the flip chart, the group then evaluates the strengths and weaknesses of each idea.
4. Group members then individually rank the ideas. Another group member tallies up the individual rankings, and produces an overall group ranking of the ideas.
5. The group then selects the most highly ranked ideas (say the top three), and the subsequent discussion focuses on those top ideas.
6. Steps 3–5 are repeated until the group reaches a decision.

> NOMINAL GROUP TECHNIQUE is a procedure in which group members generate ideas individually, share these ideas with the group, and then evaluate them as a group.
>
> The DEVIL'S ADVOCATE procedure involves assigning an individual to question the assumptions and processes the group uses to make decisions.

Convergent thinking works best when it helps group members to see differing perspectives regarding an issue. As we said earlier in this chapter, groups that make high-quality decisions are vigilant in their interactions, and explore problems from a variety of perspectives. One of the dominant approaches used to bring in the perspectives of others and explore their implications is the devil's advocate procedure.

The **devil's advocate procedure** involves assigning an individual to question the assumptions and processes the group uses to make decisions.[16] The devil's advocate challenges the group's thinking by introducing contrasting viewpoints and ideas. This role in the group is significant, in that it introduces minority views for consideration. The more minority opinions are included in the final decision, the higher quality the decision. However, the devil's advocate procedure is only effective when group members are open to criticism, and value contrasting ideas. If a group is not open to hearing divergent views, no matter how hard the devil's advocate tries, the minority views will not be heard. Even if minority opinion is present in the discussion, if it is not heard or valued by the majority of the group, it will not lead to high-quality decisions. This suggests that, when possible, decision-making groups should be constructed that emphasize heterogeneous versus homogeneous

Table 9.5: Computer-Mediated Communication (CMC) and Small Groups

Misperceptions about using computers to communicate in small groups may result in some misuse of technology. Here are four misperceptions and their corrections.

MISPERCEPTIONS	CORRECTIONS OF MISPERCEPTIONS
Misperception 1 Computer-mediated communication increases task-oriented communication.	Whether or not to communicate by computer to address a task depends on the intricacies of the task and the need for some "face time" to address it.
Misperception 2 Computer-mediated communication always increases group member participation.	In truth, some group members may not participate as much by computer as they would in a face-to-face meeting. It is easy to hide behind the technology.
Misperception 3 Communication technology allows equal participation by group members.	Communication technology can allow for equal participation, but it does not guarantee that will happen.
Misperception 4 More information is exchanged by groups using computer-mediated communication than face-to-face communication.	Just because more information may be disseminated as attachments or links to websites, that is no guarantee that group members will read or review it.

member opinions. The enrollment task force was, in fact, a heterogeneous group, in that the members held different opinions about the problem and its solution.

In addition to groups managing groupthink effectively, one final challenge to decision making relates to the impact of media and technology on groups and teams in the 21st century.

IMPACT OF MEDIA AND TECHNOLOGY ON GROUPS AND TEAMS.

Most definitions of small-group communication during the 1950s and 1960s typically included the criterion of face-to-face communication. However, most contemporary definitions of small-group communication no longer emphasize face-to-face communication. Why? The simple answer is that the explosion of communication technologies through which people exchange messages has altered the ways in which group members communicate. They no longer have to be physically present in the same room to communicate in a small group. Think of the various ways communication technology can be used to connect group members. You can now use intranets within organizations, the Internet, desktop videoconferencing, computer-based messaging and decision-making programs, and teleconferencing to exchange ideas.

In small groups, members often do communicate through computers to perform decision-making tasks such as analyzing the problem, generating solutions, and evaluating solutions. And research in several disciplines is investigating the nature of this influence.[17] The results suggest that there are several misperceptions of technology's influence on group communication, which are listed—and corrected—in Table 9.5.

What are the consequences of working in virtual teams, compared to traditional face-to-face teams?[18] Competent small-group communicators need to pay attention to four issues when using any type of communication technology. But, it should be noted, these four issues often apply to working in face-to-face groups, though face-to-face these issues are more easily monitored. First of all, group members and their leader need to determine whether they are achieving an appropriate balance between working face-to-face and with technology. Second, they should monitor whether they have enough participation from the right group members to accomplish the task. Third, they have to be sure some group members are not dominating the discussion. Fourth, they need to assess whether the group is exchanging all the relevant information needed in order to accomplish the task.

Indeed, the solutions to these issues depend on the unique circumstances of the group situation. For example, when certain group members have more expertise in a particular topic area, they may need to dominate the discussion. So when using technology, competent group communicators need to assess the context they are operating in, and make informed judgments about the kind of communication that is required, how much member participation is needed, whether it is effective for members to participate equally, and whether the necessary information is made available during discussion.

In the opening story for this chapter, you observed the inner workings of a small group, the task force for managing student enrollment at National University. Since observing that group, you have learned about how groups should make decisions, and how they should use task skills and messages to examine and solve problems. Reflect for a moment on how you would use this new information to facilitate the task force on enrollment if you were its leader. The next chapter in this book specifically discusses leadership in small groups.

CHAPTER SUMMARY

Small groups are used to make many decisions, and are central to helping get work done. A small group is three or more people who perceive themselves to be a group, are interdependent, and communicate with one another. Similarly, small-group communication is defined as the process of managing messages and media for the purpose of creating meaning in groups of three or more people who perceive themselves to be a group, are interdependent, and who communicate with one another.

Group decision making differs from group problem solving. A problem exists when there is a gap between an ideal state and the current state of events, whereas decision making involves the selection among alternative explanations or proposals. Conducting a force field analysis can help you understand what is causing the problem, and the drivers and restraining forces that are preventing the problem from being resolved. Often nested decision making is used, which involves resolution depending on making decisions regarding a variety of other issues.

Beginning with Dewey's reflective thinking model, and continuing with a functionalist approach, knowing how to make decisions must be paired with the task skills key to effective decision making:

1. Defining and analyzing the problem.
2. Identifying criteria for solving the problem.
3. Generating and evaluating solutions or alternatives.

Groupthink short-circuits the decision-making process. Groupthink occurs when group members establish a norm that makes consensus the highest priority, and diminishes the vigilant appraisal of possible alternatives to their final decision. Three factors can move the group toward groupthink: members' cohesiveness, structural factors, and the situational context. Then concurrence seeking takes place, and the group tries to achieve consensus regarding their decision.

Groups can use several procedures to structure the decision-making process. Group members and their leader need to determine whether ideas need to be generated (divergent thinking) or evaluated (convergent thinking). Brainstorming and brainwriting are two procedures that can be used to enhance divergent thinking. Nominal group technique and the devil's advocate procedure are tools that can be used to narrow down competing alternatives. In addition to managing groupthink effectively, a challenge to decision making in the 21st century relates to the impact of media and technology on virtual groups and teams.

KEY TERMS.

The key terms below are defined in this chapter, and presented alphabetically with definitions in the Glossary at the end of the book.

- small group
- small-group comunication
- problem
- problem solving
- force field analysis
- drivers
- restraining forces

- decision
- nested decision making
- reflective thinking model
- functionalist approach
- task skill
- groupthink
- concurrence seeking

- divergent thinking
- brainstorming
- brainwriting
- convergent thinking
- nominal group technique
- devil's advocate procedure

BUILDING MOTIVATION: SELF-ASSESSMENT TOOL.

Rate each of the eight communication situations described here, indicating your own typical level of small-group competence. Rate one situation all the way through for motivation, knowledge, and skills. Then rate the next situation. Use the 1–4 scale below, with 1 being minimal competence and 4 high competence.

Communication situations.

1. Working in a small group that is uncertain about the assigned task and whether it is a problem to be solved or a decision to be made.
2. Defining a problem with a group of people with very different opinions on the nature of the problem.
3. Analyzing a problem with a group of people with very different opinions on the alternative approaches to resolving the problem.
4. Identifying and deciding on criteria for a problem with a group of people with very different opinions about possible evaluative criteria.
5. Participating in a group that has a tendency to engage in groupthink.
6. Managing disagreements and conflict in a small group.
7. Encouraging group members who appear frustrated or disappointed about the progress the group is making toward accomplishing its task.
8. Leading a group productively that only communicates using computer-mediated technology.

Motivation.

   1 = Distracted, disinterested, or simply no motivation to be competent.
   2 = Somewhat distracted or disinterested, but motivated to be competent.
   3 = Somewhat interested and motivated to be competent.
   4 = Highly interested and motivated to be competent.

Knowledge.

   1 = Completely inexperienced and ignorant about what to do and how to do it.
   2 = Minimal experience and sense of what to do and how to do it.
   3 = Somewhat experienced and knowledgeable about what to do and how to do it.
   4 = Highly knowledgeable about all aspects of what to do and how to do it.

Skills.

   1 = Completely incapable of behaving competently.
   2 = Barely capable of behaving minimally competent.
   3 = Fairly capable of behaving competently.
   4 = Highly capable of behaving competently.

Interpreting your scores.

Total your score separately for each situation (motivation, knowledge, and skills). The possible range of the score for each situation is 3–12. If your total score for any of the situations is 6 or less, you see yourself as less competent in that situation than you should be. A score of 7–9 means that you are average at sending and receiving communication messages in the situation. A score of 10–12 indicates that you have a high level of communication competence in that situation.

BUILDING KNOWLEDGE: DISCUSSION QUESTIONS.

   1. How do the criteria for classifying a small group (three or more people, perception of being in the group, interdependence, and communication) connect? Is it possible to have a small group that perceives itself to be a small group, but the members do not talk or communicate with one another? Is it possible for two people who perceive themselves as a group, who are interdependent and communicate with one another, to be classified as a group? Why or why not?

   2. What are the differences between problem solving and decision making? Is it possible to solve a problem without making a decision, or to make a decision without solving a problem? Explain.

   3. Should all problems be solved using a force field analysis? Why or why not?

   4. Should all problems be solved using nested decision making? Why or why not?

   5. What kinds of communication do the reflective thinking model and the functionalist approach to decision making suggest are important for effective decision making?

   6. How does groupthink influence decision making? Are there ever times when a group leader may want to encourage groupthink?

   7. When should group members engage in divergent and convergent thinking? What strategies can they use to generate and evaluate ideas?

BUILDING SKILLS: STUDENT ACTIVITIES.

Individual activities.

1. Ask four or five friends how they define small-group communication. Do their definitions of small-group communication reflect the four characteristics of small groups: three or more people, perception, interdependence, and communication? Why do you think your friends defined communication in the way they did?

2. Select and interview two or three individuals who participate in small groups. Use the following questions for your interview:

   a. What has been your best experience in group decision making?
   b. What made it such a good experience?

   Compare the answers you get from your interviews to the material in the chapter. In what ways are your interviewees' answers similar to or different from the material in the chapter? Why do you think that is?

3. Identify a problem that concerns you. Do a force field analysis of this problem. What are the drivers? What are the restraining forces?

4. Imagine you are a member of an organization. You have been assigned to write a memo about effective decision making that will be distributed to everyone in the organization. What are five rules for effective decision making you would include in the memo?

5. Conduct an Internet search for sites that discuss decision-making procedures. Type in the keywords, "decision-making procedures," and identify two sites that discuss ways to coordinate group decision-making activities. Compare the recommendations to those identified in this chapter. In what ways are the recommendations similar and different?

Group activities.

1. Form groups of four to five students, and develop a short list of controversial topics. Brainstorm about the kinds of ground rules you would set up for a constructive discussion of the most controversial topic on your list.

2. As a group of four to five students, identify a time when one of the group members participated in a group that engaged in groupthink. Develop a set of guidelines for leading that group, if you were the appointed leaders.

3. As a group of four to five students, identify a time when one of the group members participated in a group that communicated mainly electronically to accomplish a task or address a problem. Identify the advantages and disadvantages of using technology in that situation, and develop a set of guidelines for leading that group, if you were the appointed leaders.

NOTES

1. See Bales 1950, p. 33.
2. See Socha (1996).
3. See Lewin (1951).
4. See Gouran (2003).
5. See Dewey (1910).
6. See Gouran & Hirokawa (2003).
7. See Wittenbaum et al. (2004).

8. See Gouran & Hirokawa (1996).

9. See Hirokawa (1990).

10. See Orlitzky & Hirokawa (2001).

11. See Park (2000).

12. See Chapman (2006).

13. See Janis (1982).

14. See Whyman & Ginnett (2005).

15. See Tassoul & Buijs (2007).

16. See Schwenk (1990).

17. See Walther (2009).

18. See Webster & Wong (2008).

REFERENCES

Bales, R. F. (1950). *Interaction process analysis: A method for the study of small groups*. Reading, MA: Addison-Wesley.

Chapman, J. (2006). Anxiety and defective decision-making: An elaboration of the groupthink model. *Management Decision, 44*(10), 1391–1404.

Dewey, J. (1910). *How we think*. Boston, MA: D. C. Heath.

Gouran, D. S. (2003). Reflections on the type of question as a determinant of the form of interaction in decision-making and problem-solving discussions. *Communication Quarterly, 51*(2), 111–125.

Gouran, D. S., & Hirokawa, R. Y. (1996). Functional theory and communication in decision-making and problem-solving groups: An expanded view. In R. Y. Hirokawa & M. S. Poole (Eds.), *Communication and group decision-making* (2nded., pp. 55–80). Thousand Oaks, CA: Sage.

Gouran, D. S., & Hirokawa, R. Y. (2003). Effective decision making and problem solving in groups: A functional perspective. In R. Y. Hirokawa, R. S. Cathcart, L. A. Samovar, & L. D. Henman (Eds.), *Small group communication: Theory and practice: Anthology* (8th ed., pp. 27–38). Los Angeles, CA: Roxbury.

Hirokawa, R. Y. (1990). The role of communication in group decision-making efficacy: A task-contingency perspective. *Small Group Research, 21*(2), 190–204.

Janis, I. L. (1982). *Groupthink: Psychological studies of policy decisions and fiascoes* (2nd ed.). Boston, MA: Houghton Mifflin.

Lewin, K. (1951). *Field theory in social research*. New York, NY: Harper & Row.

Orlitzky, M., & Hirokawa, R. Y. (2001). To err is human, to correct for it divine: A meta-analysis of research testing the functional theory of group decision-making effectiveness. *Small Group Research, 32*(3), 313–341.

Park, W-W. (2000). A comprehensive empirical investigation of the relationships among variables of the groupthink model. *Journal of Organizational Behavior, 21*(8), 873–887.

Schwenk, C. R. (1990). Effects of devil's advocacy and dialectical inquiry on decision making: A meta-analysis. *Organizational Behavior and Human Decision Processes, 47*(1), 161–176.

Socha, T. (1996). Group communication across the life span. In L. R. Frey & J. K. Barge (Eds.), *Managing group life: Communicating in decision-making groups* (pp. 1–28). Boston, MA: Houghton Mifflin.

Tassoul, M., & Buijs, J. (2007). Clustering: An essential step from diverging to converging. *Creativity and Innovation Management, 16*(1), 16–26.

Walther, J. B. (2009). In point of practice: Computer-mediated communication and virtual groups: Applications to inter-ethnic conflict. *Journal of Applied Communication Research, 3*(3), 225–238.

Webster, J., & Wong, W. (2008). Comparing traditional and virtual group forms: Identity, communication and trust in naturally occurring project teams. *The International Journal of Human Resource Management, 19*(1), 41–62.

Whyman, W., & Ginnett, R. (2005). A question of leadership: What can leaders do to avoid groupthink? *Leadership in Action, 25*(2), 13–14.

Wittenbaum, G. M., Hollingshead, A. B., Paulus, P. B., Hirokawa, R. Y., Ancona, D. G., Peterson, R. S., Jehn, K. A., & Yoon, K. (2004). The functional perspective as a lens for understanding groups. *Small Group Research, 35*(1), 17–43.

CHAPTER TEN

LEADERSHIP IN SMALL GROUPS

KNOWLEDGE AND SKILLS

- **What Is Leadership?**
  Defining Leadership
  Leadership and Change
  Leadership and Conflict

- **Overcoming Challenges to Competent Leadership**
  Controlling the Climate
  Exploring Multiple Positions
  Framing the Issues
  Impact of Media and Technology on Leadership in Groups

- **Chapter Summary**
  Key Terms
  Building Motivation: Self-Assessment Tool
  Building Knowledge: Discussion Questions
  Building Skills: Student Activities

Communication is the real work of leadership.— Nitin Nohria, Current Dean of Harvard Business School, b. 1962

• •
• • •

Rob is the newly hired executive director for the Arlen Arts Company, a local nonprofit group that sponsors a wide variety of adult and children's theater programs. The theater has flourished over the years, expanding its programming to include the children's theater program and summer productions. During the last five years, however, season ticket sales have plummeted, the talent pool of actors and actresses has dwindled, and volunteer support for building the sets and helping at the box office has fallen. The board of directors hired Rob to reverse the pattern of falling ticket sales, and to increase community involvement with the theater.

Rob quickly conducted an analysis of the theater's operating budget, and created a set of recommendations for the board of directors to consider. When he presented his ideas to the board, a heated discussion erupted in the board meeting. Some board members strongly disagreed with Rob's recommendations, and verbally attacked him, calling him "young and inexperienced." These board members had voted for another candidate for executive director, and had difficulty accepting Rob's ideas. Other board members did not want to talk about Rob's recommendations at all; they wanted to talk about the problems the theater was having. They had great difficulty moving beyond talking about the theater's financial difficulties to talking about actions that could address the problems. Still other members wanted to talk about the theater's history. They had belonged to the theater for over 20 years, and wanted to focus on how good things had been in the past. Any new idea Rob presented was met with the refrain of "that's not how we've done it in the past." Other board members were open to Rob's ideas, and tried to keep the discussion focused on the recommendations. Yet others sat there in silence trying to make sense of the discussion.

Rob had problems leading the discussion. He felt that some board members were "out to get him," and no matter what he said, they were going to disagree. He thought to himself, "They hire me to help straighten out the theater, and yet they fight me when I want to make changes." But just as he thought the discussion could not get any worse, one of his staff members, the director of the Children's Theater, entered the discussion, and criticized Rob's recommendations as not being sensitive to the needs of the Children's Theater. At that point, Rob suggested that they table his recommendations until the next board meeting, and adjourn.

Part of the difficulty Rob faced during the meeting emerged from having multiple groups of board members, each pursuing their own agenda. It is not surprising that the meeting became chaotic and unproductive, given such a diverse set of people, goals, and expectations. Rob felt, quite correctly, that he had been hired to change the theater's operations, but when he tried to be proactive and make recommendations to change the theater, he met resistance. This situation highlights a common dilemma for group leaders. Leaders in groups are commonly charged with creating change and innovation, yet the groups they work with deny that change is needed or desirable.

Is it fair to blame Rob for this meeting's failure? As the formally appointed leader of the group, Rob does share some responsibility for the disintegration of the meeting. Yet the individual board members also made choices about their participation in the board meeting. Some chose to pursue their own agendas and sabotage Rob's authority. Others chose to abdicate their responsibility to think about the future, and chose to remain focused on the past. Others did choose to work toward making changes that could lead to increased ticket sales and community involvement. Although it was Rob's responsibility as the leader to manage the board of directors, that does not absolve group members of the responsibility to participate constructively.

This chapter focuses on leading small groups, and managing group member participation. In any group to which we belong, as the leader or group member, we make choices about how to behave and how to communicate. We begin our discussion by examining what you need to know about competent leadership in groups.

WHAT IS LEADERSHIP?

When you think of leaders, who comes to mind? Whom do you perceive as group leaders? Organizational leaders? Community leaders? National leaders? International leaders? As you review your mental list, what characteristics do these leaders share? In Western culture, leaders are typically associated with people who manage crises and problems effectively.[1] For example, Martin Luther King, Jr. confronted the problem of racial inequality in the United States.

Although there appears to be some agreement that leadership is associated with managing difficulties and problems, there is also disagreement over what counts as effective leadership. Let us examine three questions regarding leadership:

1. How can we define leadership?
2. How can leaders help groups manage change?
3. How do leaders manage conflict?

DEFINING LEADERSHIP.

What is leadership? This is a difficult question to answer, because over 300 definitions of leadership have been recorded.[2] Some people associate leadership with formal positions of authority, such as a manager in an organization or an elected official. Others view leadership as directly tied to the personality, physical, and cognitive traits that one is born with. Still others contend that leadership can be taught—it is *not* a trait that is inborn in us. We define **leadership** as a communication process that helps groups organize themselves to achieve desirable goals. This simple definition suggests four important implications or characteristics for competent leadership that are outlined in Table 10.1 and now described in brief.

> LEADERSHIP is a communication process that helps groups organize themselves to achieve desirable goals.

First, leadership is a communication process. Early leadership research focused on the traits individuals were born with that enabled them to emerge as leaders within groups, organizations,

Table 10.1: Understanding What Leadership Is and How It Works

These four implications or characteristics of leadership help us understand the critical role leaders play in helping small groups accomplish their goals.

FOUR IMPLICATIONS	DESCRIPTION OF IMPLICATION/CHARACTERISTIC
Leadership is a communication process.	This characteristic calls attention to what leaders say and do—how they talk and how they use nonverbal communication.
Leadership is an organizing process.	This characteristic focuses on task functions and relational functions—what the leader does to keep the group on task and to maintain a positive group climate.
Leadership is a situated process.	This characteristic states that effective leadership first involves examining the situation and the group, and then doing what needs to be done.
Leadership is a social process.	This characteristic emphasizes how leaders guide and direct the group in its activities, whether the leader is appointed or emerges from social interaction in the group.

and society.[3] A variety of traits such as motivation, drive, social competence, assertiveness, and intelligence were examined to see if they allow individuals to emerge as leaders. However, researchers discovered no uniform correlation between personality traits and leadership. What happened next was that people began to view leadership as a behavioral process. The focus shifted from the question, "What are leaders like?" to "What do leaders do?" This latter question is primarily about communication. How do leaders talk? What do they say? How do they use nonverbal communication to get their point across? Contemporary leadership theory views leadership as a communication process that is directly tied to what leaders say and do.

TASK FUNCTIONS involve instrumental behavior aimed at goal achievement.

RELATIONAL FUNCTIONS emphasize the importance of building a positive group culture and managing conflict.

Second, leadership is an organizing process. The leader organizes the group to perform task and relational functions.[4] **Task functions** involve instrumental behavior aimed at goal achievement. Leaders help to clarify the purpose and scope of the group's task, maintain the group's focus on task, and manage the way information is collected, structured, and used in problem solving and decision making. **Relational functions** emphasize the importance of building a positive group culture and managing conflict. Both types of functions must be performed if a group is to be successful.

Third, leadership is a situated process. Early leadership work emphasized the importance of identifying the one best style that characterized effective leadership.[5] Many leadership experts contended that effective leaders are democratic in nature, regardless of the situation. A democratic leadership style involves two-way communication among people with equal power for making decisions. By contrast, an autocratic leadership style is about leaders having more power than followers, making independent decisions, and using communication to tell followers what to do. For many years, leadership researchers argued that democratic leadership is superior, because group members feel more included in the decision making and are more committed to the decisions that are made. But the problem with identifying one best leadership style is that a necessary skill for leaders is reading a situation and adapting what they do to thatsituation.[6] From this perspective, effective leaders need to examine the situations and groups they are leading, and then determine what needs to be done to keep the group moving forward.

Fourth, leadership is a social process that involves give-and-take among leaders and followers. In this sense, **leaders** are individuals within a group who guide and direct the group's activities. To understand this role of leaders, we need to consider how positions of group leadership get created. One way is for leaders to be appointed by some external authority to the group. For example, Rob was appointed to be the leader of the theater company. Another way leaders emerge is from the social interaction among group members. An individual may emerge as a leader if he or she participates a great deal within the group, demonstrates expertise other group members do not have, and collaborates with other group members. Both approaches to creating leaders have strengths and weaknesses. Appointed leaders may be viewed favorably by other group members if the people doing the appointing are well-respected. But if group members do not perceive the process of appointing the leader as fair, the appointed leader may be viewed as incompetent, or not deserving of the position. By contrast, leaders who emerge in the course of group discussion tend to be viewed as more credible. However, sometimes unqualified people emerge as leaders simply by virtue of being active in the group discussion. Whether a leader is appointed or emerges, all leaders need to be able to manage change and conflict.

> **LEADERS** are the individuals within a group who guide and direct the group's activities.
>
> **TECHNICAL WORK** occurs when the problem the group is working on, its solution, and its implementation are all clearly defined.
>
> **ADAPTIVE WORK** has problems and solutions that are not clearly defined, and places the responsibility for change on the group members.

LEADERSHIP AND CHANGE.

Perhaps the biggest responsibility a group leader faces is creating change within the group. In the opening story, Rob was specifically asked to lead the theater board to implement some changes. Indeed, as group tasks become more complex in rapidly changing environments, leaders must facilitate groups adapting to and meeting all kinds of environmental challenges.[7] The kind of leadership needed to create change within a group depends on the type of work a group is doing, and what kind of work needs to be changed. There are two kinds of work small-group leaders and followers do—technical and adaptive.[8]

In **technical work**, the problem the group is working on is clearly defined, and the solution and how the solution is to be implemented are also clearly defined. When leaders are involved with technical work, the leader is most responsible for making change happen. It is up to the leader to tell the group what needs to be done and how to do it. The leader has the authority to implement the change by simply informing the team about the change and asking them to do it.

However, not all group work is technical work, with the leader telling the group members what to do. Would you classify the kind of work Rob was doing with the board of directors as technical work? Probably not. The problem Rob is dealing with is not clearly defined, nor is the solution and its implementation. Such work is better labeled adaptive work.

Adaptive work has problems and solutions that are not clearly defined, and places the responsibility for change on the group members. Given the ambiguity and complexity of a problem, group members need to learn about the nature of the problem, possible solutions, and ways to implement any change. In adaptive work, the role of the leader is to facilitate the group members' learning, so they can make the change. In the case of the theater board, as much as Rob wants to encourage change, it is up to the board to decide how to make the changes. It is Rob's responsibility to create an environment where the board takes responsibility for understanding the problem and generating solutions.

A leader like Rob needs to get the group to consider questions such as these:

1. What is causing the problem?
2. What perspectives do key stakeholders in the group or organization hold that are now in conflict?
3. What is the history of the problem?
4. How do people respond to the problem?
5. In the past, when did the problem reach a breaking point such that people began to engage in self-destructive patterns?
6. How have people in the past tried to address the problem?

These kinds of questions focus the group on the tensions creating the problem, and the reasons why the group may be avoiding working on it. If Rob had worked with the board of directors on defining the problem, the group may have generated a number of problems, ranging from poor audience attendance to unmotivated board members. The group then may have decided that the issue most likely to be changed would be audience attendance. They may feel that talking about poor board member motivation may simply aggravate the situation. In the process of discussing these issues, they may reach an understanding that one of the reasons the board wants to avoid working on the problems is that they will be forced to confront their lack of motivation.

LEADERSHIP AND CONFLICT.

Although many definitions have been offered, **conflict** is typically defined as interaction among interdependent people who perceive others as opposing their goals, aims, or values, and having the potential to frustrate them in achieving these goals, aims, or values.[8] This definition contains the three "I's" of conflict:

> CONFLICT is defined as interaction among interdependent people who perceive others as opposing their goals, aims, or values and having the potential to frustrate them in achieving these goals, aims, or values.

1. Interaction.
2. Interdependence.
3. Incompatibility.

It is through interaction that people become aware of the differences among their goals, aims, or values. People are not telepathic (at least most of us are not!), and verbal and nonverbal interaction is the way we become aware of the differences that separate us. The notion of interdependence is also central to understanding conflict. Many times we disagree over a variety of issues, but these disagreements are not necessarily conflicts. Conflict emerges when people are dependent on one another, and one person can interfere with the other person achieving her or his goals. That leads us to the heart of conflict, which is the third "I"—incompatibility. In order for a conflict to exist, there needs to be real or perceived opposition to your recommendations, and incompatibility of the goals people want to achieve.

Now think back again to the meeting of the company's board of directors. What type of conflict do you think occurred? Three types of conflict typically emerge in groups—conflicts resulting from negative affect or emotions, differences in ideas, or differences in preferred procedures.

Affective conflict involves the interpersonal relationships formed among group members and the group's emotional climate. Part of a group's success depends on the ability to manage disagreements and conflict appropriately. By helping the group stay focused on issues rather than personalities, and finding ways to blend the talents of group members, group leaders can help move a group from being paralyzed by different styles of conflict to using conflict as a resource for greater productivity. Affective conflict may occur when some group members do not like one another, or there is a power struggle among them. People who do not like one another may begin sniping and insulting one another during the group meetings. Or, two group members may fight over who will be the leader of the group. Affective conflict can occur when people fight over performing the same role, or feel the role another person is performing is inappropriate.

> **AFFECTIVE CONFLICT** involves the interpersonal relationships formed among group members and the group's emotional climate.
>
> **IDEATIONAL CONFLICT** centers on the arguments and issues regarding decision alternatives.
>
> **PROCEDURAL CONFLICT** occurs when there are differences of opinion on what procedures to use during group discussion.

Ideational conflict centers on arguments and issues regarding decision alternatives. People may have conflict over which alternative is better. They may have conflict over what counts as appropriate data and assumptions to base decisions on. They may have conflict over how they define the problem, or what criteria for a solution are acceptable. Ideational conflict revolves around defining problems, generating solutions, setting and applying criteria, and selecting among competing alternatives.

Procedural conflict occurs when there are differences of opinion about what procedures to use during group discussion. Disputes may arise over how to structure the agenda, and whether to use

---

Table 10.2: Types of Conflict and Conflict Management Styles

To engage in productive conflict in a small group, leaders and group members as well need to be aware of these three types of conflict, and the three management styles for dealing with conflict.

TYPES OF CONFLICT

1. Affective conflict results from group members not liking one another, or engaging in power struggles.
2. Ideational conflict results from group members having different ideas about the group's problem and how to solve it.
3. Procedural conflict results from differences in how group members think they should proceed in order to accomplish their task.

CONFLICT MANAGEMENT STYLES

1. Group members who use an avoidance style tend to ignore conflict by not arguing for their own point of view or the points of view of others.
2. Group members who prefer a distributive style argue for and try to achieve what they want without any concern for others.
3. Group members who favor an integrative style argue for and try to achieve their own goals and the personal goals of others in the group.

a specific procedure such as brainstorming to enhance divergent thinking, or the devil's advocate procedure to enhance convergent thinking.

In the opening story, we could argue that all three types of conflict were present. Personal power struggles between Rob and the board members became emotionally charged; arguments over everyone's ideas about the problem and possible solutions were clearly evident; and effective group procedures were clearly absent. One way to avoid Rob's situation and manage conflict effectively is to adopt a communication or management style appropriate for the situation.

Conflict management styles are different patterns of behavior or approaches to managing disagreements and disputes. While many systems for categorizing conflict management styles exist, three styles are typically identified in group communication theory and research: avoidance, distributive, and integrative.[10]

Avoidance is low in both assertiveness and collaboration. Rather than engage in disputes, conflict avoiders do not want to expend energy to advocate their own view, or to collaborate with others. They may ignore the conflict, or shift the conversation to a different topic. When people say, "I don't want to get into it with you" or "Let it be," they are indicating that they do not want to get involved with the conflict.

The **distributive style** is high in assertiveness and low in cooperativeness. Group members who employ such a style want to achieve their goals, are low in cooperativeness, and are unconcerned if others achieve their goals. The most important thing is to achieve personal goals no matter the cost. Such a style emphasizes confrontation, and attempting to control the conversation by persistently arguing for one's own position.

An **integrative style** is high in both assertiveness and collaboration. Collaboration necessitates that all group members find ways that allow everyone to achieve personal goals (high assertiveness) while still allowing others to achieve their personal goals (high cooperation and collaboration). Put simply, this collaboration is about inventing creative solutions to conflict that make everybody happy.

It is tempting to think that an integrative style is always the best way to manage conflict within a small group. However, each of the styles can be appropriate depending on the situation. Several factors, such as the importance of the issue to self and other, the importance of maintaining a positive relationship, time pressures, and the level of trust, can dictate what style may be appropriate for a situation.[10] A person may want to use the avoidance style if the issue is unimportant, or if the other person has the power to punish anyone who disagrees. For example, suppose Rob believed certain recommendations were less important than others, and these less important recommendations were adamantly opposed by certain board members. Rob may want to avoid getting into a conflict over these unimportant proposals in order to achieve his more important recommendations. On the other hand, suppose one board member has special knowledge or expertise about one of the problems the board faces, that member may have good reasons for trying to achieve certain goals. In that situation, a distributive style may be appropriate. Finally, integration may be very useful when group members trust one another. High levels of trust often allow people to share information and engage in joint problem solving to work through a conflict. In general, most groups that use an integrative conflict management style tend to make better decisions than groups that use avoidance or distributive styles.[9, 10] That clearly was not the case with Rob's board of directors.

···
AVOIDANCE as a conflict management style is low in both assertiveness and collaboration.

···
THE DISTRIBUTIVE STYLE of conflict management is high in assertiveness and low in cooperativeness.

···
THE INTEGRATIVE STYLE of conflict management is high in both assertiveness and collaboration.

Review Table 10.2 summarizes the types of conflict and conflict management styles. At some time or another, all small groups are faced with managing conflict. We have no choice about whether conflict will occur, but it is the leader's responsibility to manage it competently. It is also the leader's responsibility to manage and overcome the following challenges all groups face at one time or another.

Table 10.3: Group Environment and Controlling the Climate

Leaders must recognize a group's current environment. Then they need to control the climate in the group using communication skills to create a supportive climate.

ENVIRONMENT TYPES AND COMMUNICATION SKILLS	DESCRIPTION OF ENVIRONMENT TYPES AND COMMUNICATION SKILLS
Supportive Group Environment	Communication in a supportive environment: • Describes rather than evaluates. • Focuses on the problem, not group members' actions. • Is open and honest. • Conveys empathy and concern. • Values all members' ideas. • Involves a give-and-take of those ideas.
Defensive Group Environment	Communication in a defensive environment: • Lacks trust and cooperation. • Is competitive and negative. • Evaluates the situation. • Tends to be manipulative of others. • Uses ambiguity to control others. • Demonstrates a lack of concern and caring for others and their ideas.

OVERCOMING CHALLENGES TO COMPETENT LEADERSHIP

Leading and managing the complexities of group life can be challenging. Keeping the discussion on track, analyzing problems and solutions in depth, managing conflicts, and leading change in a group are difficult tasks. Three essential communication skills allow competent leaders to address these complexities and challenges: creating a supportive group climate, exploring multiple positions on issues and problems, and framing the issues and problems in a way that engages all group members. Finally, managing these challenges is significantly impacted by the use of media and technology in today's small groups and geographically dispersed teams.

CONTROLLING THE CLIMATE.

Among the qualities of successful teams are that team members are highly motivated; have clear, elevating goals; and are supportive of one another.[11] Whether the group is a team of championship professional athletes or a high-performing work team in an organization, all such effective groups have supportive member relationships. Group members are able to offer support to other members and motivate them to higher levels of group performance. Central to constructing supportive member relationships is the creation of the group environment. A **group environment** is the social climate in which group members communicate. It is defined and shaped by the feelings and emotions of group members. Recognizing a group's current environment allows a competent leader to select messages that either affirm constructive feelings and emotions, or transform negative or hostile environments.

Two different kinds of group environments exist.[12] A **supportive group environment** exists when group members collaborate with each other to achieve group goals jointly. In contrast, **defensive group environments** are characterized by a lack of trust and cooperation among group members. Defensive group environments create competition among group members, arouse negative emotions between group members, and frustrate achieving group goals. The types of communication typical of supportive and defensive environments are outlined in Table 10.3.

Competent small-group communicators need to understand how supportive group environments can generate positive results. For example, supportive environments can help groups accomplish work by creating feelings that affirm and support all group members. On the other hand, defensive environments can frustrate group members from accomplishing their task. Returning to the opening story, one reason Rob may have had difficulty with the theater board is because of the hostile group environment. Board members acted in ways that conveyed superiority. They voiced their opinions in ways that indicated that they alone knew the correct answer. Such communication aroused negative feelings, and led to even more conflict among board members.

Two communication skills are particularly useful to helping create supportive climates within groups: acknowledging and reflecting. **Acknowledging comments**, as listed in Table 10.4, help members indicate that they understand one another, their situation, their process, and their actions. Acknowledgment serves two important functions. First, it allows group members to keep track of where they are in the discussion. By highlighting points of difference and consensus, how much progress has been made, and decisions that have been made, group members know where they are in the discussion. Second, acknowledgment can heighten motivation. When the contributions of group members are recognized, when positive moments are acknowledged, and when hard work is praised, then group members know what is expected, and will be more likely to exert the effort to accomplish the task.

A second communication skill is **reflecting**, which involves repeating someone's feelings about what they have said. Reflection helps check understanding, helps participants feel confirmed and acknowledged, and helps group members understand the emotional dimension of what others are saying. Reflecting the feelings of group members recognizes the validity of their feelings and beliefs. Reflecting also allows people

A GROUP ENVIRONMENT refers to the social climate in which group members communicate that is informed by the feelings and emotions of other group members.

A SUPPORTIVE GROUP ENVIRONMENT exists when group members collaborate with each other to achieve group goals jointly.

A DEFENSIVE GROUP ENVIRONMENT is characterized by a lack of trust and cooperation among group members.

ACKNOWLEDGING COMMENTS help members indicate that they understand one another, their situation, their process, and their actions.

REFLECTING involves repeating someone's feelings about what they have said.

Table 10.4: Two Communication Skills for Creating a Supportive Climate

Leaders can use Acknowledging Comments and Reflecting Skills to create a supportive climate in any group.

ENVIRONMENT TYPES AND COMMUNICATION SKILLS	DESCRIPTION OF ENVIRONMENT TYPES AND COMMUNICATION SKILLS
Acknowledging Comments	Communication that acknowledges sounds like this: • "It sounds like the problems you perceive are. . . ." • "Where we differ in the group over this issue is. . . ." • "I appreciate the hard work you put in on this task." • "Bob has done a tremendous job on this project." • "What we have gotten done so far is. . . ." • "It seems like most of us agree that. . . ." • "So, what we have decided to do now is. . . ."
Reflecting Skills	Communication that reflects feelings sounds like this: • "You seem very upset." • "I think you feel that all group members need to give the same level of effort to completing the project." • "So, Sandra, you feel pretty appreciative that Britney got her work in on time." • "This new deadline is kind of stressful, huh?" • "At this point, we all seem to feel positive about our progress, and accomplishing this task by the deadline."

to feel as if they have been heard, which helps build supportive climates. Some possible reflections that could be offered during a group meeting are listed in Table 10.4.

EXPLORING MULTIPLE POSITIONS.

Whether you are managing diverse points of view or conflict within a group, it is important to articulate your viewpoints in ways that are heard and understood by others. You also need to inquire into the opinions and viewpoints of other group members. Two skills are particularly useful to help understand the multiple positions on any issue in a small group: exploring other people's interests and positions, and explaining your viewpoints to others.

The ability to explore people's interests requires you to distinguish between their positions and their interests.[12, 13] A **position** is a stated course of action that the person wants to see pursued in the group. An **interest** is the underlying motivation or reason the person wants to pursue a particular position. Listening for people's interests, and differentiating those interests from their positions on an issue, allows you to identify the multiple motivations of various group members. During the theater board meeting, it was apparent that some board members did have hidden agendas and personal interests motivating what they recommended. Exploring such diverse viewpoints rests on your

> A POSITION is a stated course of action that the person wants to see pursued in the group.

> An INTEREST is the underlying motivation or reason the person wants to pursue a particular position.

Table 10.5: Exploring Perspectives and Viewpoints

All leaders and group members need to be able to explore other group members' interests and positions on issues. Leaders also need to be able to explain their own viewpoints clearly to the group.

EXPLORING OTHERS' PERSPECTIVES	EXPLAINING YOUR POINT OF VIEW
"What assumptions are you making about this situation?"	"I think the situation calls for. . . ."
"What values are important to you in this situation?"	"One of the assumptions I am making is. . . ."
"What data are you using as the basis for your interpretations?"	"It is important to me because. . . ."
"Why are you focusing on these data and not other data?"	"The data I'm using to base my inferences on are. . . ."
"How does it make sense for you to interpret the data in the way you have?"	"What these data mean to me is. . . ."
"How do your interpretations influence what conclusions you are making?"	"This leads me to conclude that. . . ."
"Why are you making the recommendations you are, given your conclusions?"	"Based on my interpretations and conclusions, I think we need to do. . . ."

ability to delve into the assumptions, values, and beliefs others use to form their opinions. Table 10.4 provides a list of the kinds of questions that can be used to explore others' points of view. By asking those kinds of questions, it is possible to gain a more detailed understanding of other group members' perspectives.

In addition to exploring the interests and positions of others, it also is critical to clearly articulate your own interest and position. You need to clarify what has influenced your perceptions of the problem, the data you find important, and how you have drawn inferences from those data and arrived at certain conclusions. In Table 10.5, we provide a list of statements that can help to clearly explain your position to other group members.

FRAMING THE ISSUES.

Sometimes group members become stuck in their own thinking. The way they have described or framed the problem or main issue may be encouraging more conflict. One way to refocus the group is to reframe the discussion topic or issue. Reframing helps soften and neutralize hostile comments, encourages progress, and clarifies and introduces creative possibilities. In addition, if the topic or issue is not framed collaboratively by all group members, the discussion will not honor everyone's concerns, and may lead to unnecessary conflict.

Issue framing consists of refining and rewording the discussion question for the group. This process involves groups beginning with a fuzzy statement of the problem, and then developing a more precise wording of it. Only after creating a precise wording of the problem can the group identify their choices to solve the problem. Reframing allows you to reinterpret what an event or issue means to all group members. It can get them to think about an event or issue in different and constructive ways.

> ISSUE FRAMING consists of refining and rewording the discussion question for the group.

Group leaders and members can help the group go through this framing process by following the four steps outlined in Table 10.5. Looking at the table, how could Rob have used issue framing to work with the board of directors? First, Rob might have asked about the board members' primary concerns. They may have agreed that it was low audience attendance. Second, Rob might have had the group work on the wording of the question. The group may have discussed the viability of the following three questions:

1. Will a new advertising campaign increase audience attendance?
2. Is a new advertising campaign or dropping ticket prices better?
3. What opportunities do we have for increasing audience attendance?

The first question violates the rule of embedding a solution into the question. The second question not only embeds a solution into the question, it also phrases the question as an "either-or." The third question is best, because it provides enough focus for the group but does not prescribe for the group what the final solution should be. Moreover, it invites all group members to engage with the issue, and work collaboratively with one another.

The three important communication skills just outlined will help any leader create a supportive climate, explore and examine all sides of an issue, and frame that issue or problem in a useful way for the group. Still, these basic leadership skills may be challenged in the 21st century by the impact of media and technology on small groups and geographically dispersed teams. We now examine this somewhat new challenge.

IMPACT OF MEDIA AND TECHNOLOGY ON LEADERSHIP IN GROUPS.

New communication technologies and Internet-based communication systems are facilitating interaction among group members of virtual teams in locations around the globe, and across departments and branches of large organizations. A **virtual team** (also known as a geographically dispersed team) is a group of geographically, organizationally, and/or time-dispersed workers who coordinate their work predominantly with electronic information and communication technologies, in order to accomplish one or more organization tasks.[14]

> A VIRTUAL TEAM is a group of geographically, organizationally, and/or time-dispersed workers who coordinate their work predominantly with electronic information and communication technologies, in order to accomplish one or more organization tasks.

Challenges to leading virtual teams relate to globalization, mobility of employees, and the need for group members to make collective but often rapid decisions.[15] Not surprisingly, software engineers have responded to this need with a proliferation of software programs for virtual decision making, including tools such as wikis, blogs, microblogs, discussion forums, and social networking platforms.

Given the continuously evolving nature of these technologies, leaders of groups with access to such tools have a unique set of responsibilities. The six technological responsibilities leaders must consider in the 21st century are arranged below in chronological order.

1. Determine if the group or team should use technology to work on the particular task or problem.
2. Choose among the various project team approaches, that is, traditional (co-located and face-to-face), virtual (completely facilitated by technology), or semi-virtual (consists of some group members working locally and some using technology).
3. Figure out the fitness between a particular technological tool and the major activities and tasks the group must undertake.
4. Motivate group members to use the particular team approach and technology chosen by the leader.
5. Provide training in the use of the communication technology.
6. Manage the impact of the use of the technology on relationships among group members, in particular, how they perceive the behaviors of other remote team members.[16]

Note that the first responsibility listed above is to decide if and when to use a virtual team to accomplish a given task or activity. To make that decision, competent leaders need to know about the advantages and disadvantages of using virtual teams. In today's global economy, organizations capable of using virtual teams can respond quickly to new business opportunities. This ability can provide organizations with a competitive advantage in tough economic times.[17]

Three advantages of virtual teams include: increased productivity, extended market opportunity, and increased knowledge transfer. Virtual teams experience increased productivity because of workers' personal flexibility, and reduction in commute time. And the work day is not limited to "9–5." Half of the work team on one side of the globe starts to work when the workers on the other side go to bed. A second benefit of geo-dispersed teams is greater access to different market opportunities. With work teams in different parts of the globe, organizations can acquire customers worldwide. Third and perhaps most important, involving people with different types of knowledge spread around the world can be very beneficial to any organization. Online meetings, remote computer access, wireless technology, and conferencing systems offer a way for all different kinds of group members to contribute to a common knowledge base.

Three disadvantages of virtual teams include: inefficient communication, poor leadership and management, and incompetent team or group members. The biggest disadvantage virtual teams experience is a lack of efficiency in communication, due to constraints in virtual communication media. Incorrect assumptions about the task may be made if messages are not clearly communicated. Failure to communicate competently online, in web conferences, or in e-mail can lead to frustration and misinterpretation of others' messages and intentions. Second, poor communication by leaders and managers can negatively affect any team, whether virtual or not; however, it becomes a bigger problem in virtual teams. The inability of the leader to effectively communicate to members of the team using technology can affect every aspect of any work project. Third, incompetence of any team members in a geo-dispersed team can have a negative effect on the entire team's ability to accomplish its tasks. And when the incompetent team member fails to perform, the rest of the team may not know it as quickly as they would in a face-to-face team. Virtual teams, therefore, should only consist of competent and experienced team members, due to the distance factor, which can affect the completion of any project.

Despite these challenges to virtual teams and the rapid diffusion of new communication technologies, the basic principles of communication competence remain the same for managing geo-dispersed groups and teams. Although the communication context and technology may change significantly and rapidly, the responsibilities of leaders of small groups remain unchanged.

In the opening story, Rob faced many of the challenges to competent leadership just outlined in this chapter. His first meeting with the board of directors of the theater group did not go well. Unfortunately, Rob was not aware of his responsibility to create a supportive climate for exploring the multiple positions and viewpoints held by the various board members. The board did not know how to frame the issues they needed to consider. As things got worse during the board meeting, all Rob could do was table his recommendations until a later date. How would you have used what you now know about leading small groups to help the board solve its problems?

With this chapter, we conclude our discussion of small group communication and leadership, and turn our attention in the next four chapters to public speaking.

CHAPTER SUMMARY

The increasing complexity of group tasks, and a rapidly changing communication environment have heightened the need for effective leadership in small groups. Competent leaders need a working knowledge of what leadership is, how to manage change in small groups, and how to manage conflict. Leadership is a communication process that helps groups organize themselves to achieve desirable goals. A focus on leadership as a communication process calls attention to what leaders do and say. A focus on leadership as an organizing process suggests that leaders need to organize groups to perform both task and relational functions. Task functions involve instrumental, goal-oriented behavior, while relational functions emphasize building a positive group culture and managing conflict. A focus on leadership as a situated process suggests that leaders first need to examine situations and groups they are leading, and then determine how to keep the group moving forward. A focus on leadership as a social process sees leaders as individuals within a group who guide and direct the group's activities.

The ability to manage change in small groups requires leaders to recognize whether their group is engaged in technical or adaptive work. When a group is engaged in technical work with a clear problem and solution, the leader informs the group members about the needed change, and asks them to do it. Whena group is involved in adaptive work with problems and solutions not clearly defined, the leader's role is to facilitate the group members' learning about the change, and engage them collaboratively in planning for how to change. Group conflicts result from the interaction among interdependent group members who perceive their goals, aims, or values as incompatible. Conflict can occur over interpersonal relationships and the group's emotional climate (affective conflict), arguments regarding decision alternatives (ideational conflict), and the procedures that should be employed during group discussion (procedural conflict). Managing these various conflicts involves mastering a variety of conflict management styles, including avoidance, distributive style, and an integrative style.

Group leaders face the challenges of keeping the discussion on track, analyzing problems and solutions in depth, managing conflicts, and leading change in the group. These challenges can be addressed by using three important communication skills. First, using the skills of acknowledging and reflecting, which lead to supportive group environments. Second, exploring group members' interests and positions helps uncover hidden agendas of group members, and provides more understanding of multiple positions on issues and problems. Leaders must also explain clearly their own interests and positions on the issues being discussed. Third, framing issues to allow group members to work collaboratively helps to build a supportive group environment, and avoid unnecessary conflict. One other challenge to leading small groups relates to the use of virtual or geographically dispersed teams. In order to decide if and when to use a virtual team, leaders need to know about the advantages and disadvantages of such teams.

KEY TERMS.

The key terms below are defined in this chapter, and presented alphabetically with definitions in the Glossary at the end of the book.

- leadership
- task functions
- relational functions
- leaders
- technical work
- adaptive work
- conflict
- affective conflict

- ideational conflict
- procedural conflict
- avoidance
- distributive style
- integrative style
- group environment
- supportive group environment

- defensive group environment
- acknowledging comments
- reflecting
- position
- interest
- issue framing
- virtual team

BUILDING MOTIVATION: SELF-ASSESSMENT TOOL.

Rate each of the eight communication situations described here, indicating your own typical level of leadership competence. Rate one situation all the way through for motivation, knowledge, and skills. Then rate the next situation. Use the 1–4 scale below, with 1 being minimal competence and 4 high competence.

Communication situations.

1. Leading a group that is uncertain about the nature of the assigned task.
2. Leading a group engaged in technical work that is not clearly defined in terms of the problem and its solution.
3. Leading a group that needs to engage in adaptive work, and change how they have been doing things for some time.
4. Leading a group in which members of the group are in conflict about how to manage their assigned task.
5. Leading a group in which the climate is not as supportive as it needs to be in order to accomplish the assigned task.
6. Leading a group in which the members hold significantly different positions on what the problem is, and how it should be solved.
7. Leading a group that needs to address an immediate problem, or make an immediate decision.
8. Leading a group competently that only communicates as a virtual and geo-dispersed team.

Motivation.

    1 = Distracted, disinterested, or simply no motivation to be competent.
    2 = Somewhat distracted or disinterested, but motivated to be competent.
    3 = Somewhat interested and motivated to be competent.
    4 = Highly interested and motivated to be competent.

Knowledge.

    1 = Completely inexperienced and ignorant about what to do and how to do it.
    2 = Minimal experience and sense of what to do and how to do it.
    3 = Somewhat experienced and knowledgeable about what to do and how to do it.
    4 = Highly knowledgeable about all aspects of what to do and how to do it.

Skills.

    1 = Completely incapable of behaving competently.
    2 = Barely capable of behaving minimally competently.
    3 = Fairly capable of behaving competently.
    4 = Highly capable of behaving competently.

Interpreting your scores.

Total your score separately for each situation (motivation, knowledge, and skills). The possible range of the score for each situation is 3–12. If your total score for any of the situations is 6 or less, you see yourself as less competent in that situation than you should be. A score of 7–9 means that you are average at sending and receiving communication messages in the situation. A score of 10–12 indicates that you have a high level of communication competence in that situation.

BUILDING KNOWLEDGE: DISCUSSION QUESTIONS.

1. How does the nature of the group task—technical or adaptive—influence the type of leadership the small group needs?
2. What are the defining characteristics of a conflict situation that is affective, ideational, or procedural?
3. Is using an integrative style the best way to manage group conflict? When might it be desirable to use avoidance and distributive conflict management styles?
4. What are the differences between supportive and defensive group environments? What kinds of communication can help create supportive group environments?
5. How does exploring multiple positions contribute to constructing a supportive group environment? What are the different strategies leaders can use to explore group members' interests and positions on an issue?
6. How does framing contribute to constructing a supportive group environment? What are the different strategies leaders can use to frame and reframe issues and problems?

BUILDING SKILLS: STUDENT ACTIVITIES.

Individual activities.

1. Think about a group you belong to where you offered suggestions or stated conclusions during the discussion. Reflect on what you said, and how you may have said it differently to be a more competent group member.

2. Identify a leader who has recently instituted some change in a group. Interview that group leader and explore what he or she did to create the change. What techniques or strategies did he or she employ to create the change? Did the leader view the change as involving technical or adaptive work?

3. Reflect on a conflict you have participated in or observed in a small group. If you were the group leader, based on the information in this chapter, how would you have managed the conflict most productively?

4. Take a group you belong to, and identify an issue or topic that is important to the group. Using the steps involved with issue framing, generate three acceptable discussion questions that could guide the group discussion.

5. Go to the website of the Center for Creative Leadership at http://www.ccl.org/leadership/programs/LDRFlash.aspx?flash=cdp. Examine the core development programs on the site. Given the information on the web site, prepare a presentation for your class summarizing what this Center thinks a competent and effective leader should know and be able to do.

Group activities.

1. In a group of four to five people, have each person describe an occasion when she or he was the appointed or emergent leader of a small group. Share what each of you did well as the group leader, and what you could have done better.

2. In a group of four to five students, select an important issue or problem currently being discussed on your campus or in the news. Would you characterize this issue as being a technical or adaptive problem? If you were to lead an effort to address the problem, what steps would you take?

3. In groups of four to five students, identify a conflict in a small group that one of you participated in or observed. Using the three conflict management styles of avoidance, distributive, and integrative, role-play in the group how that conflict could be managed using each of the three styles. Which conflict management style would work best and why?

4. In groups of two to three students, identify a small-group situation each of you has experienced recently. Have each student describe the climate—was it supportive or defensive? Have each student describe the various positions on the topic discussed by the group—were there multiple interests and positions on the issue?

5. In groups of four to five students, have each student identify and describe a virtual project team he or she has experienced. Describe how well the virtual team worked, and the advantages and disadvantages of working as a virtual team.

NOTES

1. See Kouzes & Posner (2003).
2. See Bennis & Nanus (2007).

3. See Stogdill (1948).

4. See Barge (2003).

5. See Lewin, Lippitt, & White (1939).

6. See Bolman & Deal (2003).

7. See Heifetz (2004).

8. See Putnam & Poole (1987), p. 552.

9. See Folger, Poole, & Stutman (2001).

10. See Kuhn & Poole (2000).

11. See LaFasto & Larson (2001).

12. See Gibb (1961).

13. See Stone, Patton, & Heen (2000).

14. See Ale Ebrahim, Ahmed, & Taha (2009).

15. See Turban, Liang, & Wu (2011).

16. See Bazarova & Walther (2009).

17. See Bergiel, Bergiel, & Balsmeier (2008).

REFERENCES

Ale Ebrahim, N., Ahmed, S., & Taha, Z. (2009). Virtual R & D teams in small and medium enterprises: A literature review. *Scientific Research and Essay, 4*(13), 1575–1590.

Barge, J. K. (2003). Leadership as organizing. In R. Y. Hirokawa, R. S. Cathcart, L. A. Samovar, & L. D. Henman (Eds.), *Small group communication: Theory and practice: Anthology* (8th ed., pp. 199–214). Los Angeles, CA: Roxbury.

Bazarova, N., & Walther, J. B. (2009). Attributions in virtual groups: Distances and behavioral variations in computer-mediated discussions. *Small Group Research, 40*(2), 138–162.

Bennis, W. G., & Nanus, B. (2007). *Leaders: The strategies of taking charge.* San Francisco, CA: HarperCollins.

Bergiel, B., Bergiel, E., & Balsmeier, P. (2008). Nature of virtual teams: A summary of their advantages and disadvantages. *Management Research News, 31*(2), 99–110.

Bolman, L. G., & Deal, T. E. (2003). *Reframing organizations: Artistry, choice, and leadership* (2nd ed.). San Francisco, CA: Jossey-Bass.

Folger, J., Poole, M. S., & Stutman, R. (2001). *Working through conflict: Strategies for relationships, groups, and organizations.* New York, NY: Addison Wesley Longman.

Gibb, J. (1961). Defensive communication. *The Journal of Communication, 11*(3), 141–148.

Heifetz, R. A. (2004). Adaptive work. In G. R. Goethals, G. J. Sorenson, & J. M. Burns (Eds.), *Encyclopedia of leadership.* Thousand Oaks, CA: Sage

Kouzes, J. M., & Posner, B. Z. (2003). *The leadership challenge: How to get extraordinary things done in organizations* (2nd ed.). San Francisco, CA: Jossey-Bass.

Kuhn, T., & Poole, M. S. (2000). Do conflict management styles affect group decision making? Evidence from a longitudinal field study. *Human Communication Research, 26*(4), 558–590.

LaFasto, F., & Larson, C. (2001). *When teams work best.* Thousand Oaks, CA: Sage.

Lewin, K., Lippitt, R., & White, R. K. (1939). Patterns of aggressive behavior in experimentally created "social climates." *Journal of Social Psychology, 10*(2), 269–299.

Putnam, L. L., & Poole, M. S. (1987). Conflict and negotiation. In F. M. Jablin, L. L. Putnam, K. H. Roberts, & L. W. Porter (Eds.), *Handbook of organizational communication* (pp. 549–599). Thousand Oaks, CA: Sage.

Stogdill, R. M. (1948). Personal factors associated with leadership: A survey of the literature. *Journal of Psychology, 25*(1), 35–71.

Stone, D., Patton, B., & Heen, S. (2000). *Difficult conversations: How to discuss what matters most.* New York, NY: Penguin.

Turban, E., Liang, T., & Wu, S. (2011). A framework for adopting collaboration 2.0 tools for virtual group decision making. *Group Decision and Negotiation, 20*(2), 137–154.

PART FOUR

PUBLIC SPEAKING

CHAPTER ELEVEN

SPEECH PREPARATION

BUILDING KNOWLEDGE

- **Rhetoric and History of Public Speaking**
  The Greek Period
  The Roman Period

- **What Is Public Speaking?**
  Types of Speeches
  Types of Delivery

- **Analyzing the Audience and Situation**
  The Listeners
  The Situation

- **Choosing and Narrowing the Topic**
  Finding a Good Topic
  Adapting and Narrowing the Topic

- **Developing a Speech Purpose and Thesis Statement**
  General Purpose and Specific Purpose
  Thesis Statement

- **Gathering Support Materials**
  Personal Observations and Conducting Interviews
  Using the Internet
  Evaluating Internet Sources
  Using the Library
  Support Materials and Critical Thinking

- **Organizing and Outlining**
  Organizational Patterns
  Basics of Outlining
  Types of Outlines
  Introduction, Body of the Speech, and Conclusion

- **Chapter Summary**
  Key Terms
  Building Motivation: Self-Assessment Tool
  Building Knowledge: Discussion Questions
  Building Skills: Student Activities

To speak and to speak well are two things. A fool may talk, but a wise man speaks.
—Ben Jonson, Renaissance playwright, 1572–1637

. . .

Terry approached speech preparation the way many students do, facing a blank computer screen the night before his speech. He had chosen a topic and done a little research for the speech he had to give in a marketing class on Tuesday morning. But when he got home from school at eight o'clock Monday night, he had not yet organized the support materials or prepared an outline for the speech. He found himself with a mountain of information that lacked organization and focus. By midnight, he had sifted through the research material and achieved some semblance of a speech outline, but had no energy left to practice the presentation. So he went to bed, planning to arrive early enough at school to practice with his friend, Sean, who no doubt was well prepared for his presentation.

Sean was ready to present his speech. When the assignments were given out, he took the time to get acquainted with other students in the class before choosing his speech topic. He was surprised to learn that most of his classmates were interested in job skills needed in the marketplace, but they were not well informed about the need for on-the-job communication and public speaking skills. Based on that bit of information, Sean chose the importance of public speaking in a business setting as his speech topic. The purpose of his speech would be to motivate other business majors like himself to think about the benefits of continuing to improve their public speaking skills beyond graduation. He interviewed his manager at work and also the developer of a website about public speaking in the work setting. He located several good sources of information on the Internet and in the campus library, and prepared an outline for presenting the speech. He had even practiced ahead of time using a computerized presentation as a visual aid. You can probably guess what happened in the marketing class the next morning. Not only did Sean get a higher grade than Terry, his speech was better received, and he felt more confident presenting it. Sean presented his speech competently, because he understood the importance of speech preparation.

Well-known communication researchers affirm that the amount of preparaton time, including time spent practicing and revising your speech, results in higher speech grades.[1] This competent speech preparation begins with knowledge—an understanding of the roots of public speaking in rhetoric, the various types of speeches, and different ways you can deliver a speech.

RHETORIC AND HISTORY OF PUBLIC SPEAKING

When you present your next speech, you are participating in the age-old tradition of rhetoric.[2] **Rhetoric**—the art of influencing an audience through public speech—dates back many centuries, with its roots in the Greek and Roman periods of history.

THE GREEK PERIOD.

Long ago, before 500 B.C.E., a teacher and his student, Corax and Tisias, taught ordinary citizens on the island of Sicily how to organize arguments to defend themselves in court. The work of Corax and Tisias led to the early development of rhetoric in ancient Greece. In 481 B.C.E., a group of Greek philosophers, called sophists, began to teach about thinking and speaking persuasively.[3] Isocrates carried on the traditions of the sophists. He had his students learn about a variety of subjects and then form political, social, and ethical judgments, so they would become better citizens and more eloquent public speakers.

> **RHETORIC** is the art of influencing an audience through public speech.
>
> **DIALECTIC** is a question-and-answer process used to examine all sides of an issue in search of the truth.

Plato, one of the most famous Greek philosophers, stressed participation in **dialectic**, a question-and-answer process used to examine all sides of an issue in search of the truth. Another famous Greek philosopher and writer, Aristotle, a student of Plato, was responsible for the first fully developed and unified body of rhetorical thought. His book, *Rhetoric*, is considered the foundation of the communication discipline, and he often is referred to as the father of modern communication. Aristotle saw logic as essential to understanding any subject. He was the first to describe a system of persuasion for Western culture based on logic (*logos*), emotion (*pathos*), and speaker credibility (*ethos*). He also was the first to identify the five canons of rhetoric, listed below. These classical canons for public speaking are like steps a competent speaker follows when preparing and presenting a speech.

- *Invention* is identifying—or inventing—the materials that will make up your speech, including a topic and information to support it.
- *Arrangement* is organizing—or arranging—what you have invented in a logical and effective manner to accomplish the goal of the speech.
- *Style* is the manner and way you give the speech, most particularly the way you use language.
- *Delivery* is the presentation of the speech itself, how it is actually delivered to the audience.
- *Memory*—memorizing your speech—is a rhetorical canon of less importance today, since speeches typically are not memorized by public speakers.

Aristotle's ideas about public speaking are still taught today to help students understand persuasive speaking (See Chapter Fourteen).

THE ROMAN PERIOD.

The Romans continued the tradition of public speaking that began with the Greeks. In the second century B.C.E., Cicero combined rhetoric and philosophy in his writings about public speaking. Like the Greeks, he believed good public speakers needed a comprehensive education, but his unique contribution was a refined process for analyzing issues and developing a speech.

In the first century A.D., another Roman, Quintilian, extended the Roman tradition of public speaking by developing a series of questions to encourage creative, critical thinking on important social and philosophical issues. Quintilian is credited with a concern for public speakers being ethical as well as effective. If you recall in Chapter Two, competent communication is described as containing ethics and effectivenesss. In his early writings, Quintilian described the ideal speaker as a good man (person) speaking well. By that, he meant that an effective speaker is also ethical and of good character.

The basic ideas about rhetoric introduced centuries ago by the Greeks and Romans have endured until the present day. Modern-day rhetoricians speak of the need for citizens in contemporary society to move toward greater civility as they debate and argue in public forums. They recommend using what they call an invitational form of rhetoric in order to engage in ethical exchanges in difficult situations.[4] Invitational rhetoric is less driven by trying to persuade the other side to adopt your viewpoint and more driven by respectful dialogue. Training in public speaking, such as what you are now experiencing, prepares you to participate effectively in respectful and civil public discussions. Given this goal, let us now think about what public speaking is and how it works.

WHAT IS PUBLIC SPEAKING?

Public speaking is communication from one to many. A single person—or sometimes a group of people—presents a message to a few or many people, who usually do not have speaking roles, except sometimes asking questions. These speeches can be categorized according to the type of speech—its purpose—and how the speech is delivered or presented.

TYPES OF SPEECHES.

Although in the future you may be asked to give a speech to entertain an audience or commemorate a special occasion, the two types of speeches covered in most public-speaking classes are informative and persuasive. An **informative speech** has the purpose of communicating something new or a new perspective to an audience, and moving listeners to greater understanding or insight. A **persuasive speech** has the purpose of influencing an audience's attitudes, beliefs, values, or behaviors, and moving listeners to change or to action of some kind.

TYPES OF DELIVERY.

Both types of speeches—informative and persuasive—can be presented using any one of four different methods of delivery: impromptu, extemporaneous, manuscript, or memorized. Each type of delivery involves a different amount of preparation time, and is appropriate to use in different public speaking situations.

The **impromptu speech** is delivered with the least amount of preparation, usually with little or no time to plan your

PUBLIC SPEAKING is when a single person—or sometimes a group of people—presents a message to a few or many people, who usually do not have speaking roles, except sometimes asking questions.

AN INFORMATIVE SPEECH has the purpose of communicating something new or a new perspective to an audience, and moving listeners to greater understanding or insight.

A PERSUASIVE SPEECH has the purpose of influencing an audience's attitudes, beliefs, values, or behaviors, and moving listeners to change or to action of some kind.

AN IMPROMPTU SPEECH is delivered with the least amount of preparation, usually with little or no time to plan your remarks.

remarks. Your first speech in a public-speaking class could be an impromptu. If that happens, Table 11.1 provides some good advice for this type of delivery.

Unlike the impromptu, an **extemporaneous speech** is carefully planned and prepared ahead of time. It is delivered in a conversational tone of voice using note cards or a presentational outline to remember key ideas and information. Because your note cards or outline contain only key words to remind you of what to say, the wording of the speech varies each time it is presented, creating an illusion of a spontaneous delivery. This spontaneity is key to this type of speech reaching the audience in a meaningful way. Extemporaneous speaking is one of the most popular types of delivery but, despite its advantages, it often is difficult to keep within a time limit. You can remedy this problem by including less information and practicing the speech ahead of time to be sure you can cover what is on your note cards.

AN EXTEMPORANEOUS SPEECH is carefully planned and prepared ahead of time, and is delivered in a conversational tone of voice using note cards or a presentational outline.

A MANUSCRIPT SPEECH is written out ahead of time and read word for word to the audience.

A MEMORIZED SPEECH requires the most preparation because it is fully written out and memorized ahead of time, then spoken to the audience word for word.

A **manuscript speech** is written out ahead of time and read word for word to the audience. If you were to write out the content of each note card or item from the speech outline for an extemporaneous speech, it would become a manuscript speech. This type of delivery is called for when complete accuracy is necessary, like a keynote address at an important conference or business meeting. Although accuracy and formality are advantages, a problem with this type of delivery is a lack of spontaneity—speakers sometimes make less eye contact and gesture less as they read the speech. You can handle this problem by preparing the manuscript using more adverbs and adjectives to liven up the speech, and shorter paragraphs that are easier to come back to after looking up to make eye contact. Type the manuscript in large capital letters for ease of reading. And practice with the manuscript, so you memorize some parts and can say them to the audience instead of just reading them.

A **memorized speech** requires the most preparation because it is fully written out and memorized ahead of time, then spoken to the audience word for word. Like a manuscript speech, this type of delivery is used when accuracy is crucial, but it is the most time-consuming and frequently least effective, because it can appear rehearsed and insincere. Furthermore, if the speech is interrupted for

Table 11.1: Suggestions for Impromptu Speaking

Debaters need to be skilled at organizing their remarks quickly and in the moment. These five suggestions will help you prepare an impromptu speech quickly and effectively.

DEBATERS' FIVE IDEAS FOR PREPARING PUBLIC REMARKS

1. First, keep your composure and try to relax.
2. Before you speak, jot down quick notes to focus and organize what you will say.
3. Quickly figure out your single most important point and something to illustrate and support it. Keep your remarks organized around that central theme or idea.
4. Decide on a simple introduction, middle, and conclusion to organize what you will say.
5. When you get to your conclusion, say it and stop speaking. The biggest mistake impromptu speakers make is talking on and on.

some reason, you may lose your place in the text. These problems can be avoided by practicing the speech so much that you can convey spontaneity and sincerity to the audience when you deliver it.

ANALYZING THE AUDIENCE AND SITUATION

As you learned in Chapter Two, the context in which communication takes place influences and shapes any communication event. Therefore, competence in public speaking calls for carefully preparing and adapting your speech to the particular context. To adapt your speech to the context, you must consider two critical factors—the audience or listeners, and the particular speaking situation.

THE LISTENERS.

One of the main reasons a speech fails to achieve its goal is because the speaker does not know his or her listeners well enough. **Audience analysis** is the process a speaker uses to ascertain relevant facts and information about the listeners that then shape how the speech is prepared and delivered. The key word here is relevant. You do not need to find out everything about the audience, but you do need to be aware of anything about them that will affect how they perceive and react to you and your speech. Three sets of characteristics about the listeners are important to know:

1. Personal (demographic) characteristics.
2. Cultural characteristics.
3. Psychological characteristics.[5]

As you analyze these characteristics, it is helpful to think about the audience on a scale ranging from highly similar (the audience members are much like one another) to highly diverse (the audience members are not very much alike). Greater diversity in personal, cultural, or psychological characteristics represents a greater challenge as you choose a topic and adapt it to the particular audience.

Personal characteristics include objective demographic information about the audience members. Most relevant are the listeners' ages, household types, education, occupation, and income levels.

> AUDIENCE ANALYSIS is the process a speaker uses to as certain relevant facts and information about the listeners that then shape how the speech is prepared and delivered.

Age is often an indicator of the concerns or interests of listeners. If your audience is fairly similar in age, be sure your topic is one that appeals to the average age of the listeners. If they are diverse in age, provide background information for any ideas with which they may be unfamiliar.

> PERSONAL CHARACTERISTICS include objective demographic information about the audience members.

Household type—who is actually living together in the household—is another personal characteristic that may affect audience reactions. Today's diverse household types include many people living alone, households with two working parents, single-parent families, stepfamilies, intergenerational families with grandparents and grandchildren living under the same roof, and gay and lesbian households. Choose a topic and develop your speech so that it is equally appealing and respectful regardless of listeners living in different household types.

Knowing the educational level of your listeners will also help you prepare a speech they will relate to and find engaging. The main impact of their educational background is that it represents what audience members know and do not know regarding your topic. So let their educational background guide how you develop your topic. If the topic is one the audience would only know about through more education, fill them in so they can appreciate it.

What audience members do for a living and how much they earn also can provide insights into what they will find interesting. Occupational choices sometimes indicate people's likes and dislikes, and their income may shape what they are able to do in life and what they want to hear about in a speech. If there is a high level of occupational similarity, choose a topic with appeal to those similarities. If there is a high level of economic diversity, be sure that your topic will be interesting, regardless of income level.

As we discussed in Chapter Three, culture affects and shapes everything people perceive, learn, understand, and know. Therefore, cultural characteristics of audience members influence what they expect from a speech and how they will react to it. **Cultural characteristics** of importance to public speaking come from two kinds of groups that listeners belong to: those they are born into or grow up in (such as their biological sex, race, and ethnicity), and groups they may choose to belong to (such as their religion, clubs, political parties, or other sorts of organizations). By becoming aware of the groups your listeners belong to, you can prepare a more effective speech that appeals to and respects their culturally diverse experiences and perspectives. This is particularly important in contemporary society, because today's audiences often represent a rich mix of interests and racial and ethnic backgrounds.

CULTURAL CHARACTERISTICS of audience members come from two kinds of groups that listeners belong to: those they are born into or grow up in, and groups they may choose to belong to.

Indeed, statisticians say that by the year 2050, the racial and ethnic demographics of United States society will shift significantly.[6] Their prediction is that the overall proportions of White and non-White populations will change. Whites are currently a majority, but by or before 2050, they will account for only about half the total population, and the other half will be made up of a mix of other racial and ethnic groups—African Americans, Asian Americans, Hispanic Americans, and so forth.

Here are some concrete guidelines for analyzing a diverse audience and adapting your speech, so that it is appropriate for the listeners and effective in the particular context.[7]

- Avoid stereotyping. Despite the need to consider similarities in the personal and psychological characteristics of the listeners, do not assume any characteristic is always true of all of your listeners simply because they belong to a certain group.
- Avoid ethnocentrism. Do not use your own culture or group as the standard against which others are measured and evaluated.
- Avoid bias. Do not make judgments about listeners' preferences, interests, abilities, or knowledge of certain topics based on their race, ethnicity, or gender.
- Show an interest in other cultures. Your listeners will appreciate it if you include diverse opinions or observations from members of other cultures.
- Respect differences in how other cultures communicate. Adapt your communication style to the audience, but do so without offending your listeners. If you know the audience prefers a certain communication style, use it.
- Respect how different cultures organize and present information. Some cultures prefer organizing ideas linearly, coming directly to the point, presenting the speech purpose, and moving quickly from one point to the next. Other cultures prefer a less direct approach and consider directness impolite and even aggressive.

Psychological characteristics of the audience that must be analyzed include their needs and motivation and their attitudes, beliefs, and values. These characteristics represent subjective information that frequently is more difficult to determine than objective, personal characteristics. At a glance, you can estimate the average age and even income of an audience (based on their clothing, accessories, etc.), but ascertaining what they might

PSYCHOLOGICAL CHARACTERISTICS of audience members include their needs and motivations and their attitudes, beliefs, and values.

need or value is far more difficult. Communication experts agree that it is essential to assess and understand those needs in order to develop meaningful messages and effective speeches.[8] The reason is that most people are motivated to listen more attentively if the information presented relates to a topic they need to know about.

Along with listeners' needs, their attitudes, beliefs, and values impact their reactions to a speech. For the purpose of audience analysis, the following descriptions clarify these three psychological aspects of a person. Attitudes are psychological reactions (to another person, object, or concept) that affect people's behaviors. Our attitudes represent what we like or dislike. For instance, if you have a generally positive attitude toward work, most days you go to your job cheerfully. Beliefs are people's basic convictions about what is true or false, based on their own knowledge and experience. If you hold the belief that people should work hard to get ahead, you will apply yourself at work and give your all to the job. Values are deeply rooted clusters of attitudes and beliefs that reflect what a person considers important or unimportant, worthy or unworthy.[9] If you highly value professional

Figure 11.1: Attitudes, Beliefs, and Values

Values are at the very core of a person, surrounded by her or his beliefs, and then attitudes. A public speaker will have a hard time changing or influencing listeners' core values.

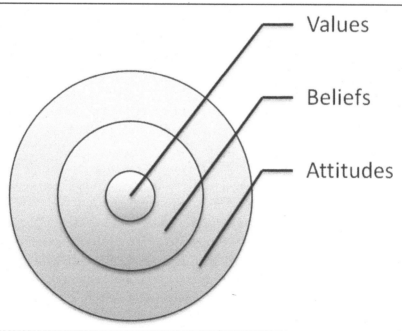

success and achieving status in the workplace, when offered a promotion, you will accept the offer regardless of any marginal negative consequences.

Your speech will be more effective if you carefully analyze your listeners' attitudes, beliefs, and values. They are more likely to listen to and remember information that supports or is at least compatible with their existing attitudes. Because beliefs are based on what people think is true, it will take presenting facts and persuasive evidence to influence their beliefs. Values are harder to change than attitudes or beliefs. However, a speech related to your audience's values will hold their attention because they really care about it.

THE SITUATION.

Besides analyzing the listeners' personal, cultural, and psychological characteristics, a competent speaker also analyzes the speaking situation. **Situation analysis** includes both time and place.

Timing involves how much time you have to speak and when the speech is scheduled to be presented. When you consider how much time you have to present, remember that two of the worst things you can do as a public speaker are to run overtime and to rush to cover everything. If your speech runs too long and you seem to be rambling on and on, you will lose your audience's attention and appear disorganized. But if your speech runs too short and you fail to fill up the time allotted, your audience may think that you do not have much to say, or that you did not gather sufficient information for the speech. The best way to stay within the time constraints, as mentioned earlier, is to prepare carefully and practice your speech out loud ahead of time to see how long it takes to present. If it runs overtime, you obviously need to cut something out. If it runs short, you need to enhance the content to lengthen the speech.

Another frequently overlooked aspect of timing is the time of day when you will speak. Listeners are more alert around midmorning but tend to become fatigued by midafternoon, so a complex topic may be poorly received later on in the day. If you are required to present complex information in the afternoon, enliven it for your listeners with effective presentational aids or with some information that is easy to pay attention to, like stories or examples.

Place relates to the context in which the speech is presented, the environment and the physical surroundings. Place includes the arrangement of furnishings and seating for the listeners, audiovisual equipment being used, and any other physical factor in the situation that could impact your speech, such as lighting.

Experienced public speakers often visit the place where they will speak ahead of time to reduce the possibility of last-minute surprises. They check out the location of the speaker's podium, where the listeners will be seated, and where they themselves will be seated before and after the speech. Most important, they examine the audiovisual equipment to be sure it will work well during the actual presentation. They examine the lighting in the room to be sure all listeners will be able to see their visual aids while taking notes. If you familiarize yourself with the speaking place, you will encounter fewer problems later, and will feel more confident when the time comes to give the speech.

As you now can see, analyzing the audience and situation for your speech is essential to public speaking competence. Using the results of that analysis, a competent speaker next turns her or his attention to the speech topic.

> SITUATION ANALYSIS includes both time and place. Timing involves how much time you have to speak, and when the speech is to be presented. Place relates to the context in which the speech is presented.

CHOOSING AND NARROWING THE TOPIC

The next preparation step is choosing and narrowing a speech topic. While this step is critical to preparing your speech competently, many speakers overlook its importance. So you need to reflect on everything you learned about the audience and then use the following guidelines to find a topic. Then you need to adapt and narrow that topic to the interests of the listeners and to the situation.

FINDING A GOOD TOPIC.

First, it is important to understand the difference between a general subject area and a speech topic. A **subject area** is a general area of knowledge such as the American Civil War, college or work life, contact sports, or organic chemistry. A **topic** is a specific facet or aspect of a subject area. For example, the subject area of Sean's speech was public speaking. Based on analyzing his audience's needs and interests, he chose the importance of presenting speeches effectively in a business setting as his topic.

> A SUBJECT AREA is a general area of knowledge, whereas a TOPIC is a specific facet or aspect of a subject area.

The best place for you to start is with a subject area you find interesting or know something about. A good topic is one that appeals to you; if you are interested in it, you will prepare and present a much better speech. Besides searching your own mind and experiences for a topic, you also could browse through newspapers or magazines, or go to one of several websites on the Internet that includes an idea generator. An example of a useful idea generator can be found at this website: http://www.lib.odu.edu/researchassistance/ideagenerator/. You use an idea generator to search main categories or subject areas such as arts and humanities, business and public administration, sports, recreation, and leisure, etc. For each category, the idea generator provides an extensive list of possible speech topics.

ADAPTING AND NARROWING THE TOPIC.

After finding and choosing a topic, next it must be adapted and narrowed so that it is appropriate for the audience and speaking situation. Based on your audience analysis, decide on an approach to the topic that will appeal to the listeners. Then narrow and limit what you will cover in the speech. You narrow the topic by getting more and more specific about what you will cover until it reaches a manageable level for the time constraints. A common mistake is preparing a speech that contains too much information. If your speech is fairly narrow in its focus, your listeners will find it easier to understand and follow. And narrowing the topic simplifies the preparation process. A speech topic that is too broad is difficult to research.

DEVELOPING A SPEECH PURPOSE AND THESIS STATEMENT

Once you are satisfied with your speech topic, the next step is to clarify what you hope to accomplish by speaking. All successful speeches are built around a general and a specific purpose, and they contain a thesis statement or central idea. Without these, your listeners will not understand why you are speaking, and they will not be able to follow what you say. Even the best speakers sometimes fail to distinguish between the purpose and thesis of a speech; they tend to think these are the same thing, which they are not. So please read this short description carefully.

GENERAL PURPOSE AND SPECIFIC PURPOSE.

Speeches can have any one of several **general purposes** or goals, as discussed earlier in this chapter under types of speeches. The two main types of speeches, based on their general purpose, are speeches to inform (covered in detail in Chapter Thirteen) and speeches to persuade (covered in Chapter Fourteen). In addition to this general purpose, every speech also has its own **specific purpose**, a statement of the response the speaker would like from the audience. The specific purpose is written as a single infinitive statement that summarizes what you want the audience to know, do, or feel as a result of listening to your speech. Sean's speech, from the opening story in this chapter, provides this example of a specific purpose:

> *To persuade the audience to continue to develop and improve their public speaking skills beyond graduation, and for the benefit of their careers in the business world.*

As this example illustrates, a good specific purpose is clear, realistic, and focused on what the speaker wants to accomplish with the audience.

THESIS STATEMENT.

Building on the specific purpose, the next step is to formulate a thesis statement, which is said out loud to the audience when you deliver the speech. The **thesis statement**, in one or two sentences, tells the audience exactly what you want them to know, understand, and remember when your speech is done. Write it as a simple, declarative sentence (or two) that restates the speech purpose and states the main points that support the purpose. Although you may formulate a thesis statement early in the speech development process, you may revise and reword it as you research your topic. Sean's speech provides the following thesis statement:

> *Today, by highlighting the value of public speaking skills in business and at work, and by providing specific resources for continued skills development, I hope to persuade you to continue to improve your skills beyond this class and after graduation.*

••••••••••••••••••••••••••••••••••

THE GENERAL PURPOSE of a speech is its general goal, such as to inform or to persuade, whereas the SPECIFIC PURPOSE is a statement of the response the speaker would like from the audience.

••••••••••••••••••••••••••••••••••

THE THESIS STATEMENT, in one or two sentences, tells the audience exactly what you want them to know, understand, and remember when your speech is done.

••••••••••••••••••••••••••••••••••

CRITICAL THINKING involves evaluating evidence, assumptions, and ideas as you prepare your speech.

GATHERING SUPPORT MATERIALS

After you choose and narrow a topic and develop a purpose and thesis statement, the next step is to find information to support and accomplish the speech purpose. To help you with this step, we now discuss various sources of information, including personal observations, interviews, the Internet, and the library.

PERSONAL OBSERVATIONS AND CONDUCTING INTERVIEWS.

Information you gather firsthand, from your own observations and experiences, lends support and credibility to factual information. Moreover, telling a story or recounting an experience helps you relax and relate better to your listeners. To come up with a personal experience for your speech, think about your topic and whether you have done something, known someone, or witnessed something that relates to it. Tell the audience that story, and because it is personal to you, you will tell it like an experienced storyteller.

Interviewing is another effective way to gather information for your speech, either from an expert or from someone whose life experience relates to your topic. An informational interview can help you gather testimony and useful evidence such as an example or a quotation. For instance, Sean interviewed his manager at work to get her viewpoint on the importance of public-speaking skills in a business setting. Also consider the possibility of conducting an electronic interview, by e-mail or Skype, for example. Electronic interviewing is considered important to such an extent that some students have received specialized training in this skill.[10] You could locate an expert on your speech topic using the Internet, and submit your interview questions by e-mail. Sean did such an interview with an expert he found on a website on public speaking in business.

Preparation is the key to a successful interview, so plan carefully what you will ask and how you will ask it. Include open-ended questions that the interviewee cannot answer with a simple yes or no, and prepare several follow-up questions for each open-ended question. During the interview itself, be prepared to skip questions if the discussion moves in an unexpected direction. Review your notes immediately after the interview, looking for themes or major ideas that support your purpose and thesis. Is there a meaningful quotation that will enliven your speech? If so, contact the interviewee and ask for permission to use it.

USING THE INTERNET.

In addition to personal experiences and interviewing, the Internet can be a great resource for researching a speech. Used effectively, the Internet provides avenues for researching your speech by contacting experts directly, and by visiting any one of an overwhelming number of websites.

E-mail, listservs (electronic mailing lists), blogs, and websites like *Facebook* (www.facebook.com) are useful for communicating directly with people who can help you research your speech. When contacted electronically, people often go to great lengths to help students looking for information. E-mail lists, chat rooms, and the addresses of experts in a subject area are frequently available from associations or organizations. On the Internet, you can locate a blog related to your speech topic at websites like this one that identifies the Top Ten Blogs in various subject areas (http://www.blogs.com/topten/).

The Internet does provide access to an amazing number of topic-specific websites, any of which may contain useful information for your speech. To simplify and expedite your use of the Internet for speech research, consult with your school's librarian about specialized search engines. For instance, *SearchEdu.com* is a metasearch engine that indexes and searches over 20 million websites in the educational domain, including links to the Library of Congress, world census data, and websites librarians themselves use to locate information. Consider using the U.S. government's official search engine (http://search.usa.gov/) that serves as a metasearch engine for all governmental websites. Finally, sites linked to universities and colleges (.edu) are good places to look for scholarly research or experts in a subject area. Nonprofit organizations (.org) can be an additional source of information, because they have access to large volumes of research data in a particular field. The National Communication Association, for example, is www.natcom.org.

EVALUATING INTERNET SOURCES.

Sean, in the opening story, used the Internet to search for information on his speech topic. He visited the website of the U.S. Department of Labor, and found a government document on career projections for the 21st century that stated that college graduates need more training in communication and public-speaking skills (www.labor.gov). But Sean not only found interesting information on the Internet, he also made sure that the websites were credible sources. It is your responsibility as a public speaker to validate all sources of materials you use in your speech, and information from the Internet has its limitations. Often it is not clear whether the developer of a particular website is credible and well-informed about the topic of the site. On the contrary, articles published in academic journals or well-respected magazines or newspapers typically are credible. Therefore, the support materials and/or information from any website need to be scrutinized carefully.

If you are using a website as a source of information for your speech, ask the following questions about the validity and credibility of the site. Use what you learn about the site to let listeners know that your sources are credible.

- What is the goal of the site, and is it stated anywhere? Who is the audience?
- How accurate and reliable is the information on the site when compared to similar information from other sources?
- Are sources for the information provided? Is the origin of the content documented, and are facts verifiable?
- Is the information on the site current, and is there an indication of when it was posted or updated?
- How broad is the coverage of the topic, and is it also explored in depth?
- Is the information on the site presented objectively, or does it appear to be biased? Is the information fact, opinion, or propaganda?
- Finally, who are the developers of the site, and what are their credentials? How reputable is the organization or institution with which the site is associated? Is it clear who is responsible for the site, and can the author(s) be contacted?

The above questions are typical of what college librarians ask about websites.[11]

USING THE LIBRARY.

While the Internet provides some sources of support materials for your speech, much excellent information also can be accessed in printed form and computerized databases in the library on your campus. A computerized database contains abstracts and full-text versions of documents and publications or indexes to information that is located elsewhere. Such online databases are housed in the library computer system or accessed using the Internet. They are typically fully and easily searchable. Most school libraries can provide detailed lists of the computerized databases they have available.

Libraries also contain an array of other resources including reference books, newspapers and periodicals, and government documents. Reference works include almanacs, biographies, dictionaries, directories, encyclopedias, and collections of quotations—most of which are available in print, online, and on CD-ROM. Almanacs are compilations of statistics and other facts about nations, politics, the labor force, natural phenomena, and so on. If you want biographical information about a famous person, living or dead, you could check a biographical reference book. Dictionaries help clarify unfamiliar terminology, but you also can sometimes use the definition of a word in the speech itself. Directories contain information about various professions, special interest groups, and organizations. Encyclopedias can serve as good starting points for research because they cross-reference subjects, and list additional readings and names of experts in a field. Books of quotations, organized by subject, topic, or source, could provide a clever or meaningful quote for opening or ending your speech.

Newspapers and periodicals are good sources of current and historical information about politics, business, media, crime, fashion, weather, and the many events that shape and influence society. Periodicals include popular magazines, trade journals, business magazines, and academic journals. Indexes to newspapers and periodicals can be searched by topic or keyword to find an article on practically any speech topic.

Government documents are available from most U.S. government departments and offices, which regularly collect and publish data to keep the public informed. The subjects covered in government publications are endless, ranging from college enrollment, to the unemployment rate to census data, population projections, and economic forecasts. Like other large sources of information, indexes and catalogs are available in the library to simplify the process of searching for the right government document.

Sean did not assume that the Internet was the only and easiest source of information for his speech. Rather, he also visited the school library to find support materials. Heeding the advice of his helpful librarian, he used a computerized database to research communication literature and found a journal article and a book that talked about how important commmunication and public-speaking skills are to professional success.

SUPPORT MATERIALS AND CRITICAL THINKING.

As you examine the wide array of sources of information—from other people, from the Internet, and from the library—you use critical-thinking skills to evaluate and determine which support materials are most useful for your speech. **Critical thinking** involves evaluating evidence, assumptions, and ideas, which is precisely what you must do as you prepare your speech. Researchers have learned that critical thinking and communication are intertwined and intimately related to one another. They have found that training in public speaking, discussion, and debate has a significant positive impact on critical-thinking abilities. To illustrate, even beginners in a public-speaking course significantly improved their critical-thinking skills by working on the depth and breadth of the content of their speeches.[12] So if you actively engage in researching and preparing your speech, you also will become a better critical thinker. Your ability to think critically about your topic will be obvious to your listeners, and they will judge you and your speech to be highly credible.

> CRITICAL THINKING involves evaluating evidence, assumptions, and ideas as you prepare your speech.

Here are some suggestions for thinking critically when researching and gathering support materials for your speech.

WHAT YOU SHOULD DO. . .

- Seek to understand new ideas by examining all the information and evidence.
- Consider all ideas, whether your own or someone else's, from different viewpoints.
- Probe and examine assumptions by questioning and challenging them.

- Understand the difference between a fact and an opinion. You can verify a fact but not an opinion.
- Explore contradictions and differences in opposing viewpoints.
- Weigh all the evidence before forming a judgment.
- Draw conclusions only after examining all alternatives and possibilities.

WHAT YOU SHOULD NOT DO . . .

- Rush to judgment and form an opinion without examining the evidence.
- Accept unsupported claims or assertions.
- Assume all information posted on the Internet is authoritative and reliable.

ORGANIZING AND OUTLINING

The last step in competent speech preparation is to organize the support materials and develop an outline for your speech. The importance of this step was emphasized by the Roman rhetorician, Quintilian, referenced earlier in this chapter, who said, "In speaking, however abundant the matter may be, it will merely form a confused heap unless arrangement be employed to reduce it to order and to give it connection and a firmness of structure."[13] To give your speech connection and structure, we first consider several ways to organize the support materials. Then we will look at several types of speech outlines that are useful for preparing and presenting your speech.

ORGANIZATIONAL PATTERNS.

A variety of patterns can be used to organize and structure the main part or body of your speech. Certain patterns lend themselves more easily to informative speeches and others to persuasion, but this is not an absolute rule. Your job is to choose the right organizational pattern to accomplish the purpose of your speech.

The most common patterns are topical and chronological, which are very effective for informative speeches. **Topical speech organization** arranges information according to a logical set of subtopics or subcategories of the speech topic. While the subtopics do not have to occur in any particular order, often a preferred order becomes obvious as you organize your materials. **Chronological speech organization** presents information based on time, so it is important to order the subtopics in the sequence they might occur. Other patterns, such as problem-solution and a technique called the motivated sequence, lend themselves more to persuasive speeches. Table 11.2 introduces you to the various organizational patterns for informative and persuasive speeches that are covered in detail in Chapters Thirteen and Fourteen. For now, we discuss a basic approach to organizing and outlining that will work with any organizational pattern for any speech.

> **TOPICAL SPEECH ORGANIZATION** arranges information according to a logical set of subtopics or subcategories of the speech topic.

> **CHRONOLOGICAL SPEECH ORGANIZATION** presents information based on time, and orders the subtopics in the sequence they might occur.

Table 11.2: Organizing Informative and Persuasive Speeches

Organizational patterns for these two types of speeches are discussed in detail in Chapters Thirteen (informative speeches) and Fourteen (persuasive speeches). You can look ahead to those chapters, but here is an overview of organizing to help with your first few speeches

TYPES OF ORGANIZATIONAL PATTERNS FOR SPEAKING TO INFORM AND SPEAKING TO PERSUADE

ORGANIZING THE INFORMATIVE SPEECH

1. Topic: Divides information about the topic into subtopics or subcategories.
2. Chronology: Describes changes or developments in any situation or circumstance, historical or sequential.
3. Space: Organizes information based on the positioning of objects in physical space or relationships among locations.
4. Comparison and contrast: Describes or explains how a subject is similar to or different from something else.
5. Cause and effect: Examines why something happens or happened and the results.

ORGANIZING THE PERSUASIVE SPEECH

1. Problem-solution: Identifies a problem and then proposes a solution for it.
2. Motivated sequence: Moves through a sequence of five steps designed to motivate and persuade listeners psychologically (attention, need, satisfaction, visualization, action).
3. Claim-warrant-data: Moves audience from accepting data that is presented through a warrant that links the data to the speaker's claim.
4. Refuting the opponent: Dismantles the opponent's argument to indicate the superiority of the speaker's argument.
5. Comparing alternatives: Examines two or more alternatives, and then makes an appeal for the speaker's preferred choice.

BASICS OF OUTLINING.

Most outlines look much like the basic structure for a speech presented in Figure 11.2. They contain an introduction, a body, and a conclusion. This approach to organizing speeches dates back to the Greek orators, Corax and Tisias, mentioned earlier, who taught citizens how to organize arguments for presentation in court. Their centuries-old model contained three main parts—a prologue, an argument or proof, and an epilogue—that parallel the introduction, body, and conclusion approach still used today. Remember—and this is important—that the organizational pattern you choose, such as by topic and subtopics or by time, is used to structure the *body* of your speech outline and not the introduction and conclusion.

Based on the simple structure of introduction, body, and conclusion, the outline itself should resemble the standard outline format presented in Box 11.1. This format makes use of an alphanumeric system with a consistent pattern of numbers and letters to indicate subordination of ideas. Indented headings and subheadings indicate how the points in the outline relate to each other, with main points to the extreme left and subpoints indented in a consistent manner throughout the outline.

Figure 11.2: Basic Structure for a Speech Outline

The notion of organizing a speech with three main parts—a beginning, a middle, and an end—dates back to the days of the Greek and Roman philosophers and writers.

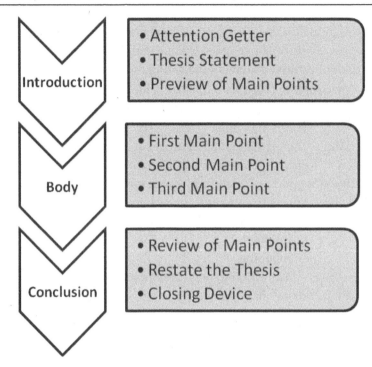

Introduction
- Attention Getter
- Thesis Statement
- Preview of Main Points

Body
- First Main Point
- Second Main Point
- Third Main Point

Conclusion
- Review of Main Points
- Restate the Thesis
- Closing Device

Here are a few suggestions to help you develop your outline. Always have at least two main points in the body of any speech. And for each main point, have at least two subpoints. So if you have an "A," you always have a "B." If you have a "1," you always have a "2." Also, the main parts of the speech—the introduction, body, and conclusion—are identified with Roman numerals. Examine the standard outline format in Box 11.1 very carefully for further clarification of this outlining process.

TYPES OF OUTLINES.

As you go through the process of developing your speech, you will do a far better job of organizing it if you make use of three different types of outlines: a working outline, a formal outline, and a presentational outline.

A **working outline** contains brief references to the support materials gathered through your research efforts arranged in the order you plan to use them in your speech. This outline acts as a vehicle for organizing and reorganizing your main ideas and support materials. As you develop the working outline, you identify the main points, and decide on the best way to organize them to accomplish the purpose of the speech. This outline is, in essence, a very preliminary, rough draft of your speech. You will change

> A WORKING OUTLINE contains brief references to the support materials gathered through your research efforts arranged in the order you plan to use them in your speech.

Box 11.1: Standard Outline Format for a Speech

Most public speakers benefit by using a format such as this to help organize speeches.

STANDARD OUTLINE FORMAT

Speech Title: Indicate the speech topic, pique curiosity, and be concise.
General Purpose: To inform, persuade, or entertain.
Specific Purpose: Infinitive statement indicating the goal of the speech.

  I. **Introduction** (Written out in full sentences).
     A. Attention-getting or lead-in device.
     B. Thesis statement (Declarative sentence stating the central idea or claim of the speech and its significance to the audience).
     C. Preview of main points (Serves as transition to the body of the speech).

  II. **Body** (Support materials that help accomplish the speech purpose, organized into 3–4 main points with subpoints for each main point).
     A. First main point (Can be a complete sentence).
       1. Subpoint.
       2. Subpoint.
         *Transition to next main point (Verbal or nonverbal).
     B. Second main point (Can be a complete sentence).
       1. Subpoint.
       2. Subpoint.
         *Transition to conclusion.

  III. **Conclusion** (Written out in full sentences).
     A. Review of main points.
     B. Restatement of the thesis statement.
     C. Closing device.

---

it often as you experiment with different ways of organizing the information, and then it will serve as the foundation for creating a formal outline.

A **formal outline** contains all of the information from the final version of your working outline, organized and presented in more detail using the alphanumeric system for main and subpoints in the standard outline format in Box 11.1. Use this formal outline to examine your main points visually, to check whether you have enough but not too many subpoints under each main point, and to review the logic of how your ideas are arranged and relate to one another. Orderliness, neatness, and logic are essential, and often professors require that this outline include references for the sources of information used in the speech.

A speaking or **presentational outline** is an abbreviated version of the formal outline, and it is what you use when you give your speech. It contains only enough information to remind you of what

A FORMAL OUTLINE contains all of the information from the final version of a working outline, organized and presented in more detail using an alphanumeric system for main and subpoints in the standard outline format.

A SPEAKING or PRESENTATIONAL OUTLINE is an abbreviated version of the formal outline, and it is what you use when you give your speech.

to say at a glance. You prepare it from the formal outline, selecting just enough details to jog your memory. This outline could take the form of a brief keyword outline on a single sheet of paper, or you could put notes on one side of a 3x5 notecard.Using either method, including too much information on the presentional outline will not allow you to see key points at a glance, and may cause you to lose your place in the speech. You also want to avoid becoming note dependent—meaning you refer to your notes too often, and lose contact with the audience when giving the speech.

As these three types of outlines confirm, most speeches do have three main parts: an introduction, a body, and a conclusion. We now discuss these three main parts of any speech. As the parts are discussed, refer back to the standard outline format in Box 11.1 where each of the three parts is summarized concisely.

INTRODUCTION, BODY OF THE SPEECH, AND CONCLUSION.

The **introduction** sets the tone for the speech, and motivates the audience to become involved in what is about to be presented. The main functions of the introduction are to capture your listeners' attention, establish your credibility as a speaker, present your main claim (the thesis statement), say why this claim is important, and preview what the speech will be about.

An attention-getting device for the introduction could be a startling statement, a question, a quotation, a personal experience, a story, or a reference to the audience or speaking occasion. An important point to remember about the attention getter is that it should be just that. Do not start by saying your name or stating the purpose of your speech. Instead, start right out by saying your attention getter to the audience. In Sean's speech, he used a quotation from a famous industrialist and financial leader, Charles Schwab, as an attention getter:

> The INTRODUCTION sets the tone for the speech, and motivates the audience to become involved in what is about to be presented.

> The BODY OF THE SPEECH supports your central claim through the presentation of a series of main points.

> The MAIN POINTS are key ideas that, when taken together, prove the claim and support the thesis statement.

I'll pay more for a man's ability to speak and express himself than for any other quality he might possess.

The thesis statement, the central idea of the speech, follows the attention-getting device in the introduction. In addition to stating the single most important idea of the speech, a good thesis indicates why the speech is important to the audience.

After you capture the listeners' attention, establish credibility, and present the thesis, you then provide a preview of the content of the speech. The purpose of the preview is to indicate what your listeners should anticipate and be listening for. Sometimes the preview specifically states the main points of the speech that are to follow, but not always. If your speech is designed to build to a suspenseful conclusion, or if you first want to impress a hostile audience with your evidence, you may not want to mention your main points in the preview.

The **body of the speech** supports your central claim through the presentation of a series of main points. The **main points** are key ideas that, when taken together, support the claim and thesis statement. They are ordered based on the organizational pattern you selected for the body of the speech—like topically, chronologically, or problem-solution. An effective speech contains at least two main points but no more than five, because listeners can pay attention to only a limited amount of information at one time. All main points should try to contain approximately the same amount of information and number of subpoints.

Within the body of the speech, the main points are connected using **transitions**—words, phrases, or sentences that demonstrate how the main points relate to each other. Transitions are also used to connect the introduction to the body of the speech, and the body to the conclusion. Transitions, like couplings between train cars, connect main points, and indicate to listeners that you are ending one idea and going on to the next. They also can serve as an internal summary, telling the audience what you have covered so far. A transition could be something as simple as saying, "Next, I would like to describe . . ." or Having examined the problem of . . . , let's consider a solution."

The **conclusion** lets the listeners know that your speech is ending, and reminds them of your central idea. An effective conclusion brings a sense of finality to your speech, and emphasizes the significance of your message. Its main functions are to review the content of the speech and summarize its meaning and purpose, refer back to the introduction and reinforce the thesis, and leave the audience with a final attention-getting message. Like the opening statement in the introduction, the closing device can be a question, a short story, a quotation, or an inspirational appeal. In closing his speech, Sean called on his classmates to continue to improve their public-speaking skills, and he used a quotation from the CEO of Pier 1 Imports as an impressive closing device:

> As I moved up in business, starting at the bottom as a lumber salesman, I watched how successful executives dressed and behaved. I saw that there was a strong correlation between their ability to express ideas (publicly) and to get ahead!

Not surprisingly, presenting an effective conclusion is one of the biggest challenges a speaker can face. There are a few pitfalls you need to avoid. Try not to start your conclusion with a phrase like, "Now, in conclusion . . ." or "To wrap up. . . ." Instead, just begin your concluding comments, and the audience will immediately know you are ending the speech. Avoid presenting new information in the conclusion because the conclusion should end the speech and not expand it, and do not apologize or make excuses for anything you said. When you have finished the conclusion, just stop talking and avoid comments like, "Well, I guess that's all I have to say." Finally, if you plan to take questions, pause briefly after the conclusion, and then ask if anybody has questions or comments.

The steps to competent speech preparation just outlined in this chapter helped Sean prepare a speech that turned out well. Preparation is key to an effective presentation, which is why we just spent a lot of time talking about it. In one recent study, overall preparation time—and practice—correlated significantly with higher speech grades.[11] So now you know how to prepare a good speech and thereby get a good grade. Next, Chapter Twelve discusses the skills essential to presenting a speech with competence.

The **MAIN POINTS** are key ideas that, when taken together, prove the claim and support the thesis statement.

TRANSITIONS are the words, phrases, or sentences that demonstrate how the main points relate to one another, and how the introduction and the conclusion are connected to the body of the speech.

The **CONCLUSION** lets the listeners know that your speech is ending, and reminds them of your central idea.

CHAPTER SUMMARY

Public speaking is communication from one to many. A single person—or sometimes a group of people—presents a message to a larger number of people. Competent speech preparation starts with an understanding of the roots of public speaking in rhetoric, which is the art of influencing an audience through public speech. A competent speaker also is familiar with the various types of speeches, the most common being informative and persuasive, and the different ways to present a speech, the most popular being extemporaneous.

Speech preparation begins by analyzing the speech context—the listeners and the speaking situation. Audience analysis involves ascertaining relevant facts and information about the listeners with a consideration of their personal, cultural, and psychological characteristics. Situation analysis includes an examination of both time and place. Based on audience analysis, the speaker then chooses a subject area and speech topic appropriate to the speaking situation. A good topic may be found in personal experiences and interests, outside print sources, or on the Internet. The speaker adapts and narrows the topic, identifies a general and specific purpose for the speech, and then writes a thesis statement, the central idea or claim of the speech. Using critical thinking skills, support materials gathered from personal observations and experiences, interviews, the Internet, and the library are used to accomplish the purpose and support the thesis. It is the speaker's responsibility to validate the authenticity of all sources of support materials, but most important is the authenticity of any Internet sources included in the speech.

The next step in speech preparation is organizing the support materials in outline form. Organizational patterns, such as topical and chronological, order information for the body of the speech in the most effective way for speaking to inform or speaking to persuade. A working outline serves as a vehicle for organizing and reorganizing the support materials into main points. A formal outline contains all the information from the final version of the working outline, organized and presented using an alphanumeric system to label main points and subpoints. A presentational outline contains only enough information from the formal outline to remind the speaker of what to say at a glance, when presenting the speech.

Most speeches have three main parts: an introduction, a body, and a conclusion. The introduction sets the tone for the speech, and motivates the audience to become involved in what is about to be presented. The body of the speech supports the central claim through the presentation of a series of main points. Within the body of the speech, transitions indicate how the main points are related to each other. The conclusion lets the listeners know that the speech is ending and reminds them of the central idea of the speech.

KEY TERMS.

The key terms below are defined in this chapter, and presented alphabetically with definitions in the Glossary at the end of the book.

- rhetoric
- dialectic
- public speaking
- informative speech
- persuasive speech
- impromptu speech
- extemporaneous speech
- manuscript speech
- memorized speech
- audience analysis
- personal characteristics

- cultural characteristics
- psychological characteristics
- situational analysis
- subject area
- topic
- general purpose
- specific purpose
- thesis statement
- critical thinking
- topical speech organization

- chronological speech organization
- working outline
- formal outline
- presentational outline
- introduction
- body of the speech
- main points
- transitions
- conclusion

BUILDING MOTIVATION: SELF-ASSESSMENT TOOL.

Rate each of the eight public-speaking situations described here, indicating your own typical level of preparation competence. Rate one situation all the way through for motivation, knowledge, and skills. Then rate the next situation. Use the 1–4 scale below, with 1 being minimal competence and 4 high competence.

Public-speaking situations.

1. Preparing a speech on a topic that seems too broad or big to be presented in the time allotted for its presentation.
2. Preparing a speech on a required topic that you think most of the audience members may find boring.
3. Figuring out the specific purpose and an appropriate thesis statement for a speech to be given in class or at work.
4. Gathering objective support materials to accomplish effectively the purpose of your next speech.
5. Gathering subjective support materials to accomplish effectively the purpose of your next speech.
6. Evaluating and providing credible sources from the Internet for your next speech.
7. Choosing an organizational pattern for your next speech, and developing an outline.
8. Figuring out an effective way to open and close your next speech—the introduction and conclusion.

Motivation.

1 = Distracted, disinterested, or simply no motivation to be competent.
2 = Somewhat distracted or disinterested, but motivated to be competent.
3 = Somewhat interested and motivated to be competent.
4 = Highly interested and motivated to be competent.

Knowledge.

1 = Completely inexperienced and ignorant about what to do and how to do it.
2 = Minimal experience and sense of what to do and how to do it.
3 = Somewhat experienced and knowledgeable about what to do and how to do it.
4 = Highly knowledgeable about all aspects of what to do and how to do it.

Skills.

1 = Completely incapable of behaving competently.
2 = Barely capable of behaving minimally competently.
3 = Fairly capable of behaving competently.
4 = Highly capable of behaving competently.

Interpreting your scores.

Total your score separately for each situation (motivation, knowledge, and skills). The possible range of the score for each situation is 3–12. If your total score for any of the situations is 6 or less, you see yourself as less competent in that situation than you should be. A score of 7–9 means that you are average at sending and receiving communication messages in the situation. A score of 10–12 indicates that you have a high level of communication competence in that situation.

BUILDING KNOWLEDGE: DISCUSSION QUESTIONS.

1. Why is the history of rhetoric of any relevance to public speakers in the 21st century?
2. If a speaker uncovers a source of information that contradicts the claim in his or her thesis statement, what should be done and why?
3. Based on how diverse the United States is becoming, what are the ramifications for a speaker when gathering evidence and support materials for a speech?
4. How apparent should the speaker's organizational pattern be to the listeners?
5. How can a speaker effectively let the audience know how the speech is organized?
6. How might an introduction or conclusion be most appropriate and most offensive? What kinds of introductions and conclusions should a speaker avoid?
7. Some speakers prefer to write out their speeches in manuscript form and then develop a speaking outline. Why is an extemporaneous speech more effective?

BUILDING SKILLS: STUDENT ACTIVITIES.

Individual activities.

1. Engage in audience analysis of your classmates by visiting the Beloit College Mindset List for the Graduating Class of 2015, which is located at http://www.beloit.edu/mindset/2015/. Each August since 1998, Beloit College releases a list of 75 cultural hallmarks that shape the lives of students now entering college. Determine what background or information you need to include in your next speech, if most of your listeners include this generation of students.
2. Develop a list of speech topics by using personal brainstorming. Take three sheets of paper and label the sheets as these subject areas: Work Life and Academics, Leisure Activities, and Social Concerns and Issues. Then write one word or phrase that relates to you or that you find interesting under each subject area. Under Academics, you might write psychology; under Leisure Activities, maybe music or sports; under Social Concerns, perhaps the environment. Next, list five possible speech topics for each subject area for your next speech.
3. Use the idea generator at this website to choose several possible topics for your next speech: http://www.lib.odu.edu/researchassistance/ideagenerator
4. Locate a site on the Internet that contains support materials that appear useful for your next speech. Evaluate the quality of that site using the evaluative criteria at http://www.lib.umd.edu/guides/webcheck.html.
5. Locate support materials for your speech topic by searching with a keyword at http://www.infoplease.com, which is a website that searches almanacs and dictionaries, a thesaurus, and an encyclopedia.
6. Take the sources of information gathered from Activities 4 and 5 above and organize them for the body of a speech using the standard outline format described in this chapter.

Group activities.

1. Break into small groups of three to four students. Choose a controversial speech topic such as: Do violent video games cause users to commit violent acts? Have each team gather support materials to support or refute the topic. Establish a time limit (one class period or the week between class meetings) for gathering information. Have each team present its findings and vote on whose support materials are most effective.

2. In small groups of three to four students, discuss the next speech you will present in class. Exchange ideas about your possible topic, speech purpose, thesis statement, possible major points, support materials, and organizational pattern.

3. In small groups of three to four students, discuss your next speech, and the introduction and conclusion you plan to use to make it effective.

4. In small groups of four to five students, work on your audience analysis skills using cereal boxes. Have each student in the class bring in a different cereal box. Each student in a small group should identify the demographic characteristics, interests, and needs of the people who would most likely buy that particular cereal. Then all students in the small group can come up with speech topics based on who they think would buy each of the various types of cereals.[14]

NOTES

1. See Pearson, Child, & Kahl (2006).
2. See Keith (2008).
3. See Heidlebaugh (2008).
4. See Bone, Griffin, & Scholz (2008).
5. See Morreale (2010).
6. See U.S. Census Bureau (2011).
7. See Nolan (1999).
8. See Monroe & Nelson (2004).
9. See Johannesen, Valde, & Whedbee (2008).
10. See Crawford, Henry, & Dineen (2001).
11. See University of Colorado, Kraemer Family Library (2011).
12. See Sellnow & Ahlfeldt (2005).
13. See Butler (1950).
14. See Gibson & Hanson (2007).

REFERENCES

Bone, J., Griffin, C., & Scholz, T. (2008). Beyond traditional conceptualizations of rhetoric: Invitational rhetoric and a move toward civility. *Western Journal of Communication, 72*(4), 434–462.

Butler, H. E. (Trans). (1950). *The institutio oratoria of Quintilian* (Vol. 3, Book VII). Cambridge, MA: Harvard University Press.

Crawford, M., Henry, W., & Dineen, F. (2001). Developing interviewing skills of accounting students on the Web: A case study approach. *Accounting Education, 10*(2), 207–218.

Gibson, J., & Hanson, T. (2007). The breakfast of champions: Teaching audience analysis using cereal boxes. *Texas Speech Communication Journal, 31*(1), 49–50.

Heidlebaugh, N. (2008). Invention and public dialogue: Lessons from rhetorical theories. *Communication Theory, 18*(1), 27–50.

Johannesen, R. L., Valde, K. S., & Whedbee, K. E. (2008). *Ethics in human communication* (6th ed.). Long Grove, IL: Waveland Press.

Keith, W. (2008). On the origins of speech as a discipline: James A. Winans and public speaking as practical democracy. *Rhetoric Society Quarterly, 38*(3), 239–258.

Monroe, M., & Nelson, K. (2004). The value of assessing public perceptions: Wildland fire and defensible space. *Applied Environmental Education and Communication: An International Journal, 3*(2), 109–117.

Morreale, S. P. (2010). *The competent public speaker.* New York, NY: Peter Lang.

Nolan, R. W. (1999). *Communicating and adapting across cultures: Living and working in the global village.* Westport, CT: Bergin & Garvey.

Pearson, J. C., Child, J. T., & Kahl, D. H. (2006). Preparation meeting opportunity: How do college students prepare for public speeches? *Communication Quarterly, 54*(3), 351–366.

Sellnow, D. D., & Ahlfeldt, S. (2005). Fostering critical thinking and teamwork skills via a problem-based learning (PBL) approach to public speaking fundamentals. *Communication Teacher, 19*(1), 33–38.

University of Colorado, Kraemer Family Library. (2011). *Evaluating web resources.* Colorado Springs, CO: Author.

U.S. Census Bureau. (2011). *PEOPLE: Race and ethnicity.* Retrieved from http://factfinder.census.gov/jsp/saff/SAFFInfo.jsp?_pageId=tp9_race_ethnicity

CHAPTER TWELVE

SPEECH PRESENTATION

DEVELOPING SKILLS

- **Presenting with Competence and Credibility**
  Becoming a Credible Speaker
  Becoming a Competent Presenter

- **Using Words**
  Clarity, Vividness,
  and Appropriateness

- **Using Your Voice**
  Rate, Pitch, and Volume

- **Speaking Correctly and Appropriately**
  Pronunciation, Articulation,
  and Grammar

- **Using Nonverbal Cues in Public Speaking**
  Appearance
  Posture and Body Movement
  Gestures
  Facial Expression
  Eye Contact

- **Using Presentation Aids**
  Types of Aids
  Computerized Presentations

- **Overcoming Challenges to Public-Speaking Competence**
  Public Speaking Anxiety
  Public Speaking on the Web

- **Chapter Summary**
  Key Terms
  Building Motivation: Self-Assessment Tool
  Building Knowledge:
  Discussion Questions
  Building Skills: Student Activities

You can have brilliant ideas, but if you can't get them across, your ideas won't get you anywhere. —Lee Iacocca, Industrialist and Developer of Ford Mustang, b. 1924

•
• • •

Wen Shu and Sergio were pleased when the chancellor of their campus invited them to accompany her on a speaking tour around the state to promote the university. At every stop on the tour, each of them would present a five-minute speech to encourage students from rural areas to come to the city to attend their school. After the excitement of the invitation subsided, Wen Shu and Sergio started to prepare what they would say. When their speeches were fully outlined, they practiced together and critiqued each other's performances. Then they revised their outlines based on each other's reactions, and presented the revised speeches to their public-speaking course instructor.

The professor said that Sergio projected his voice extremely well, but she had a few concerns with language and word choice—how he said what he said. Sergio used fancy words and jargon that might be unfamiliar to the students to whom he would be speaking. Furthermore, he mispronounced some words, did not articulate some sounds correctly, and tended to use some uhms and uhs without knowing it. The professor told Sergio to rework several parts of the speech, and practice it more with Wen Shu before embarking on the tour.

The professor liked Wen Shu's use of language, and commended her excellent pronunciation and use of grammar, particularly because English was not her first language. Wen Shu chose her words carefully, and spoke at just the right level for the students in the audience. Despite those strengths, the professor said that Wen Shu communicated nervousness and a lack of confidence nonverbally. She rocked from one foot to the other, and, unlike Sergio, she spoke quietly, and kept looking down and doodling nervously on her speech outline. In addition, no matter what content she presented, her face was almost expressionless, even when she told an emotional story about being the first in her family to leave China for college in the United States. The professor told Wen Shu to videotape her speech, and concentrate on improving several of the nonverbal cues she found most challenging.

Both Wen Shu and Sergio did a great job on the tour. Sergio watched the students' reactions to his speech, and when he thought something he said was unclear, he modified his remarks right then and there. Wen Shu succeeded in using nonverbal cues much more effectively. Their public-speaking skills training had paid off, and both students were pleased with a job well done.

Perhaps you have experienced some of the same difficulties as Sergio and Wen Shu when giving a speech. If so, you are not alone. Until most people receive training in public speaking, they have no way of knowing how to present a speech effectively. It is like any other skill—skiing, playing tennis, or even using a computer—training and practice are essential to competence. In fact, formal training in public speaking is the best way for people in the workplace and students to improve their public-speaking skills. When you are faced with the challenge of presenting a speech, this chapter will help you present it with competence and credibility.

PRESENTING WITH COMPETENCE AND CREDIBILITY

Competent speech presentation today involves what the Roman orator, Cicero, centuries ago described as style and delivery.[1] By **style**, Cicero meant the distinctive way a speech is presented that makes it memorable, which is achieved primarily through the speaker's use of language. Wen Shu's instructor was giving her advice on style by encouraging her to use language more effectively. By **delivery**, Cicero was referring to the actual presentation of the speech to the audience. A skillful delivery involves the effective use of the voice, and all the nonverbal cues Sergio incorporated in his presentation. The presentation skills described in this chapter are similar to the principles introduced by Cicero, and they are crucial to being perceived as competent and credible by your listeners.

BECOMING A CREDIBLE SPEAKER.

Speaker credibility is the impression listeners form of a speaker in a given public speaking context and at a given time. These impressions can change over time, as Figure 12.1 illustrates. Your initial credibility is based on what the audience knows about you before hearing you speak. If they have heard that you are well informed on your topic, your initial credibility is higher than if it is based on their first impression of you. That is why the introduction to your speech needs to help establish your credibility. Derived credibility, based on what you say and how you behave, develops as the audience listens to you speak. The credibility of the information you present, as discussed in Chapter Eleven, and your presentation skills discussed in this chapter, both affect derived credibility. Finally, terminal credibility is the long-term impression

STYLE is the distinctive way a speech is presented that makes it memorable, which is achieved primarily through the speaker's use of language.

DELIVERY is the actual presentation of the speech to the audience.

SPEAKER CREDIBILITY is the impression listeners form of a speaker in a given public-speaking context and at a given time.

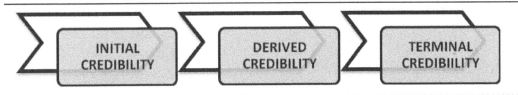

Figure 12.1: How Speaker Credibility Develops over Time

Your initial credibility is what you bring with you to the speaking situation. You develop derived credibility as you speak, and your terminal credibility is what the audience takes away with them.

INITIAL CREDIBILITY → DERIVED CREDIBILITY → TERMINAL CREDIBIILITY you leave behind—what happens after the listeners go home and think about your speech. As they reflect on what you said and how you said it, their impressions of your credibility and competence as a speaker will change and solidify.

BECOMING A COMPETENT PRESENTER.

Some communication experts say that perceptions of a speaker's competence and credibility—including perceptions of trustworthiness and dynamism—are highly influenced by the speaker's voice, posture and movements, gestures, facial expression, and eye behavior.[2] We agree, though it may sound like we are suggesting that you will become an actor giving a performance. To clarify, when you learn and are able to use these skills competently, you will do so with a sense of authenticity. You will present your best self to the audience. We will now discuss in detail the five presentation skills that will assist an effective delivery of your speeches. A competent public speaker is likely to:

1. Use language and words that are clear, vivid, and appropriate.
2. Vary the rate, pitch, and volume of the voice.
3. Apply correct and appropriate pronunciation, articulation, and grammar.
4. Incorporate a variety of nonverbal cues in the presentation: appearance, posture, body movement and gestures, facial expression, and eye contact.
5. Develop and use presentation aids to enhance the speech.

USING WORDS

The importance of spoken language and the use of words is a topic that has been studied and discussed extensively by communication scholars. One such scholar, Frank Dance, studies the relationship of speech and thought.[3] Dance postulated that as we learn to speak more competently, we also learn to think more competently.

Martin Luther King Jr.'s celebrated 1963 "I Have a Dream" speech is an excellent example of using words competently and effectively. King's speech, before a crowd of 200,000 gathered at the Lincoln Memorial in Washington, DC, often is the number one speech in rankings of the top 100 speeches of the 20th century.[4] Just reading the following section of the speech will give you an idea of how he used language:

> Let freedom ring from the prodigious hilltops of New Hampshire. Let freedom ring from the mighty mountains of New York. Let freedom ring from the heightening Alleghenies of Pennsylvania!
>
> Let freedom ring from the snowcapped Rockies of Colorado!
>
> Let freedom ring from the curvaceous slopes of California!
>
> But not only that; let freedom ring from Stone Mountain of Georgia!
>
> Let freedom ring from Lookout Mountain of Tennessee!
>
> Let freedom ring from every hill and molehill of Mississippi. From every mountainside, let freedom ring.

Competent language, such as King demonstrated, enhances listeners' understanding and enthusiasm for a speech by the use of words that are clear, vivid, and appropriate. Although most

••••••••••••••••••••••••••••••••••••
COMPETENT LANGUAGE enhances the listeners' understanding and enthusiasm for a speech by the use of words that are clear, vivid, and appropriate.

people could not deliver the "I Have a Dream" speech as well as Dr. King, the use of clear, vivid, and appropriate language is nonetheless essential for all competent speakers.

CLARITY, VIVIDNESS, AND APPROPRIATENESS.

Clear language uses words in such a way that listeners understand and can easily comprehend the meaning of your message. If your listeners have to try to figure out what you mean, they will be distracted from listening to your speech. You achieve clarity by being sensitive to how the meanings of words and phrases vary from one person to another, and by using words that are concrete and familiar to your listeners. When you present a speech to an audience of 20 people, there are 20 opportunities for what you say to mean something different.

One effective way to achieve clarity is to use words that are less open to various interpretations. To help your listeners interpret your words as you intend, use language and words that are more concrete than abstract. In Chapter Four, we described a *Ladder of Abstraction* with the most concrete words or concepts on the lower rungs, and more abstract words on the upper rungs. A concrete word refers to something specific your audience can visualize, such as an object, person, or spe-

> **CLEAR LANGUAGE** uses words in such a way that listeners understand and can easily comprehend the meaning of the speaker's message.
>
> **VIVID LANGUAGE** promotes enthusiasm for a speech by bringing the speaker's message to life, and moving the audience emotionally.
>
> **IMAGERY** is the creation of mental pictures and imagined sensory experiences through description.
>
> **FIGURES OF SPEECH** include simile, metaphor, analogy, the rhetorical question, alliteration, and repetition
>
> **SIMILE** is an explicit comparison that compares two unlike things using the words *like* or *as*.

cific place. Apple, for instance, is a concrete word and easily visualized, whereas fruit—a category of objects—is more abstract. Unfamiliar terms also can confuse people from different social or professional groups. Although it may be tempting to use jargon or fancy words to impress your audience, you run the risk of mispronouncing or misusing a fancy word, which would damage your credibility. Furthermore, if you make a point clearly the first time, you then can pay attention to using vivid language later to liven up your speech.

Vivid language promotes enthusiasm for a speech by bringing the speaker's message to life, and moving the audience emotionally. It makes a speech and its main points memorable, engaging, and real for the listeners. Vivid language can be achieved through the use of imagery, figures of speech, and other techniques.

Imagery is the creation of mental pictures and imagined sensory experiences through description. When listeners can almost see, feel, taste, smell, or hear something, they are much more likely to be impressed by it and remember it. For example, when Wen Shu described leaving China to come to college in the United States, she might have talked about her feelings on the very first day on a new campus, including details about how big the campus seemed at first, and how she sat nervously in the back of the room on the first day of class.

In addition to imagery, **figures of speech** (such as simile, metaphor, and analogy) and other rhetorical techniques (such as the rhetorical question, alliteration, and repetition) bring the style Cicero talked about to your speech. These figures of speech and rhetorical techniques help the listeners visualize, identify with, or really think about the points you are trying to make. You probably use these in everyday conversation without realizing it, but their intentional use in a speech is quite effective.

A **simile** is an explicit comparison that compares two unlike things using the terms *like* or *as*. Wen Shu could have used a simile by saying that stepping on to the new campus on the first day of class was *like* a Broadway star stepping on to the stage for the first time on opening night.

A **metaphor** also implies a comparison between two unlike things, but it does so without using *like* or *as*. Here is an example: "Communication apprehension can be the anchor that weighs you down or the wind that carries you to new heights in public speaking."

> METAPHOR, like SIMILE, implies a comparison between two unlike things, but it does so without using the words *like* or *as*.

An **analogy** is an extended simile or metaphor that asks the listeners to accept that things that seem alike in most respects will be alike in the respect being discussed. Here is an example:

> ANALOGY is an extended simile or metaphor that asks the listeners to accept that things that seem alike in most respects will be alike in the respect being discussed.

> Overcoming public speaking anxiety, for most of us, is a journey to an unknown place. The first step is always the hardest, and perhaps a bit scary. But as you travel along and become familiar with the new terrain, your anxiety subsides. And when you reach your destination, you think it was not so hard getting there after all.

> RHETORICAL QUESTIONS are asked for effect rather than to get a real answer from the listeners.

A **rhetorical question** is asked for effect rather than to get a real answer from the listeners. When you ask a rhetorical question in your speech, you are inviting your listeners to answer silently to themselves, and then continue thinking about the question while you speak. Speakers frequently use this technique as the attention-getting device in the introduction to a speech. Wen Shu could have used a rhetorical question directed at potential students to start her speech by asking:" Have you begun to ask yourself where you want to be 10 years from now?"

> ALLITERATION involves the repetition of the same consonant sound in a series of words or phrases to draw attention to certain ideas, and help listeners remember what is said.

Alliteration is the repetition of the same consonant sound in a series of words or phrases to draw attention to certain ideas, and help listeners remember what is said. When you use

> REPETITION occurs when the speaker repeats the same word or phrase several times in a section of a speech.

alliteration, the sounds add a subtle but memorable dimension to your message. Sergio might have appealed to the students by saying: "The key to *prosperity* is *preparing*, *planning*, and *placing yourself* in the front row of class this fall."

When a speaker repeats the same word or phrase several times in a section of a speech, it is called **repetition**. This repetition helps emphasize or tie several ideas together, so that your audience remembers and understands the connections you have made. It also helps to reinforce your point and make it memorable. Martin Luther King's "I Have a Dream" speech is full of repetition. Here is but one example:

> Go back to Mississippi, go back to Alabama, go back to South Carolina, go back to Georgia, go back to Louisiana, go back to the slums and ghettos of our northern cities, knowing that somehow this situation can and will be changed.

Anyone can use vivid language in a speech, but the key is to plan ahead. You could write out a rhetorical question and use it to open your speech, or you could use a simple simile or metaphor to illustrate an important point. If you choose to use a simile or metaphor, try to personalize it for the audience by using personal pronouns such as *you*, *us*, *we*, or an informal verb form such as *let's*. For instance, it would be more effective to say, "Most of us experience opening-night jitters during our first speeches," rather than "Many students experience anxiety during their first speeches."

In addition to clarity and vividness, language is guided by rules and expectations that govern what we must, may, or cannot say—more simply, what is appropriate. In a public-speaking situation, **appropriate language** presents information in a way that respects and treats all audience members as equals without being condescending or using biased language and stereotypes.

To be respectful and treat your audience members as equals, adapt what you say to their knowledge of your topic, and avoid the use of **condescending language** that speaks down to them. If your audience is unfamiliar with the topic, provide details about anything they may not understand, but do so without setting yourself up as the only expert on the topic. Also avoid the use of **biased language**, words or phrases that derive their meaning from stereotypes based on gender, race, ethnic group, age, sexual orientation, or disability. Most people know to avoid overt racial slurs, but they may hold certain stereotypes that will subtly influence what they say, and thus insult others. Gender-biased language, for instance, can result from something as simple as referring to *he* more often than *she*, which may suggest that the speaker respects men more than women. The guidelines for avoiding gender-biased language apply equally to other types of bias. Unless your audience needs to know the gender, race, or age of the person you are talking about, omit that information from your speech. Likewise, leave out references to a person's disability unless that information is relevant. By contrast, the use of unbiased language makes a positive statement about your credibility, and serves to encourage open discussion of even the most controversial topics.

APPROPRIATE LANGUAGE presents information in a way that respects and treats all audience members as equals without being condescending or using biased language and stereotypes.

CONDESCENDING LANGUAGE is language that speaks down to your audience and may be offensive.

BIASED LANGUAGE uses words or phrases that derive their meaning from stereotypes based on gender, race, ethnic group, age, sexual orientation, or disability.

Table 12.1: Suggestions for Using Language

A competent speaker uses words and language appropriately and effectively to promote understanding and enthusiasm for the speech and its message.

CLEAR, VIVID, AND APPROPRIATE LANGUAGE

1. **Clear language promotes understanding and comprehension of meaning.**
   - Be sensitive to variations in meaning.
   - Use concrete rather than abstract words.
   - Use familiar words.
2. **Vivid language promotes enthusiasm, brings the message to life, and moves the audience emotionally.**
   - Use imagery to create visual pictures.
   - Use figures of speech.
     - Simile compares unlike things using *like* or *as*.
     - Metaphor compares dissimilar things without using *like* or *as*.
     - Analogy extends a simile or metaphor.
3. **Appropriate language respects and treats listeners as equals, and avoids biased language and stereotypes.**
   - Adapt language to listeners' knowledge base, but avoid being condescending.
   - Avoid biased words or phrases based on stereotypes about gender, race, ethnic group, age, or disability.

At this point, you may be thinking that it is quite a challenge to use language effectively in your speech. However, by developing ahead of time a few well-planned and effective phrases or sentences that draw mental pictures and evoke emotions, you can improve your speech immensely. By carefully wording and writing out these parts of your speech ahead of time, you will ensure that you say them just as you intend. Use the suggestions in Table 12.1 for using language competently and deciding which techniques suit you and your speech the best.

USING YOUR VOICE

A popular communication axiom calls our attention to the second presentation skill by stating, "It isn't what you say but how you say it that counts." As a competent speaker, you use **vocal variety** to heighten and maintain audience attention and interest in your speech, varying the rate (fast versus slow), pitch (high versus low), and volume (loud versus soft) of your voice.

RATE, PITCH, AND VOLUME.

Rate is the speed at which a speaker delivers a speech. Good public speakers vary their rate, sometimes talking fast and sometimes slower, but always speaking at a pace that allows the audience to understand the words. But many beginning public speakers talk too fast because they are nervous, which makes it difficult for listeners to absorb what they say. By contrast, a speaker who talks too slowly bores listeners, and gives them time to shift their attention away from the speech. Also, a speech delivered at the same rate throughout sounds monotonous, and the listeners may tune out.

VOCAL VARIETY heightens and maintains audience attention and interest in your speech by varying the rate (fast vs. slow), pitch (high vs. low), and volume (loud vs. soft) of your voice.

RATE is the speed at which a speaker delivers a speech.

PITCH is the highness or lowness of the speaking voice.

Two keys to avoiding these problems in rate are to slow down sufficiently to gain control of your speech, and to pause silently to allow listeners a moment to think about it. Silent pauses also act as transitions from one thought to the next, letting listeners know you have completed one idea and you are moving on to another. Another benefit of pausing silently is that it helps you reduce your use of vocalized or filled pauses, such as *like*, *uh*, *you know*, and *okay*. These filled pauses, which usually result from nervousness, interrupt the flow of a speech and can be distracting. The easiest way to learn to substitute a silent pause for a filled pause is to record yourself giving a speech. Once you become aware of the filled pauses you tend to use, you can train yourself to take a quick breath instead. When you are about to present your next speech, repeat this phrase silently to yourself:

SLOW DOWN A LITTLE TO GAIN CONTROL!

Pitch is the highness or lowness of the speaking voice. All speakers have a natural or habitual pitch they tend to use in most situations.[5] But competent speakers try to achieve a more effective pitch by adjusting it to a slightly lower or higher timbre. Raising your pitch at the end of a sentence, for example, indicates it is a question. So do not do this at the end of a sentence, unless you intend to ask a question. Anxiety also may cause vocal pitch to rise to a squeaky level, giving away the fact that the speaker is nervous. Equally distracting is a speaker who uses a monotone pitch, or stays in a narrow, unchanging range for an entire speech. By varying your pitch, you keep your listeners' attention, and can emphasize important points in your speech.

Table 12.2: Suggestions for Varying your Voice

A competent speaker uses the voice to maintain listeners' attention and interest in the speech and its message.

RATE, PITCH, AND VOLUME OF THE VOICE

1. **Vary Rate.**
    - Speak to be understood, sometimes fast and sometimes slow.
    - Talk slower and more deliberately for a serious subject.
    - Talk faster for less serious subject matter.
    - Use silent pauses.
    - Avoid filled pauses.
2. **Vary Pitch.**
    - Adjust pitch to slightly lower or higher timbre.
    - Do not raise pitch at the end of a sentence, except to ask a question.
3. **Vary Volume.**
    - Vary volume but always speak loud enough to be heard.
    - Do not overpower listeners with an overly loud voice.
    - Develop a public voice for presenting speeches.

Volume is the intensity, the loudness or softness, of the speaker's voice. Because of a lack of confidence in themselves or their voice, new public speakers often do not talk loudly enough, or they let their voices quietly fade out at the end of a thought. Effective speakers vary their volume based on the size of the audience, the size of the room, and the amount of background noise they may be speaking against. Being heard is so important that experienced speakers often arrive early for speaking engagements to test audio equipment and acoustics. They speak so that everyone can hear them without straining, but they are also careful not to overpower listeners with a booming, loud voice. In the opening story, Wen Shu had a problem with volume that many beginning speakers have. When in doubt, increase your volume somewhat, then you and Wen Shu will automatically appear more confident.

> VOLUME is the intensity, the loudness or softness, of the speaker's voice.

> A PUBLIC VOICE makes use of increased variety in volume, rate, and pitch, so that your words are easily heard and understood by the entire audience.

As a public speaker, you can use volume and vocal variety most effectively by developing the use of your public voice. A **public voice** makes use of increased volume and variety in rate and pitch, so that everything you say is easily heard and understood by the entire audience. Your private voice is the one you use in interpersonal conversations or small groups. Although your private voice seems quite natural, you need to become accustomed to a louder public voice for giving speeches, even though it may sound strange at first. The three aspects of vocal variety are briefly summarized in Table 12.2 to help you remember how important your voice is to competent public speaking.

SPEAKING CORRECTLY AND APPROPRIATELY

The third presentation skill also relates to the voice, and calls for speaking correctly and appropriately for the context. Your listeners may not understand what you are saying if, for example, you mispronounce a word. An error in pronunciation, articulation, or grammar calls attention to itself, distracts listeners from your message, and damages your credibility as a speaker. **Pronunciation** means stressing and accenting the right syllables in a word. **Articulation** is forming individual speech sounds correctly with your mouth, so they combine to produce an understandable word. **Grammar** refers to the rules and structure for putting words together in sentences.

PRONUNCIATION, ARTICULATION, AND GRAMMAR.

Most speakers try to pronounce words correctly and appropriately for the given audience. But people grow up pronouncing words as others around them do; plus, regional and ethnic dialects affect pronunciation patterns. As a result, without knowing it, we may mispronounce many familiar words, saying, for instance "lyberry" for *library*, "ax" for *ask*, or "jis" for *just*. If you have any doubt about how to pronounce a word, look it up in the dictionary to see which syllables should be accented.

Besides pronunciation problems, speakers frequently fail to articulate speech sounds correctly. Most people know that *oughtuh* should be "ought to." They know the right way to pronounce it, but they may not bother to articulate it correctly. Clear and correct articulation depends on how the speaker's mouth actually forms sounds, which could be affected by factors such as chewing gum while speaking, or even wearing braces. More often, poor articulation results from simply not paying attention to how you form sounds when you speak. Most pronunciation and articulation problems for public speakers will benefit considerably from the earlier recommendation to simply "slow down to gain control."

Finally, speaking correctly and appropriately also calls for avoiding grammar errors. If listeners are distracted by a mistake in grammar, their attention turns from what you are saying to the error itself. Moreover, if you commit an error in grammar, the listeners will think, perhaps wrongly,

> PRONUNCIATION focuses on stressing and accenting the right syllables in a word.
>
> ARTICULATION is about forming individual speech sounds correctly with your mouth, so they combine to produce an understandable word.
>
> GRAMMAR includes the rules and structure for putting words together in sentences.

Table 12.3: Suggestions for Speaking Correctly and Appropriately

A competent speaker uses pronunciation, articulation, and grammar to ensure that all listeners understand the speech and its message.

PRONUNCIATION, ARTICULATION, AND GRAMMAR

1. **Pronounce words correctly.**
   - Avoid regionalisms and ethnic dialects.
   - Look up words you cannot pronounce ahead of time.
2. **Articulate speech sounds correctly.**
   - Pay attention to how you form sounds when you speak.
   - Slow down to gain control of how you are speaking.
3. **Use correct grammar.**
   - Avoid the wrong use of the verb *to be*.
   - Use correct subject-verb agreement for problem words like *data* and *media*.

that you do not know enough about the topic to be talking about it. And, while most of us pay close attention to the grammatical structure of sentences when we are writing, we are less careful about grammar when we speak in public. The typical kinds of errors most people make are simple ones, such as the erroneous use of the verb, *to be*: "All of them was there," and "Sergio and Wen Shu was late for class" are incorrect uses of the verb *to be*. *All* is a plural noun, so it should take the plural form of the verb. "All of them were there," and "Sergio and Wen Shu were late for class" are grammatically correct.

Subject-verb agreement errors also happen often when a word is confusing in regard to its plural and singular forms. *Data* and *media* are good examples. *Datum* and *medium* are the singular forms of these nouns; data and media are the plural forms. Examples of this correct subject-verb agreement are: "The data from the study are interesting; the media were expected to wait until the speaker arrived." Incorrect would be: "The data is interesting and the media was expected."

A summary of the recommendations for the use of pronunciation, articulation, and grammar is presented in Table 12.3.

USING NONVERBAL CUES IN PUBLIC SPEAKING

The fourth presentation skill, understanding and using nonverbal cues, is crucial to public-speaking competence. In Chapter Five, you learned that nonverbal cues have a large impact on how people react to messages. The nonverbal cues important to public speaking are: appearance, posture and body movement, gestures, facial expression, and eye contact.

APPEARANCE.

The discussion of first impressions in Chapter Five suggests that you should modify your **appearance**—including your clothing, shoes, jewelry, and even hairstyle—appropriately for the speaking occasion. All these nonverbal cues influence what the audience thinks of you before you even begin to speak. In a study conducted in a public speaking classroom, students rated other student public speakers more favorably as a result of the greater formality of their attire.[6] But even though you want to present

APPEARANCE includes your clothing, shoes, jewelry, hairstyle, and even hair adornments.

POSTURE is defined as a position or attitude of body parts, and that is just what it communicates—your attitude.

yourself in the best possible light, do not manipulate your appearance in any way that would seem artificial to the audience, or make you uncomfortable. Instead, a relaxed yet professional and attractive appearance is best with any audience.

POSTURE AND BODY MOVEMENT.

You are dressed to impress, and there you sit, waiting to present your first speech. When it is your turn, stand up straight, hold your head up, shoulders back, and walk with confidence to the front of the room. After arriving at the lectern, stand relaxed, but maintain an alert body posture, with your shoulders held up and in line with your hips and knees. This posture will communicate that you are in control and ready to speak. **Posture** is defined as a position or attitude of body parts, and that is just what it communicates—your attitude. During your speech, move about purposefully within the speaking area. If you are about to tell a story, move closer to the audience to draw them in, and then back to your notes as you conclude the story and move on. By contrast, nervous pacing, or letting your body rock unconsciously from one foot to the other, distracts listeners, and makes a nonverbal statement that you are nervous and would walk away if you could. Only use body movement intentionally, and try to become aware of any unconscious movements that may take attention away from your message.

GESTURES.

Gestures reinforce what you say, emphasize important points, and make presentations more interesting to watch, as well as more natural and relaxed. Gestures also communicate openness to the audience and a sense of involvement—a small gesture communicates less involvement, and a larger gesture more. Whether standing or moving, keep your hands and arms free and relaxed. Do not fiddle with a pen, a clicker, or even a button on your jacket. Rather, you want to be ready to incorporate natural movements of arms and hands into the presentation. The most important thing is to gesture in a way that is natural for you, and matches the content of what you are saying. Avoid gesturing in a way that appears artificial to the audience. If you feel that your gestures are contrived, they will certainly appear that way to the audience.

GESTURES are the large and small movements of the hands and arms that communicate meaning. They reinforce what you say, emphasize important points, and make presentations more interesting to watch as well as more natural and relaxed.

FACIAL EXPRESSION is the vehicle you use to communicate how you feel about what you are saying to the audience.

EYE CONTACT is a tool you can use to promote a sense of involvement with audience members that can make you seem credible, dynamic, believable, likeable, and persuasive.

FACIAL EXPRESSION.

Facial expression is the vehicle you use to communicate how you feel about what you are saying to the audience. If you do not believe in your claim, your facial expression will reveal your doubt. If you are nervous, your facial expression may be too strained, and you will not appear enthusiastic about the topic. Instead, try for a facial expression to match and reflect the content of your speech. If it is on a lighthearted topic, your facial expression should say so. If your topic is serious, look serious. Moreover, try to avoid either a deadpan expression—no feeling at all—or a smile pasted on your face, like some newscasters. As we mentioned in Chapter Five, research indicates that men and women use facial expressions differently when speaking. Women express more emotion on their faces and smile more, even if they are unhappy, or the message is not worth smiling about. The way to get around these gender differences is simply to match your facial expression to the content of what you are saying at the moment. Whether you are a man or a woman, use facial expressions that are appropriate to your topic and communicate your true feelings about it.

EYE CONTACT.

Like gestures, **eye contact** is an important tool for promoting a sense of involvement with audience members. Even a computational biologist recently emphasized the importance of making eye contact during presentations in that field of work.[7] To get better at using eye contact as a public speaker, mentally divide your audience into four quadrants, like a window with four panes. Look directly at and speak to at least one person in each quadrant at some point during the speech. Do not just gaze in their direction, but actually stop and make eye contact with a specific member of the audience seated in each quadrant. Not only will this communicate interest and involvement to the entire audience, you also will be able to observe how your listeners are reacting to your speech.

TRANSPARENT DELIVERY means presenting a speech in such a way that the audience does not focus on the elements of the delivery, but instead pays full attention to the message.

By now you may need some kind of guideline for making decisions about using all the presentation skills just described in this chapter. Frank Dance offered a useful recommendation for using these skills most effectively.[8] Dance coined the phrase, **transparent delivery**, which means presenting a speech in such a way that the audience does not focus on the delivery, but instead pays full attention to the message—thus, the delivery itself is invisible or transparent. In other words, do what works as a public speaker, and avoid what does not work well. To achieve a transparent delivery, rehearsing your speech several times ahead of time is critical. In fact, students who practice their speeches before a live audience actually receive better grades than students who practice without an audience.[9] And, speakers who start practicing earlier have less anxiety, and are more fluent in delivering their speeches than those who start practicing later.[10]

Table 12.4: Suggestions for Using Nonverbal Communication

A competent speaker uses nonverbal communication to support and enhance the verbal message.

NONVERBAL CUES AND PUBLIC SPEAKING

1. **Appearance**
   - Modify your appearance to make a good first impression.
   - Do not modify your appearance in a way that looks artificial, or makes you uncomfortable.
2. **Posture and body movement**
   - Walk confidently.
   - At the lectern, relax but maintain an alert body posture.
   - Move about in the speaking area voluntarily and purposefully.
   - Avoid pacing, body rocking, or fiddling with objects.
3. **Gestures**
   - Keep hands and arms free and relaxed.
   - Do not fiddle around with anything.
   - Make use of both hands, and gesture in a way that matches what you are saying.
4. **Facial expressions**
   - Use your face to communicate how you feel about your speech.
   - Let your facial expression match and reflect the content of the speech.
   - Avoid a deadpan expression, or smiling all the time.
5. **Eye contact**
   - Use eye contact to promote involvement with the audience.
   - Make eye contact with at least one listener in each of four quadrants of the audience.
   - Use eye contact to gauge how the audience is reacting to your speech.

Table 12.4 summarizes the nonverbal cues you can use to help present your speech in a transparent manner. Review that summary, and next we will discuss how presentation aids, the fifth presentation skill, can enhance your speech.

USING PRESENTATION AIDS

Presentation aids are any materials you show to or share with the audience that assist in illustrating or supporting the content of your speech, and add interest and excitement to it. Any of the information from support materials described in Chapter Eleven could be effectively presented using an aid. But incorporating a presentation aid of any kind in your speech can be challenging. If poorly used, an aid detracts from your speech; but effectively used, it enhances it. While computerized aids like

> PRESENTATION AIDS are any materials you show to or share with the audience that assist in illustrating or supporting the content of your speech, and add interest and excitement to it.

PowerPoint and Prezi are the most popular today, we begin our discussion with an overview of various types of aids, and then we focus on computerized presentations, since they are the most popular.

TYPES OF AIDS.

Your choice of a presentation aid is limited only by your imagination, creativity, and the amount of time you spend preparing it. Types of presentation aids include: objects and models; diagrams and drawings; pictures, photographs, and maps; charts and graphs; and tables and lists. Any of these aids can be incorporated in a computerized presentation.

Objects are useful aids when you want to show your listeners what something looks like or how it works. A set of gardening tools would be helpful if you are explaining aspects of horticulture. If you use an object of any kind, be sure that it is large enough for everyone to see, but small enough so you can conceal it until the point in your speech when it becomes relevant. To avoid distracting the audience from what you are saying, show the object only when you are talking about it, and try not to pass it around during the speech. If the object is too large and cumbersome to bring in, or too small for the listeners to see clearly, you can show a model rather than the object itself.

If you prefer not to create a model, you can use a diagram or a drawing to explain how something looks or operates. These types of aids are particularly useful for explaining steps in a process, or for simplifying and clarifying relationships, but they must be clear and accurate. For example, if you want to explain how a car engine works, a diagram will help listeners follow your explanation.

If your speech would benefit from a realistic depiction of a person or a place, a picture or photo can bring it to life more effectively than a diagram or drawing. For example, a photograph of the face of a young child would humanize a request to contribute to a charity for children. The picture or photograph needs to be large enough to be seen by everyone, and it should be cropped or framed to eliminate distracting details. If you want to pinpoint a location or highlight a geographical area, you could use a map as a presentation aid. If your speech is about a historical period, a map of what the world looked like at that time makes an intriguing aid for your speech.

When you are planning to present statistics or a series of numbers to support a point in your speech, you need a presentation aid that will help your listeners easily grasp the meaning of the figures. Just saying a lot of numbers out loud to the audience without an aid can be confusing. Charts

Figure 12.2: Types of Charts and Graphs

Here are a typical line graph, a pie chart, and a bar graph of columns. In most popular word processing programs, you can easily create a graph or chart to present your data.

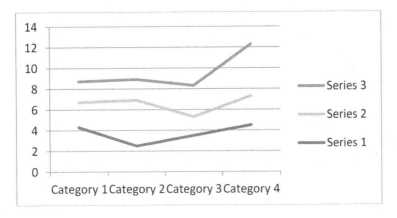

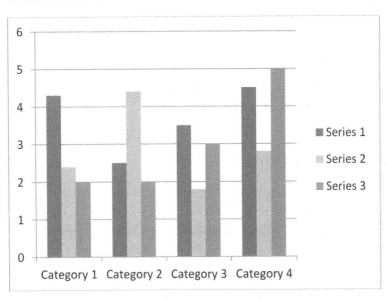

and graphs can be used to clarify therelationships among numbers, and reveal any trends or patterns. Among the most frequently used are line graphs, bar graphs, pie charts, and flow charts (see Figure 12.2 for several examples).

When you want to organize and summarize detailed information, use a table, an all-text presentation aid in which numbers or words are arranged in a grid of columns and rows. Articles in academic journals often present the results of research studies in table form. In a speech, you can use color or highlighting in a table to focus your audience's attention on specific information. Like tables, lists are all-text presentation aids that can communicate a lot of information in a simple way, showing at a glance which items are most important, by arranging them in ascending or descending order. If the items on your list are of equal importance, arrange them in the order you will talk about them. Lists are most effective if you keep them short and to the point.

Once you have chosen the type of presentation aid to use, then decide on the method you will use to present it. You can choose between two methods: un-projected aids and projected aids. Un-projected aids, including the chalkboard, flip charts, poster boards, and handouts, do not require the use of electricity. Projected aids make use of electricity, and include slides, transparencies, videotapes, audio tapes, and computer-generated images and computerized presentations.

Public relations professionals tell us that if you decide to use any presentation aid as part of your speech, include it in at least one practice session before you actually present with it.[11] Here is a summary of suggestions for using presentational aids most effectively:

- Speak to the audience, not to the presentation aid. If you face the aid, the audience will not hear what you are saying, and your eye contact with listeners will be limited.
- Use a pointer, a pencil, or a laser pointer if you want to focus audience attention on a part of the aid you are talking about.
- If possible, cover up the sections of the aid you have yet to discuss. Reveal each section just as you begin to talk about it.
- Do not read the entire text of the aid (or a slide) to the audience, unless you want to emphasize a particular definition or description of something.
- Do not shuffle through handouts while you are presenting, or fiddle around with a pointer or the remote.
- If you are using a projected image of some kind, try standing next to the podium or lectern, or next to the projected image, and decide which feels most comfortable to you.

For more suggestions specifically about using un-projected aids, see Table 12.5.[12] Of equal importance is the following discussion of projected and computerized presentation aids, the most popular being PowerPoint.

COMPUTERIZED PRESENTATIONS.

Computerized presentations, particularly PowerPoint, are increasingly the most popular form of projected aids in classrooms and offices. If you have not used a presentation software program before, an easy way to get started is with the tutorial assistant built into most programs. Nonetheless, despite its popularity, some critics say that PowerPoint takes the life and vitality out of public speaking. They refer to getting bored with computerized presentations as "Death by PowerPoint." While that criticism is somewhat valid, if you do not allow the aid to upstage you as a speaker, using a program like PowerPoint can be essential to public speaking competence. In fact, one well-respected communication scholar, Dale Cyphert, said that public discourse is entering an age of "electronic eloquence," in which students need to be able to use presentation technology far more effectively.[13] They need to be able to fully integrate visual tools (like PowerPoint) and verbal tools (the spoken message) in order to participate fully as good citizens in the media age.

So if PowerPoint and similar presentation aids are here to stay, an important question is, what are they good for?[14] PowerPoint can serve as a useful organizing and pacing tool. The slides allow listeners to follow along with what is being said, and they can provide correct citations and other important names and definitions. However, despite the pervasiveness of PowerPoint, research studies have not yet tested and provided a complete set of best practices for the use of PowerPoint.[15] There is some preliminary consensus, though, for how to use visuals and graphic images to enliven and enhance the spoken message.

The old saying, "One picture is worth a thousand words," applies here. But use relatively simple yet powerful visual graphics—photographs for example—and limit the quantity of text, the number of words and number of lines, on each slide. Also, control the amount of action in the form of transitions and fly-ins of images and lines of text. Just because PowerPoint is capable of it does not mean that a lot of action makes for a better presentation. When actually presenting, it is important to know how to navigate smoothly and seamlessly between slides, and to and from links to videos and the Internet.[16] Embedded videos in PowerPoint presentations are effective, but only if you access the video smoothly and without any problems. In addition, if you use a remote clicker to change slides, conceal its use, and try not to look at the slides to know when it is time to change. You divert attention away from yourself as the speaker every time you look up at a slide.

Certainly, the ability to use a computerized aid like PowerPoint will set you apart as a public speaker in any 21st-century organization. However, you also need to be aware of the challenges PowerPoint presents, and how to manage those challenges to your advantage. Read over the list below of 13 concerns for computerized aids provided below. Then we will turn our attention to two other equally important challenges to competent public speaking.

1. It is too easy to create slides. Speakers often make more than are needed for the presentation, and are rushed to cover them all. Speakers also use up precious preparation time tweaking a presentation's bells and whistles.
2. It is too easy to start the presentation with PowerPoint, instead of starting with ideas and using PowerPoint to reinforce them.
3. The computer program puts tools in average hands that were once reserved for visual artists. Often the result is ugly, cluttered presentations rather than strong visual graphics enhancing the spoken message.
4. PowerPoint actually can impede attention. Audience members attend to the messenger— the "flying" transitions—and not the message.
5. It becomes a replacement for the presenter. Instead of a visual aid for the speaker, the speaker becomes an audio aid for the slides.
6. PowerPoint sometimes masks that the presentation does not have enough intrinsic value in itself.
7. It lends itself to unnecessary competition. Presenters, particularly students, become distracted with "dueling PowerPoints."
8. It does not lend itself to spontaneous discussions in the classroom or boardroom.
9. Speakers end up reading what is on the slide, which results in a flat and uninspiring delivery.

10. Presenters rely too much on the slides for structure. Clear structure should still be part of what the speaker says. The aids should reinforce the structure, not replace it.
11. Presenters rely too much on the visual slide, and neglect repetition, examples, metaphors, and other figures of speech that make a message memorable.
12. Presenters fail to establish their own credibility. They let the slides speak for them.
13. Speakers do not look at the audience, and the audience does not look at the speaker; they look at the slides instead. Subtle nonverbal cues are lost, such as eye contact, posture, and gesturing.

OVERCOMING CHALLENGES TO PUBLIC-SPEAKING COMPETENCE

The remaining challenges to making successful presentations relate to feeling confident and self-assured about giving a speech, and becoming aware of the complexities of presenting and speaking on the Web.

PUBLIC SPEAKING ANXIETY.

Public speaking anxiety, popularly referred to as stage fright, refers to a person's fear or anxiety associated with an expected or actual public-speaking event. Generally, the more formal and unfamiliar the occasion, the larger the audience, and the more important the goals, the more nervous people become about giving a speech. But in general, fear of public

PUBLIC SPEAKING ANXIETY, popularly referred to as stage fright, refers to a person's fear or anxiety associated with an expected or actual public-speaking event.

Table 12.5: Suggestions for Using Un-projected Presentation Aids

A competent speaker knows how to use an array of un-projected aids to support and enhance the delivery of the speech.

FLIP CHARTS AND POSTERS, AND HANDOUTS

1. **Flip Charts and Posters**
   - Investigate the degree of formality and guidelines or limitations concerning size and space for the poster or chart.
   - Decide where you'll display the chart or poster ahead of time.
   - Don't block the audience's view of the chart or poster.
   - Don't face the chart or poster while you're speaking.
   - Conceal material and then reveal it as you talk about it.
2. **Handouts**
   - Use handouts to help listeners follow or recall your main points, but don't let them take over.
   - Decide carefully when and how to distribute the handouts, including copies of *PowerPoint* slides.
     - Before the speech, if the handout is essential to understanding what you have to say.
     - At the end of the speech, if you don't want the audience reading the handout as you speak.

Source: Hazard (2007).[12]

speaking has been at or near the top of Gallup's annual poll of "things Americans fear most" for years. Public speaking, at least for some, is more fearsome than heights, claustrophobia, spiders, needles, mice, crowds, thunderstorms, and even flying.[17]

Given the widespread nature of this fear, it is helpful to know why people have public speaking anxiety in the first place. One cause of anxiety is the psychological threat to your self-esteem, which sometimes results from remembering previous negative experiences when you spoke in pub-

Table 12.6: Addressing the Challenge of Public Speaking Anxiety

Three causes of anxiety are previous negative experiences, identification with the wrong public-speaking role models, and unrealistic attitudes and expectations about public speaking. Look at these causes and the solutions for handling each cause.

CAUSE OF ANXIETY AND SPEAKER'S REACTION TO IT	POSSIBLE SOLUTIONS TO EACH CAUSE OF ANXIETY
Cause: Previous negative experiences with public speaking. **Reaction:** You avoid public speaking so you will not look foolish and stupid.	Forget the past, and do not allow it to shape the present.
Cause: Identification with the wrong public-speaking role models. **Reaction:** You avoid public speaking, because you expect to make mistakes and embarrass yourself.	Make a conscious effort to identify with speakers who appear confident and in control. Watch those people, and think about yourself being a public speaker just like them.
Cause: Unrealistic attitudes and expectations about public speaking. **Reaction:** You avoid public speaking, because you think you will not do well, and you expect a catastrophe to occur.	Become aware of which unrealistic expectations affect you as a public speaker. Realize that it is unlikely that anything catastrophic will occur. And if something goes wrong, it is not the end of the world, and listeners probably do not notice or care.
1. Desire for total acceptance.	Realize that it is impossible to please everyone all the time, just as it is impossible for everyone to please you all the time. Be yourself, and do the best job you can.
2. Desire for absolute perfection.	Do not expect perfection. Realize that no speech is perfect, then accept your imperfections, and learn from mistakes. Do not dwell on what goes wrong.
3. Desire for total confidence.	Expect anxiety. Realize that fear is natural, and everyone has it. Accept your insecurities, knowing that the audience cannot see your fears, and they are probably supportive of you.

lic. Perhaps someone laughed, or failed to take your comments seriously. Or perhaps you forgot the most important points you wanted to make. In either case, you learned a negative lesson: When I speak publicly, I feel foolish or stupid.

A second cause of anxiety is identifying with the wrong public speakers as your role models. You watch people speak in public who appear nervous and make mistakes. You identify personally with them, rather than with someone who speaks with confidence and competence. You say to yourself, "Now that's the kind of speaker I am." The lesson is learned: When I speak in public, I make mistakes, embarrass myself, and appear inept.

A third cause of public speaking anxiety is the tendency to hold unrealistic attitudes and expectations about public speaking, and about yourself as a speaker. You may expect some disaster or catastrophic failure to occur when you speak, such as blanking out and forgetting everything you want to say. Or you may have an unrealistic desire to please everybody, and to have all of the listeners like you. You may think that your speech has to be flawless in content and delivery, and that you need to feel totally confident and in control when you present your speech. All of these attitudes and expectations are unrealistic.

Table 12.6 summarizes these three causes of public speaking anxiety, and suggests ways to handle each. See which causes you relate to most, and note the suggestions for handling them. In addition to understanding these causes, communication scholars and educators have developed other techniques for reducing public speaking anxiety, the most popular being systematic desensitization, cognitive modification, and skills training.[18] Each of these assumes a different cause for the anxiety— anxious emotions, negative thoughts, or lack of skills—and then focuses treatment on that cause.

Systematic desensitization assumes that anxiety results from becoming overly emotional, and therefore nervous. So it desensitizes a speakers's feelings and emotional reactions to public speaking by using positive visualization. Before giving a speech, you visualize yourself speaking competently, and in full control of the situation. Cognitive modification assumes that negative thoughts are the root of anxiety. So it changes or modifies any unrealistic beliefs about public speaking. Before giving a speech, you work on changing any negative thoughts to positive ones. Skills training assumes that anxiety stems from a speaker's inadequate public skills repertoire. So it targets the improvement of speaking behaviors. Skills training, such as provided in a public-speaking course, exemplifies this technique or approach to reducing anxiety. If you repeatedly stand up to speak and practice the skills you are taught, you definitely will become more confident. But if you feel particularly anxious about public speaking, the course instructor could help you with these or other approaches to reducing anxiety.

For now, we offer two final suggestions you may find helpful. Several leading researchers on anxiety discovered that 38.2% of student worries about giving a speech can be predicted by their concerns about receiving evaluative feedback after their performance.[19] Instead of worrying about the feedback you may receive, concentrate all your energy on preparing and delivering your speech effectively—not on what others will say to you afterward. Also, read the student's true story in Box 12.1 about giving her first speech. You may find her experience with anxiety helpful.

PUBLIC SPEAKING ON THE WEB.

A final challenge to you as a public speaker is becoming aware of the increased use of Internet conferencing and presentation technologies in business communication.[20] It is quite likely that one day you will find yourself presenting to audiences in several countries, as your technology-assisted

Box 12.1: A True Tale of Anxiety and Presenting a Classroom Speech

The student who provides this tale of overcoming anxiety and giving an "A" speech is now a public-speaking instructor herself. See if her story helps you with any public speaking anxiety you may be experiencing.

I cleared my throat for the third time as my instructor continued to give instructions about how the presentations were going to go for the day. "After you speak, please stand up front and wait for the class to give you verbal feedback about your presentation." But the pounding of my heart was already overriding the sound of her cheery voice. Why did I have to spill coffee on the front corner of my light pink shirt today? Will the class even hear what I am saying, or will everyone be secretly laughing at me and my glaring coffee stain? What if my topic is too boring? Is my introduction good enough to get everyone's attention? Do I even want their attention, because then they will be staring at me the whole time I'm talking.

"Lindsey McCormick, it looks like you are first today! Please hand me a copy of your outline and take as much time as you need to get situated up front for your presentation." Oh no, it's time... why am I first? I swallow hard once more and move to the front of the classroom. I feel myself smiling at my peers, thankful they cannot hear my inner dialogue of fear. I look back at my instructor and see she is ready, and still smiling. Yeah, because she's not giving a speech. I hear myself start by saying:

"There once was a young man who believed in something more than the status quo. From a young age, he knew most people underestimated their ability to overcome differences and come together in a world of division and divisiveness. He also knew coming together around controversial issues was the biggest problem facing the U.S. in the 1960s. Today, we are going to talk about three major steps Martin Luther King, Jr. took to become one of the greatest leaders and activists for human rights in our country's history."

Nailed it! My introduction went just as I practiced, but it seemed to roll off my tongue as if I had just thought of it! Three deep breaths into my speech and I was on a roll. I was walking intentionally toward my audience as I shared another exciting example, and at the same time, I was even making eye contact with a few of my classmates scattered around the room. I collected myself silently between each major point instead of filling the room with my usual "uhms," "likes," and "OK?" I heard myself speaking with passion and openness that felt unfamiliar, but I liked it. I was being myself; natural, clear, and even a little funny at times. As I heard myself concluding, I could see the approval on my instructor's face and I knew I had done as well as I hoped I would. Why was I so nervous? As everyone clapped, I realized I am my own worst enemy when it comes to this whole public speaking thing. Nobody wanted me to fail or do poorly. They wanted me to do my best, and I did.

Source: Lindsey McCormick, M.A. (2012). University of Colorado at Colorado Springs.

presentation is translated into one or more languages. While this may sound like a unique situation, it is, in fact, the norm in many multinational organizations.

Not surprisingly, training is not abundant in the use of virtual presentation skills. And, as soon as you are trained in one technology, a new program may have replaced it. As a result, these presentations often are not done well, and many of us just do not know how to use the technologies competently. So the most important thing you can do is become familiar with and prepared to learn about any presentation technologies available where you work. To that end, it is best to understand the terminology and the various types of technologies currently in use. Here, we briefly distinguish among the current, most common types of web-based technologies.

Webcast presentations involve information and data transmission over the web that is one way, and does not allow for interaction between the presenter and the audience. Web conferencing involves information and data transmission over the web that is two way, and does allow for interaction between the presenter and the audience. Webinars are web-based seminars, workshops, or trainings transmitted over the web. Webcasts and web conferences typically are informative or per-

---

Box 12.2: Instructors' Pet Peeves about Student Speeches

Teachers find some behaviors during speeches so bothersome that they qualify as pet peeves—minor irritants—to public-speaking instructors.

---

1. **Practices to avoid during the introduction and conclusion**
   - Beginning a speech with "OK, ah. . . ."
   - Apologizing or making excuses for not being ready for a speech.
   - Beginning a speech with "Hello, my speech is on . . ." or a question such as "How many of you. . . ."
   - Ending a speech with "Thank you," "in conclusion," or "Are there any questions?"

2. **General offenses regarding the class or when presenting**
   - Inappropriate attire (exposed midriff, holes in jeans, wearing hats or dirty and rumpled clothing).
   - Not being prepared on the assigned speech day.
   - Excessive absenteeism.
   - Reading a manuscript of the speech.

3. **Annoying delivery problems**
   - Vocalized pauses (ah, um, you know, like . . .).
   - Slang and profanity.
   - Citing *Yahoo, Google, Wikipedia*, or a website with insufficient validation.
   - Chewing gum while speaking.
   - A tongue-piercing clicking against teeth.
   - Using the podium as a conga drum.

4. **Ineffective use of presentation aids**
   - Poorly prepared presentation aids.
   - Passing photos or other aids around during the speech.
   - Standing in front of the projection screen or other speech aid.
   - Talking to the aid rather than the audience.
   - Speech aids that are alive.

5. **General concerns**
   - Using sexist language like "you guys . . ." to an audience including women.
   - Writing out the speech on notebook paper.
   - Choosing speech topics that are used too often (abortion, gun control, marijuana).

Source: Adapted from Taylor (2005).[21]

suasive presentations or a combination of both. Webinars typically are instructional and focused on education or training.

Regardless of which of the presentation technologies you may be asked to use, understanding their functions and capacities, what they can and cannot do, and being comfortable with their use is critical to an effective delivery. Like any presentation, personal preparation ahead of time includes getting training from technology staff, or reading the manual, if such staff members are not available. Rehearse using the technology, prepare presentation notes or an outline, and time the presentation using the technology itself, if possible.

At this point, you should be quite ready to give a speech in a highly competent manner, just as Wen Shu and Sergio did in the story at the start of this chapter. But just in case you would like to avoid the public-speaking behaviors speech teachers find most distracting, take a glance at the list in Box 12.2. The next two chapters will focus on preparing and presenting the two most common types of speeches—informative and persuasive.

CHAPTER SUMMARY

The Roman orator Cicero stated that style and delivery is the best way to improve public-speaking skills. The use of language and words, vocal variety, pronunciation, articulation, grammar, nonverbal cues, and presentation aids are all essential to speaker credibility and becoming a competent presenter.

Competent language enhances the listeners' understanding and enthusiasm for a speech by the use of words that are clear, vivid, and appropriate. Vividness is achieved through the use of imagery; figures of speech (simile, metaphor, and analogy) and techniques such as the rhetorical question, alliteration, and repetition. It also is necessary to use language appropriately by avoiding condescending or biased language and stereotypes. In addition to language, vocal variety is used to heighten and maintain audience attention and interest in a speech by varying the rate (fast versus slow), pitch (high versus low), and volume (loud versus soft) of the voice. A public voice makes use of increased vocal variety. A competent speaker also pronounces words and articulates speech sounds correctly, and uses correct grammar. Beyond words and how they are spoken, a competent speaker uses the following nonverbal cues to support and enhance the spoken message: appearance, posture and body movement, gestures, facial expression, and eye contact. These cues are incorporated into a transparent delivery, which means that the audience does not focus on the delivery, but instead pays full attention to the speaker's message. Finally, a competent speaker uses presentation aids (un-projected, projected, or computerized) to enhance the delivery of the speech.

To make best use of these presentation skills, it is critical to address the challenge of public speaking anxiety, which often is caused by concern about psychological threats to self-esteem, identifying with the wrong public speakers, or holding unrealistic attitudes and expectations about giving a speech. Public speaking anxiety can be reduced by using any one of three approaches: systematic desensitization, cognitive modification, or skills training. Finally, competent speakers address the challenge of using presentation technologies, such as PowerPoint, and speaking on the web by practicing and becoming comfortable with any technology before presenting.

KEY TERMS.

The key terms below are defined in this chapter, and presented alphabetically with definitions in the Glossary at the end of the book.

- style
- delivery
- speaker credibility
- competent language
- clear language
- vivid language
- imagery
- figures of speech
- simile
- metaphor
- analogy

- rhetorical question
- alliteration
- repetition
- appropriate language
- condescending language
- biased language
- vocal variety
- rate
- pitch
- volume
- public voice

- pronunciation
- articulation
- grammar
- appearance
- posture
- gestures
- facial expression
- eye contact
- transparent delivery
- presentation aids
- public speaking anxiety

BUILDING MOTIVATION: SELF-ASSESSMENT TOOL.

Rate each of the eight public-speaking situations described here, indicating your own typical level of presentational competence. Rate one situation all the way through for motivation, knowledge, and skills. Then rate the next situation. Use the 1–4 scale below, with 1 being minimal competence and 4 high competence.

Public-speaking situations.

1. Presenting a speech to a group of people from cultures very different from your own.
2. Talking to a group of senior citizens about crime prevention in the neighborhood.
3. Presenting the toast to the bride and groom at a wedding.
4. Presenting a group project in class, and serving as the main speaker for the group.
5. Presenting a project summary at your new job to all of upper management.
6. Presenting the student speech at your college graduation.
7. Giving an impromptu speech at a political meeting to gather support for a cause.
8. Presenting a web conference or a training webinar at your job.

Motivation.

1 = Distracted, disinterested, or simply no motivation to be competent.
2 = Somewhat distracted or disinterested, but motivated to be competent.
3 = Somewhat interested and motivated to be competent.
4 = Highly interested and motivated to be competent.

Knowledge.

1 = Completely inexperienced and ignorant about what to do and how to do it.
2 = Minimal experience and sense of what to do and how to do it.
3 = Somewhat experienced and knowledgeable about what to do and how to do it.

4 = Highly knowledgeable about all aspects of what to do and how to do it.

Skills.

1 = Completely incapable of behaving competently.
2 = Barely capable of behaving minimally competently.
3 = Fairly capable of behaving competently.
4 = Highly capable of behaving competently.

Interpreting your scores.

Total your score separately for each situation (motivation, knowledge, and skills). The possible range of the score for each situation is 3–12. If your total score for any of the situations is 6 or less, you see yourself as less competent in that situation than you should be. A score of 7–9 means that you are average at sending and receiving communication messages in the situation. A score of 10–12 indicates that you have a high level of communication competence in that situation.

BUILDING KNOWLEDGE: DISCUSSION QUESTIONS.

1. In what creative ways can a novice speaker, not well-known to her or his audience, improve initial credibility with those listeners?
2. Competent language calls for using words that are clear, vivid, and appropriate. However, words that are clear may not be very vivid, and words that are vivid may not be appropriate for the particular audience or speaking situation. How can a speaker balance the use of all three types of words?
3. As speakers strive for variety in rate, pitch, and volume, how can they retain the genuineness of their own voices?
4. Is it always appropriate for a speaker to use correct pronunciation, articulation, and grammar? When not, and why?
5. Of all the nonverbal cues a speaker can use—appearance, posture, body movement, gestures, facial expression, and eye contact—which is the most important and why?
6. What aspects of a speech help decide which type of presentation aid to use?
7. Of all the suggestions in this chapter for reducing public speaking anxiety, which would work best for you, and why?
8. How can a speaker manage to keep up with all the innovations in presentation technologies?

BUILDING SKILLS: STUDENT ACTIVITIES.

Individual activities.

1. Make a videotape of your next speech during one of your practice sessions. Watch yourself, and evaluate your presentation skills, based on the content of this chapter. Identify your key strengths and weaknesses, and make a list of what you will try to improve when you actually present the speech to an audience.
2. Attend a live lecture or speech. Evaluate the speaker's presentation skills using the content of this chapter.

3. Go to this website that contains the Top 100 Speeches of the 20th century: http://www.americanrhetoric.com/top100speechesall.html. Find a speech that appeals to you and examine the speaker's use of language. Is it clear, vivid, and appropriate? Does the speaker use correct grammar and effective figures of speech?

4. On the Internet, access the White House website that provides manuscripts of the president's recent major speeches: http://www.whitehouse.gov. Select a speech that interests you, and present an analysis of it in a speech to your class.

5. Try employing some of the techniques in this chapter for reducing public speaking anxiety. See which works best for you.

Group activities.

1. Get another student to be your rehearsal and practice partner. Ask your partner to watch carefully how you present your speech. Then have that person critique your posture, body movement, gestures, facial expression, and eye contact. Reverse roles, and critique your partner's nonverbal cues.

2. Ask your practice partner to provide you feedback after your in-class presentation regarding your voice, in particular, your volume, speaking rate, and filled pauses.

3. In small groups of six or seven students, practice your ability to walk to, stand in, and move around in the speaking area. Have each student take a turn walking to the speaking platform, standing at the lectern, and moving deliberately away from the lectern to another part of the speaking area. Group members should provide feedback to each student.

4. In small groups of three or four students, practice presenting your speech using your presentation aid. Again, the group should provide feedback to each student.

NOTES

1. See May (1988).

2. See Fatt (1999).

3. See Dance (2002).

4. See *American Rhetoric: Top 100 speeches* (2011).

5. See Zraick, Gentry, Smith-Olinde, & Gregg (2006).

6. See Sellnow & Treinen (2004).

7. See Bourne (2007).

8. See Dance (1999).

9. See Smith & Frymier (2006).

10. See Goberman, Hughes, & Haydock (2011).

11. See Williamson (2006).

12. See Hazard (2007).

13. See Cyphert (2007).

14. See Nemec & Sullivan-Soydan (2008).

15. See Katt, Murdock, Butler, & Pryor (2008).

16. See Howell (2008).

17. See Bruggen (2004).

18. See Bodie (2010).

19.   See Kopecky, Sawyer, & Behnke (2004).

20.   See Flatley (2007).

21.   See Taylor (2005).

REFERENCES

American rhetoric: Top 100 speeches. (2011). Retrieved from http://www.americanrhetoric.com/top100speechesall.html

Bodie, G. D. (2010). A racing heart, rattling knees, and ruminative thoughts: Defining, explaining, and treating public speaking anxiety. *Communication Education, 59*(1), 70–105.

Bourne, P. E. (2007). Ten simple rules for making good oral presentations. *PLOS Computational Biology, 3*(4), 77–79.

Bruggen, H. (2004, September 10). Taking the fear and boredom out of public speaking.*Washington Business Journal* [Online]. Retrieved from http://www.bizjournals.com/washington/stories/2004/09/13/smallb5.html

Cyphert, D. (2007). Presentation technology in the age of electronic eloquence: From visual aid to visual rhetoric. *Communication Education, 56*(2), 168–192.

Dance, F. E. X. (1999, July). Successful presenters master the art of being transparent. *Presentations, 13*(7), 80.

Dance, F. E. X. (2002). Speech and thought: A renewal. *Communication Education, 51*(4), 355–359.

Fatt, P. T. (1999). It's not what you say, it's how you say it. *Communication World, 16*(6), 37–41.

Flatley, M. (2007). Teaching the virtual presentation. *Business Communication Quarterly, 70*(3), 301–305.

Goberman, A., Hughes, S., & Haydock, T. (2011). Acoustic characteristics of public speaking: Anxiety and practice effects. *Speech Communication, 53*(3), 867–876.

Hazard, B. (2007). A recipe for successful poster sessions. *International Journal of Listening, 21*(2), 162–165.

Howell, D. (2008). Four key keys to powerful presentations in PowerPoint: Take your presentations to the next level. *TechTrends: Linking Research & Practice to Improve Learning, 52*(6), 44–46.

Katt, J., Murdock, J., Butler, J., & Pryor, B. (2008). Establishing best practices for the use of PowerPoint as a presentation aid. *Human Communication, 11*(2), 193–200.

Kopecky, C. C., Sawyer, C. R., & Behnke, R. R. (2004). Brief reports. *Communication Education, 53*(3), 281–286.

May, J. M. (1988). *Trials of character: The eloquence of Ciceronian ethos.* Chapel Hill, NC: University of North Carolina Press.

McCormick, L. (2012). A true tale of anxiety and presenting a classroom speech [Student speech]. University of Colorado at Colorado Springs, Colorado Springs, CO.

Nemec, P., & Sullivan-Soydan, A. (2008). The medium isn't the message. *Psychiatric Rehabilitation Journal, 31*(4), 377–379.

Sellnow, D. D. & Treinen, K. P. (2004). The role of gender in perceived speaker competence: An analysis of student peer critiques. *Communication Education, 53*(3), 286–297.

Smith, T., & Frymier, A. B. (2006). Get "real": Does practicing speeches before an audience improve performance? *Communication Quarterly, 54*(1), 111–125.

Taylor, K. (2005). Speech teachers' pet peeves: Student behaviors that public speaking instructors find annoying, irritating, and unwanted in study speeches. *Florida Communication Journal, 33*, 54–59.

Williamson, S. (2006). Creating presentatons that get results. *Public Relations Quarterly, 51*(4), 31–32.

Zraick, R., Gentry, M., Smith-Olinde, L., & Gregg, B. (2006). The effect of speaking context on elicitation of habitual pitch. *Journal of Voice, 20*(4), 545–554.

CHAPTER THIRTEEN

SPEAKING TO INFORM

Good communication does not mean that you have to speak in perfectly formed sentences and paragraphs. It isn't about slickness. Simple and clear go a long way.
—John Kotter, Author and Harvard Business School Professor, b. 1947

.:
• • •

By the time Zak started to prepare his informative speech, he already had learned a lot about speaking with competence. Now it was time to apply his newly learned preparation and presenting skills to the informative assignment in his public speaking class. He chose a topic he knew something about—the popularity of coffeeshops and coffee drinking in American society. Because of his job as a manager at the Starbucks near school, Zak had observed how much business had grown over the last few years. Plus, he thought the topic would appeal to his classmates, most of whom dropped by frequently for a cup of coffee. He located some impressive statistics in the library, demonstrating a year-by-year increase in coffee consumption, so he decided to describe how much coffee drinking had increased in the United States during the past decade, and why that happened. To support his speech, he interviewed students, who explained why they liked coming to Starbucks.

When he presented the speech in class, "The Joy of Java," Zak expected the other students to be fascinated with his speech, but that did not happen. Some of them even appeared a little bored as Zak told them about the increase in coffee drinking. His grade improved over the last speech, as he had hoped, but he wondered why his classmates were not more attentive. After class, he was anxious to review the professor's feedback form to find out what he did well and what he could have done better. He was sure his topic was a good one for the audience. But had he provided too much or too little information—and was it the right information? Was the speech organized in a way that was easy to follow? Why weren't his listeners motivated to learn more about the dramatic increase in coffee drinking?

The instructor said that Zak's presentation style was fine, and he definitely had chosen a topic the other students could relate to. He had organized the speech well, and it was easy to follow as he talked about his two main points—how much coffee consumption had increased, and why that had happened. But to gain and maintain the attention of the other students, the instructor said that Zak needed to be more creative in his use of stories and examples to liven up the facts and statistics. She told Zak about a recent study that examined whether a story or a statistical message has more effect on listeners' attitudes.[1] Indeed, stories and narrative messages, compared to statistics, were significantly more effective. The instructor also said that while his testimonies from interviews were effective, he could have used a better attention getter to open his speech, maybe giving out a coffee sample, or a coupon for a free cup. His support materials also could have included some information and quotations from highly credible sources in the coffee industry. Zak had done a good job, but he still had something to learn about giving an informative speech.

This chapter covers key ideas about speaking to inform that will help you prepare and present an informative speech most competently. We begin by clarifying what an informative speech is, and why it is an important form of public-speaking competence.

UNDERSTANDING THE INFORMATIVE SPEECH

An informative speech may range from a description of the intangible, like understanding the law of gravity, to a set of tangible instructions, like how to prepare for final exams. Whether the speech is intended to describe or explain something, or to instruct the audience about how something works, it is considered informative.

WHAT IS AN INFORMATIVE SPEECH?

As we stated in Chapter Eleven, the general purpose of an **informative speech** is to communicate new information or a new perspective on a topic to an audience, and bring the listeners to greater understanding or insight. Given that general purpose, an informative speech may be about an object, process, event, person, concept, or issue.

If you choose to present a speech about an object, it is usually about something tangible that can be seen, touched, or otherwise experienced through the physical senses, such as a car, a computer, a place, or even a monument of some kind, like the Lincoln Memorial or the World War II Memorial. If you decide to describe a system or sequence of steps that lead to a result or change taking place, such as the steps involved in applying for a loan or shopping for a new smart phone, that is an informative speech about a process. An event speech describes something that has occurred, such as a historical event—the collapse of the twin towers on 9/11 in New York City or a noteworthy event that has happened in your community—like the results of an election, or reactions to a local catastrophe. A speech about a person describes an individual in much the same way that an object speech describes an object.

A **concept speech** is about abstract ideas—theories, principles, or values—such as the theory of relativity, or the principles underlying democracy, like freedom of the press or human rights. If you choose to present an **issue speech**, it would examine a debatable topic from various points of view, such as the right to die, or varying perspectives on environmental concerns. To better understand these six possibilities for your informative speech, Table 13.1 suggests topics for each of the six.

The issue speech brings up an important concept any competent public speaker must understand—that there is a fine

An INFORMATIVE SPEECH communicates new information or a new perspective on a topic to an audience, and brings the listeners to greater understanding or insight.

A SPEECH ABOUT AN OBJECT is usually about something tangible that can be seen, touched, or otherwise experienced through the physical senses.

A SPEECH ABOUT A PROCESS describes a system or sequence of steps that lead to a result or change taking place.

AN EVENT SPEECH describes something that has occurred.

A SPEECH ABOUT A PERSON describes an individual.

A CONCEPT SPEECH is about abstract ideas—theories, principles, or values.

AN ISSUE SPEECH examines a debatable topic from various points of view.

Table 13.1: Possible Topics for Informative Speeches

This is a list of possible topics for each of the six different content types of speeches.

TYPE OF SPEECH	POSSIBLE TOPICS FOR EACH TYPE OF SPEECH
• An object speech	Things you collect—books, stamps, antiques; an extraordinary place you have visited or know about—a town, city, state, or country; electronic devices or a household item.
• A process speech	Things you do or know how to do—snowshoeing, skiing, hiking, traveling, refinishing furniture, cooking, saving money, spending money, getting along with others, living in another country, planning your life.
• An event speech	A local or national current event, a noteworthy event from history, an event that marked a turning point in history, an event that occurred in the life of a noteworthy person, a special event that occurred in your life.
• A people speech	A contemporary or historical person of significance to the audience, someone you know or have known of particular interest.
• An issue speech	Texting while driving, recycling, conservation laws and practices, violence in the media, grading systems, substance abuse and regulation, health care, political and governmental policies or programs, unions and strike policies, alternative lifestyles.
• A concept speech	Nuclear power and reactors, inclusiveness and/or diversity, the world ecosystem, media literacy and convergence, ethical communication, theory of evolution, principles of communication, democracy, friendship, love.

line between informative speaking and persuasive speaking. Some public-speaking experts say that all public speeches—including speeches to inform—are partly persuasive. According to this point of view, whenever you present information, you are attempting to persuade the audience that the information is true and right. Because you believe you are telling the truth about the information, and because you are trying to convince the audience of that truth, perhaps any informative speech could be considered persuasive to some degree. To clarify, speeches that are more objective and less opinionated may be considered informative. Speeches that are more subjective and more opinionated are considered persuasive. When you prepare an informative or persuasive speech, keep this concept in mind, or you may lose points on your speech grade.

THE IMPORTANCE OF INFORMATIVE SPEAKING SKILLS.

Developing the ability to present an informative speech may be one of the most important public-speaking competencies you will learn, because you will use these skills frequently. The majority of us earn our living by handling information in some way and conveying it to one another, and often we are conveying that information using some kind of technology. Consequently, presenting information in all sorts of ways is a crucial aspect of most people's professional and personal lives.

A professor's lecture obviously is an informative speech, and at community meetings and political gatherings, we often have to stand up and present our ideas informatively.

Businesspeople often are called on to present information as well. In the corporate world, informative speaking can take the form of a briefing that summarizes large amounts of information, a report of progress on projects and activities, or a training that provides instructions about how to carry out a task or assignment.

In giving any of these informative speeches, the goal is to promote understanding of the information presented, as well as to encourage the audience to retain a significant amount of the message. Retention of information is a very real problem. According to one listening trainer, who tested adults for their ability to retain information, most retain only 26% of what is presented.[2] The older or more educated a person was, the poorer their retention. The listening trainer's conclusion was that as we grow older and learn more, our mind is stuffed with information, and it interferes with what we are hearing. This problem is made worse now, as we are truly overloaded with information in the 21st century.

Given these realities, improving your informative speaking competence is a must, and that begins with understanding the three different types of informative speeches.

TYPES OF INFORMATIVE SPEECHES.

Informative speeches can be categorized based on their objective. Three possible objectives for an informative speech are speaking to describe, explain, or instruct. These are general objectives, similar to the general purpose for a speech discussed in Chapter Eleven, but they are tailored to informative speaking. They emphasize audience understanding or abilities—what the audience should know or be able to do by the end of the speech.

> DESCRIPTIONS are used when the listeners are unfamiliar with the topic of the speech, and need new information in order to understand it.

> EXPLANATIONS are necessary to tell listeners how something works, or to clarify something that is already known but not well understood.

Descriptions are used when the listeners are unfamiliar with the topic of the speech, and need new information in order to understand it. If you want the audience to become aware of and remember something new, your objective is to describe or provide a verbal picture of it. For example, if you want to introduce a new product line to a sales force, you need to describe the new items and their advantages over older products. This informative objective could be stated as follows. Take note in this example of how concrete the speaker's expectation of the audience is:

> Sales force members will understand and be able to describe four advantages of the new product line in comparison to last year's products.

Explanations are necessaary to tell listeners how something works, or to clarify something that is already known but not well understood. If you want the listeners to understand why something exists or has occurred, or how it operates, your objective is to explain it. If your speech is about an increase in violent crime or drug usage, you could explain why the problem exists, and what measures are being taken to address the situation. But if you were to move beyond explaining the problem of increased drug usage, and take a position on how to decrease it, your speech would become persuasive. An informative objective for this particular speech would be this:

The audience will be able to explain the underlying causes of the increase in drug use, as well as two strategies now in use to combat this problem.

Instructions are useful when the objective is to teach the audience something, or to tell them how to use it. If you want the listeners to be able to apply what is presented, then your objective is to instruct. Let us say that you want the other students to be able to use a particular method for reducing public speaking anxiety. You then need to provide instructions for applying the various methods. Here is an informative objective statement for that speech:

> INSTRUCTIONS are useful when the objective is to teach the audience something, or tell them how to use something.

Each student will understand and be able to use one of the three most popular methods for reducing public speaking anxiety.

Depending on the content of your speech—object, process, event, people, issue, or concept—the speech is more likely to lend itself to one objective more than the other two—describe, explain, or instruct. To make this easy to understand, Table 13.2 tells you which objective works best for a particular type of content speech.

To appreciate the importance of clarifying the objective of an informative speech, think about Zak's speech at the beginning of this chapter. After choosing the topic of coffee consumption, Zak decided, perhaps unintentionally, that his speech was to be both descriptive and explanatory. His objectives were to describe the surprising changes in coffee drinking patterns in the United States, and to explain why those changes occurred. Given that he had two objectives, Zak needed to provide sufficient information to accomplish both effectively. He provided statistics to support his claim of an increase in coffee drinking, but he only had testimonial evidence from students who frequent Starbucks to explain why the increase occurred. That oversight may have accounted in part for his speech not being quite as effective as he would have liked. If he decided to stay with both objectives, he should have researched the second objective more, perhaps contacting marketing experts at coffee companies for additional explanations of the increase in coffee consumption.

Table 13.2: Content of Speeches and Possible Objectives

Each of the informative speeches, based on their content, is more likely to lend itself to one of the three objectives rather than the others. For each type of speech based on its content, the three objectives—describe, explain, instruct—are placed in rank order to indicate which is best for that speech.

CONTENT OF SPEECH	MOST LIKELY OBJECTIVE BY RANK ORDER		
• An object speech	1. Describe	2. Explain	3. Instruct
• A process speech	1. Explain	2. Describe	3. Instruct
• An event speech	1. Describe	2. Explain	
• A people speech	1. Describe	2. Explain	
• An issue speech	1. Explain	2. Describe	
• A concept speech	1. Describe	2. Explain	

ORGANIZING AND OUTLINING AN INFORMATIVE SPEECH

The general recommendations for speech organization and outlining discussed in Chapter Eleven, although important for all speeches, are especially helpful for a competent speaker who wants to achieve the objective of an informative speech. Because the goal is often to communicate an abundance of new information, clear organization is essential for the audience to understand what is presented, and not be overwhelmed by it.

One communication researcher, Kathy Rowan, summarized why it is difficult to organize and present informative speeches.[3] Information in a speech may be confusing if it involves difficult concepts or language, structures or processes that are hard to envision, or ideas that are difficult to understand because they are hard to believe. In all of these cases, the researcher suggested first analyzing the informative topic to discover what aspects of it will be most difficult for your listeners to understand, and then organizing and outlining your speech accordingly. Developing a working outline for your speech (see Chapter Eleven) will help you with this task. You will be able to determine what complex information must be included, the best location for it in your speech, and what form of support or presentation aid is essential to understanding it.

The five common ways to organize the body of an informative speech are by topic, chronology or time, space, comparison and contrast, and cause and effect. These five organizational patterns are most often used for informative speaking, but several of them clearly could be used for a persuasive speech. Cause and effect, for example, is frequently recommended for both informative and persuasive speeches.

Figure 13.1: Organizing the Informative Speech

The body of an informative speech is structured using any one of five different organizational patterns. The introduction and conclusion remain the same, as we discussed in Chapter Eleven.

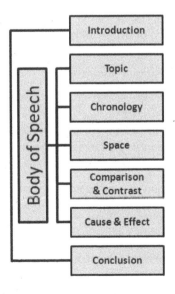

As you learn about these five organizational patterns, understand that an informative speech outline has the same basic parts discussed in Chapter Eleven—an introduction, body, and conclusion. However, the main points of the body of an informative speech are organized using one of the

---

Box 13.1: Example of an Outline for an Informative Speech

Zak's informative speech about coffee drinking in the United States is organized topically with two main points making up the body of the speech. The Standard Outline Format from Chapter Eleven was used to develop this outline easily and quickly. Try it yourself.

Speech Title: "The Joy of Java."
General Purpose: To inform (describe and explain).
Specific Purpose: To describe changes in coffee drinking patterns in the United States, and to explain why those changes occurred.

I. INTRODUCTION (full sentences: attention getter, thesis statement, preview of main points).
   A. You may be one of the few students on campus who has not yet visited the Starbucks at First and Main, where I am a barista. A barista (from the Italian for "bartender") is a person, usually a coffeehouse employee, who prepares and serves espresso-based coffee drinks.
   B. The coffee business is booming for some very good reasons. Today, I want to explain this boom, and give you a free coupon for one of the drinks I concoct.
   C. First, I will describe some surprising changes in coffee drinking patterns in the U.S., and then I will explain why those changes occurred.

II. BODY (support materials that help accomplish the speech purpose).
   A. I am glad to report a significant increase in coffee drinking that started in the mid-80s and continues to be on the rise.
       1. Statistics describing the year-by-year increase in coffee consumption using a bar graph to illustrate the changes.
       2. Story about a student who increased her visits to Starbucks, taking her computer along to work, and having a cup of coffee in the relaxing atmosphere.
   *Transition: Despite a sluggish economy, coffee drinking is on the rise. That is good news for me and my job. But, you may wonder why it is happening.

   B. I got an explanation about the increase from some of you, and from some experts in marketing in the coffee industry.
       1. Testimonies from students saying why they like coming to Starbucks.
       2. Quotations from interviews with marketing experts at coffee companies.
   *Transition: I now rest my case about the true "Joy of Java!"

III. CONCLUSION (full sentences: review of main points, restate thesis, closing device).
   A. Yes, coffee drinking has increased significantly, since the mid-80s, and clearly there are some good reasons why.
   B. Maybe now you may want to join your friends and come by Starbucks and use your free coupon.
   C. As your personal barista, I look forward to welcoming you to your friendly neighborhood coffee shop!

five patterns, as shown in Figure 13.1. Knowing which of these organizational patterns you are using is absolutely key to preparing and presenting an effective informative speech.

BY TOPIC.

Topical organization, as suggested in Chapter Eleven, divides information about a subject and topic into subtopics or subcategories that will constitute the main points of the body of the speech. Business reports often use this straight-forward organizational pattern to good advantage in briefings and other informative meetings.[4] This structure is advantageous when your topic naturally clusters into subtopics or lists of items you want the listeners to understand or know how to use. Various aspects of an object or a person, steps in a process, or dimensions of a concept are subcategories that can be effectively organized by topic.

TOPICAL ORGANIZATION divides information about a subject and topic into subtopics or subcategories.

CHRONOLOGICAL ORGANIZATION is used to describe changes or developments in any situation or circumstance.

One problem with topical organization is that the main points may sound unrelated if you fail to provide clear transitions as you move from one point to the next. Also, you risk boring the audience, and sounding as though you are droning on and on, from one topic of discussion to another. To avoid this problem, structure an introduction that builds a strong case for the importance of your topic, use transitions between main points, and use a presentation aid of some kind—statistics on a chart or an intriguing picture—to help your listeners stay involved.

Zak's speech about coffee drinking naturally clustered into two main points, so topical organization worked best for him. An outline of that speech is presented in Box 13.1, to illustrate how informative organizational patterns work with the introduction and conclusion. Also, transitions and the suggestions provided to Zak by his instructor are incorporated in this illustrative outline.

BY TIME.

Chronological organization, as mentioned in Chapter Eleven, is used to describe changes or developments in any situation or circumstance. The speech could be historical—linked to actual dates of when something occurred and started and ended—or sequential—related to a sequence of steps that occur or are performed over time. A historical structure would work well if you are describing an event like a war, the founding and development of your college or company, or the development and decline of the labor movement in the United States. In a speech about the labor movement, a historical structure could be used to structure the main points of the body of the speech in this way:

I. 1792 to 1929: Labor unions grew to be a powerful economic force in the US.
II. 1930 to 1950: Union membership grew in the 1930s and 1940s, and began to decline in the 1950s.
III. 1960 to present: Membership has continued to decline; labor unions are searching for a new foothold in the information-age economy.

Two problems can occur if you organize a speech historically. First, the audience may not think something that happened in the past is relevant to them. If that is the case, demonstrate early in the speech the relevance of the speech topic to their lives. Second, you will bore the audience if your speech is little more than a recounting of dates and times. To avoid that problem, include precise dates only to provide a context for appreciating the significance of the event. Also, try to make the particular time in history memorable, using lively and colorful examples of life back then.

A sequential time structure is effective in describing the steps in a process. You could use this pattern to describe how the stock market ebbs and flows, or how weather systems form and move around the globe. A topic such as the steps a graduate takes to finding a new job could be presented using the following sequential pattern:

I. Gather information about job possibilities that align with your qualifications.
II. Develop or revise your résumé, highlighting your strengths that match the job of your dreams.
III. Circulate your résumé to employment agencies.
IV. Apply to your top three choices, and await acceptance notification.

BY SPACE.

Spatial organization presents information based on the positioning of objects in physical space, or relationships among locations. This structure works well when you want the listeners to visualize the arrangement of objects, locations, or distances. For example, if you are describing what your home is like, or the architectural design of a building, you would structure your speech spatially around the layout of the building. Space organization also would work well to describe the shifting battle lines held by the North and South during the Civil War, or the the best places to visit in a major city like London or New York.

> SPATIAL ORGANIZATION presents information based on the positioning of objects in physical space, or relationships among locations.

> ORGANIZATION BY COMPARISON AND CONTRAST is used to describe or explain how a subject is similar to, or different from, something else.

The main problem with space organization is making certain that the listeners follow along, and can visualize the spaces you are describing. If you are describing New York City, also referrred to as Manhattan, talking about Midtown or the Upper East Side is not enough. Providing a map, layout, or diagram of the city will solve the problem.

COMPARISON AND CONTRAST.

Organization by comparison and contrast is used to describe or explain how a subject is similar to, or different from, something else. Comparison means pointing out the similarities; contrast means pointing out the differences. This structure is useful when significant similarities or differences between the subject of discussion and something else will help the audience understand and appreciate the subject better. It works particularly well if the topic of the speech is unfamiliar but can be easily related to something the audience already knows about.

For example, a speech on health care reform could both compare and contrast programs in the United States to those in other countries by using these two main points as the body of the speech:

I. How the U.S. health care program is like (compares to) that in Canada and England.
II. How the U.S. health care program is unlike (contrasts to) programs in Canada and England.

One problem when using comparison and contrast is structuring the speech so the listeners know when you are talking about a similarity or a difference. You could present all the comparisons first, followed by all the contrasts; then your speech would be like the health care speech. Another approach would be to select important aspects of the topic, and talk about the similarities or the differences of each aspect. Then, the body of the speech would have as many main points as aspects that you choose to talk about.

CAUSE AND EFFECT.

Organization by cause and effect examines why something happens (the causes), and what happens as a result (the effects). This structure is good for understanding an event or an action of an individual, an organization, or an institution. It also is useful for describing a controversial issue, because it can illustrate connections between the issue and its consequences. A

> ••••••••••••••••••••••••••••••
> ORGANIZATION BY CAUSE AND EFFECT examines why something happens (the causes), and what happens as a result (the effects).

cause-and-effect speech could be used to describe a significant historical event, or the emergence of a communication phenomenon, such as an increase in the use of social media and websites like Facebook and YouTube.

Be aware that you may want to reverse the order, and describe the effects or results first, and then their cause. This reverse approach is recommended when the audience is already interested in the topic, and knows something about it. By first calling attention to the significant impact of the effects, you heighten interest in the causes before you discuss them. In a speech about social media, you could first describe the effects—increased usage and less face-to-face communication—before you proceed to the causes—easy access to social media websites, and big profits for the developers from advertisers. Here is how the body of that speech could be structured:

I. Statistics on the increase in use of social media (effect).
II. Story about a young person who rarely interacts personally with others (effect).
III. New forms of social media easily accessed and constantly being enhanced by developers (cause).
IV. Technology companies reaping great profits from advertising on social media websites (cause).

Two cautions are in order when using cause-and-effect organization. First, be sure you are clear about whether you are speaking to inform or to persuade, because this organizational pattern lends itself to both types of speeches. For instance, the informative speech about social media would become persuasive if you urged the audience to take some action about the situation. Second, be certain that you have a true cause-and-effect relationship, and that the situation (cause) you are describing is really what is causing the result (effect).

To decide which of the five organizational patterns will work best for organizing and outlining the body of your informative speech, think about the actual content of the speech. Depending on whether the speech is about an object, process, event, person, issue, or concept, one or more of the organizational patterns just described will be most effective. Table 13.3 summarizes suggestions for organizing the body of your informative speech based on what the speech is about—its content.

Table 13.3: Organizing Informative Speeches

Depending on the content of the informative speech, certain organizational patterns will work better than others.

TYPE OF SPEECH BASED ON CONTENT	ORGANIZATIONAL STRUCTURES FOR EACH TYPE OF SPEECH
• An object speech	**By Topic/Category**: Use if aspects of the object you are describing naturally cluster into categories. **By Space**: Use if aspects of the object can easily be visualized in a spatial relationship to one another.
• A process speech	**By Time**: Use if the process you are describing occurs sequentially over time or as a sequence of steps. **By Space**: Use if the steps in the process can be easily visualized as connected to each other.
• An event speech	**By Time**: Use when an event or a series of events can be described as they occurred over time. **By Cause and Effect**: Use when the event can be understood by describing why it happened and what resulted.
• A people speech	**By Topic/Category**: Use when you want to describe various aspects, characteristics, achievements, or actions of a person. **By Comparison and Contrast**: Use to understand a person based on how she or he is either like or unlike someone else. **By Cause and Effect**: Use to understand the cause and effects of the person's actions or decisions.
• An issue speech	**By Cause and Effect**: Use to promote understanding of an issue by presenting why the issue exists, and what is happening as a result. **By Comparison and Contrast**: Use to provide insights into an issue, based on how it is like or unlike another issue. **By Topic/Category**: Use to describe the main ideas that comprise the issue.
• A concept speech	**By Category**: Use to describe main ideas that comprise the concept. **By Comparison and Contrast**: Use to provide insights into an unfamiliar concept by describing how it is like or unlike something else.

USING SUPPORT MATERIALS TO INFORM

Deciding how to organize your informative speech is a crucial step. But to make your speech as effective as possible, you also need to be creative in how you use support materials. In Chapter Eleven you learned about the sources of information for gathering support materials, such as your own experiences and those of other people, the Internet, and the library. From these sources of information, the support materials you have access to include: definitions and descriptions, examples and stories, testimonies and quotations, and facts and statistics. These forms of support are essential to informative speaking, but they are equally effective in persuasive speeches.

DEFINITIONS AND DESCRIPTIONS.

Clarity and understanding in an informative speech are achieved in part by providing definitions and descriptions. In Chapter Two, you learned that clarity contributes to communicating competently, whether with one person or a large audience. To achieve clarity, first realize that uncommon terms, which are new or unfamiliar to the listeners, must be explained. So

> A HYPOTHETICAL EXAMPLE is about something that has not actually happened but could happen.

define any new word or term, and provide a description of it early in your speech. Also, members of the audience may interpret common or familiar words differently from what you mean. Therefore, if a familiar word or phrase is serving as a key term in your speech, provide a simple and concise definition of it to let your listeners know exactly how you are using it. As stated in Chapter Four on language, words mean different things to different people. Somewhat controversial words or terms like *global warming*, *abortion*, or *affirmative action* need to be defined. Use a dictionary to determine the most acceptable definition for the key term. In Zak's speech, he provides a simple definition of *barista* in his introduction (see Box 13.1).

EXAMPLES AND STORIES.

Another simple but effective form of support is the example. An example in a speech, such as a specific item, person, or event, helps explain or illustrate an idea, clarify a difficult concept, or make anything you say more interesting and real to the audience. You can choose between using real examples or hypothetical ones. A **hypothetical example** is about something that has not actually happened but could happen, which can be just as effective as a real example. In using a hypothetical example, you ask your listeners to imagine a situation related to the speech topic. It is important that a hypothetical example be plausible. For instance, in Zak's speech about drinking coffee at Starbucks, he could have said, "Imagine relaxing this weekend after our final speeches, enjoying a cup of cappuccino with a few friends!"

A competent speaker carefully plans the use of powerful examples, realizing that one strong example is more effective than several inadequate ones. But even though an example is effective, it is not ethical to use an example to prove a point if you know it is only an isolated incident. If it is true on a larger scale, then use statistics or other information that demonstrates the widespread nature of the problem or situation.

When you tell a story, which is actually just a long example, it serves the same purpose—to illustrate an idea, clarify a concept, or make a point more interesting and real. The ability to tell a good story is one of the most valuable skills a public speaker can have. A story fuels a speech with energy, and inspires and influences the listeners through their involvement in the tale.[5] It also is an ideal tool for eliciting an emotional response from the audience, and setting the tone or mood for a speech as part of the introduction.

A story in the introduction certainly would grab the audience's attention. However, a story that is either poorly told or not relevant to the content of your speech can have a negative impact. To avoid this situation, choose your story carefully, be sure it is relevant to your topic, and do not include it just to fill up time or amuse the audience. Keep the story short and concise, and, if possible, describe real people and events. Create a mental picture of the action that takes place in the story by describing what actually happened or what someone actually did. Most important, be sure that you are comfortable telling the story by practicing it a couple of times before you give the speech.

TESTIMONIES AND QUOTATIONS.

Two more valuable forms of support make use of someone else's words to support the ideas in your speech. **Testimony** utilizes the opinion of an expert, or the account of an event by a witness to it. A **quotation** makes use of a person's exact words. Either or both of these techniques can be used to provide authoritative evidence for your speech when your own credibility is not as impressive as you would like. In Zak's speech about drinking coffee, he provided both testimonies and quotations.

For a testimony or quotation to be effective, choosing the right source is imperative. Find experts or people who hold respected positions in the subject area you are speaking about, preferably someone your listeners will recognize. You can use a person who is not highly expert if she or he has experience relevant to your speech topic. You can use a person who is not well known if you tell the audience why the individual's opinion is important.

TESTIMONY utilizes the opinion of an expert, or the account of an event by a witness to it.

A QUOTATION makes use of a person's exact words.

A FACT is an individual piece of information that listeners could verify for themselves if they wanted to.

STATISTICS are numerical summaries of facts, figures, and research findings that provide pictures of data about people, ideas, or patterns of behavior.

FACTS AND STATISTICS.

A final way to provide support for an informative speech is to present facts and statistics. A **fact** is an individual piece of information that listeners could verify for themselves if they wanted to. The ability to verify the information, perhaps in the library or on a legitimate website, is what makes a piece of information a fact. Therefore, you need to tell the listeners the source of any claim you make based on a fact. **Statistics** are numerical summaries of facts, figures, and research findings that provide pictures of data about people, ideas, or patterns of behavior. To be effective, a fact or statistic should be highly relevant to the speech topic, and it should contain enough evidence so that it can stand on its own as a solid piece of information.

If you use statistics, select your figures carefully, and do not overwhelm the audience with the numbers. More is not necessarily better—in fact, it can be confusing. One recent study found that journalists' use of statistics led to messages that confused readers rather than informed them.[6] But if you do want to present a lot of numbers, provide a simple interpretation of the statistics. An effective way to simplify a statistic is to use a presentation aid. Chapter Twelve discussed the use of charts and graphs to present statistics more clearly. Look back at Figure 12.2 that shows how to use a typical line graph, pie chart, or bar graph. Also, consider strengthening your statistical evidence by combining it with a strong example or story, as Zak did in his main point about the increase of coffee drinking. An example makes a situation or event real and personal, and statistics indicate that the example is a common occurence.

ETHICS AND INFORMATIVE PUBLIC SPEAKING

Just as ethics is important to communication competence in general (See Chapter Two), it also plays a crucial role when preparing an informative speech. As you plan your informative speech and choose support materials and evidence, you will be obligated to make some ethical decisions. Should you use statistics or other support materials that would accomplish your informative objective, but perhaps misrepresent the truth, or lead your listeners to faulty conclusions? If you discover some evidence that could be manipulated ever so slightly to make your informative speech more interesting, is this use of information really unethical?

The discussion of ethics in Chapter Two helps to answer questions such as these. Recall that we said competence involves balancing effectiveness and achieving your own personal goals, with appropriateness and with respect for others. So deciding what support materials to use and how to present your informative speech most ethically relates to achieving an optimal balance of appropri-

---

Box 13.2: Beloit College Mindset List for the Class of 2014

Most students who will graduate in 2014 were born in 1992. Here is a list of 20 of the 75 cultural references that characterize students in this age group.

---

1. Email too slow, and they seldom if ever use snail mail.
2. "Caramel macchiato" and "venti half-caff vanilla latte" have always been street corner lingo.
3. In a country where a quarter of young people under 18 have at least one immigrant parent, they aren't afraid of immigration . . . unless it involves "real" aliens from another planet.
4. Colorful lapel ribbons have always been worn to indicate support for a cause.
5. Korean cars have always been a staple on American highways.
6. They never twisted the coiled handset wire aimlessly around their wrists while chatting on the phone.
7. DNA fingerprinting and maps of the human genome have always existed.
8. Unless they found one in their grandparents' closet, they have never seen a carousel of slides for presenting speeches.
9. They've never recognized that pointing to their wrists was a request for the time of day.
10. The first home computer they probably touched was an Apple II or Mac II; they are now in a museum.
11. Czechoslovakia has never existed.
12. Secondhand smoke has always been an official carcinogen.
13. "Assisted Living" has always been replacing nursing homes, while Hospice has always offered an alternative to the hospital.
14. Once they got through security, going to the airport has always resembled going to the mall.
15. American companies have always done business in Vietnam.
16. The dominance of television news by the three networks passed while they were still in their cribs.
17. Rock bands have always played at presidential inaugural parties.
18. Having hundreds of cable channels but nothing to watch has always been routine.
19. They first met Michelangelo when he was just a computer virus.
20. The nation has never approved of the job Congress is doing.

Source: *Beloit College* (2011).[7]

ateness and effectiveness. It is acceptable to attempt to achieve the objective of your speech, but not at the price of disrespecting the listeners by distorting the truth, or presenting information inaccurately. As an ethical informative speaker, you must provide sufficient information so listeners can make informed decisions about any matter of importance to them that you mention in your speech. In fact, this explanation is a good description of ethical communication, in general.

OVERCOMING CHALLENGES TO INFORMATIVE SPEAKING

When a speaker fails to present an informative speech competently, it is usually because of one or more of the following three reasons: The speaker chose an inappropriate subject or topic, faulty information was used to support the topic, or, the speech was poorly organized. Novice speakers are most likely to have problems with these challenges, whereas more experienced speakers have learned through trial and error how to overcome them.

INAPPROPRIATE SUBJECT OR TOPIC.

The process of topic selection was thoroughly discussed in Chapter Eleven. With regard to informative speaking, choosing from the wrong subject area, or selecting an inappropriate topic because of poor audience analysis is a serious mistake that will result in a speech with little audience appeal. This challenge can be well illustrated by thinking about what an audience of today's college freshmen is probably like. If you fail to consider these students' life experiences and their cultural knowledge base, you will not choose a topic they will find engaging. A list of cultural references that characterize many, if not most, of today's college students is presented in Box 13.2.

When you decide on a topic for your informative speech, particularly if it evolves from your own knowledge and experience, examine it in light of the listeners' possible interests. Does it represent information they will care about and want to know more about? Or will you have to work too hard to motivate them to care? As a competent informative speaker, you should either choose a topic to which your listeners will easily relate, or take responsibility for providing background information to help them appreciate and understand it.

FAULTY INFORMATION.

In addition to topic selection, another challenge to informative speaking is the use of faulty information. Three problems can occur with this challenge—too much information, too little information, or the wrong information. Information overload is a common problem: You include more information than is necessary to accomplish the objective of the speech, more than can be covered in the time allotted, or too much high-level information. On the other hand, including too little information also can be a problem. You may assume you already know enough about the topic, so you do not need to research it, and a lack of adequate support materials results. Figuring out how much or how little information to include is important, but the quality of that information is also a concern. Each minute of an informative speech is precious, so you should only present information the audience can relate to, and that helps accomplish the informative objective.

As you choose support materials, be sure they represent information that will be perceived as meaningful and relevant by the particular listeners. Also, be sure you use an appropriate amount of information, not too much and not too little. As mentioned elsewhere, practice your speech ahead of time to know if you can comfortably present the amount of information it contains in the time allowed.

POOR ORGANIZATION.

A third challenge to giving an informative speech competently is failing to organize the speech so the listeners can easily understand it. A common mistake new speakers make is not realizing how hard it is for listeners to follow and absorb a large amount of new information. Because you become familiar with the content of your informative speech, you may not realize how overwhelming it may sound when your listeners hear it for the first time. If they have to spend time figuring out the maze of new information you present, your informative speech just will not be effective.

Regardless of which organizational pattern you use for your informative speech, err on the side of simplicity. While the temptation may be great to impress the audience with lots of information presented in a complex way, instead present a clear and uncomplicated, informative message that is easily understood. Pare it down to the essentials, to what is simple, basic, and necessary for accomplishing your informative objective.

The steps to giving an informative speech outlined in this chapter would have helped Zak present his "Joy of Java" speech with a bit more competence. They will help you as well, as you determine the type of informative speech to present, how to organize it, and how to use support materials most effectively. The next and final chapter on public speaking will introduce you to similar concepts, but as they apply to persuasive speaking.

CHAPTER SUMMARY

The purpose of speaking to inform is to communicate new information or a new perspective on a topic to an audience about an object, process, event, person, concept, or issue. Being able to present an informative speech competently is important to people's professional and personal lives.

Informative speeches can be categorized based on their objective, including speeches to describe, explain, or instruct. Descriptions are used when the listeners are unfamiliar with the topic of the speech, and need new information in order to understand it. Explanations are used to tell listeners how something works, or to clarify something that is already known but not well understood. Instructions are useful when the objective is to teach the audience something, or tell them how to use something.

Organizing an informative speech clearly is essential to achieving its objective. However, it is difficult to organize and present complex ideas in informative speeches. The five ways to organize the body of an informative speech are by topic, chronology or time, space, comparison and contrast, and cause and effect. Organization by topic divides information about a subject and topic into subtopics or subcategories. Organization by time is used to describe changes or developments in any situation or circumstance, which can be historical or sequential. Organization by space presents information based on the positioning of objects in physical space, or relationships among locations. Organization by comparison and contrast is used to describe or explain how a subject is similar to, or different from, something else. Organization by cause and effect examines why something happens (the causes) and what happens as a result (the effects).

To present an informative speech most effectively, a competent speaker is creative in the use of these support materials: definitions and descriptions, examples and stories, testimonies and quotations, and facts and statistics. In choosing support materials and evidence, a speaker has to make some ethical decisions about how to use some of the information. An ethical informative speaker provides sufficient information so that listeners can make informed decisions about any matter of importance to them that is mentioned in your speech.

Three challenges to informative public speaking are as follows: the speaker chooses an inappropriate subject or topic, faulty information is used to support the topic, or the speech is poorly organized.

KEY TERMS.

The key terms below are defined in this chapter, and presented alphabetically with definitions in the Glossary at the end of the book.

- informative speech
- speech about an object
- speech about a process
- event speech
- speech about a person
- concept speech
- issue speech
- descriptions
- explanations

- instructions
- topical organization
- chronological organization
- spatial organization
- organization by comparison and contrast
- organization by cause

- and effect
- hypothetical example
- testimony
- quotation
- fact
- statistics

BUILDING MOTIVATION: SELF-ASSESSMENT TOOL.

Rate each of the eight communication situations described here, indicating your own typical level of competence in informative speaking. Rate one situation all the way through for motivation, knowledge, and skills. Then rate the next situation. Use the 1–4 scale below, with 1 being minimal competence and 4 high competence.

Communication situations.

1. Present an informative speech to a group of people from cultures very different from your own.
2. Describe to a group of neighbors your plan to renovate a local park.
3. Explain to a group of other students how to solve a statistical problem.
4. Outline the events to a group of voters that resulted in a current problem they face.
5. Instruct a group of your coworkers in the use of a new computer software program.
6. Present the convocation speech at a big college or university.
7. Give an informative speech that needs facts and statistics to be effective.
8. Present a talk using Web conferencing technology.

Motivation.

1 = Distracted, disinterested, or simply no motivation to be competent.
2 = Somewhat distracted or disinterested, but motivated to be competent.

3 = Somewhat interested and motivated to be competent.

4 = Highly interested and motivated to be competent.

Knowledge.

1 = Completely inexperienced and ignorant about what to do and how to do it.

2 = Minimal experience and sense of what to do and how to do it.

3 = Somewhat experienced and knowledgeable about what to do and how to do it.

4 = Highly knowledgeable about all aspects of what to do and how to do it.

Skills.

1 = Completely incapable of behaving competently.

2 = Barely capable of behaving minimally competently.

3 = Fairly capable of behaving competently.

4 = Highly capable of behaving competently.

Interpreting your scores.

Total your score separately for each situation (motivation, knowledge, and skills). The possible range of the score for each situation is 3–12. If your total score for any of the situations is 6 or less, you see yourself as less competent in that situation than you should be. A score of 7–9 means that you are average at sending and receiving communication messages in the situation. A score of 10–12 indicates that you have a high level of communication competence in that situation.

BUILDING KNOWLEDGE: DISCUSSION QUESTIONS.

1. Is informative speaking an important communication skill for a person to acquire? Whether your answer is yes or no, explain your reasoning.
2. Could one informative speech have all three objectives: to describe, explain, and instruct? If yes, provide an example. If no, explain why not.
3. Of the five ways to organize an informative speech—by topic, chronology or time, space, comparison and contrast, and cause and effect—is any one of them more likely to be useful than the others? Explain your answer.
4. In your opinion, which of the various types of support materials are most essential for giving an effective informative speech? Explain your reasoning.
5. How can a public speaker know when he or she has crossed the line and is presenting an informative speech in an unethical manner?

BUILDING SKILLS: STUDENT ACTIVITIES.

Individual activities.

1. Make three columns on a piece of paper. Label your columns "Types of Informative Speeches," "Speech Topic," and "Organizational Pattern," from left to right. In column 1, list the three types of informative speeches (describe, explain, instruct) based on objective. In column

2, come up with one speech topic that appeals to you for each type of speech. In column 3, decide which organizational pattern would work best for each topic you listed.

2. Attend an informative public speech or lecture. Identify the type of speech that it is, how it is organized, and evaluate the support materials used. Write up a summary of your evaluative comments.

3. Visit The Quotations Home Page at http://www.theotherpages.org/quote.html. This site contains links to other collections, and over 24,000 quotes. Find a quotation that could be used for the topic you are considering for your next speech.

4. Attend an informative public speech or lecture. Evaluate how effectively the speaker managed the three challenges to informative speaking outlined in this chapter—inappropriate subject or topic, faulty information, and poor organization.

Group activities.

1. Attend an informative speech in a small group with several other students (a lecture will do). Each student should analyze the speech based on the speaker's use of an organizational pattern and support materials. After you leave the presentation, compare your evaluations.

2. With one other student, identify the topic for your next informative speech. Collaborate to determine the best organizational pattern and potential support materials for both speeches.

3. In a small group of four to five students, practice telling a personal story to the group. First, have each group member choose one of these topics for his or her story: (a) your most memorable communication experience, (b) an event that influenced the course of your life, or (c) a person who contributed something memorable to your life. Take five minutes to organize and make notes about your story. Then have each person tell his or her story, and the rest of the group provides feedback to the storytellers.

NOTES

1. See Reinhart & Feeley (2007).
2. See Mobley (2011).
3. See Rowan (2003).
4. See Yeung (2007).
5. See Simmons (2002).
6. See Amberg & Hall (2010).
7. See *Beloit College: The Mindset List* (2011).

REFERENCES

Amberg, S. M., & Hall, T. E. (2010). Precision and rhetoric in media reporting about contamination in farmed salmon. *Science Communication, 32*(4), 489–513.

Beloit College: The mindset list. (2011). Retrieved from http://www.beloit.edu/mindset/2014/

Mobley, P. (2011). *Listening.* Retrieved from http://ezinearticles.com/?Listening&id=397732

Reinhart, A., & Feeley, T. (2007). Comparing the persuasive effects of narrative versus statistical messages: A meta-analytic review. Paper presented at the National Communication Association Conference. Retrieved from EBSCO*host*, www.ebsco.com

Rowan, K. E. (2003). Informing and explaining skills: Theory and research on informative communication. In J. O. Greene & B. R. Burleson (Eds.), *Handbook of communication and social interaction skills* (pp. 403–438). Mahwah, NJ: Erlbaum.

Simmons, A. (2002). *The story factor: Inspiration, influence and persuasion through the art of storytelling*. Philadelphia, PA: Perseus Books.

Yeung, L. (2007). In search of commonalities: Some linguistic and rhetorical features of business reports as a genre. *English for Specific Purposes, 26*(2), 156–179.

CHAPTER FOURTEEN

SPEAKING TO PERSUADE

- **Understanding the Persuasive Speech**
  What Is a Persuasive Speech?
  The Importance of Persuasive Speaking Skills
  Types of Persuasive Speeches

- **Organizing and Outlining a Persuasive Speech**
  By Problem-Solution and the Motivated Sequence
  By Refuting the Opponent
  By Comparing Alternatives

- **Making Your Argument Persuasive**
  Logical Appeals
  Emotional Appeals
  Character Appeals

- **Ethics and Persuasive Public Speaking**

- **Overcoming Challenges to Persuasive Speaking**
  Persuasion Failure Rate
  Audience Reaction Factor

- **Chapter Summary**
  Key Terms
  Building Motivation: Self-Assessment Tool
  Building Knowledge: Discussion Questions
  Building Skills: Student Activities

Speech is power; speech is to persuade, to convert, to compel. —Ralph Waldo Emerson, poet and essayist, 1803–1882

• •
• • •

Vanden was about to finish his first semester at Southeast University. He took a public speaking class because he knew it would help him give better presentations at work and in other classes. The final assignment in the class involved preparing and presenting a persuasive speech. The instructor recommended that students choose a significant topic or issue they felt strongly about, but also one that would interest the student audience. Vanden reviewed the list of suggested topics, but did not see anything on the list that excited him. Two weeks before the assignment was due, Vanden ran into Cyndy, a classmate who was quite involved in campus politics. As she had done before, Cyndy tried to persuade Vanden to help her fight for the interests and needs of students on campus. She described a few of the current problems she was working on with a student activist organization, such as insufficient parking and the latest tuition increase. She said that if Vanden and other students did not organize to fight for their rights, campus administrators would assume they did not care what was happening, and tuition would continue to go up.

Cyndy's persuasive argument impressed Vanden, and he agreed to attend a meeting of the student activist group with her that afternoon. Later that evening, Vanden thought about how Cyndy had persuaded him, a relatively nonpolitical type of person, to get involved in campus life. He felt that his eyes had been opened to the administration's shifting priorities and their indifference to students' concerns. He had even signed a petition to protest tuition hikes and to protect other important student rights. But how did Cyndy motivate him to overcome his ambivalence and finally attend the student meeting?

Cyndy effectively persuaded Vanden by changing what he believed to be true, and thereby moving him to action. She had presented a logical argument, reminding Vanden that the last tuition increase was only a year ago, and the size of this year's increase would be greater than the inflation rate. She appealed to him emotionally by explaining how hard it can be for some students at Southeast to handle the repeated tuition hikes. A committed and credible role model herself, Cyndy appeared to care genuinely about the welfare of others. She stressed the importance of Vanden's contribution to the united voice for all students. Not only was Vanden glad to be working with Cyndy and the other students, he realized there was another immediate benefit—he had found a topic for his persuasive speech. He would try to persuade his classmates in the public speaking class to sign the petition, and join him in protesting the tuition hike. This was a topic Vanden could get excited about and make relevant to his audience.

This chapter covers the key elements and techniques of competent persuasion, similar to what Cyndy used to influence Vanden to become more of a student activist. We begin by building an understanding of persuasive speaking and its importance.

UNDERSTANDING THE PERSUASIVE SPEECH

A persuasive speech may range from a politician's appeal for your vote to a sales person's pitch to get you to buy a new car to replace your old clunker. Whether the speech is intended to present a problem and tell you how to solve it, or refute the rhetoric of an opposing candidate for public office, both are considered persuasive.

WHAT IS A PERSUASIVE SPEECH?

We defined persuasion in Chapter One as the use of communication to influence an audience's attitudes, beliefs, values, or behaviors, and move the listeners to change or to action. Experts in persuasive communication identify four critical components in this process—the source, the appeal(s), the receivers, and the setting.[1] Therefore, a **persuasive speech** is a speech presented by a speaker (the source), using the right appeals for the setting to influence the attitudes, beliefs, values, or actions of the audience (receivers).

> A PERSUASIVE SPEECH is a speech presented by a speaker (the source), using the right appeals for the setting to influence the attitudes, beliefs, values, or actions of the audience (receivers).

As you saw in Chapter Thirteen, an informative speaker uses information purely to promote understanding. By contrast, as you will see in this chapter, a persuasive speaker uses information to influence listeners. As a result, persuasive speeches are organized differently from informative ones. Furthermore, although both types of speakers are concerned with the audience's attitudes toward the information presented, the listeners' specific position on the topic is even more vital to persuasive speaking, because the ultimate goal is to influence that position.

THE IMPORTANCE OF PERSUASIVE SPEAKING SKILLS.

Persuasion has been considered an important aspect of social life for centuries. In fact, rhetoric and persuasive speaking are central and vital to the actual practice of any democracy.[2] Think about any election or political campaign you have observed. It is mainly through using persuasive speaking skills that a candidate is chosen by the electorate. In his famous book on persuasion, *The Rhetoric*, the Greek philosopher, Aristotle, wrote about how important it is for people to discover and be able to use the available means of persuasion in any situation.[3] Aristotle identified four social values for rhetoric and persuasion.

First, persuasion prevents the triumph of fraud and injustice. It is not enough just to know what is right; people must be able to argue for what is right. Second, rhetoric and persuasion are an effective method of instruction for the public. It is not sufficient just to understand a matter; a speaker must also be able to instruct the audience about it in a persuasive manner. Third, persuasive rhetoric helps people see and understand both sides of an issue. They determine what they believe to be true by listening to persuasive arguments on all sides. Fourth, rhetoric and persuasion are a viable means of defense. According to Aristotle, just as people need to be able to defend themselves physically, they should also be able to fend off verbal attacks persuasively. If, for instance, another person is unfairly criticizing you—publicly or privately—it would be useful to be able to persuade the person to cease the criticizing.

Indeed, the effective use of communication, including persuasive speaking skills, continues to be the foundation of a free and open society. Whether at the local or national level—in legislatures, schools, businesses, or public meetings—people use persuasive speaking to debate, and then set organizational and public agendas for their communities. At the college level, students who learn to formulate compelling persuasive arguments are able to think more cogently about their arguments, and then "show" the validity of their position and "tell" that position to others.[4] By learning to develop and deliver persuasive speeches, students also learn to understand and respect different points of view—as Aristotle suggested—and to support their beliefs with evidence, and present their opinions effectively.

TYPES OF PERSUASIVE SPEECHES.

As with informative speeches, persuasive speeches can be categorized based on the speaker's objective. The objective of Vanden's speech to his class was to motivate his classmates to sign a petition opposing tuition hikes. Three types of persuasive speeches, based on their objective, attempt to:

1. Reinforce listeners' attitudes, beliefs, and values,
2. Change their attitudes, beliefs, and values, or
3. Move the listeners to action.

Table 14.1: Analyzing Listeners' Attitudes, Beliefs, Values, and Behaviors

When preparing a persuasive speech topic, you first must determine the audience's attitudes, beliefs, values, and behaviors with regard to the topic or issue. That information will help you develop a speech that is more likely to achieve your persuasive objective.

TOPIC	ATTITUDE	BELIEF	VALUE	BEHAVIOR
Prostitution	Favorable toward allowing prostitutes to work their trade	It is the responsibility of everyone to earn a living in any way possible	Personal autonomy free of government control	Encourage legislators to vote against control of prostitution
Capital Punishment	Favorable toward life sentences for those committing murder or other violent crimes	It is wrong to take another person's life	Sacredness of all human life	Vote against putting people to death by use of the electric chair or lethal injection
First Amendment Rights	Favorable toward no control or interference by the government on the Internet	Everyone has a right to express their opinions in any way they prefer	Individual liberty	Vote for a hands-off policy relative to Web pages and pornography on the Internet
Euthanasia	Favorable toward assisted suicide	People have a right to control their own destiny	Freedom of choice	Encourage the use of living wills that allow people to die as they choose

This categorization system for persuasive speeches may be a bit misleading in that it suggests the three types are discrete and unrelated to one another. In reality, the types of speeches sometimes overlap. You may find yourself presenting a speech that has more than one objective. For example, in the opening story, Cyndy's objective was to change Vanden's attitudes and beliefs, but also move him to action.

As you will recall from Chapter Eleven, these audience characteristics—attitudes, beliefs, and values—were discussed as crucial to audience analysis (See Figure 11.1). Now you must use what you know about analyzing these characteristics of your audience to develop an effective persuasive speech.[5] This analysis entails figuring out the audience's potential reaction to your persuasive attempt.[6] Your job is to identify any resistance, and motivate them to want to change. So you need to figure out whether you want to reinforce *or* change their attitudes, beliefs, and values, or move them to act. Table 14.1 provides a few examples of how to analyze potential audience reactions to some typical persuasive topics. We now examine these three types of persuasive speeches more closely.

A speech to reinforce is intended to influence listeners by strengthening their convictions, and taking advantage of their tendency to seek out and attend to messages with which they already agree. Most listeners are more likely to pay attention to and remember information that supports or resembles their own attitudes and opinions. So by reinforcing your listeners' attitudes, beliefs, or values, you will increase the likelihood that they will pay attention and remember what you say. This type of speech works well if there is a need to raise your listeners' consciousness about an issue or concern. They may already agree with your position, but have no sense of urgency about the topic. So you want to encourage them to care more about it.

> A SPEECH TO REINFORCE is intended to influence listeners by strengthening their convictions, and taking advantage of their tendency to seek out and attend to messages with which they already agree.

> A SPEECH TO CHANGE is intended to convince the audience to change what they like or dislike, what they hold to be true or untrue, or what they consider important or unimportant.

To reinforce listeners' attitudes and beliefs, provide them with additional information that supports their existing attitudes and what they already believe to be true. Reinforce their values by indicating your respect for what they hold to be right or important. You should not say that you agree with them, if you do not. But merely by respecting their values, you build rapport and goodwill, which enhances your credibility, and helps accomplish the objective of speaking to reinforce.

A speech to change is intended to convince the audience to change what they like or dislike, what they hold to be true or untrue, or what they consider important or unimportant. To change listeners' attitudes—what they like or dislike—you first have to provide them with information that motivates them to listen to you, and then try to modify or change their attitudes. You could accomplish this by reinforcing an attitude they already hold to get their attention and establish mutual understanding, and then make your own point.

The best way to change listeners' beliefs—what they hold to be true or untrue—is to present them with solid facts and evidence from highly credible sources. Because beliefs are based on what people know, if you want to change beliefs, you need compelling evidence to counteract their previous experiences and knowledge. Information from credible sources, as well as your own credibility as a speaker, are essential to convince the audience that their current beliefs are not necessarily true, and that they should change them.

To change your listeners' values—what they consider important or unimportant—is to make a fundamental change in something very basic to each individual.[7] Because values are rooted in a person's self-concept, they are much harder to change than attitudes or beliefs. Therefore, success in changing listeners' values is rare, but appealing to values is an effective technique for influencing attitudes and beliefs.

A speech to move to action is intended to influence listeners to either engage in a new and desirable behavior, or discontinue an undesirable behavior. If you give a speech and ask your listeners to vote for your candidate, buy a product, or start recycling their trash, you are asking them to adopt a new behavior. If your speech asks them to stop smoking or littering, the action you are recommending is one of discontinuance.

To change people's behaviors, it is important to realize that attitudes, beliefs, and values shape and direct behaviors. For example, you may hold a favorable attitude toward environmental concerns, believe that recyling is a good idea, and value personal involvement in community life. As a result of these attitudes, beliefs, and values, you could be persuaded to adopt behaviors such as supporting sustainability efforts at your school or at work.

If you want to change people's behaviors—which is hard to do—you must demonstrate that their current behaviors are not consistent with their attitudes, beliefs, or values. Most people prefer to think they are acting according to what they believe and value. If you can demonstrate to your listeners that another set of behaviors is more consistent with their attitudes, beliefs, and values, your speech is more likely to result in at least some behavioral change.

Once you have decided on the type of persuasive speech you are presenting—to reinforce or change listeners' attitudes, beliefs, and values, or move them to action—then you need to determine the best way to organize the speech.

> A SPEECH TO MOVE to action is intended to influence listeners to either engage in a new and desirable behavior, or discontinue an undesirable behavior.

> PROBLEM-SOLUTION ORGANIZATION first identifies a problem, and then proposes a workable solution to it.

ORGANIZING AND OUTLINING A PERSUASIVE SPEECH

The general recommendations for speech organization discussed in Chapter Eleven apply to the persuasive speech as well. An effective persuasive speech is carefully organized, and is structured to accomplish its objective based on what you already have learned about the audience.[8] While there are a variety of ways to organize a persuasive speech, four patterns are best known and most accessible for beginning speakers. The problem-solution pattern and the motivated sequence are arguably the most popular. Refuting the opponent and comparing alternatives are useful when it is necessary to take opposing arguments into account.

BY PROBLEM-SOLUTION AND THE MOTIVATED SEQUENCE.

Problem-solution organization first identifies a problem, and then proposes a workable solution to it. This organizational pattern can be used to plan the body of the speech, using the basic structure introduced in Chapter Eleven. Draft an introduction, body, and conclusion, but cover only two main points in the body of the speech. Your first main point describes the problem, and persuades the audience that the problem must be overcome. The second main point proposes a solution to overcome the problem. For an outline of problem-solution organization, see Figure 14.1.

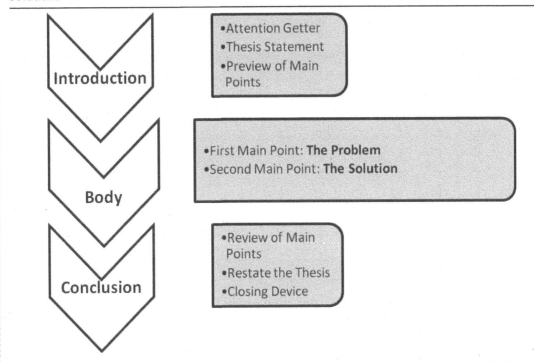

Figure 14.1: The Problem-Solution Pattern

This organizational pattern for a persuasive speech is structured similarly to the standard outline format described in Chapter Eleven. The body of the speech is organized as a problem and a solution.

Introduction
- Attention Getter
- Thesis Statement
- Preview of Main Points

Body
- First Main Point: **The Problem**
- Second Main Point: **The Solution**

Conclusion
- Review of Main Points
- Restate the Thesis
- Closing Device

Cyndy may have attempted to get Vanden involved in campus life by using problem-solution organization. She might have described what she saw as a crucial problem on campus, and then offered a constructive solution to it.

Problem: Campus administrators make decisions with too little concern for the students' welfare.

Solution: Get involved in campus life, and contribute to policy-making decisions.

An enhanced version of problem-solution organization has dominated public-speaking instruction for years, since it was first introduced in 1935 by Alan Monroe, a professor at Purdue University.[9] The **motivated sequence** organizational pattern is a model for persuasive speaking that moves through a sequence of five steps that are designed to motivate and persuade listeners psychologically.[10] This pattern is effective, because it makes use of a natural sequential pattern of human thought: gaining the listeners' attention, convincing them of a need or problem, offering a solution to satisfy the need or solve the problem, and then helping them visualize the solution and take action qualified to it.

MOTIVATED SEQUENCE is a model for persuasive speaking that moves through a sequence of five steps, designed to motivate and persuade listeners psychologically.

Returning to the basic speech structure you learned from Chapter Eleven, you present the attention step in your introduction, the need and satisfaction steps in the body of the speech, and the

Box 14.1: Outline of Motivated Sequence Organizational Pattern

As with any speech, your outline for this organizational pattern should state the title, general purpose, and specific purpose of the speech. Then the motivated sequence goes on to include five sequential steps: attention, need, satisfaction, visualization, and action.

Speech Title: Indicate the issue of persuasion, pique curiosity, be concise.
General Purpose: To persuade.
Specific Purpose: Infinitive statement indicating whether the speech has the objective to influence the audience's beliefs, attitudes, values, or behaviors.

INTRODUCTION

I.   ATTENTION STEP: Grab the audience's attention and forecast theme of the speech.

BODY

II.   NEED/PROBLEM: Describe the problem or need, provide evidence of its importance, and relate it to the audience's desires and/or needs.
III. SATISFACTION/SOLUTION STEP: Present a plan of action to address the problem or the need.

CONCLUSION

IV. VISUALIZATION STEP: Describe the results of the proposed plan, or the consequences of the audience's failure to change or to act.
V.   ACTION STEP: Summarize main ideas, and call for the audience to change their beliefs or to act or react in the desired manner.

visualization and action steps in your conclusion. These five steps are outlined in Box 14.1, and here we provide a short description of each step.

Step 1: Get the audience's attention. In this first step, create interest in the topic of your speech, and a desire on the part of your listeners to hear what you have to say. A management expert from Harvard University emphasized the importance of creating word pictures in listeners' minds by opening with a surprising or dramatic situation.[11] Also in this step, provide a statement of the purpose of your speech, and forecast the importance of the need or problem that will be the general theme of your speech.

Step 2: Establish that a need or problem exists. In this step, describe and develop the need or problem by providing evidence of its existence and importance. Use examples, testimony, statistics, and other forms of support to emphasize the seriousness of the situation. Explain why the problem exists, and relate it to the listeners by pointing out how it affects them. Provide visual images to make the problem "real." Motivate the audience to feel that a decision needs to be made or some action taken.

Step 3: Propose a satisfying solution. This step is used to present a plan of action to meet the need or solve the problem you established in the previous step. Explain to the listeners how your plan addresses the situation better than any other solution. To do this, you may have to actually demonstrate how your solution is superior to others.

Step 4: Help the audience visualize the solution. This step helps the audience to imagine the benefits of the solution you propose, or the negative consequences of not adopting your solution. You ask your listeners to picture the proposed plan being implemented, or what the world will look like if they fail to act. Again, the use of visual images will bring this step to life for your listeners.

Step 5: Motivate the audience to take action. Finally, ask the audience to act on the solution that you proposed to solve the problem. Summarize your main ideas as you would in any conclusion. Then clearly identify the specific action that is called for. If your objective is to change attitudes or beliefs, try to motivate the audience to reconsider their past positions, and believe what you propose instead. If you want the listeners to change their behaviors, urge them to take the specific actions you recommend to solve the problem.

Box 14.2 demonstrates how Vanden's speech urging his classmates to get involved in campus issues could use the motivated sequence pattern.

BY REFUTING THE OPPONENT.

Refuting the opponent organization dismantles your opponent's argument in order to persuade the audience that your argument is superior. In using this type of organizational pattern, your goal is to convince the audience that the opposition's ideas are false, misinformed, or in some way harmful.

There are two basic approaches for refuting the opponent, either of which can be used as the main points to structure the body of your speech. The first is to convince the audience that the other argument is flawed—that something is wrong with your opponent's line of reasoning. You examine his or her argument for any inconsistencies or errors in how evidence is used. The second approach is to convince the listeners that the actions recommended by your opponent will lead to undesirable results or consequences. You refute your opponent's argument by stressing its negative results or impact on the audience.

> REFUTING THE OPPONENT ORGANIZATION dismantles your opponent's argument in order to persuade the audience that your argument is superior.

> COMPARING ALTERNATIVES organization first asks listeners to examine two or more alternatives, and then it makes a strong appeal for the preferred choice.

A word of caution if you decide to use refuting the opponent. Avoid engaging in personal attacks, and stay strictly with the issues involved. Use solid evidence to criticize only your opponent's argument, because attacking a person can backfire and damage your own credibility. Besides, mudslinging and personal attacks are unethical approaches to persuasion, and therefore not competent.

BY COMPARING ALTERNATIVES.

Comparing alternatives organization first asks listeners to examine two or more alternatives, and then it makes a strong appeal for the preferred choice. This organizational pattern is designed to convince the audience that among all the possible ways to solve a problem, there is but one choice that has significant advantages over the others.

To use this organizational pattern, you present a series of alternatives, and provide reasons to reject each alternative, except the one you are persuading the audience to favor or adopt. You present all the other alternatives, and then present the alternative you prefer last. Just as with refuting the opponent, you can use comparing alternatives to structure the body of your speech. You would

Box 14.2: A Working Outline for Vanden's Persuasive Speech Using the Motivated Sequence

Vanden's speech urging his classmates to get involved in campus issues lends itself well to the use of this structure.

Speech Title: No More Tuition Hikes!
General Purpose: To persuade.
Specific Purpose: To change students' attitudes about tuition hikes, and take action by signing a petition opposing the hikes.

INTRODUCTION

I. ATTENTION STEP:
    Cyndy is a senior here at Southeast U. who is about to graduate. But she may not be able to afford to keep going and complete her degree. Cyndy won't be able to pay for the last few credits she needs, if S.U. administrators increase tuition, as they are planning to do. You may not know how much of an increase is in the works right now— if it happens, it is a serious problem for many students.

BODY

II. NEED/PROBLEM:
    a. Administrators plan to increase revenue by raising tuition by 20%; statistics on tuition increases over last ten years.
    b. Need for a plan to cut expenses, rather than continue to raise tuition; budgets showing expenses over last ten years.
    c. Description of personal impact on finances of students in the class.
III. SATISFACTION/SOLUTION STEP:
    a. Let administrators know how many students will stop or drop out if tuition hikes continue at current pace.
    b. Ask administrators to develop a new approach that increases revenue by more fund-raising in the community and fewer tuition hikes.

CONCLUSION

IV. VISUALIZATION STEP:
    a. If administrators fail to change their approach to tuition hikes, more students stopping and dropping out will have a profound, negative impact on revenues.
    b. If administrators change their approach, S.U. can continue to grow, and students like ourselves can complete our degrees in a timely manner.
V. ACTION STEP:
    Administrators here at Southeast U. are on our side, but they are not aware of the financial realities some of us face. If we continue down the path of more increases in tuition hikes, we will only see more decreases in the size of the student population. Today I am asking you to do two things. Please sign our petition urging administrators to put a stop to increasing tuition and come up with a new approach to fund-raising. Join us this Friday at 2:00 p.m. to participate in a peaceful protest at the administration building.

then have several main points, each containing a different alternative, and ending with the presentation of your preferred choice.

A word of caution also is in order for using this organizational pattern. It may not always work as you expect. One recent study found that a one-sided message—presenting only one desired alternative—may work best.[12] These researchers learned that one-sided messages induced more positive perceptions and attitudes than comparing alternatives.

MAKING YOUR ARGUMENT PERSUASIVE

Regardless of the structure you choose for your speech, you can make your argument much more persuasive by using one or more of three types of persuasive appeals. An **appeal** is the subtle technique speakers use to get the audience to accept their persuasive argument. Current thinking on this topic is derived from the classical tradition of rhetoric, when in the fourth century B.C.E., Greek rhetoricians recommended that persuasive speakers use *logos*—a form of logical appeals, *pathos*—emotional appeals, and *ethos*—credibility appeals.

> An APPEAL is the subtle technique speakers use to get the audience to accept their persuasive argument.

> A LOGICAL APPEAL is based on knowledge and reasoning, which involves how people think.

> DEDUCTION is a process of reasoning in which a specific conclusion follows from a general principle that is often made up of a major and a minor premise.

Although there is some debate about which of these appeals is most effective—logic, emotion, or credibility—persuasion experts agree that all three techniques can be effective depending on the situation, the audience, and the persuasive goal. For example, in the persuasive enviroment of religious retailing, several rhetoric researchers came up with a thought-provoking finding. They analyzed persuasive appeals associated with various forms of merchandise associated with Jesus. They found that Jesus's name is used in logical or rational appeals designed to change beliefs and promote positive attitudes toward the Christian faith, while Jesus's visual image is used in emotional appeals.[13] Let us take a closer look at the three types of appeals.

LOGICAL APPEALS.

A **logical appeal** is based on knowledge and reasoning, which involves how people think. It consists of presenting evidence, and encouraging listeners to draw a conclusion based on that information. Logical arguments are particularly effective for audiences made up of people from Western or North American cultures, who prefer to make decisions based on examining evidence and information.

Despite the usefulness of this appeal, three public speaking teachers recently discovered that their students did not clearly understand how to use reasoning, or logos, in a persuasive argument.[14] As a result, their students' speeches were not very persuasive. These instructors now stress how important it is for students to learn to effectively construct a convincing and ethical argument that contains a well-articulated claim or problem, and valid and reliable evidence. Indeed, a logical appeal works best and is most effective when it includes a very specific claim, as oppposed to weak or ineffective claims.[15]

Logical arguments can be made in two ways—using deductive or inductive reasoning. **Deduction** is a process of reasoning in which a specific conclusion follows from a general principle that is often made up of a major and a minor premise. If the audience accepts the two premises as true, then they must also accept that the specific conclusion is true. Here is a classic example that teachers of rhetoric use to illustrate deductive reasoning:

> Major premise: *All humans are mortal.*
>
> Minor premise: *Socrates is human.*
>
> Specific conclusion: *Therefore, Socrates is mortal.*

Using the topic of opposition to tuition hikes, here is how Vanden might use deductive reasoning:

> Major premise: *Inappropriate tuition hikes on many college campuses are rendering students unable to complete their degree programs.*
>
> Minor premise: *Administrators at Southeast University are considering inappropriate tuition hikes.*
>
> Specific conclusion: *Students at Southeast University must unite to oppose any inappropriate tuition hikes on our campus.*

Induction is a process of reasoning in which a general conclusion follows from considering a series of specific instances or examples. If the listeners accept the specific instances and examples as true, then they must also accept the general conclusion as true. The more credible the specific examples and illustrations, the more logical the conclusion will seem to the listeners. Vanden could use an inductive argument to come to a general conclusion in this manner:

> Instance: *Northeast University raised tuition substantially last year, and witnessed an immediate decrease in student enrollment.*
>
> Instance: *Southwest University raised tuition at the start of this academic year, and spring semester enrollment figures are showing signs of a decrease.*
>
> Instance: *I myself will need to cut back on the number of courses I take, if Southeast raises tuition next year.*
>
> General conclusion: *To avoid decreased enrollment, students at Southeast University must unite to oppose any tuition hikes on our campus.*

As you consider the use of logical appeals, you need to be aware of and avoid the use of logical fallacies. **Logical fallacies** are errors in reasoning and logic that lead listeners to false conclusions. The speakers are so intent on achieving their persuasive goals that they present evidence or information that is in error, unreasonable, or misrepresents the truth in some way. Whether intentional or unintentional, if fallacies in reasoning are detected, they reflect negatively on your credibility, and call into question your integrity. Researchers have identified literally hundreds of logical fallacies to avoid.

Here are some examples of the more common forms of faulty reasoning.

- *Ad hominem.* This fallacy occurs when a speaker attacks another person, as opposed to the argument the person is making. *Ad hominem* is Latin for "to the man." Candidates in political campaigns sometimes commit this error in reasoning by attacking their opponents per-

---

INDUCTION is a process of reasoning in which a general conclusion follows from considering a series of specific instances or examples.

LOGICAL FALLACIES are errors in reasoning and logic that lead the listeners to false conclusions.

sonally, and failing to stick to the issues. Unfortunately, some candidates for public office have discovered that this approach to negative campaigning has a benefit—it often works.

- *Non sequitur.* When a claim does not directly follow from the presented support material, a non sequitur occurs. While the claim may be correct and true, it does not necessarily follow from the evidence presented. *Non sequitur*, literally, means that a statement does not follow from anything previously said.

- *Red herring.* This fallacy diverts the audience's attention from the real issue by presenting irrelevant arguments or issues. The expression, "red herring," derives its meaning from the practice of dragging a smelly fish across a trail to divert the attention of hunting dogs.

- *Slippery slope.* When a speaker suggests that one event automatically leads to a series of other undesirable events, it is called slippery slope reasoning. The speaker implies that if the listeners take one action, they are setting themselves up to slide down a slope from which there is no return. This implication that a situation results from a single cause, when in fact it had multiple causes, is another way of misleading an audience. If you know there are additional causes, you have an obligation to describe them to the audience.

- *Straw man argument.* With this type of logical fallacy, the speaker attacks an entire argument by selecting a weak example or aspect of it, challenging that example, and thus discrediting the entire argument. The speaker sets up a "straw man" that is easy to challenge and knock over.

- *Sweeping or hasty generalization.* A sweeping generalization, that clusters ideas, people, or objects into one group and implies that all of the items in the group are the same, obscures vital and relevant differences. A hasty generalization results from moving to a conclusion too quickly, and based on too few specific cases or examples.

EMOTIONAL APPEALS.

An **emotional appeal** is based on psychology and passion, which involves how people feel. Despite what most people would like to think, they are not always logical. If your argument appeals to your listeners' emotions, it will get their attention and hold it. By reaching them emotionally and convincing them they should care about your topic, you will be more likely to achieve your persuasive goal.

> An EMOTIONAL APPEAL is based on psychology and passion, which involves how people feel.
>
> A FEAR APPEAL is based on changing listeners' attitudes or behaviors through the use of an anxiety-arousing message.

To use emotional appeals effectively, you can appeal to any of a variety of your listeners' emotions, such as love, hate, sympathy, guilt, or even fear. A **fear appeal** is based on changing listeners' attitudes or behaviors through the use of anxiety-arousing messages. This type of appeal is useful in situations where you really need to motivate the audience to pay attention and get more involved in your topic.

A fear appeal is not inherently ethical or unethical. For example, antismoking campaigns appropriately use fear appeals to convince people of the danger of this health issue. Fear appeals, however, should be used cautiously. Too strong a fear appeal may backfire if the listeners are not provided information for dealing with the fear-inducing situation or problem. In addition, a fear appeal must include information that poses a real threat or danger, the listeners must believe the threat could actually happen, and the speaker and his or her information must be perceived as highly credible.

Finally, emotional and logical appeals can be used effectively together to accomplish the objective of a persuasive speech. Listeners typically respond to the emotional content of a speech first, and then examine the logical evidence. In the opening story, Cyndy may have started out by emotionally describing the plight of several unfortunate students who could no longer take a full load of courses because of the latest tuition hike. Then she may have provided concrete evidence of the pattern of increases in tuition over recent years.

CHARACTER APPEALS.

A **credibility appeal** relates to how listeners perceive the reputation, prestige, and authority of the speaker. If you establish the credibility of your sources of information and of yourself as a speaker, you are more likely to be believable, and therefore persuasive. By contrast, if the audience disrespects or distrusts you, you will have a harder time persuading them, regardless of any logical or emotional appeals you use. Furthermore, if you lack credibility, they may not even have an interest in what you have to say.

> A CREDIBILITY APPEAL relates to how listeners perceive the reputation, prestige, and authority of the speaker.

Because their reputations precede them, some speakers are automatically perceived as more credible. But how can a novice speaker establish credibility with an audience? Three factors influence whether you will impress your audience as credible: expertise, trustworthiness, and charisma.

- Expertise. You need to be perceived by the listeners as someone who is competent and an expert on the subject of your speech. This kind of competence involves knowing the topic well, being prepared to talk about it, and bringing your own experience to the discussion. If you prepared your speech according to the guidelines in Chapter Eleven, and include credible sources of information, the audience will respect you as an expert on the topic. Or if you have any personal experience relevant to the topic, they will be more likely to listen to your advice.

- Trustworthiness. You need to be perceived as a person the listeners can trust, so they know they can believe what you say. Trust involves honesty, openness, and objectivity.[16] Being honest and open enhances your credibility, and quickly builds the trust crucial to audience respect. You also build a sense of trustworthiness by speaking objectively about your speech topic, sharing real stories, and using concrete descriptions.[17] In addition, acknowledging opposing viewpoints and any alternative values of the listeners will communicate to the audience that you are a person who can be trusted.[18]

- Charisma. In addition to appearing expert and trustworthy, you need to be perceived as a speaker with charisma, which means the audience finds you engaging, likable, and enthusiastic. All of the nonverbal cues for competent public speaking outlined in Chapter Twelve will help you become more charismatic, and therefore a more credible speaker. Such a speaker is dynamic, energetic, and enthusiastic, and therefore able to gain and hold the audience's attention. In the world of politics, we have seen many charismatic speakers over the years. And whether you agree with their politics or not, their ability to impress audiences is due in part to their personal charisma.

By now you are better informed about both organizing a persuasive speech and using appeals to make it most effective. Given that you are able to sway opinions and change attitudes, you have a responsibility to use these skills ethically.

ETHICS AND PERSUASIVE PUBLIC SPEAKING

Over many years, scholars have studied the topics of ethics, communication, and persuasion. Some say that persuasive speaking can be easily misunderstood and confused with coercion or manipulation, which are not ethical ways of influencing others. **Coercion** is a negative form of influence that occurs when a speaker persuades others to act in a particular way out of fear, or by using force, or giving the listeners no choice but to cooperate. In Nazi Germany, some people were coerced by Hitler's speeches to betray their friends and family members who were providing safe havens for Jews. **Manipulation** is also a negative and unethical form of influence that is used to control people's actions or reactions, but in a devious or deceitful way. A speech borders on manipulation when the speaker deliberately distorts or misrepresents an opponent's position on an issue. Again, in the world of politics, we sometimes see this type of negative persuasion, with one candidate distorting the policies of another.

COERCION is a negative form of influence that occurs when a speaker persuades others to act in a particular way out of fear, or by using force, or giving the listeners no choice but to cooperate.

MANIPULATION is a negative and unethical form of influence that is used to control people's actions or reactions, but in a devious or deceitful way.

ETHICAL PERSUASION leaves the decision about what to think or do up to the other person or the audience members.

By contrast to these unethical approaches, **ethical persuasion** leaves the decision about what to think or do up to the other person or the audience members. The speaker presents information, without coercing or manipulating the listeners, and allows them to make up their own minds. Building on the information about ethics introduced in Chapter One, Box 14.3 highlights some ethical dilemmas professionals and public speakers often face. We conclude this chapter with two other challenges you need to know about.

OVERCOMING CHALLENGES TO PERSUASIVE SPEAKING

Persuasive speeches can represent a great challenge to a public speaker. You are attempting to influence your listeners and, as we said before, most people are highly resistant to being influenced. So your speech may fail for the same reason most persuasion fails—it is difficult to get people to change the attitudes, beliefs, values, and behaviors they have spent years developing. Still, by understanding why the persuasive failure rate is high, and how the audience may react to your topic, your speech likely will be more persuasive.

PERSUASION FAILURE RATE.

Most important to know is that human beings tend to selectively expose themselves to information that is consistent with their own opinions.[19] We watch news shows we agree with, and we log onto

Box 14.3. Ethics and Speaking to Persuade

Public speakers face challenging ethical dilemmas when they are speaking to persuade. An ethic based on objectivity says share only the truth with your audience. But a persuasion ethic suggests that you may want to present your argument in its most favorable light. Here are some pitfalls to avoid when making decisions about ethical persuasive speaking.

ETHICAL DILEMMAS

- Don't allow the end to justify the means. Your end in a persuasive speech is to accomplish your persuasive goal. But if you withhold information in order to accomplish that goal, you're assuming the audience isn't capable of weighing all the evidence and making a good decision. If you suppress or distort information or deliberately lie in order to adapt your speech to the audience, that is unethical. As a public speaker, you are ethically responsible to present all viewpoints—openly and fairly—so your listeners will be in a position to form their own opinions.
- Don't use numbers or statistics to mislead the audience. Most people think statistical studies are precise and reliable, so they're easily persuaded by the use of numbers to support an argument. However, researchers who generate statistics, and public speakers who make use of them, can interpret and slant what numbers mean. Using the persuasive ability of statistics to misrepresent what is true is not ethical. If you discover statistics that contradict your position, you have an ethical responsibility to report that evidence to your listeners.
- Don't misrepresent your position on the topic to the listeners. If the listeners strongly disagree with your position, it may be tempting to distort or misrepresent your claim or position. To say what you do not mean, to fabricate enthusiasm for a topic, or to endorse a policy with which you disagree is unethical.
- Don't use emotion to distract the listeners from the truth. Emotional evidence can sometimes be more effective than a logical argument. Therefore, you may be tempted to use an emotional story or example to persuade the audience of the rightness or importance of your claim. That is acceptable only if you have carefully considered the impact of that evidence on the audience. Moreover, to use emotion as a substitute for sound reasoning is unethical.

Source: Murray (2004).[21]

---

websites and participate in chats and blogs with like-minded others. So when we are presented with a persuasive argument containing information we may disagree with, we often unconsciously engage in a form of *inner speech* or counterargument. **Counterargument** argues against the persuasive message being presented and for the listener's entrenched position or point of view. This silent counterargument encourages audience members to build a case against your persuasive message rather than listening to the arguments for it. As a result, they may be even more committed to their own position after hearing you argue against it.

COUNTERARGUMENT or INNER SPEECH argues against the persuasive message being presented and for the listener's entrenched position or point of view.

Since counterargument represents such a challenge to persuasion, you want to prevent it from even getting started. One way to accomplish this is to present information early in your speech that builds toward a positive response. If the audience's attitude toward your topic is negative, do not state a straightforward claim or thesis in your introduction that will get that counterargument started. If you state a claim or viewpoint with which the listeners disagree, that could prejudice them against your message, before they even hear your argument. Instead, use the thesis to forecast the general theme of your speech. Present neutral yet valid information first, and state your claim only after the audience really has listened to your good evidence.

AUDIENCE REACTION FACTOR.

In addition to counterargument, communication researchers are investigating the very nature of people's resistance to being persuaded.[20] They refer to this resistance as **reactance**, which is an emotional reaction in direct contradiction to any rules or regulations that may threaten a person's behavioral freedom. This emotional reaction often occurs when a person is pressured to accept a contrary viewpoint or attitude. Because of counterargument, this reactance can cause listeners to adopt or strengthen views or attitudes very contrary to what the persuasive speaker is presenting.

Since listeners may engage in counterarguments and have contrary reactions to persuasive messages during presentations, it is extremely important to consider their position on your persuasive topic well ahead of time. When the majority of the audience members strongly disagree with your position, or have an unfavorable attitude toward you, your topic, or the particular situation, you need to address this challenge early in the preparation process. You must anticipate all possible audience reactions to your speech, and prepare your speech in a way that deals with, if not overcomes, the challenges of counterargument and reactance. The goal of such preparation is to use information and support materials in such a way that you avoid alienating the listeners at any point during your speech.

> REACTANCE is an emotional reaction in direct contradiction to rules or regulations that threaten a person's behavioral freedom.

> A TWO-SIDED APPEAL in a persuasive speech presents two alternative points of view, and then presents arguments to counter the opposing view and support the speaker's view.

Some communication instructors favor an approach to managing counterargument and negative reactance that is very similar to the comparing alternatives organizational pattern discussed earlier in this chapter. A persuasive speech that presents two alternative points of view, and then presents arguments to counter the opposing view and support the speaker's view is called a **two-sided appeal**. Despite the study mentioned earlier that found one-sided messages work best, a two-sided message can be effective with an audience that is strongly opposed to your side, or may be be exposed to strong arguments for the other side. That kind of audience must first be persuaded to abandon their present view before a new view can be presented. When using such a two-sided appeal, the speaker should establish a sense of rapport with the listeners by emphasizing commonalites and shared values. After seeing what they have in common with the speaker, the listeners are more likely to pay attention to an alternative point of view.

Being fully aware of the challenges of counterargument and reactance puts you at an advantage over other public speakers. You are able to figure out how to develop and present your persuasive argument most favorably, and the likelihood of your persuasive speech accomplishing its objective is enhanced.

Cyndy and Vanden followed this advice, and it helped Cyndy get Vanden involved in student activism. It also helped Vanden convince his classmates to rally against tuition hikes on the campus.

Like Cyndy and Vanden, if you follow the guidelines provided in this chapter, you, too, will influ-ence your listeners, and reinforce, modify, and change their attitudes, beliefs, values, and behaviors.

We turn your attention in the final chapter of this book to a discussion of a pervasive commu-nication context in the 21st century—mass communication and media convergence.

CHAPTER SUMMARY

A persuasive speech is a speech presented by a speaker (the source), using the right appeals for the setting to influence the attitudes, beliefs, values, or actions of the audience. Aristotle emphasized the importance of persuasive speaking skills in society, which continue to be crucial today. Because of its goal to influence, a persuasive speech is more concerned with the listeners' specific position on the speech topic, and is organized differently from an informative speech.

The three types of persuasive speeches, based on the speaker's objective, attempt to:

1. Reinforce the listeners' attitudes, beliefs, and values,
2. Change attitudes, beliefs, and values, or
3. Move the listeners to action.

A persuasive speech can be organized in any one of four ways. Problem-solution organization first identifies a problem and then proposes a solution. The motivated sequence consists of five sequen-tial steps: attention, need, satisfaction, visualization, and action. Refuting the opponent organization dismantles the opposing argument in order to prove your argument superior. Comparing alterna-tives examines two or more alternatives and makes an appeal for the preferred choice.

Whether a persuasive speech is intended to influence attitudes, beliefs, values, or actions, a com-petent speaker uses one or more of three types of appeals. An appeal is the subtle technique speakers use to get the audience to accept their persuasive argument. A logical appeal is based on knowledge and reasoning—how people think—and makes use of deductive or inductive reasoning to influence listeners. When using a logical appeal, a competent speaker avoids logical fallacies, errors in reason-ing and logic that lead listeners to false conclusions. An emotional appeal is based on psychology and passion, which involves how people feel. A third type of appeal, credibility, is based on the lis-teners' perceptions of the reputation, prestige, and authority of the speaker. The speaker's perceived expertise, trustworthiness, and charisma affect perceptions of credibility.

In using all of these public-speaking skills, an ethical speaker avoids using coercion or manip-ulation to influence the audience, and instead uses ethical persuasion, which leaves the decision about what to think or do up to the person or audience members being persuaded. In addition to the challenge of ethical dilemmas, persuasive speeches often fail for two reasons. Listeners engage in counterargument or inner speech, which argues against the persuasive message being presented and for their entrenched position or point of view. Reactance occurs, which is an emotional reac-tion in direct contradiction to rules or regulations that threaten a person's behavioral freedom. A two-sided appeal in a persuasive speech, which is similar to the comparing alternatives organiza-tional pattern, presents two points of view, and then presents arguments to counter the opposing view and support the speaker's view.

KEY TERMS.

The key terms below are defined in this chapter, and presented alphabetically with definitions in the Glossary at the end of the book.

- persuasive speech
- speech to reinforce
- speech to change
- speech to move to action
- problem-solution
- motivated sequence
- refuting the opponent
- comparing alternatives

- appeal
- logical appeal
- deduction
- induction
- logical fallacies
- emotional appeal
- fear appeal
- credibility appeal

- coercion
- manipulation
- ethical persuasion
- counterargument
- reactance
- two-sided appeal

BUILDING MOTIVATION: SELF-ASSESSMENT TOOL.

Rate each of the eight communication situations described here, indicating your own typical level of competence in persuasive speaking. Rate one situation all the way through for motivation, knowledge, and skills. Then rate the next situation. Use the 1–4 scale below, with 1 being minimal competence and 4 high competence.

Communication situations.

1. Present a persuasive speech about recycling to reinforce the attitudes and beliefs of a group of people in your neighborhood.
2. Present a persuasive speech about recycling to change the attitudes and beliefs of a group of people in your neighborhood.
3. Present a persuasive speech about recycling in order to change behaviors and move a group of people in your neighborhood to action.
4. Motivate a group of other students to take a statistics class as part of their degree program.
5. Convince your friends to take one day off a week from texting, tweeting, and using e-mail.
6. Persuade a group of coworkers to use a new computer software program.
7. Convince a group of citizens at a political rally to support the candidate you prefer.
8. Present a speech to motivate a group of people to give a donation to a charity you support.

Motivation.

1 = Distracted, disinterested, or simply no motivation to be competent.
2 = Somewhat distracted or disinterested, but motivated to be competent.
3 = Somewhat interested and motivated to be competent.
4 = Highly interested and motivated to be competent.

Knowledge.

1 = Completely inexperienced and ignorant about what to do and how to do it.
2 = Minimal experience and sense of what to do and how to do it.

3 = Somewhat experienced and knowledgeable about what to do and how to do it.

4 = Highly knowledgeable about all aspects of what to do and how to do it.

Skills.

1 = Completely incapable of behaving competently.

2 = Barely capable of behaving minimally competently.

3 = Fairly capable of behaving competently.

4 = Highly capable of behaving competently.

Interpreting your scores.

Total your score separately for each situation (motivation, knowledge, and skills). The possible range of the score for each situation is 3–12. If your total score for any of the situations is 6 or less, you see yourself as less competent in that situation than you should be. A score of 7–9 means that you are average at sending and receiving communication messages in the situation. A score of 10–12 indicates that you have a high level of communication competence in that situation.

BUILDING KNOWLEDGE: DISCUSSION QUESTIONS.

1. Of the three types of persuasive speeches—to reinforce, change, or move to action—which poses the greatest challenge for a public speaker, and why?
2. Is any one of the persuasive organizational patterns better to use or more effective than the others? Explain your answer.
3. When considering the use of appeals in a persuasive speech—logical, emotional, or credibility appeals—what aspects of the speech or the speaking situation will help you decide what appeals will work best?
4. Which of the logical fallacies do you see used most frequently in contemporary organizations? In contemporary political life? Provide examples.
5. If there is a fine line between ethical persuasion and manipulation or coercion, what might a persuasive speaker say or do to avoid becoming manipulative or coercive?

BUILDING SKILLS: STUDENT ACTIVITIES.

Individual activities.

1. Identify several topics for a persuasive speech. Label five columns on a piece of paper as follows: topics, attitudes, beliefs, values, and actions. List your speech topics in the left-hand column, and then answer these questions for each topic in the remaining four columns. What would the other students in the class believe about the topic? What attitude would they hold toward it? What values might be related to the topic? What actions or behaviors might they demonstrate regarding the topic?
2. On the Internet, visit a site that contains links to historical or contemporary speeches, such as The National Gallery of the Spoken Word at http://www.ngsw.org/. Find a persuasive

speech that interests you. Read the speech, and identify what type of persuasive speech it is, what types of appeals are used, and its organizational pattern. Based on your analysis, decide how effective you think the speech is.

3. Make a list of the occasions you can remember during the last year or so, when you changed your mind or your behavior in some way. What happened that persuaded you to change?

4. Make a list of the occasions you can remember when someone or something (like an advertisement) tried to influence or persuade you but failed. Why did that persuasive act fail, and what could have improved its effectiveness?

Group activities.

1. Form groups of four students, and choose a topic for a persuasive speech that appeals to all of you—something you all know or care about, and that the other students in your class would find interesting. As a group, decide on a position on the topic, and state that position as a specific purpose statement for a persuasive speech. Decide what type of persuasive speech to develop for the topic and what type(s) of appeals will work best. Choose the best way to organize the speech.

2. With one other student, develop a case for your credibility as public speakers. Each person should choose a topic for a persuasive speech, and determine how to build his or her credibility when presenting that speech. Compare how each student would build a case for his or her expertise, trustworthiness, and charisma.

3. Attend a persuasive speech either on or off campus with a small group of students, and evaluate its effectiveness, based on the contents of this chapter. After you leave the presentation, compare your evaluations.

4. In a group of four to five students, have each student describe his or her personal opinion of what it means to engage in ethical persuasion. Have each student provide a personal example of an occasion when she or he had to make a choice about ethically persuading someone else.

NOTES

1.   See Stiff & Mongeau (2003).

2.   See Kane & Patapan (2010).

3.   See Roberts (1954).

4.   See Miller (2004).

5.   See Werder (2005).

6.   See Pavey & Sparks (2009).

7.   See Johannesen (2008).

8.   See Sawyer (2007).

9.   See Monroe (1935).

10.   See McDermott (2004).

11.   See Genard (2005).

12.   See Lin, Lim, Kiousis, & Ferguson (2006).

13.   See Hirdes, Woods, & Badzinski (2009).

14.   See Rolain-Jacobs, Kirkham, & Norris (2008).

15. See Lang & Yegiyan (2006).

16. See Shockley-Zalabak, Morreale, & Hackman (2010).

17. See Larrimore, Li, Larrimore, Markowitz, & Gorski (2011).

18. See Skinner (2009).

19. See Turner, Shuo, Baker, Goodman, & Materese (2010).

20. See Dillard & Lijiang (2005).

21. See Murray (2004).

REFERENCES

Dillard, J., & Lijiang, S. (2005). On the nature of reactance and its role in persuasive health communication. *Communication Monographs, 72*(2), 144–168.

Genard, G. (2005). Picture it: The power of visual speaking. *Harvard Management Communication Letter, 2*(1), 3–5.

Hirdes, W., Woods, R., & Badzinski, D. M. (2009). A content analysis of Jesus merchandise. *Journal of Media & Religion, 8*(3), 141–157.

Johannesen, R. L. (2008). *Ethics in human communication* (8th ed.). Long Grove, IL: Waveland Press.

Kane, J., & Patapan, H. (2010). The artless art: Leadership and the limits of democratic rhetoric. *Australian Journal of Political Science, 45*(3), 371–389.

Lang, A., & Yegiyan, N. (2006). Understanding the interactive effects of message production features and claim effectiveness in health messages. Paper presented at the International Communication Association Conference. Retrieved from EBSCO*host*, www.ebsco.com

Larrimore, L., Li, J., Larrimore, J., Markowitz, D., & Gorski, S. (2011). Peer to peer lending: The relationship between language features, trustworthiness, and persuasion success. *Journal of Applied Communication Research, 3*(19), 19–37.

Lin, S., Lim, J., Kiousis, S., & Ferguson, M. (2006). The effect of message sidedness on CSR perceptions and company evaluations. Paper presented at the International Communication Association Conference. Retrieved from EBSCO*host*, www.ebsco.com.

McDermott, V. M. (2004). Using motivated sequence in persuasive speaking: The speech for charity. *Communication Teacher, 18*(1), 13–14.

Miller, V. R. (2004). "Show and tell" persuasion. *Communication Teacher, 18*(1), 28–30.

Monroe, A. H. (1935). *Principles and types of speech*. Glenview, IL: Scott, Foresman.

Murray, J. (2004). The face in dialogue, Part II: Invitational rhetoric, direct moral suasion, and the asymmetry of dialogue. *Southern Communication Journal, 69*(4), 333–347.

Pavey, L., & Sparks, P. (2009). Reactance, autonomy and paths to persuasion: Examining perceptions of threats to freedom and informational value. *Motivation and Emotion, 33*(3), 277–290.

Roberts, W. R. (Trans.). (1954). *The rhetoric, by Aristotle*. New York, NY: Modern Library.

Rolain-Jacobs, S., Kirkham, S., & Norris, N. (2008). Unconventional lessons in logic. Paper presented at the National Communication Association. Retrieved from EBSCO*host*, www.ebscohost.com

Sawyer, J. (2007). Speaking to strangers: How the voice of political mobilization necessarily changes when targeting youth audiences. Paper presented at the National Communication Association. Retrieved from EBSCO*host*, www.ebscohost.com

Shockley-Zalabak, P. S., Morreale, S. P., & Hackman, M. Z. (2010). *Building the high trust organization: Five key dimensions of trust*. San Francisco, CA: Jossey-Bass.

Skinner, C. (2009). "She will have science": Ethos and audience in Mary Gove's lectures to ladies. *RSQ: Rhetoric Society Quarterly, 39*(3), 240–259.

Stiff, J. B., & Mongeau, P. A. (2003). *Persuasive communication* (2nd ed.). New York, NY: Guilford.

Turner, M., Shuo, Y., Baker, R., Goodman, J., & Materese, S. A. (2010). Do lay people prepare both sides of an argument? The effects of confidence, forewarning, and expected interaction on seeking out counter-attitudinal information. *Argumentation & Advocacy, 46*(4), 226–239.

Werder, K. (2005). An empirical analysis of the influence of perceived attributes of publics on public relations strategy: Use and effectiveness. *Journal of Public Relations Research, 17*(3), 217–266.

PART FIVE

21ST-CENTURY COMMUNICATION

CHAPTER FIFTEEN

MASS COMMUNICATION AND MEDIA CONVERGENCE

I'm a great believer that any tool that enhances communication has profound effects in terms of how people can learn from each other. —Bill Gates, Chairman of Microsoft, business magnate and philanthropist, b. 1955

• • •

Sitting in a coffee shop on Sunday morning, Madison had just played a high-scoring word on her smart phone in a Scrabble game with a friend, who was still on vacation. Using the shop Wi-Fi, Madison then checked her e-mails—three from friends, a half dozen pushed from various services, ads, and groups she subscribed to, and 18 e-mails from coworkers exchanging messages about an upcoming sales proposal at work, where she chairs the team working on the contract. Given that it is Sunday, she decides to return to the novel she downloaded on her tablet, while listening to her music files.

After two coffees and a bagel, she decides it is time to call her parents and sister for her routine weekend conversation. She finds out from her sister that a mutual friend from high school is getting married, and that she should expect an invitation. While conversing, Madison goes online on her tablet, and checks flights and fares back to her hometown.

Finished with her family conversation, Madison texts her boyfriend Michael, that she would like to get together that night before the workweek begins. While texting, she hears a song on the coffee shop soundtrack, opens her music recognition application on her phone, and downloads the song. She then tweets how much she likes the song, places the cover on her Facebook, checks up on her notifications, and finally decides to sum up the dialogue so far on the sales proposal so that her team will know the agenda for their meeting in the morning. Just before leaving the coffee shop, and not having heard from Michael, she opens SMS to see if there is a message saying where he is, in case they can get together before she starts her day. She then taps her SceneTap application, which uses facial recognition software to see which nearby restaurants have an age demographic similar to her own, so she can think about where she wants to go later on when she finds Michael.

How many communication acts did Madison engage in during her two cups of coffee? How many different roles did she perform during this time? How many redundant conversations occurred—one, two, three, more than a dozen? Madison, it turns out, represents a relatively typical young person in the United States.

According to Pew Internet & American Life Project, a Pew Research Center project for research on the role of communication technologies in the US, approximately 60% of Americans have cell phones, and of those in the 18–29 age bracket, over 80% of cell phone owners engage in text messaging and taking pictures with their phone, and two-thirds access the Internet with their phones.[1] Almost 90% of Americans now have Internet access, and about two-thirds of homes with Internet access also have a Wi-Fi connection.[2] Over a third of Americans own not just a cell phone, but a smart phone, capable of Internet access and multitasking activities.[3] Most smart phone owners use their phones for text messaging and a number of other functions, such as accessing the Internet, sending and receiving mail, playing music, recording videos, watching videos, and playing games.[4] And over a third have used their smart phones to access or check their bank accounts. Almost a third of people who use text messaging say they prefer text messages to voice calls—a good thing, given that the average text messenger sends or receives over 40 text messages a day.[5] Two-thirds of Americans who are online in some way say they belong to and engage in some amount of social networking, meaning that over half of Americans now use social network sites.[6]

We are a wired, wireless, and highly networked society. Indeed, most people on the planet are only a few links or clicks apart from one another.[7] We have come a long way down the technology and communication superhighway in a surprisingly short time. This final chapter of your textbook discusses the nature of this technological superhighway, and the communication revolution you may take for granted. We start with an overview of mass media and mass communication, and then explore technology and computer-mediated communication.

MEDIA AND MASS COMMUNICATION: FROM ONE-TO-ONE TO ONE-TO-MANY

As described in the first chapter of this book, the word *media* refers to the channel(s) through which any message or symbolic behavior is transmitted. When most people refer to media today, they are thinking about manufactured electronic and digital technologies. The term, **technological media**, refers to any apparatus or tool assembled by human intervention for the purpose of communicating messages. In ancient times, however, beating on logs, painting on cave walls, lighting fires, carving bones, tattooing skin, waving flags or objects, and perhaps a variety of other undiscovered media were used to communicate. Beating a particular set of sounds on a log or lighting signal fires, if seen or heard by many people able to interpret such signals, could be considered mass communication.

In reality, since the invention of the printing press, the development of various forms of mass communication has exposed wider and wider audiences to technologically delivered messages. **Mass communication** refers to any form of mediated message exchange with a large audience. There is no absolute designation of "large audience," but generally the idea is that more people can be exposed to a set of messages than could be exposed through unmediated communication channels.

TECHNOLOGICAL MEDIA refers to any apparatus or tool assembled by human intervention for the purpose of communicating messages.

MASS COMMUNICATION refers to any form of mediated message exchange with a large audience.

MASS MEDIA commonly refers to television, radio, advertising, public relations, newspapers, book and magazine publishing, music publishing, movies, as well as Internet publishing and advertising, and the organizations that own, produce, and distribute mass communication.

So a text message to a loved one is mediated, but not a form of mass communication. However, a tweet sent by a celebrity that reaches thousands of followers is a form of mediated mass communication. As technologies have evolved to improve our ability to send messages to large audiences, mass media have evolved in a parallel manner. The term, **mass media**, commonly refers to television, radio, advertising, public relations, newspapers, book and magazine publishing, music publishing, movies, as well as Internet publishing and advertising, and the organizations that own, produce, and distribute mass communication. We now take a closer look at the fascinating evolution of mass communication.

Table 15.1: Evolution of Communication and Human History

As early as 40,000 B.C.E. and clearly in 6000 B.C.E., our early ancestors used forms of mediated communication to send and receive messages. These two figures trace the evolution of communication behaviors all the way up to how we use contemporary media.

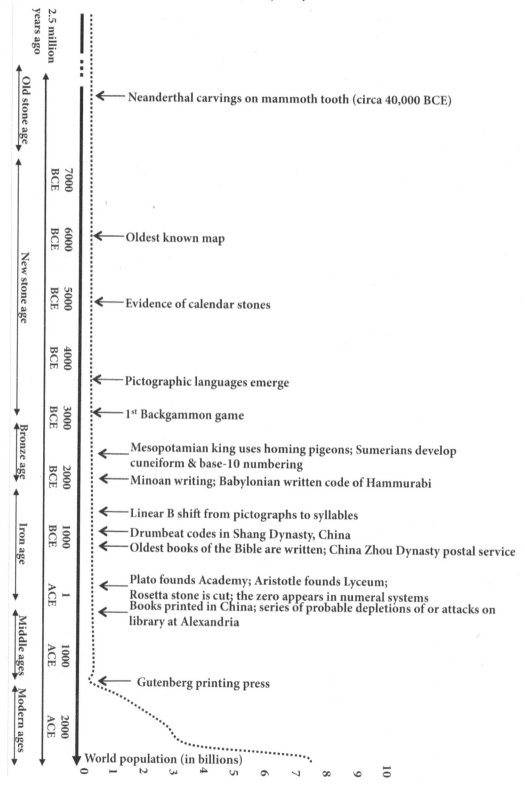

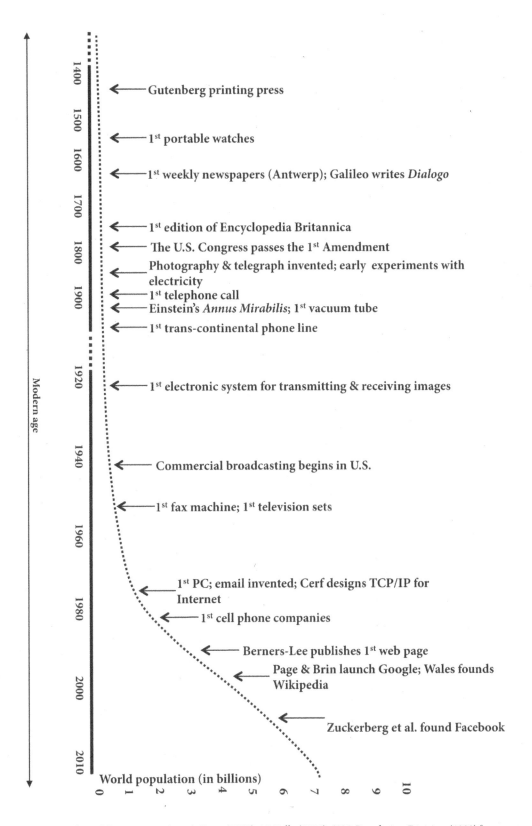

Sources: Adapted from Börner (2010); Fang (2008); McFalls (1991); U.N. Population Division (1999).[8]

HISTORY OF MASS COMMUNICATION.

Any history of media or mass communication is confronted with a problem of evidence during the earliest times. However, we can say that *the arc of media history is the arc of human history, which is largely about collapsing time and physical space while expanding our information space.* While detailed evidence of this evolution may not be readily available, we can say that in recent decades, changes in mass media are affecting the nature of individuals, society, and the planet.

One historical trend we can identify in mass communication over time is greater flexibility in the sending and receiving of messages. In the 1700s, messages had to travel by foot, horse, and ship over great distances. In the 1800s, news would often take months to travel across oceans, languages, and national borders. Even in the days of the telegraph, people on the west coast of the United States might discover events on the east coast weeks or months after their occurrence. But the advent of radio, satellite communications, and digital transfer of visual, textual, and auditory information has collapsed time and space to make information available virtually, in real time, almost anywhere. Clearly, communication is less and less dependent on physical proximity. As a result, our everyday environments are saturated with exposure to mass communication and media, as well as the contents of those media. Table 15.1 visually illustrates the advance of communication technologies alongside human history.

Now, in the 21st century, technological developments are pushing the envelope for how we communicate using language, images, and sounds, simultaneously and interactively. Research indicates that among U.S. adults, 85% have a cell phone, 76% have a desktop or laptop computer, 47% have an MP3 player, and 42% have a home gaming system or console.[1] All told, surveys indicate that young people today spend an average of 6.5 hours a day using media, and about a quarter of that time they are using more than one medium at a time.[9] A case in point is Madison's use of multiple media in the coffee shop, as described in this chapter's opening story. Given the omnipresence of media in our lives, we now take a look at two theories that explain the impact and actual effects of media on all of us—agenda-setting theory and cultivation theory.

MAJOR THEORIES OF MASS COMMUNICATION.

Media do have effects—perhaps some good and some not so good. The exact nature of their effects has been a central question of mass communication theory for over a century.[10, 11] Given the rapid pace of change, and society's adoption of mass communication and media in the early 20th century, it is not surprising that many theories of media effects evolved along with the evolution of media technologies.[12] Early theorists anticipated that mass communication and media would have **strong effects**. This is the prediction that media operate with direct causal force on audience attitudes, beliefs, and behaviors. To some extent, strong effects models viewed mass communication messages as a hypodermic needle or magic bullet that inserted the desired messages into the passive minds of the audience. These models proposed a one-step flow process in which mass communication messages flow directly from the sender to the receivers.

Such models did not last long, because it became obvious that audiences play an active role in processing information and images from mass communication. **Moderated effects** models viewed both

STRONG EFFECTS predict that media operate with direct causal force on audience attitudes, beliefs, and behaviors.

MODERATED EFFECTS models view both mass communication and the audience as having influence on the impact of messages, with the media and its messages having more limited influence.

mass communication and the audience as having influence on the impact of messages, with the media and its messages having more limited influence. Some of the earliest research suggested, for example, that a large part of the influence of mass communication was based on opinion leaders. **Opinion leaders** are people who receive mass communication messages, form an opinion on the basis of those messages, and then influence others who may or may not have received the messages. Opinion leaders' influence is based more on credibility and interpersonal persuasion. Thus, media can have strong, but indirect effects. Their effects are substantial, but depend on people interpreting the messages, and interacting with others in a way that creates meanings for those others.[13]

The idea that opinion leaders serve as a filter of media influence led theorists to think about how society processes media content. Media and media industries may have significant control in selecting what we are exposed to, but we then gather at home, at work, and in coffee shops, and talk about what is in the news. Despite exposure to an array of information sources, audience members generally are able to reach their own conclusions, based on the messages and their own personal opinions and values. However, there is little doubt that large segments of the population do think about and talk about the topics identified as important by the media—which leads us to two more theoretical explanations of how mass media work.

> **OPINION LEADERS** are people who receive mass communication messages, form an opinion on the basis of those messages, and then influence others who may or may not have received the messages.

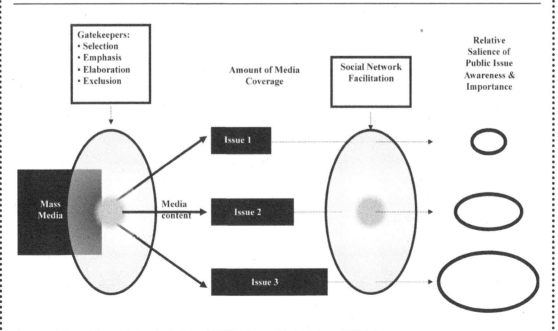

Figure 15.1: Agenda-Setting Theory

Agenda-setting theory says that media do not tell us *what* to think, but they do tell us what to think *about*

Sources: Adapted from McCombs & Shaw (1976); Nguyen Vu & Gehrau (2010).[13]

Agenda-setting theory claims that the mass media do not determine *what* we think, but they do have significant influence over what we think *about*.[14] Figure 15.1 depicts how this process works. The degree to which we consider topics important corresponds to how much coverage those topics receive in the media. If most newscasts are about the economy, the environment, health care, or foreign policy initiatives, then people tend to talk about these topics. If most media content is about superstars or the latest political scandal, then that is what people tend to talk about. Thus, the basic prediction of agenda-setting theory is that people are aware of ideas and topics based on the amount of media coverage they are given.

Some agenda-setting effects are short-lived. However, the media also can have subtle, long-term effects on society and culture.[15] Unlike agenda-setting theory, **cultivation theory** predicts that people not only are more aware of the ideas the media present, but media consumers' beliefs are affected by the media content as well. For example, studies indicate that video games systematically overrepresent (relative to the world population) White adult males as characters, and underrepresent females, Hispanics, Native Americans, elderly persons, and children.[16, 17] And video games tend to distort the typical body dimensions of female characters relative to the body shapes of the actual population.[17] As a result, those who play these games will misconstrue the numbers of different kinds of people in the world, and the body shapes of real females.

The general prediction of cultivation theory is that people who consume high amounts of a particular medium are more strongly influenced than light consumers of the same medium. In addition, this effect is particularly expected for people with personal experiences that make certain media content more relevant and meaningful. As an example, the best researched cultivation effect is the "mean world" hypothesis, which predicts that mainstream television consumers will have unrealistic beliefs about crime and violence. Research shows that the more people watch television that publicizes both real and fictional violence and crime, the more they will significantly overestimate their risk of becoming the victim of a violent crime.[18] This effect would be especially true of people who have previously been victims of violent crime, or who know somebody who has been a victim. Figure 15.2 gives a picture of how the process described by cultivation theory works.

The early views of mass media effects, described by agenda-setting theory and cultivation theory, have been refined by more audience-centered models that view the process of persuasion as residing more in the minds of the audience than just in the messages or media.

MODELS OF MASS COMMUNICATION.

Most early views of mass communication tended to view the media and their contents as a dominant influence, with the audience only buffering or filtering those messages. Now however, the audience is increasingly recognized as playing a primary role in selecting and choosing what media to use. Different individuals seek different *uses* and *gratifications* from the media they consume.[19, 20]

Uses and gratifications are the needs or goals being served by media consumption.[20] We become conscious of certain issues, needs, or uncertainties we experience in life, and we anticipate the kinds of solutions needed to address these concerns. Often, we are motivated to use some sort of media as

AGENDA-SETTING THEORY claims that the mass media do not determine what we think, but they do have significant influence over what we think about.

CULTIVATION THEORY predicts that people not only are more aware of the ideas the media present, but media consumers' beliefs are affected by the media content as well.

USES AND GRATIFICATIONS are the needs or goals being served by media consumption.

Figure 15.2: Cultivation Theory

Cultivation theory shows how our views of the world can come to reflect the world we see depicted in the media.

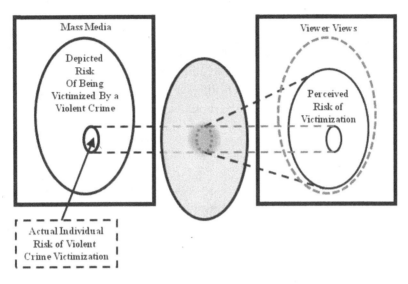

Sources: Adapted from Gerbner (1998); Morgan & Shanahan (1997); Morgan & Shanahan (2010).[14, 15]

part of the process we use to satisfy our needs and manage uncertainties. For example, people who have been lonely for a short while may be more inclined to seek entertaining sources of media, such as prime-time soap operas and comedies, to compensate for their lack of a social life. By contrast, chronically lonely people may give up on using media to enhance their social life, finding the relationships displayed to be frustrating depictions of what they lack.[21] Consumers of media are satisfied or dissatisfied with media to the extent that the gratifications they seek are obtained, or not, from those media.

People may seek media to be entertained, to find out what is going on around them (news shows), to escape the stresses of everyday life, to develop self-concept or identity, or even to develop parasocial relationships with those portrayed in the media. **Parasocial relationships** are perceived attachments to characters, real or fictional, portrayed in the media. For example, people who follow certain television shows often experience feelings like those in a real relationship breakup when they know a character is leaving the show, or breaking up with someone on the show.[22] They may mourn or be glad to get out of a relationship with one character, and be glad to begin a new relationship with that character's replacement.

PARASOCIAL RELATIONSHIPS are perceived attachments to characters, real or fictional, portrayed in the media.

These audience-centered models of mass communication all predict that as exposure to mass-mediated messages increases, the effects of the messages also increase. But while there is agreement about such effects occurring, understanding the precise nature of some of the effects can be difficult. Consider, for example, the influence of the commercial music industry, and the various forms of music it distributes and plays.

It is difficult, at best, to identify the many different effects listening to all different kinds of music may have on the general population, much less on particular segments of the population.

The theories and models we discussed so far tend to focus on a somewhat outdated view of human communication. Mass communication traditionally has been about relatively few people producing, distributing, and sending messages to a very large number of people. But new technology and new media are dissolving the distinction between one-to-many (mass media), and one-to-one (interpersonal) forms of communication. Due to the availability of all kinds of communication technologies, these two ways to communicate appear to be merging with one another. Now, what seems to be interpersonal (sending a tweet) can also be mass communication (a tweet reaching out to the masses). In this process of interpersonal communication and mass media "converging," we are witnessing a transformation of significant features of communication. We now describe this process of convergence, which you are probably part of, but take somewhat for granted.

MEDIA CONVERGENCE: FROM ONE-TO-MANY TO ONE-TO-ANY

One of the most significant trends in mass communication is **media convergence**, which refers to the integration of media technologies across platforms, functions, and capabilities. In the most typical sense, convergence means an integration of online, print, and broadcast forms of information.[23] More broadly, convergence refers to the extent to which new communication technologies are multimodal,[24] that is, capable of communicating and connecting across hardware and software platforms, and across types of sensory experiences (e.g., vocal, visual, auditory, tactile, etc.).

MEDIA CONVERGENCE refers to the integration of media technologies across platforms, functions, and capabilities.

With regard to mass media, this convergence is connecting print versions of magazines and newspapers, like *The New York Times*, with online subscriptions to the same publication. The benefit offered to readers of the electronic versions is the ability to follow links to streaming video and other related sources on the topic of any article, and to influence others by forwarding, noting, or otherwise commenting on any article or its topic. Traditional broadcast media, like newscasts, also are converging by sending their viewers to their websites, inviting them to participate on their Facebook pages, or by newscasters tweeting their opinions on issues in the news.

With regard to interpersonal communication, convergence also is a reality. Your cell phone has camera and video, instant messaging, and e-mail capability. You can have wireless Internet access, calendar, and personal data assistant (PDA) capabilities. Some phones and tablets have two-way interactive video and Skype capabilities that allow you to see the person with whom you are talking. Even as this chapter was being written, cell phone companies were competing to create and sell yet newer phones, tablets, and blends of those two communication technologies.

Without a doubt, convergence is creating a multimedia environment in which we all live, by vastly increasing our access to various media. One positive effect of this convergence is greater convenience for the user, but also consider the pop-up advertising that now populates most media with corporate and product messages. Increasingly, convergence means that average media consumers can find no place in which their media are not saturated with an array of sales messages.

Despite the importance of media convergence, it is important to remember that communication competence in the new media environment still depends significantly on face-to-face competence. The basic skills of writing, speaking, listening, organizing ideas well, understanding and adapting to others—these are still the building blocks of any set or repertoire of media-related skills.[25] So while employers may increasingly expect media literacy skills and abilities, they are unlikely to compromise on the more fundamental communication skills already outlined in this book.[26] We now explore how to integrate and apply the basic communication competencies you already know to the computer-mediated communication environment of the 21st century.

COMPUTER-MEDIATED COMMUNICATION COMPETENCE

Computer-mediated communication, generally referred to as **CMC**, is any human, symbolic interaction that takes place through digitally based technologies. *Digital* simply means that the information contained in sounds, images, and procedures is converted into combinations of the digits 1 and 0. The word *mediated* comes from the Latin word *media* meaning *middle*. It has come to mean anything that comes between one person's message and the receiver or audience. Computers in one way or another are the channels or intermediaries through which CMC messages travel from one person to other persons.

Computers are technological media, which we can contrast with natural media. **Natural media** are those that send and translate symbols using only our bodies and minds, such as spoken words, gestures, posture, and all the other verbal, nonverbal, and listening processes examined in the previous chapters. Technological media, defined at the start of this chapter, typically include telephones, instant messaging, teleconferencing, videophones, videoconferencing, e-mail, and other computer-assisted interactions such as telemarketing, group-decision support systems, computer chatlines, blogging, multiuser domains (MUDs), and some virtual reality systems. Virtually all of these technologies are dependent upon digital software processes to function. The prevalence of technological media today calls our attention to the importance of this form of communication.

> COMPUTER-MEDIATED COMMUNICATION, generally referred to as CMC, is any human, symbolic interaction that takes place through digitally based technologies.

> NATURAL MEDIA are those that send and translate symbols using only our bodies and minds, such as spoken words, gestures, posture, and all the other verbal, nonverbal, and listening processes.

THE IMPORTANCE OF TECHNOLOGY AND MEDIATED COMMUNICATION.

As the history presented in Table 15.1 illustrates, the invention of the printing press made the transfer and accumulation of knowledge and information far more available than ever before. As a result, the Industrial Revolution gave way to a service economy dependent on access to information. Most contemporary observers believe that the microchip and computers are ushering in the next big revolution—an Information Technology Revolution—characterized by far more extensive use of media. The pace of change in media usage is difficult to comprehend fully. As can be seen in Table 15.2, the use of print is decreasing, whereas audio or music, TV, computers, and video games all increased substantially over time. Then Table 15.3 presents some surprising statistics, showing how widespread and omnipresent computers and technology have become in the daily lives of most Americans.

This new revolution appears to be transforming our lives in positive, negative, and even surprising ways. In fact, there is some evidence that the number of friends we claim to have on our Facebook

Table 15.2: Media Use Over Time

Among 8- to 18-year-old Americans, average hours and minutes of media use in any typical day has increased significantly over the last ten years.

TYPE OF MEDIA	1999	2004	2009
TV content	3:47	3:51	4:29
Music/audio	1:48	1:44	2:31
Computer	0:27	1:02	1:29
Video games	0:26	0:49	1:13
Print	0:43	0:43	0:38
Movies	0:18	:25	0:25
Total media use time in any day	6:19	6:21	7:38
Total media exposure time in any day	7:29	8:33	10:45

Source: Adapted from Rideout, Foehr, & Roberts (2010, p. 2).[9]

Table 15.3: Prevalence of Technology Media Use in U.S. Society

Statisticians now tell us that communication technologies of all sorts are now a permanent and constant fixture in our lives.

STATISTICS ON TECHNOLOGY MEDIA USAGE IN THE U.S.

- 88% of U.S. households have Internet access, about two-thirds of which have Wi-Fi access (Webster, 2011).[2]
- 65% of adult U.S. Internet users also now use a social network site (SNS), more than double the number reported in 2008, meaning that over 50% of all U.S. adults now use one or more social networking sites. Over 40% of those on the Internet claim to use such sites in a typical day. Although most SNS users report positive experiences, one in five volunteered negative experiences (Madden & Zickuhr, 2011).[6]
- 51% of Americans over the age of 11 have a Facebook site, one-third of them check it several times a day (Webster, 2011).[2]
- 59% of U.S. adults go online wirelessly, either through laptops (47% of adults) or cell phones (40% of adults) (Smith, 2010a).[3]
- 35% of U.S. adults own a smartphone, which is 42% of all cell phone owners, and 25% of smartphone owners claim to go online "mostly" through the phone (Smith, 2011a).[4]
- 51% of cell phone owners have used it to access information they needed immediately, 40% have used it in emergency situations, and 42% use it for entertainment or to avoid boredom. By comparison, 20% have experienced frustration with their phone, and 13% have pretended to be interacting with their phone as a way to avoid interacting with someone near them (Smith, 2010b).[1]
- 73% of cellphone owners engage in text messaging, and 55% of heavy texters (those who send over 50 text messages a day), or 31% of all text messengers, prefer texting to calling (Smith, 2011b).[5]
- There are over 100 million users posting over 230 million tweets every day (Miller, 2011).[29]

page is directly reflected in the actual structure of our brains.[27] This finding suggests that the new media actually may be affecting our basic nature as human beings. Another recent study found that perceptions of attractiveness are affected by the number of friends we claim on Facebook.[28] Those with around 300 friends are viewed as more socially attractive than those with significantly fewer friends (100), or with significantly more friends (900).

Statisticians call our attention to some questionable changes and practices now occurring in our everyday lives because of new communication technology—they refer to this as "The Dark Side of New Media." Here are some questionable changes and negative effects of new media.

- There is a correlation (-.05) between high Internet use and psychological well-being, meaning that high levels of Internet use is slightly but significantly associated with less overall well-being.[30] However, it appears it could be the lower well-being that leads to the Internet use, rather than the other way around.[31]
- 18% of Americans report negative effects of using Facebook, such as unwanted advances, harassment, stalking, harmful gossiping, or data theft.[32]
- 27 to 31% of Facebook users have used it to "keep tabs" on an ex-intimate (former significant other), and 2 to 7% indicate that they have shown up at events an ex-intimate indicated they might attend. 11 to 17% of Facebook users say they have experienced an ex-intimate "keeping tabs" on them through Faccbook, and 9 to 11% say an ex-intimate has used it to show up at events.[33] Time spent on Facebook also is associated with increased jealousy.[34]
- 32% of online teenagers have been contacted by a stranger online, and 23% of online teens say they felt scared or uncomfortable when contacted by the stranger.[35]
- 27% of social network site users have been denied a friend request, 16% have experienced a discrepancy of friend rankings, 7% have experienced personal surveillance of their profile, and at least 4% have experienced disparaging remarks or gossip when social networking.[36]
- 81% of online dating participants lie to some degree about their weight or height in their online descriptions.[37] Still, lying through media does not appear to occur any more than it does in face-to-face encounters.[38]
- 54% of Americans have experienced a "mean or hurtful" text message in the last year from a friend or dating partner, and 72% have experienced some kind of "electronic hostility".[39]
- 54% have experienced hurtful cyber-teasing to a "moderate or greater degree from their current relational partner".[40]

If you feel as though you have got it made because you have media access and some level of competence in using new media, do not be fooled. Having access and some knowledge does not necessarily imply competence in using these technologies. Looking back, the first programmable computer, named ENIAC (for Electronic Numerical Integrator And Computer), was unveiled in 1946. It was 10 feet tall and 150 feet wide. ENIAC cost millions of dollars, and executed about 5,000 operations per second. Today's personal computers execute millions of operations per second using microchips the size of thumbnails. All of this computing power is potentially useless without a real understanding of the nature of computer-mediated communication and its competent use.

CHARACTERISTICS OF COMPUTER-MEDIATED COMMUNICATION.

Certain basic characteristics of communication are particularly important to understanding communication using computers. Four such characteristics important to computer-mediated communication (CMC) are richness, presence, interactivity, and openness. Note, as we describe these four characteristics, that they tend to work together and complement one another.

When you talk with people face-to-face, you see them, hear them, and perhaps even touch and smell them. Such natural media are rich in sensory information. **Richness** is the extent to which a medium represents all the information available in the original message. Richer media allow for more feedback; greater immediacy; more types of verbal, visual, and audio cues; more tailoring of messages to the other person; and more use of informal language.[41] For example, a videophone offers more richness than a regular telephone because you can see the other person(s) and, therefore, the expanded amount of information available. A competent communicator needs to realize that the concept of richness is the foundation for understanding any and all forms of mediated communication.

Presence is the extent to which a medium represents the nonverbal and emotional content of messages in real time and sensation.[42, 43] Presence describes the potential for a medium

RICHNESS is the extent to which a medium represents all the information available in the original message.

PRESENCE is the extent to which a medium represents the nonverbal and emotional content of messages in real time and sensation.

INTERACTIVITY is the extent to which people can communicate simultaneously in response to each other's messages.

OPENNESS is the extent to which messages sent through the medium are publicly accessible and the authorship is identifiable or, in some cases, anonymous.

to permit communicators to feel as though they are in the physical space of the other person. The telephone provides a wider range of vocalic cues about speaker intent and emotion than letters and e-mail, but all these media are less complete and present than videophones. Yet, even videophones provide only a fairly flat, two-dimensional picture of a person. Presence obviously is related to richness, but it is not the same thing. Richness is more about providing information, while presence is about the "feel" of the communication encounter. A telephone call could be rich in information but not quite as present, because it uses only the vocalic channel of nonverbal communication, not other nonverbal cues like facial expression and eye contact.

Interactivity helps to determine the richness and presence of a medium. **Interactivity** is the extent to which people can communicate simultaneously in response to each other's messages.[44] "Poor" or "lean" media lack the two characteristics of richness and presence, and are less interactive. Standard e-mail and instant messages are not very interactive because a writer must complete an entire message, send it, and wait for the message to be deposited in the recipient's inbox. Many chat rooms, in contrast, are more interactive, because they allow a recipient to see the words the other person is typing, and they permit midsentence interruptions, almost like a face-to-face conversation. So, interactivity is related to richness and presence in that the more interactive the medium, the richer and more present it is.

Openness is the extent to which messages sent through the medium are publicly accessible and the authorship is identifiable or, in some cases, identified as anonymous. To some extent, computer-based media have begun to blur the lines between private and public communication. Virtually everything sent by e-mail is recorded somewhere. Unlike letters that can be burned, voicemail that can be erased, and telephone and face-to-face conversations that are rarely recorded, computer-based messages are often copied, manipulated, forwarded, and reproduced for many eyes to see. The fact that computerized messages can take on a life of their own makes openness one of the basic characteristics or capabilities any communicator needs to consider when choosing how to send a message. We may want some messages to remain private or not to go viral, so to speak. You need to ask yourself if the message being sent is one you would be comfortable with the whole world reading. If not, reword it, or just do not send it.

Any competent communicator needs to be fully aware of the impact of richness, presence, interactivity, and openness on computer-mediated communication. An awareness of these characteristics helps you choose the right medium to send and receive any given message, and it will help you to manage certain challenges to CMC.

OVERCOMING CHALLENGES TO COMPUTER-MEDIATED COMMUNICATION COMPETENCE

Communicators around the world and of all ages are just beginning to understand the challenges to communicating using technology. Given the evolving nature of communication technology, how can a communicator know the most effective and appropriate way to use all of the new media? One of the keys to competence in a mediated context is understanding how to select the optimal media for the particular message that needs to be communicated.[45] What medium is effective and appropriate for initiating or ending a relationship? What about questioning a grade a professor gives you on a paper? What about offering condolences to a friend who just experienced a death in the family? Some answers to these questions can be derived from understanding the critical challenges to competent mediated communication posed by ambiguity, complexity, and emotionality.

CHALLENGES OF MESSAGE AMBIGUITY, COMPLEXITY, AND EMOTIONALITY.

Message ambiguity is the extent to which a message has either unknown or multiple meanings. Most people assume that ambiguous messages are incompetent, but that is not always true. Every day of our lives we get through conversations, group decisions, and public presentations by relying on ambiguity. For example, voters are more likely to support political candidates who speak about vague and ambiguous concepts such as freedom and democracy than candidates who speak in concrete terms about the cost of a program or amendments to a particular policy.

MESSAGE AMBIGUITY is the extent to which a message has either unknown or multiple meanings.

MESSAGE COMPLEXITY refers to the amount of detail, density, and integration of information in a message.

CMC is challenging because it is less present than face-to-face communication, and therefore it is more open to message ambiguity. When nonverbal information cannot be included in a message, like in e-mail or text messages, the receiver has more ways to interpret what is being said or sent. The result, of course, is misinterpretation of CMC messages and misunderstandings among communicators. Sarcasm and humor, for example, may not work well in e-mail, because the intended meaning of the ambiguous message is lost without accompanying nonverbal information.

Message complexity refers to the amount of detail and the density of information in a message. More meaning, of course, can be derived from messages rich in detail and containing a large amount of information. Some uses of CMC, like text messages and instant messaging, are not suffi-ciently rich, which represents a challenge for their use. To compensate, e-mail and other CMC mes-sages now routinely include visual, video, or sound files, as well as some introductory text from the sender—even just a quick "Hi, how are you?" For instance, a picture sent by smart phone conveys far more than many words in a text message can say. Meanwhile, highly complex messages may bene-fit from media that permit careful production of the entire message, and time for review and edit-ing before the message is sent.

Message emotionality is the extent to which a message attempts to communicate feelings and a sense of presence. Using CMC to communicate an emotional message does rep-resent a challenge and, in fact, may not always be a good idea. Messages that have a strong emotional component are likely to require different media than messages that are emotionally

> MESSAGE EMOTIONALITY is the extent to which a message attempts to communicate feelings and a sense of presence.

"lean." Despite the convenience and appeal of breaking off a relationship by letter, e-mail, IM, or leaving a phone message, most receivers would probably consider such media inappropriate for such an emotionally charged message. In general, for more emotional messages, using a medium that is rich, present, and capable of interactivity is the best idea. Conversely, breaking up or dissolving a long-term relationship in a medium high in openness, like Facebook, would be considered less than competent—to say nothing of being unkind.

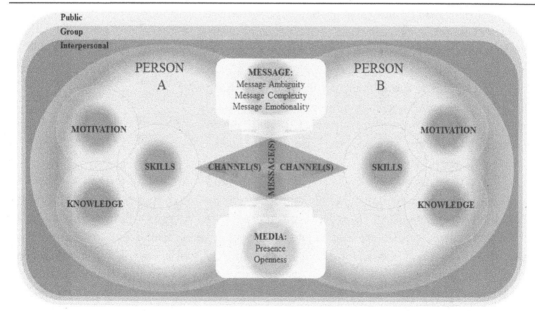

Figure 15.3: Model of Computer-Mediated Communication (CMC) Competence

The motivation, knowledge, and skills of Persons A and B, with regard to computer-mediated communication, determine the extent to which any mediated communication interaction is considered competent.

OVERCOMING THE CHALLENGES.

Recall that communication is more likely to be perceived as competent when a person is motivated, knowledgeable, and skilled at communicating in a given context. These same components—motivation, knowledge, and skills—apply to computer-mediated communication. The model in Figure 15.3 shows how the basic model of communication competence applies to CMC. Person A and Person B are communicating using some type of computer-mediated channel. The middle components of the model represent the context in which the media are used and the characteristics of the message (ambiguity, complexity, emotionality) and of the media (presence and openness). The motivation, knowledge, and skills of Persons A and B will determine how competent they are at computer-mediated communication, whether the desired outcomes are achieved, and whether the mediated communication interaction is competent. We now discuss motivation, knowledge, skills, context, and outcomes as these components of competence relate to CMC.

Motivation.

Motivation in the mediated world has two sides: positive and negative. Positive motivation in mediated communication is the feeling or belief that a given medium can help us to achieve our preferred outcomes. If you believe a PowerPoint or Prezi presentation will be more likely to land a big contract or motivate your sales force than a chalkboard or flip charts, you are positively motivated to use that software in a computer-based medium. There are many positive motives for using media, including to seek support, escape, achieve some distance or privacy, experience pleasure, and to influence someone.

Negative motivation is the feeling or belief that you are incapable of using a given medium competently. The fear of incompetence in sending or receiving computer-mediated messages is **technophobia**, or CMC apprehension.[46] In societies in which technology is common but relatively new, such as the United States, the average eighth grader may know more about computers than his or her parents. Such familiarity makes the younger generation more comfortable, and less afraid to use and experiment with the technology.

TECHNOPHOBIA is the fear of incompetence in sending or receiving computer-mediated messages; it also is termed CMC apprehension.

Various aspects of any medium can affect people's motivation to adopt and use it. In general, the greater the richness, the more useful and easy a medium is, and the more a person's social network uses the medium, the more motivated a person will be to obtain and use it.[47] Many of these features result in a person tending to have a positive attitude and feeling more competent at using a given medium,[48] which relates to the other two components of knowledge and skills.

Knowledge.

One of the main reasons people are afraid of technology is that they lack the knowledge for using it, and few people ever learn how by reading the users' manual for hardware or software. With CMC, most people tend to use one of two strategies for gaining knowledge and achieving their goals. They engage in tinkering and experimenting, using trial and error, pushing buttons, exploring drop-down menus, and trying options until they find something that works or gets them a little closer to their goal. Or they use social resources by learning from others, perhaps using a helpdesk or online resource, or by having a knowledgeable friend show them what to do and how to do it. Many people are more comfortable with this informal learning, but may not gain critical knowledge that does not seem important at the time. Many of us favor solving our immediate problem, rather than attending a long training session covering what seems to be irrelevant knowledge. But then we may not know what to do if we accidentally delete a file, or a projector cuts out in the middle of a presentation, or a hyperlink does not work. We had gained knowledge about how to use the technology in the best possible situation when everything was working the way it should. But we lacked the knowledge and the skills to maximize our use of the particular technology or medium.

Skills.

Skills, as explained in Chapter Two, are the repeatable, goal-oriented behaviors a person uses to communicate. In any mediated context, particularly in the computer-mediated context, the four interpersonal skills defined in Chapter Eight—attentiveness, composure, coordination, and expressiveness—are most important.

Attentiveness is the ability to show interest in, concern for, and attention to others when communicating. CMC is generally a much colder and more impersonal medium than face-to-face or telephone communication, which makes attentiveness difficult. Even so, there are many ways of being attentive and adding a personal touch to a message, even when communicating by computer. For example, in a traditional business message you can direct questions to the particular recipient and display your awareness of past correspondence. To show interest, you might begin a business e-mail memo with a question or comment about the recipient's recent business trip. As with natural media, responding rapidly and relevantly to someone's message is one of the best ways to show attentiveness.

Composure is the ability to display comfort with, control of, and confidence in communication. In the mediated environment, composure reflects knowledge and mastery of both the medium and your communication behavior using that medium. A person who knows more about a medium and has overcome technophobia is generally going to come across as more composed, as will a person who uses new programs and technologies with confidence. Some people, for instance, go out of their way to learn how to scan images and set up their own Web pages. Others may only enter online environments, "lurking" rather than contributing. Other examples of composure include composing messages with fewer qualifiers (e.g., "maybe," "perhaps," "sometimes," etc.) and fewer stumbles or errors when talking in a Skype or interactive media context like a Web conference or webinar.

Coordination in the computer-mediated environment is the management of time and relevance. Senders, who manage their time competently, send and respond to messages when they should, and send messages that are neither too long nor too dense to process. Managing relevance means that messages are about what they are supposed to be about. If you have ever sent an urgent message by email requesting an answer to a question, only to get a response a few days later that does not respond to the original question, then you have experienced the sender's poor coordination in two ways. First, the response was not topically connected with the message you had sent. Second, it was not sent immediately in response to a message titled "urgent," which calls for a timely reply.

An explanation for this failure to manage time and relevance competently is not an excuse but often is the reason. An increasing challenge to coordination is multitasking, which means coordinating messages and information processing across the many media we all use every day—including cell phones. For example, by one estimate, cell phone-related traffic deaths increased 28% from 2005 to 2008, and accounted for 16,000 deaths between 2001 and 2007.[49] Driving with no conversation at all is the safest, but conversing with a passenger in the front is safer than having a cell phone conversation.[50]

Expressiveness in the computer-mediated environment is about the vividness of the message. Vividness describes how alive and how animated a message is. Many forms of mediated communication—e-mail, texting, instant messaging—are very dependent on using language and linguistic expressiveness, but are not as rich in the use of nonverbal cues. When e-mail first became popular for day-to-day communication, people realized the limited extent to which it could convey emotions. They began to invent **emoticons**—or icons that frame the emotion underlying a verbal statement—and acronyms and abbreviations to make messages more efficient. Look at Table 15.4 for some popular acronyms and emoticons for enhancing the expressiveness of a message in any cold medium.

EMOTICONS are icons that frame the emotion underlying a verbal statement.

Context.

In Chapter Two, we stated that context has several levels—culture, relationship, situation, and function—all of which impact how communication occurs. Mediated communication is affected by all four of these levels.

Regarding the impact of culture, it is easy for people in the United States to take CMC for granted, and assume that how we use CMC is how the world uses it. But some cultures may value ambiguity or politeness more than those of us in the US, a preference that should govern if and how you use CMC with people of that background. Other cultures, such as the Japanese, may value the slow development of trust in business relationships, a preference that is not compatible with the impersonal feel of e-mail.

The relational level of context also is extremely important to how we use various media. Facebook allows us to define friends and family groups, and only allow certain groups access to certain messages. But Facebook also allows for de-friending, which is a mediated form of relationship breakup

Table 15.4: Acronyms and Emoticons

The expressiveness and vividness of any computerized message can be enhanced by the appropriate use of these quick ways to make nonverbal statements.

ACRONYM (MEANING OF ACRONYM)	EMOTICON	(MEANING OF EMOTICON)
BTW (by the way)	:-)	smile
F2F (face to face)	:- (	frown
FAQ (frequently asked question)	:'	cry
FWIW (for what it's worth)	;-)	wink
IIRC (if I recall correctly)	:D	laughter
IMO (in my opinion)	:P	sticking out tongue
IOW (in other words)	:-o	yell
IRL (in real life)	:-	anger
LOL (laughing out loud)	:X	my lips are sealed
MEGO (my eyes glaze over)	:Q	smoking
OTOH (on the other hand)	:*	a kiss
TMOT (trust me on this)	%-)	confusion

Sources: Adapted from http://www.computeruser.com/resources/dictionary/emoticons.html; http://www.computeruser.com/resources/dictionary/chat.html; and http://www.netlingo.com/smiley.cfm

that may be made public to many others. E-mail tends to encourage rapid development of relationships, at least in terms of disclosure of personal information. However, it is not yet known whether disclosure and relational development through computers promotes relationships as normal and healthy as those that follow the traditional face-to-face path. Moreover, e-mail also allows users to send "flaming" messages, because they may feel less emotionally involved with the receiver. Such flames often are disrespectful, and escalate anger, resulting in needless conflict.

••••••••••••••••••••••••••••••••
MEDIA ACCESS is the extent to which CMC technologies are available to an intended audience.

In contrast to the impact of culture and relationship, the situational level of CMC is obviously different from face-to-face communication by virtue of the physical medium itself. Consider **media access**, which is the extent to which CMC technologies are available to your intended audience. If you are in the situation of coordinating a family reunion, it makes little sense to operate strictly through e-mail if only a fraction of your extended family uses or has access to e-mail. The often-heard query, "Didn't you get my e-mail?" will not work with those whose life situation does not include regular use of e-mail.

The functional level of the context refers to the purpose of the message, and to pressures that may affect it, such as time. When a message has to get to someone immediately, a smart communicator uses multiple media—sending an e-mail and leaving a voicemail at the same time. Even though overnight mail takes only a day to reach the recipient, most people are choosing to attach files to an e-mail message instead, because it is even faster.

Like the frame of a painting, the context of CMC shows us what is and what is not part of the picture, but it is not the picture itself. The message is the picture. Competence in CMC requires attention to the message as much as the context. One of the most influential writers on media in the last century, Marshall McLuhan, claimed that the medium *is* the message.[51] That is, the medium influences a message so much that the meaning itself changes. To some extent, seeing a video of a tsunami crushing whole villages on TV creates a very different experience of the disaster than if it had been reported only by radio or newspaper. The medium made the tsunami emotionally "hot," real, and intense. The medium is certainly part of the message, but the message itself is at least as important.

People who use one medium to communicate with another person tend to use multiple media to communicate with that person. We often do not select a single medium for a given receiver; instead we use multiple media to communicate what we need to with a given receiver. And as media in general become richer, the lines between face-to-face and mediated communication will continue to blur. But competence in all these media is not achieved in a vacuum. We have seen that messages, communication behaviors, and media are not competent or incompetent in and of themselves. Rather, communication is competent in a given context based on the extent to which the desired outcomes are achieved.

Outcomes.

The appropriateness and effectiveness of outcomes determine whether the communication and medium are perceived as competently chosen and used. Again, recall from Chapter Two that a message is *effective* if it accomplishes preferred goals, and *appropriate* if it is acceptable to the participants in the context. These outcomes are not really different in the mediated context. They may, however, depend on slightly different factors. Instead of evaluating only the appropriateness of the message, as in a face-to-face encounter, the recipient in a CMC encounter often evaluates the sender's competence based on the choice and use of the medium. If you send an emotionally rich message with important consequences through an inappropriate medium, you risk incompetence. Firing an employee—an emotionally charged message—via e-mail is likely to be seen as far less competent than doing so face-to-face. It may be efficient and effective to fire an employee or end an intimate relationship using some kind of computerized message, but it is hardly appropriate, respectful, or considerate. Obviously, appropriateness and effectiveness still serve as the touchstones of competence even in computerized-communication situations.

In today's mass-communicated and mass-mediated world, communication competence is more critical than ever. Its importance is evident in personal well-being, and in the extent to which societies survive and thrive. For example, communication competence, in its various forms, often accounts for whether individuals in the United States participate in their communities, and engage in civic and political affairs.[52] Further, the common denominator supporting social unrest and social change in the world continues to be the extent to which citizens' voices are heard; and, in many cases, their voices are expressed using the latest communication technologies. Indeed, we all need and want to live in a society that respects the right to communicate freely, and values the ability to communicate competently.

Consider again the ambitious claim we made at the start of Chapter One—"Your communication competence is the single most important factor in determining your quality of life." We stand by that claim, and hope the motivation, knowledge, and skills for communicating more competently, as described in this book, will play a critical role in enhancing the quality of your life!

CHAPTER SUMMARY

The history of mass communication, which refers to any form of mediated message exchange with a large audience, has advanced alongside human history. Technological media, any apparatus or tool assembled by human intervention for the purpose of communicating messages, has resulted in media's omnipresence in our lives in the 21st century. This mass communication refers to any form of mediated message exchange with a large audience. Media theorists refer to both strong effects—direct causal force on audience attitudes, beliefs, and behaviors—and moderated media effects—the media and its messages have a more limited influence on audiences. Opinion leaders are people who influence others who may or may not have received the media messages.

Two theories help to explain media's influence on people and on society. Agenda-setting theory claims that mass media do not determine *what* we think, but they do have significant influence over what we think *about*. Cultivation theory predicts that people not only are more aware of the ideas the media present, but their beliefs are affected by the media content as well. Other theorists refer to a mass communication model of uses and gratifications, which are the needs or goals being served by media consumption. Parasocial relationships are perceived attachments to characters, real or fictional, portrayed in the media.

Some contemporary observers believe that the microchip and computers are ushering in the next big revolution that is characterized by far more extensive use of media—an information technology revolution. A significant, contemporary trend in mass communication is media convergence, which refers to the integration of media technologies across platforms, functions, and capabilities. But despite media convergence, it is important to remember that competence in the new media environment still depends significantly on face-to-face competence. Computer-mediated communication refers to any human, symbolic interaction that takes place through digitally-based technologies. By contrast, natural media are those that send and translate symbols using only our bodies and minds.

Four basic characteristics of communication are particularly important to computer-mediated communication: richness, presence, interactivity, and openness. Richness is the extent to which a medium represents all the information available in the original message. Presence is the extent to which a medium represents the nonverbal and emotional content of messages in real time and sensation. Interactivity is the extent to which people can communicate simultaneously in response to each other's messages. Openness is the extent to which messages sent through the medium are publicly accessible and the authorship is identifiable.

Aspects of computerized messages that represent critical challenges to competent mediated communication are: ambiguity, complexity, and emotionality. Message ambiguity is the extent to which a message has either unknown or multiple meanings. Message complexity refers to the amount of detail, density, and integration of information in a message. Message emotionality is the extent to which a message attempts to communicate feelings and a sense of presence.

The same components—motivation, knowledge, and skills—that result in being perceived as competent in most communication situations also apply to computer-mediated communication. A model of computer-mediated competence considers these three components, as well as the context in which the media are used and the outcomes of the mediated communication interaction. With regard to motivation, technophobia is the fear of incompetence in sending or receiving computer-mediated messages. One of the main reasons people are afraid of technology is that they lack the knowledge for using it. With regard to skills, the four interpersonal skills of attentiveness, composure, coordination, and expressiveness are most important. Emoticons, icons that frame the emotion underlying a verbal statement, are used to add vividness to an e-mail or text message. In addition to considering motivation, knowledge, and skills, mediated communication is impacted by four levels of context—culture, relationship, situation, and function. Finally, the appropriateness and effectiveness of outcomes determine whether the communication and medium are perceived as competently chosen and used.

KEY TERMS.

The key terms below are defined in this chapter, and presented alphabetically with definitions in the Glossary at the end of the book.

- technological media
- mass communication
- mass media
- strong effects
- moderated effects
- opinion leaders
- agenda-setting theory
- cultivation theory

- uses and gratifications
- parasocial relationships
- media convergence
- computer-mediated communication
- natural media
- richness
- presence

- interactivity
- openness
- message ambiguity
- message complexity
- message emotionality
- technophobia
- emoticons
- media access

BUILDING MOTIVATION: SELF-ASSESSMENT TOOL.

Rate each of the eight communication situations described here, indicating your own typical level of technology and computer-mediated communication competence. Rate one situation all the way through for motivation, knowledge, and skills. Then rate the next situation. Use the 1–4 scale below, with 1 being minimal competence and 4 high competence.

Communication situations.

1. Using e-mail to inform employees or a group of friends about an upcoming party.
2. Contacting someone you want to start flirting with, but you only have her or his e-mail address.
3. Getting started with a new software program you think is not as good as what your organization or company was using before.
4. Finding your e-mail inbox overflowing, and having little time to respond to all the messages.
5. Responding to a text message you find somewhat inappropriate.
6. Answering the person who calls you by phone and starts the conversation with the classic line, "Didn't you get my e-mail?"
7. Hitting "reply to all" by mistake, and unintentionally sending out a message not intended for everyone.
8. Organizing a group of people to work on a project as a geographically dispersed team.

Motivation.

1 = Distracted, disinterested, or simply no motivation to be competent.
2 = Somewhat distracted or disinterested, but motivated to be competent.
3 = Somewhat interested and motivated to be competent.
4 = Highly interested and motivated to be competent.

Knowledge.

1 = Completely inexperienced and ignorant about what to do and how to do it.
2 = Minimal experience and sense of what to do and how to do it.
3 = Somewhat experienced and knowledgeable about what to do and how to do it.
4 = Highly knowledgeable about all aspects of what to do and how to do it.

Skills.

1 = Completely incapable of behaving competently.
2 = Barely capable of behaving minimally competently.
3 = Fairly capable of behaving competently.
4 = Highly capable of behaving competently.

Interpreting your scores.

Total your score separately for each situation (motivation, knowledge, and skills). The possible range of the score for each situation is 3–12. If your total score for any of the situations is 6 or less, you see yourself as less competent in that situation than you should be. A score of 7–9 means that you are average at sending and receiving communication messages in the situation. A score of 10–12 indicates that you have a high level of communication competence in that situation.

BUILDING KNOWLEDGE: DISCUSSION QUESTIONS.

1. How do communication media and computers affect your everyday interactions and relationships? To what extent are you satisfied or dissatisfied with the effect?

2. Some people think that media are changing the fundamental ways we relate to one another. Do you think the changes are fundamental, or only superficial? Why?

3. Where do you feel most comfortable relating to people, online or in person? Why? Does it depend on the type of situation, the person you are communicating with, or something else?

4. Think about where communication technology seems to be going in our society. What changes do you think technology and media will bring in the foreseeable future? If you see changes occurring, will these be mainly positive or negative?

5. CMC includes all forms of formal or informal computer-based networks that we use for sending and receiving messages. How competent do you think you are in relating to people using these various communication technologies and media? What are your strengths and weaknesses?

BUILDING SKILLS: STUDENT ACTIVITIES.

Individual activities.

1. Find out more about CMC by searching the Internet. Enter "computer-mediated communication" into a search engine. Among other things, you should find an entire journal devoted to the study of this phenomenon: *Journal of Computer-Mediated Communication.* Change your search slightly in order to find a topic or article related to CMC that is of particular interest to you.

2. Some say that the average person is only six degrees of separation from anyone else in the world. For example, you probably do not know Lady Gaga, but you probably know someone (first degree), who knows someone else (second degree), who knows someone else (third degree), and so on to a sixth someone who actually knows Lady Gaga. Technology may have reduced the number of degrees you are from contacting someone you do not already know personally. Search for information about yourself on the Internet using all the search tools available to you. How accessible do you think you are to others because of technology? How much privacy do you have, and do you need more, or less?

3. Based on the number of different media you know how to use, how competent are you? How dependent upon media are you, and how comfortable are you with this level of media dependence? Do you feel highly connected to or disconnected from communication media? Are your friends and acquaintances more or less media connected than you? Why?

4. What is your level of computer-mediated competence? How good are you at making choices about when one medium will be more competent to use than another? How good are you at structuring messages for various media, and for various recipients? If you lack skills in using a form of communication technology or media, how could you learn more about how to use it competently?

Group activities.

1. In a group of four to five students, decide which medium or communication technology would be most effective and appropriate for each of the following types of encounters.

   - Informing people of an upcoming party.
   - Asking someone out on a date.
   - Criticizing someone for something.
   - Lifting the spirits of a friend who is feeling poorly.
   - Introducing yourself to other employees in your organization who do not work in your department.

2. Form a group of six to seven students and compare past group assignments or projects accomplished by computer to those accomplished face-to-face or by telephone. Analyze what differences there were in the way group members related to one another. Decide what approach to group projects worked best and why.

3. In groups of four to five students, develop a list of strategies for addressing each of the three challenges to computer-mediated competence: message ambiguity, complexity, and emotionality. Have each group report on their recommended strategies, and look for common recommendations across the groups.

4. Form two groups of students that will debate utopia and dystopia. A *utopia* is a world in which everything meets some ideal sense of what is best. A *dystopia* is a world in which everything is disastrous or dysfunctional. Scholars have been debating the world that communication technology is likely to create. Each group of students will argue for a utopian vision or for a dystopian vision of communication technology. Each group will have time to research the topic. Then, as teams, they will present arguments for their side, and will provide a rebuttal. Which vision seems more probable, and why?

NOTES

1. See Smith (2010b).
2. See Webster (2011).
3. See Smith (2010a).
4. See Smith (2011a).
5. See Smith (2011b).
6. See Madden & Zickuhr (2011).
7. See Dodds, Muhamad, & Watts (2003).
8. See Börner (2010); Fang (2008); McFalls (1991); and U.N. Population Division (1999).
9. See Rideout, Foehr, & Roberts (2010).
10. See Katz (2010).
11. See Potter & Riddle (2007).
12. See Bryant & Miron (2004).
13. See McCombs & Shaw (1972); and Nguyen Vu & Gehrau (2010).
14. See Morgan & Shanahan (1997); and Gerbner (1998).
15. See Morgan & Shanahan (2010).
16. See Williams, Martins, Consalvo, & Ivory (2009).

17. See Martins, Williams, Harrison, & Ratan (2009).

18. See Romer, Jamieson, & Ada (2003).

19. See Rubin & Windahl (1986).

20. See Ruggiero (2000).

21. See Canary & Spitzberg (1993).

22. See Cohen (2004).

23. See Adams (2008).

24. See Yzer & Southwell (2008).

25. See Pierce & Miller (2007) & Spitzberg (2006).

26. See McCleneghan (2006).

27. See Kanai, Bahrami, Roylance, & Rees (2012).

28. See Tong, Van Der Heide, & Langwell (2008).

29. See Miller (2011).

30. See Huang (2010).

31. See Tokunaga & Rains (2010).

32. See Debatin, Lovejoy, Horn, & Hughes (2009).

33. See Chaulk & Jones (2011).

34. See Muise, Christofides, & Desmarais (2009).

35. See Lenhart (2008).

36. See Tokunaga (2011).

37. See Toma, Hancock, & Ellison (2008).

38. See George & Robb (2008).

39. See Bennett, Guran, Ramos, & Margolin (2011).

40. See Madlock & Westerman (2011).

41. See Trevino, Lengel, & Daft (1987).

42. See Witmer & Singer (1998).

43. See Insko (2003).

44. See Miczo, Mariani, & Donahue (2011).

45. See Palvia, Pinjani, Cannoy, & Jacks (2011).

46. See Kelly, Keaten, Hazel, & Williams (2010).

47. See Kwon & Wen (2010).

48. See Ledbetter (2009).

49. See Wilson & Stimpson (2010).

50. See Charlton (2009).

51. See McLuhan, Gordon, Nevitt, & Innis (2005).

52. See Shah, McLeod, & Lee (2009).

REFERENCES

Adams, J. W. (2008). Industry guidance could help J-programs prepare print majors for convergence. *Newspaper Research Journal, 29*(4), 81–88.

Bennett, D. C., Guran, E. L., Ramos, M. C., & Margolin, G. (2011). College students' electronic victimization in friendships and dating relationships: Anticipated distress and associations with risky behaviors. *Violence and Victims, 26*(4), 410–429.

Börner, K. (2010). *Atlas of science: Visualizing what we know.* Cambridge, MA: MIT Press.

Bryant, J., & Miron, D. (2004). Theory and research in mass communication. *Journal of Communication, 54*(4), 662–704.

Canary, D. J. & Spitzberg, B. H. (1993). Loneliness and media gratifications. *Communication Research, 20*(6), 800–821.

Charlton, S. G. (2009). Driving while conversing: Cell phones that distract and passengers who react. *Accident Analysis and Prevention, 41*(1), 160–173.

Chaulk, K., & Jones, T. (2011). Online obsessive relational intrusion: Further concerns about Facebook. *Journal of Family Violence, 26*(4), 245–254.

Cohen, J. (2004). Parasocial break-up from favorite television characters: The role of attachment styles and relationship intensity. *Journal of Social and Personal Relationships, 21*(2), 187–202.

Debatin, B., Lovejoy, J. P., Horn, A-K., & Hughes, B. N. (2009). Facebook and online privacy: Attitudes, behaviors, and unintended consequences. *Journal of Computer-Mediated Communication, 15*(1), 83–108.

Dodds, P. S., Muhamad, R., and Watts, D. J. (2003). An experimental study of search in global social networks. *Science, 301*(5634), 827–829.

Fang, I. (2008). *Alphabet to Internet: Mediated communication in our lives.* St. Paul, MN: Rada Press.

George, J. F., & Robb, A. (2008). Deception and computer-mediated communication in daily life. *Communication Reports, 21*(2), 92–103.

Gerbner, G. (1998). Cultivation analysis: An overview. *Mass Communication and Society, 1*(3–4), 175–194.

Huang, C. (2010). Internet use and psychological well-being: A meta-analysis. *CyberPsychology, Behavior, and Social Networking, 13*(3), 241–249.

Insko, B. E. (2003). Measuring presence: Subjective, behavioral and physiological methods. In G. Riva, F. Davide, & W. A. Ijsselsteijn (Eds.), *Being there: Concepts, effects and measurements of user presence in synthetic environments* (pp. 109-119). Amsterdam, The Netherlands: Ios Press.

Kanai, R., Bahrami, B., Roylance, R., & Rees, G. (2012). Online social network size is reflected in human brain structure. *Proceedings of the Royal Society B: Biological Sciences, 279*(1732), 1327–1334.

Katz, E. (2010). On sixty years of research and theorizing on mass communication. *Romanian Journal of Journalism and Communication, 5*(2), 5–8.

Kelly, L., Keaten, J. A., Hazel, M., & Williams, J. A. (2010). Effects of reticence, affect for communication channels, and self-perceived competence on usage of instant messaging. *Communication Research Reports, 27*(2), 131–142.

Kwon, O., & Wen, Y. (2010). An empirical study of the factors affecting social network service use. *Computers in Human Behavior, 26*(2), 254–263.

Ledbetter, A. M. (2009). Measuring online communication attitude: Instrument development and validation. *Communication Monographs, 76*(4), 463–486.

Lenhart, A. (2008). *Teens, stranger contact & cyberbullying.* Washington, DC: Pew Internet & American Life Project. Retrieved from http://cyber.law.harvard.edu/sites/cyber.law.harvard.edu/files/Pew%20Internet%20teens.pdf

Madden, M., & Zickuhr, K. (2011, August 26). *65% of online adults use social networking sites.* Washington, DC: Pew Internet & American Life Project. Retrieved from http://pewInternet.org/Reports/2011/Social-Networking-Sites.aspx

Madlock, P. E., & Westerman, D. (2011). Hurtful cyber-teasing and violence: Who's laughing out loud? *Journal of Interpersonal Violence, 26*(17), 3542–3560.

Martins, N., Williams, D. C., Harrison, K., & Ratan, R. A. (2009). A content analysis of female body imagery in video games. *Sex Roles, 61*(11–12), 824–836.

McCleneghan, J. S. (2006). PR executives rank 11 communication skills. *Public Relations Quarterly, 51*(4), 42–46.

McCombs, M. E., & Shaw, D. L. (1972). The agenda-setting function of mass media. *Public Opinion Quarterly, 36*(2), 176–187.

McFalls, J. A., Jr. (1991). Population: A lively introduction. *Population Bulletin, 46,* 2–41.

McLuhan, M., Gordon, W. T., Nevitt, B., & Innis, H. A. (2005). *Marshall McLuhan: The medium is the message.* Corte Madera, CA: Gingko Press.

Miczo, N., Mariani, T., & Donahue, C. (2011). The strength of strong ties: Media multiplexity, communication motives, and the maintenance of geographically close friendships. *Communication Reports, 24*(1), 12–24.

Miller, G. (2011, September 30). Social scientists wade into the tweet stream. *Science, 333*(6051), 1814–1815.

Morgan, M., & Shanahan, J. (1997). Two decades of cultivation research: An appraisal and meta-analysis. In B. Burleson (Ed.), *Communication yearbook* (Vol. 17, pp. 1–45). Thousand Oaks, CA: Sage.

Morgan, M., & Shanahan, J. (2010). The state of cultivation. *Journal of Broadcasting & Electronic Media, 54*(2), 337–355.

Muise, A., Christofides, E., & Desmarais, S. (2009). More information than you ever wanted: Does Facebook bring out the green-eyed monster of jealousy? *CyberPsychology and Behavior, 12*(4), 441–444.

Nguyen Vu, H. N., & Gehrau, V. (2010). Agenda diffusion: An integrated model of agenda setting and interpersonal communication. *Journalism & Mass Communication Quarterly, 87*(1), 100–116.

Palvia, P., Pinjani, P., Cannoy, S., & Jacks, T. (2011). Contextual constraints in media choice: Beyond information richness. *Decision Support Systems, 51*(3), 657–670.

Pierce, T., & Miller, T. (2007). Basic journalism skills remain important in hiring. *Newspaper Research Journal, 28*(4), 51–61.

Potter, W. J., & Riddle, K. (2007). A content analysis of the media effects literature. *Journalism and Mass Communication Quarterly, 84*(1), 90–104.

Rideout, V. J., Foehr, U. G., & Roberts, D. F. (2010, January). *Generation M2: Media in the lives of 8- to 18-year-olds.* Menlo Park, CA: Henry J. Kaiser Family Foundation. Retrieved from http://www.kff.org/entmedia/upload/8010.pdf

Romer, D., Jamieson, K. H., & Ada, S. (2003). Television news and the cultivation of fear of crime. *Journal of Communication, 53*(1), 88–104.

Rubin, A. M, & Windahl, S. (1986). The uses and dependency model of mass communication. *Critical Studies in Mass Communication, 3*(2), 184–199.

Ruggiero, T. E. (2000). Uses and gratifications theory in the 21stcentury. *Mass Communication and Society, 3*(1), 3–37.

Shah, D., McLeod, J. M., & Lee, N-J. (2009). Communication competence as a foundation for civic competence: Processes of socialization into citizenship. *Political Communication, 26*(1), 102–117.

Smith, A. (2010a, July 7). *Mobile access 2010.* Washington, DC: Pew Internet & American Life Project. Retrieved from http://pewInternet.org/Reports/2010/Mobile-Access-2010.asp

Smith, A. (2010b, October 14). *Americans and their gadgets.* Washington, DC: Pew Internet & American Life Project. Retrieved from http://pewInternet.org/Reports/2010/Gadgets.aspx

Smith, A. (2011a, July 11). *Smartphone adoption and usage.* Washington, DC: Pew Internet & American Life Project. Retrieved from http://pewInternet.org/Reports/2011/Smartphones.aspx

Smith, A. (2011b, September 19). *Americans and text messaging.* Washington, DC: Pew Internet & American Life Project. Retrieved from http://pewInternet.org/Reports/2011/Cell-Phone-Texting-2011.aspx

Spitzberg, B. H. (2006). Preliminary development of a model and measure of computer-mediated communication (CMC) competence. *Journal of Computer-Mediated Communication, 11*(2), 629–666. Retrieved from http://jcmc.indiana.edu/vol11/issue2/spitzberg.html

Tokunaga, R. S. (2011). Friend me or you'll strain us: Understanding negative events that occur over social networking sites. *CyberPsychology, Behavior, and Social Networking, 14*(7–8), 425–432.

Tokunaga, R. S., & Rains, S. A. (2010). An evaluation of two characterizations of the relationships between problematic Internet use, time spent using the Internet, and psychosocial problems. *Human Communication Research, 36*(4), 512–545.

Toma, C. L., Hancock, J. T., & Ellison, N. B. (2008). Separating fact from fiction: An examination of deceptive self-presentation in online dating profiles. *Personality and Social Psychology Bulletin, 34*(8), 1023–1036.

Tong, S. T., Van Der Heide, B., Langwell, L., & Walther, J. B. (2008). Too much of a good thing? The relationship between number of friends and interpersonal impressions on Facebook. *Journal of Computer-Mediated Communication, 13*, 531-549.

Trevino, L. K., Lengel, R. K. & Daft, R. L. (1987). Media symbolism, media richness and media choice in organizations. *Communication Research, 14*(5), 553–574.

U.N. Population Division. (1999, October). *The world at 6 billion.* Department of Economic and Social Affairs, United Nations Secretariat (ESA/P/WP.154). Retrieved from http://www.un.org/esa/population/publications/sixbillion/sixbilpart1.pdf

Webster, T. (2011). *The social habit II: The Edison research/Arbitron Internet and multimedia study 2011.* Somerville, NJ: Edison Research. Retrieved from http://www.slideshare.net/webby2001/the-social-habit-2011-by-edison-research

Williams, D., Martins, N., Consalvo, M., & Ivory, J. D. (2009). The virtual census: Representations of gender, race and age in video games. *New Media & Society, 11*(5), 815–834.

Wilson, F. A., & Stimpson, J. P. (2010). Trends in fatalities from distracted driving in the United States, 1999 to 2008. *American Journal of Public Health, 100*(11), 2213–2219.

Witmer, B. G.,& Singer, M. J. (1998). Measuring presence in virtual environments: A presence questionnaire. *Presence, 7*(3), 225–240.

Yzer, M. C., & Southwell, B. G. (2008). New communication technologies, old questions. *American Behavioral Scientist, 52*(1), 8–20.

GLOSSARY

ACKNOWLEDGING COMMENTS help members indicate that they understand one another, their situation, their process, and their actions.

ACTIONS are the behaviors performed by a person.

ADAPTABILITY is the ability to alter skills appropriately as contexts and conversations evolve and change.

ADAPTIVE means messages are altered to fit particular situations in ways designed to produce better outcomes.

ADAPTIVE WORK has problems and solutions that are not clearly defined, and places the responsibility for change on the group members.

AFFECT BLEND occurs when a person blends two or more facial expressions into one affect display. Typical affect blends are fear/anger and surprise/happiness.

AFFECTIVE CONFLICT involves the interpersonal relationships formed among group members and the group's emotional climate.

AGENDA-SETTING THEORY claims that the mass media do not determine *what* we think, but they do have significant influence over what we think *about*.

AGGRESSIVE COMMUNICATION refers to the expression of your rights or views in a way that violates another person's rights or views.

ALLITERATION involves the repetition of the same consonant sound in a series of words or phrases to draw attention to certain ideas, and help listeners remember what is said.

ANALOGY is an extended simile or metaphor that asks the listeners to accept that things that seem alike in most respects will be alike in the respect being discussed.

APPEAL is the subtle technique speakers use to get the audience to accept their persuasive argument.

APPEARANCE includes your clothing, shoes, jewelry, hairstyle, and even hair adornments.

APPROPRIATE COMMUNICATION occurs when you act in ways suitable to the norms and expectations of contexts and situations you encounter.

APPROPRIATE LANGUAGE presents information in a way that respects and treats all audience members as equals without being condescending or using biased language and stereotypes.

ARRANGEMENT is organizing—or arranging—what you have invented in a logical and effective manner to accomplish the goal of the speech.

ARTICULATION is about forming individual speech sounds correctly with your mouth, so they combine to produce an understandable word.

ARTIFACTS are the objects in the environment that make nonverbal statements about the identity and personality of their owner.

ASSERTIVENESS is the skill of expressing one's rights or views without violating another person's rights or views.

ATTENTIVENESS is the skill of showing interest in, concern for, and attention to the other person or persons in the interaction.

ATTRIBUTION THEORY provides people with a framework for determining the motives underlying others' behavior.

AUDIENCE ANALYSIS is the process a speaker uses to ascertain relevant facts and information about the listeners that then shape how the speech is prepared and delivered.

AVOIDANCE as a conflict management style is low in both assertiveness and collaboration.

AVOIDANCE SKILLS function to displace conflict.

BIASED LANGUAGE uses words or phrases that derive their meaning from stereotypes based on gender, race, ethnic group, age, sexual orientation, or disability.

BODY LANGUAGE or kinesics, focuses on how people communicate through movement, posture, gestures, and expressions of the face and eyes.

BODY MOVEMENT AND POSTURE can communicate three things in any situation: how people see power operating, how they feel about themselves in the situation, and how they feel about the topic of discussion.

BODY OF THE SPEECH is the section of the speech that supports your central claim through the presentation of a series of main points.

BRAINSTORMING is a group procedure in which each individual in a group generates ideas, and adds them to the group discussion.

BRAINWRITING is a written method for brainstorming, in which a grid is created and passed along for each member to contribute new ideas while reviewing what previous group members have written.

BREADTH relates to the number of different types of roles a person can play.

CHANNEL is the medium through which a message is sent.

CHRONOLOGICAL ORGANIZATION is used to describe changes or developments in any situation or circumstance. (Chapter Thirteen)

CHRONOLOGICAL SPEECH ORGANIZATION presents information based on time, and orders the subtopics in the sequence they might occur. (Chapter Eleven)

CLEAR LANGUAGE uses words in such a way that listeners understand and can easily comprehend the meaning of the speaker's message.

CLOSED-ENDED QUESTIONS give the respondent very limited options in answering.

COERCION is a negative form of influence that occurs when a speaker persuades others to act in a particular way out of fear, or by using force, or giving the listeners no choice but to cooperate.

COMMUNICATION is the process of managing messages and media for the purpose of creating meaning.

COMMUNICATION APPREHENSION is the fear or anxiety an individual experiences as a result of either real or anticipated communication with another person or other persons.

COMMUNICATION AS INFORMING is an informational transfer model that identifies a source, channel, receiver, noise, and feedback loop.

COMMUNICATION AS PERSUADING sees communication as a process of influencing others to achieve your own goals.

COMMUNICATION AS RELATING focuses on the power of communication to create, maintain, and dissolve relationships with others.

COMMUNICATION CLIMATE refers to the tone, general mood, or feeling that colors any interpersonal relationship.

COMMUNICATION CODES are the set of principles and meanings underlying and guiding the language used by members of any social group.

COMMUNICATION COMPETENCE is the extent to which speakers achieve desired outcomes through communication behavior acceptable to a situation.

COMMUNITY is a group of people who come together in the same physical, mental, or virtual space to interact or pursue a common goal.

COMPARING ALTERNATIVES is an organizational pattern that first asks listeners to examine two or more alternatives, and then it makes a strong appeal for the preferred choice.

COMPETENT COMMUNICATION is appropriate and effective for a particular situation.

COMPETENT LANGUAGE enhances the listeners' understanding and enthusiasm for a speech by the use of words that are clear, vivid, and appropriate.

COMPOSURE is the skill of appearing in control of one's communication behavior.

COMPUTER-MEDIATED COMMUNICATION, generally referred to as **CMC**, is any human, symbolic interaction that takes place through digitally based technologies.

COMPUTER-MEDIATED CONTEXT is technologically facilitated communication.

CONCEPT SPEECH refers to a speech that is about abstract ideas—theories, principles, or values.

CONCLUSION is the component of the speech that lets the listeners know that your speech is ending, and reminds them of your central idea.

CONCURRENCE SEEKING occurs when groups try to achieve a consensus regarding their decision.

CONDESCENDING LANGUAGE is language that speaks down to your audience and may be offensive.

CONFLICT is defined as interaction among interdependent people who perceive others as opposing their goals, aims, or values, and having the potential to frustrate them in achieving these goals, aims, or values.

CONNOTATIVE MEANING refers to the personal associations people make with a signified symbol.

CONSISTENCY means maintaining similar ways of behaving across contexts and conversations.

CONSTITUTIVE RULES take the basic content of the message, its words, and tell us what they mean, and how we are to make sense of them.

CONSTRUCTING MEANING involves assigning meaning to a speaker's message, and mentally clarifying your understanding of it.

CONTENT KNOWLEDGE refers to understanding of topics, words, meanings, and so forth, required in a communication situation.

CONTENT LEVEL of a message is what the words mean in a literal or denotative sense. (Chapter Seven)

CONTEXT is the frame within which the communication action occurs.

CONTEXT APPREHENSION is anxiety about communicating in a particular context such as interpersonal, small groups, or public speaking.

CONTEXT LEVELS refer to the number of communicators in the encounter or event, and the direction of the communication among them.

CONTEXT TYPES are routine, socially negotiated understandings of what is going on in a communication encounter or event.

CONVERGENCE is about the extent to which any given technology incorporates multiple or additional forms of communication.

CONVERGENT THINKING involves evaluating the ideas, narrowing a wide range of alternatives, and selecting the one most appropriate to the task at hand.

CONVERSATIONAL NARCISSISM is the appearance in your communication of caring only about yourself.

COORDINATION is the skill of managing the ebb and flow of the interaction.

COSMOPOLITAN COMMUNICATORS recognize that the meanings they have created for certain words are unique to them, and are not shared by others.

COUNTERARGUMENT or inner speech argues against the persuasive message being presented and for the listener's entrenched position or point of view.

CREDIBILITY APPEALS relate to how listeners perceive the reputation, prestige, and authority of the speaker.

CRITICAL THINKING involves evaluating evidence, assumptions, and ideas as you prepare your speech.

CULTIVATION THEORY predicts that people not only are more aware of the ideas the media present, but media consumers' beliefs are affected by the media content as well.

CULTURAL CHARACTERISTICS of audience members come from two kinds of groups that listeners belong to: those they are born into or grow up in, and groups they may choose to belong to.

CULTURE consists of the enduring patterns of thought, value, and behavior that define a group of people.

DECISION is the selection among alternative explanations or proposals.

DEDUCTION is a process of reasoning in which a specific conclusion follows from a general principle that is often made up of a major and a minor premise.

DEEP INTERRUPTIONS are interruptions that take over a speaker's turn in the middle of that person's statement.

DEFENSIVE GROUP ENVIRONMENTS are characterized by a lack of trust and cooperation among group members.

DELIVERY is the actual presentation of the speech to the audience.

DENOTATIVE MEANING refers to the "dictionary definition" of words.

DEPTH refers to the level of familiarity a person has with any given role in a repertoire.

DESCRIPTIONS are used when the listeners are unfamiliar with the topic of the speech, and need new information in order to understand it.

DEVIL'S ADVOCATE PROCEDURE involves assigning an individual to question the assumptions and processes the group uses to make decisions.

DIALECTIC is a question and answer process used to examine all sides of an issue in search of the truth.

DISTRIBUTIVE SKILLS attempt to divide, that is, distribute, the outcomes of the conflict so that you win more than the other person.

DISTRIBUTIVE STYLE of conflict management is high in assertiveness and low in cooperativeness.

DIVERGENT THINKING involves generating multiple ideas and alternatives about issues, problems, and solutions.

DRIVERS are the causes of a particular problem, or the sources that create the problem.

EFFECTIVE COMMUNICATION occurs when you are able to achieve the most desirable objectives or outcomes in given contexts.

EMOTICONS are icons that frame the emotion underlying a verbal statement.

EMOTIONAL APPEALS are based on psychology and passion, which involves how people feel.

EMPATHY is the ability to experience feelings similar to or related to those of another person.

ETHICAL PERSUASION leaves the decision about what to think or do up to the other person or the audience members.

ETHNOCENTRIC COMMUNICATORS recognize as valid only their own meanings for words, and reject alternative meanings as wrong.

EVENT SPEECH refers to a speech that describes something that has occurred.

EXPLANATIONS are necessary to tell listeners how something works, or to clarify something that is already known but not well understood.

EXPRESSIVENESS is the skill of animating verbal and nonverbal communication.

EXTEMPORANEOUS SPEECHES are carefully planned and prepared ahead of time, and are delivered in a conversational tone of voice using note cards or a presentational outline.

EYE CONTACT is a tool you can use to promote a sense of involvement with audience members that can make you seem credible, dynamic, believable, likeable, and persuasive.

FACIAL EXPRESSION is the vehicle you use to communicate how you feel about what you are saying to the audience. (Chapter Twelve)

FACIAL EXPRESSIONS, also called "affect displays," communicate six basic, universal emotions that the human face is capable of displaying: sadness, anger, disgust, fear, surprise, and happiness. (Chapter Five)

FACT refers to an individual piece of information that listeners could verify for themselves if they wanted to.

FEAR APPEALS are based on changing listeners' attitudes or behaviors through the use of an anxiety-arousing message.

FEEDBACK LOOP represents the information that allows communicators in the system to interpret the effects of their messages.

FENG SHUI is a 3,000-year-old Chinese approach to spatial arrangement and the use of artifacts in homes and offices.

FIGURES OF SPEECH include simile, metaphor, analogy, the rhetorical question, alliteration, and repetition.

FILLED PAUSES are the nonfluencies or distracters that slip out when you speak, particularly when you are nervous (*uh, um, y'know,* and *OK*).

FORCE FIELD ANALYSIS is a process for analyzing the reasons for a problem, as well as what is preventing the problem from being eliminated.

FORMAL OUTLINES contain all of the information from the final version of a working outline, organized and presented in more detail using an alphanumeric system for main and subpoints in the standard outline format.

FUNCTIONAL means messages are enacted so as to accomplish preferred outcomes.

FUNCTIONALIST APPROACH assumes that particular decision-making functions can be identified that, when performed, will lead to high-quality decision making.

FUNCTIONS OF COMMUNICATION are what the communication behavior attempts to accomplish or actually accomplishes.

GENDER-BIASED LANGUAGE tends to favor one sex over another.

GENERAL PURPOSE refers to the general goal of a speech, such as to inform or to persuade.

GESTURES are the large and small movements of the hands and arms that communicate meaning. (Chapter Five)

GESTURES are the large and small movements of the hands and arms that communicate meaning. They reinforce what you say, emphasize important points, and make presentations more interesting to watch as well as more natural and relaxed. (Chapter Twelve)

GRAMMAR includes the rules and structure for putting words together in sentences.

GROUP CONTEXTS include a larger number of people, typically 3 to 12, and usually take place in a more formal, task-oriented context.

GROUP ENVIRONMENT refers to the social climate in which group members communicate that is informed by the feelings and emotions of other group members.

GROUPTHINK occurs when group members establish a norm that makes consensus the highest priority, and that diminishes the vigilant appraisal of possible alternatives to a final decision.

HATE SPEECH has been defined as "speech that (1) has a message of racial inferiority, (2) is directed against a member of a historically oppressed group, and (3) is persecutory, hateful, and degrading" (Nielsen, 2002)

HOLISTIC means the entire communication process forms a system in which all the parts of the system attempt to collaborate in helping the system work.

HYPOTHETICAL EXAMPLE refers to an example about something that has not actually happened but could happen.

IDEATIONAL CONFLICT centers on the arguments and issues regarding decision alternatives.

IMAGERY is the creation of mental pictures and imagined sensory experiences through description.

IMPLICIT PERSONALITY THEORY suggests that we use one or a few personality traits to draw inferences about what people are like.

IMPROMPTU SPEECHES are delivered with the least amount of preparation, usually with little or no time to plan your remarks.

INDUCTION is a process of reasoning in which a general conclusion follows from considering a series of specific instances or examples.

INFORMATIVE SPEECHES communicate new information or a new perspective on a topic to an audience, and brings the listeners to greater understanding or insight. (Chapter Thirteen)

INFORMATIVE SPEECHES have the purpose of communicating something new or a new perspective to an audience, and moving listeners to greater understanding or insight. (Chapter Eleven)

INSTRUCTIONS are useful when the objective is to teach the audience something, or to tell them how to use something.

INTEGRATIVE SKILLS attempt to bring your goals and the other person's goals together so both of you can achieve what you want.

INTEGRATIVE STYLE of conflict management is high in both assertiveness and collaboration.

INTERACTION refers to the interdependence among sequential behaviors or moves made by communicators in a situation.

INTERACTION BARRIERS arise as a result of engaging in verbal battles and using inflammatory language, or because of individual and cultural differences between the speaker and listener.

INTERACTIVITY is the extent to which people can communicate simultaneously in response to each other's messages.

INTEREST refers to the underlying motivation or reason the person wants to pursue a particular position.

INTERPERSONAL COMMUNICATION is the process of managing messages and media for the purpose of creating meaning in interactions among people in social or personal relationships.

INTERPERSONAL CONTEXT is an informal interaction among people in social or personal relationships.

INTRODUCTION sets the tone for the speech, and motivates the audience to become involved in what is about to be presented.

INVENTION is identifying—or inventing—the materials that will make up your speech, including a topic and information to support it.

ISSUE FRAMING consists of refining and rewording the discussion question for the group.

ISSUE SPEECH refers to a speech that examines a debatable topic from various points of view.

JOHARI WINDOW outlines four possible types of openness, and is defined by two dimensions: the self-dimension and the other-dimension.

JUDGMENTAL EMPATHIC RESPONSE provides support but also helps to interpret and evaluate the speaker's situation.

KNOWLEDGE consists of all the mental processes involved in awareness, accessibility, and organization of information relevant to enacting a communication behavior.

KNOWLEDGE-GAINING STRATEGIES are behaviors people use to obtain information about others or about situations.

LADDER OF ABSTRACTION places the most concrete words on the lower rungs, and arranges words on the upper rungs as they increase in abstraction.

LANGUAGE is a verbal symbol system that allows us to take messages and utterances, in the form of words, and translate them into meaning.

LANGUAGE COMMUNITY is a group of people who have developed a common set of constitutive and regulative rules, which guide the meaning of words and the appropriate reactions, based on interpreting those words.

LEADERS are the individuals within a group who guide and direct the group's activities.

LEADERSHIP is a communication process that helps groups organize themselves to achieve desirable goals.

LEVEL OF ABSTRACTION refers to the range of communication behaviors from specific or micro-level skills to general or macro-level skills.

LINGUISTIC DETERMINISM says that language determines what we see or notice in the world, and how and what we think about what we see.

LISTENING "is the process of receiving, constructing meaning from, and responding to spoken and/or nonverbal messages" (International Listening Association, 2011).

LISTENING TO EMPATHIZE AND UNDERSTAND focuses on the speaker's *feelings and attitudes* while gaining information.

LISTENING TO EVALUATE AND CRITIQUE calls for critically analyzing the meaning and merit of a speaker's message.

LISTENING TO LEARN AND COMPREHEND includes a search for facts and ideas, and a quest for information.

LOGICAL APPEALS are based on knowledge and reasoning, which involves how people think.

LOGICAL FALLACIES are errors in reasoning and logic that lead the listeners to false conclusions.

LOOKING-GLASS SELF assumes that people imagine the perception others hold of them, and this act of perceiving the self as an object through the eyes of others creates the sense of self.

MACRO-LEVEL SKILLS represent the assembly of specific or micro-level skills to create the performance of general skills such as assertiveness, self-disclosure, social support, conflict management, deception, and wit.

MAIN POINTS are key ideas that, when taken together, prove the claim and support the thesis statement.

MANAGING is the handling or supervising of people or some process or material.

MANIPULATION is a negative and unethical form of influence that is used to control people's actions or reactions, but in a devious or deceitful way.

MANUSCRIPT SPEECHES are written out ahead of time and read word for word to the audience.

MASS COMMUNICATION refers to any form of mediated message exchange with a large audience.

MASS MEDIA commonly refers to television, radio, advertising, public relations, newspapers, book and magazine publishing, music publishing, movies, as well as Internet publishing and advertising, and the organizations that own, produce, and distribute mass communication.

MAXIMIZING COMMUNICATION is effective but inappropriate communication.

MEANING is the interpretation people assign to a message—how it is recognized or understood.

MEDIA are any means through which symbols are transmitted and meanings are represented.

MEDIA ACCESS is the extent to which CMC technologies are available to an intended audience.

MEDIA CONVERGENCE refers to the integration of media technologies across platforms, functions, and capabilities.

MEMORIZED SPEECHES require the most preparation because they are fully written out and memorized ahead of time, then spoken to the audience word for word.

MEMORY—memorizing your speech—is a rhetorical canon of less importance today, since speeches typically are not memorized by public speakers.

MESSAGE refers to the words, sounds, actions, and gestures that people express to one another when they interact.

MESSAGE AMBIGUITY is the extent to which a message has either unknown or multiple meanings.

MESSAGE COMPLEXITY refers to the amount of detail, density, and integration of information in a message, i.e., how complicated it is.

MESSAGE EMOTIONALITY is the extent to which a message attempts to communicate feelings and a sense of presence.

MESSAGE OVERLOAD refers to the sheer quantity of the message.

METAPHOR, like simile, implies a comparison between two unlike things, but it does so without using the words *like* or *as*.

MICRO-LEVEL SKILLS include such behaviors as gestures, eye contact, smiling, vocabulary, articulation, vocal variety, and so forth.

MICRO-MOMENTARY FACIAL FLASH is an expression that flashes across the face so quickly that it is imperceptible.

MIDDLE-LEVEL SKILLS include such behaviors as the ability to engage in disagreements or agreements, greetings, promises, threats, requests, assertions, and various other communication acts that language enables.

MINDFULNESS involves paying close attention to the task at hand, absorbing each bit of detail that you possibly can.

MINIMIZING COMMUNICATION is inappropriate and ineffective communication.

MODERATED EFFECTS models view both mass communication and the audience as having influence on the impact of messages, with the media and its messages having more limited influence.

MODERN SELF refers to the Western tradition of viewing people as having a core single self whose character and personality are stable over time.

MOTIVATED SEQUENCE is a model for persuasive speaking that moves through a sequence of five steps, designed to motivate and persuade listeners psychologically.

MULTIPLE SELF, in a postmodern perspective, means we create many different versions of self across various contexts.

NARCISSISM is a tendency to be outgoing, self-absorbed, but also arrogant.

NATURAL MEDIA are those that send and translate symbols using only our bodies and minds, such as spoken words, gestures, posture, and all the other verbal, nonverbal, and listening processes.

NEGATIVE MOTIVATION refers to the experience of anxiety about a communication action or the perception of low reward potential, in a real or imagined communication situation.

NESTED DECISION MAKING involves prioritizing interdependent questions and issues a group faces.

NOISE is any type of interference coming from the environment that distorts the message or distracts us from the communication.

NOMINAL GROUP TECHNIQUE is a procedure in which group members generate ideas individually, share these ideas with the group, and then evaluate them as a group.

NONJUDGMENTAL EMPATHIC RESPONSE helps both people better understand and probe what is going on.

NONVERBAL COMMUNICATION consists of those sounds, actions, or gestures—other than words—to which people attribute meaning. (Chapter One)

NONVERBAL COMMUNICATION includes all behaviors, attributes, and objects of humans—other than words—that communicate messages and have shared social meaning. (Chapter Five)

NONVERBAL CUES are nonverbal behaviors or objects to which meaning is assigned.

NONVERBAL SYMBOLS are sounds, actions, or gestures that people agree have a common meaning.

ONLINE AND ELECTRONIC BARRIERS involve any communication messages that are sent or received using blogs, wikis, social networking, computers, and the like.

OPEN-ENDED QUESTIONS permit the other person wide discretion in how to answer.

OPENNESS is the extent to which messages sent through the medium are publicly accessible and the authorship is identifiable or, in some cases, anonymous.

OPINION LEADERS are people who receive mass communication messages, form an opinion on the basis of those messages, and then influence others who may or may not have received the messages.

OPTIMIZING COMMUNICATION is appropriate and effective communication.

ORGANIZATION BY CAUSE AND EFFECT examines why something happens (the causes), and what happens as a result (the effects).

ORGANIZATION BY COMPARISON AND CONTRAST is used to describe or explain how a subject is similar to, or different from, something else.

PARASOCIAL RELATIONSHIPS are perceived attachments to characters, real or fictional, portrayed in the media.

PASSIVE COMMUNICATION is the avoidance of self-expression, or the accommodation to other's concerns over your own.

PERCEPTION is the process of noticing, organizing, and interpreting data about people, events, activities, and situations.

PERSONAL CHARACTERISTICS include objective demographic information about the audience members.

PERSONAL SPACE involves how people distance themselves from one another.

PERSPECTIVE TAKING means seeing the world cognitively as the other person sees it.

PERSUASION is the use of communication to reinforce, change, or modify an audience's attitudes, values, beliefs, or actions.

PERSUASIVE SPEECHES are presented by a speaker (the source), using the right appeals for the setting to influence the attitudes, beliefs, values, or actions of the audience (receivers). (Chapter Fourteen)

PERSUASIVE SPEECHES have the purpose of influencing an audience's attitudes, beliefs, values, or behaviors, and moving listeners to change or to action of some kind. (Chapter Eleven)

PHYSICAL APPEARANCE includes everything you notice about a person, including degree of attractiveness, race and ethnicity, age, gender, height, weight, body shape, clothing, and even how the person smells.

PHYSICAL BARRIERS to listening include interferences from the physical environment, and distracting characteristics or behaviors of the speaker, the listener, or both.

PITCH is the highness or lowness of the speaking voice.

PLAN is an intentional description of the actions and means needed to achieve a communication goal.

PLANNING is the process of anticipating and formulating possible strategies for achieving some communication goal or goals.

POLITICALLY CORRECT LANGUAGE intends to rid our minds of discriminatory thoughts by removing from our language any words or phrases that could offend people by the way they reference differences among us.

POSITION refers to a stated course of action that the person wants to see pursued in the group.

POSITIVE MOTIVATION refers to the perception of high potential reward in pursuing a communication action.

POSTMODERN SELF suggests that the self is actually made up of multiple personal constructions of self.

POSTURE is defined as a position or attitude of body parts, and that is just what it communicates—your attitude.

PRESENCE is the extent to which a medium represents the nonverbal and emotional content of messages in real time and sensation.

PRESENTATION AIDS are any materials you show to or share with the audience that assist in illustrating or supporting the content of your speech, and add interest and excitement to it.

PRESENTATIONAL OUTLINES, or speaking outlines, are abbreviated versions of the formal outline, and they are what you use when you give your speech.

PROBLEM is what exists when there is a gap between an ideal state and the current state of events.

PROBLEM-SOLUTION is an organizational pattern that first identifies a problem, and then proposes a workable solution to it.

PROBLEM SOLVING involves a group process in which members assess problems, and formulate solutions to resolve the problems.

PROCEDURAL CONFLICT occurs when there are differences of opinion on what procedures to use during group discussion.

PROCEDURAL KNOWLEDGE tells us how to assemble, plan, and perform content knowledge in a particular communication situation.

PRONUNCIATION focuses on stressing and accenting the right syllables in a word.

PROTOTYPE is the best example of some concept.

PSYCHOLOGICAL BARRIERS to listening reside within the listener, and include mental and emotional distractions to listening such as boredom, daydreaming, and thinking about personal concerns.

PSYCHOLOGICAL CHARACTERISTICS of audience members include their needs and motivations and their attitudes, beliefs, and values.

PUBLIC SPEAKING is when a single person—or sometimes a group of people—presents a message to a few or many people, who usually do not have speaking roles, except sometimes asking questions.

PUBLIC SPEAKING ANXIETY, popularly referred to as stage fright, refers to a person's fear or anxiety associated with an expected or actual public-speaking event.

PUBLIC-SPEAKING CONTEXTS include one person or a small group of people speaking to a larger number of people who have little or no speaking role.

PUBLIC VOICE makes use of increased variety in volume, rate, and pitch, so that your words are easily heard and understood by the entire audience.

QUOTATION is the use of a person's exact words.

RATE is the speed at which a speaker delivers a speech.

REACTANCE is an emotional reaction in direct contradiction to rules or regulations that threaten a person's behavioral freedom.

RECEIVER is the person or group of people who are the ultimate audience for the message.

RECEIVING means tuning in to the speaker's entire message, including both its verbal and non-verbal aspects, and consciously paying attention to it.

REFERENT is the thing to which symbols refer.

REFLECTING involves repeating someone's feelings about what they have said.

REFLECTIVE THINKING MODEL profiles a series of steps that decision makers follow in order to make high-quality decisions.

REFUTING THE OPPONENT is an organizational pattern that dismantles your opponent's argument in order to persuade the audience that your argument is superior.

REGULATIVE RULES help you determine the appropriate response, given your interpretation of the message.

RELATIONAL FUNCTIONS emphasize the importance of building a positive group culture and managing conflict.

RELATIONSHIP is any actual or perceived interdependence between or among communicators. (Chapter One)

RELATIONSHIP is the sense of relative positioning to one another, that is, how you orient yourself or connect to one another. (Chapter Seven)

RELATIONSHIP LEVEL is what a message implies about the relationship. (Chapter Seven)

REPERTOIRE is the set of roles a person is capable of playing or enacting, along with behaviors or actions that comprise those roles.

REPETITION occurs when the speaker repeats the same word or phrase several times in a section of a speech.

RESPONDING completes the interaction between the listener and speaker, and is the step in which the listener lets the speaker know the message has been received and understood.

RESTRAINING FORCES are forces that prevent the resolution of a problem.

RHETORIC is the art of influencing an audience through public speech.

RHETORICAL QUESTIONS are asked for effect rather than to get a real answer from the listeners.

RICHNESS is the extent to which a medium represents all the information available in the original message.

ROLES are the patterns and the style of statements and behaviors a person is able to perform across contexts.

RULES are prescriptions you can follow for what should or should not be done in a given type of situation.

SAPIR-WHORF HYPOTHESIS maintains that reality is already embedded in the structure of our language, and that this structure determines how we perceive our world.

SCHEMA is a framework that helps people organize information and place it into a coherent and meaningful pattern.

SCRIPT is an expected sequence of events that appears logical to the individual.

SELF-DISCLOSURE is the process of intentionally and voluntarily providing others with information about yourself that you believe is honest and accurate, and unlikely to be discovered elsewhere.

SELF-FULFILLING PROPHECY occurs when you make assumptions about yourself or another person and then behave or interact with the person as if these assumptions were true.

SELF-TALK denotes internal conversations in which we reflect on what we are doing well or what we are doing poorly.

SHYNESS is a tendency to withdraw from social activities.

SIGNIFIED is the term used for referent.

SIGNIFIER is the term used for symbol.

SIMILE is an explicit comparison that compares two unlike things using the words *like* or *as*.

SITUATION ANALYSIS includes both time and place. Timing involves how much time you have to speak, and when the speech is to be presented. Place relates to the context in which the speech is presented.

SKILLS are behaviors directed toward the achievement of preferred outcomes in a context. (Chapter Eight)

SKILLS are repeatable, goal-directed, proficient behaviors enacted in a given context. (Chapter Two)

SMALL GROUP can be defined as three or more people who perceive themselves to be a group, who are interdependent, and who communicate with one another.

SMALL-GROUP COMMUNICATION is the process of managing messages and media for the purpose of creating meaning in groups of three or more people who perceive themselves to be a group, are interdependent, and who communicate with one another.

SOCIAL ANXIETY is the real or imagined fear of interacting in an interpersonal encounter.

SOCIAL CONSTRUCTIONISM states that people create their reality and relationships through the process of interaction with others.

SOCIAL NORMS are the explicit or implicit rules specifying what behaviors are acceptable within a society or group. (Chapter Seven)

SOCIAL SELF comes into being through interaction with others, and can be determined only through relationships with other people.

SOURCE is the original producer of the message, and in human communication it is a person.

SPACE, also called proxemics, is the study of how people move around in and use space to communicate.

SPATIAL ARRANGEMENT is the way spaces are laid out and relate to one another, as well as how objects and furniture are placed in the spaces. (Chapter Five)

SPATIAL ORGANIZATION presents information based on the positioning of objects in physical space, or relationships among locations. (Chapter Thirteen)

SPEAKER CREDIBILITY is the impression listeners form of a speaker in a given public-speaking context and at a given time.

SPECIFIC PURPOSE refers to a statement of the response the speaker would like from the audience.

SPEECH ABOUT AN OBJECT refers to a speech that is usually about something tangible that can be seen, touched, or otherwise experienced through the physical senses.

SPEECH ABOUT A PERSON refers to a speech that describes an individual.

SPEECH ABOUT A PROCESS refers to a speech that describes a system or sequence of steps that lead to a result or change taking place.

SPEECH TO CHANGE refers to a speech intended to convince the audience to change what they like or dislike, what they hold to be true or untrue, or what they consider important or unimportant.

SPEECH TO MOVE TO ACTION refers to a speech intended to influence listeners to either engage in a new and desirable behavior, or discontinue an undesirable behavior.

SPEECH TO REINFORCE refers to a speech intended to influence listeners by strengthening their convictions, and taking advantage of their tendency to seek out and attend to messages with which they already agree.

STATISTICS are numerical summaries of facts, figures, and research findings that provide pictures of data about people, ideas, or patterns of behavior.

STEREOTYPES are schemas that connect a variety of characteristics we believe to be true of a category, to a person or situation we see as an example of that category.

STORY is a narrative of what is expected or needs to occur sequentially in the given situation. A story is also known as a script.

STRONG EFFECTS predict that media operate with direct causal force on audience attitudes, beliefs, and behaviors.

STYLE is the distinctive way a speech is presented that makes it memorable, which is achieved primarily through the speaker's use of language.

SUBJECT AREA refers to a general area of knowledge.

SUFFICING COMMUNICATION is appropriate but ineffective communication.

SUPPORTIVE GROUP ENVIRONMENTS exist when group members collaborate with each other to achieve group goals jointly.

SYMBOL is a word, sound, action, or gesture that refers to something else.

SYMPATHY is a desire to offer support to another, generally when the person is in a difficult situation.

TALKOVERS are instances in which you say something during someone else's turn to talk.

TASK FUNCTIONS involve instrumental behavior aimed at goal achievement.

TASK SKILL is any communication message or behavior a person sends that helps the group make a decision.

TECHNICAL WORK occurs when the problem the group is working on, its solution, and its implementation are all clearly defined.

TECHNOLOGICAL MEDIA refers to any apparatus or tool assembled by human intervention for the purpose of communicating messages.

TECHNOPHOBIA is the fear of incompetence in sending or receiving computer-mediated messages; it also is termed CMC apprehension.

TERRITORIALITY is about how people stake out space for themselves.

TESTIMONY utilizes the opinion of an expert, or the account of an event by a witness to it.

THESIS STATEMENT refers to one or two sentences that tell the audience exactly what you want them to know, understand, and remember when your speech is done.

TIME, nonverbally referred to as chronemics, involves the intentional and unintentional use of time to communicate.

TIME MANAGEMENT refers to the skill of balancing the amount of time each communicator gets to speak during a conversation.

TOPIC refers to a specific facet or aspect of a subject area.

TOPIC DEVELOPMENT is the management of the subject under discussion in the conversation.

TOPIC INITIATION refers to introducing topics for discussion.

TOPIC SHIFT is the move of the conversation away from one subject of discussion to another.

TOPICAL ORGANIZATION divides information about a subject and topic into subtopics or subcategories. (Chapter Thirteen)

TOPICAL SPEECH ORGANIZATION arranges information according to a logical set of subtopics or subcategories of the speech subject. (Chapter Eleven)

TOUCH, which social scientists call haptics, involves physical contact between people, and communicates support, power, and the intimacy level of a relationship.

TRANSITIONS are the words, phrases, or sentences that demonstrate how the main points relate to one another, and how the introduction and the conclusion are connected to the body of the speech.

TRANSPARENT DELIVERY is presenting a speech in such a way that the audience does not focus on the elements of the delivery, but instead pays full attention to the message.

A TWO-SIDED APPEAL presents two alternative points of view, and then presents arguments to counter the opposing view and support the speaker's view.

USES AND GRATIFICATIONS are the needs or goals being served by media consumption.

VIRTUAL TEAM refers to a group of geographically, organizationally, and/or time-dispersed workers who coordinate their work predominantly with electronic information and communication technologies, in order to accomplish one or more organization tasks.

VIVID LANGUAGE promotes enthusiasm for a speech by bringing the speaker's message to life, and moving the audience emotionally.

VOCAL VARIETY heightens and maintains audience attention and interest in your speech by varying the rate (fast vs. slow), pitch (high vs. low), and volume (loud vs. soft) of your voice.

VOCALICS, or paralanguage, includes all the nonverbal elements of the voice that contribute to communication competence.

VOLUME is the intensity, the loudness or softness, of the speaker's voice.

WORKING OUTLINES contain brief references to the support materials, gathered through your research efforts, and arranged in the order you plan to use them in your speech.

SUBJECT INDEX

AUTHOR INDEX